Operation Take-Over The Day

365 Days Prayer Devotional

Deliverance, healing, wisdom, prayers, and devotion for each day of the year

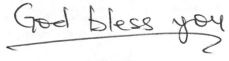

Apostle A.O. Solomon

authorHOUSE®

AuthorHouse™
1663 Liberty Drive
Bloomington, IN 47403
www.authorhouse.com
Phone: 1-800-839-8640

First published by AuthorHouse   12/6/2011

ISBN: 978-1-4670-6990-8 (sc)
ISBN: 978-1-4670-6989-2 (hc)
ISBN: 978-1-4670-6988-5 (e)

Library of Congress Control Number: 2011919132

Printed in the United States of America

Understanding Devotion and Prayers

I believe God is about to change the story of your life as you connect yourself to wisdom and power through the devotions in this book. There are certain things you must understand as a child of destiny. Studying your Bible requires discipline and time, and prayer is no different. Every child of God should have a daily quiet time and should be constantly developing his or her prayer life. It is sad but true that many of God's children wake up and don't pray. Some do not even know how to pray or what to pray about. It's time for a change in your prayer and devotional life. When God wants to change your situation, the first thing he does is to change your prayer life.

Devotion can mean a lot of things, such as studying your Bible, but in this book I want to focus on prayer and quiet time as a chance to communicate with God. Most people would tell you that, in any situation, communication is the most important step to having a healthy and open relationship. When people communicate, no one person should do all the talking or all the listening. Communication requires that all participants share equal parts talking and listening. Prayer is no different. Prayer is our means of communication with our heavenly father. And just as communicating with your family, friends, or spouse is one of the most important aspects of that relationship, so it is in our relationship with God. And because it is so important, it is imperative that we do it on a regular basis—not just when we have spare time or when it's convenient, but at all times. Our challenge and motivation, as disciples and God's children, comes from the bible, Ephesians 6:18 *"Pray in the spirit on all occasions with all kinds of prayers and requests. With this in mind, be alert and always keep on praying for all the saints."* And also the Bible says in Ist Thessalonians 5:17 *"Pray without ceasing."* As disciples, we must pray every day and on all occasions, and we must do so without ceasing!

Jesus provides us with numerous examples the importance of prayer and quiet time with God. The first chapter of Mark gives us a great example of how important Jesus felt it was to spend his time with God. Starting in verse 21, we see that Jesus was in Capernaum teaching in the synagogue. He also healed the demon-possessed man in the synagogue. As soon as he finished there, he went to the home of Simon and Andrew, where he healed Simon's mother-in-law, who had been ill. The word spread quickly about what he was doing that day, and by that evening, most of the town had gathered at Simon and Andrew's house with the sick and demon possessed. Jesus took the time to heal everyone. Jesus actions in verse 35 reveal to us how much importance we should put on prayer. The bible says, in Mark 1:35 *"Very early the next morning, while it was still dark, Jesus got up, left the house and went off to a solitary place, where he prayed."*

As far as we can tell in the book of Mark, Jesus had a very busy day the day before, teaching, healing, and visiting with others. Most of us after a day like that would want to stay in bed, and sleep in the next morning. But instead, Jesus did something that most of us have probably never done—he got up while it was still dark. And what did he do? He went to a solitary place and prayed. Jesus had been busy well after sunset the night before and he still took the time to get up before sunrise so he could have his quiet time alone with God. You too must show the same dedication to God in your quiet times.

It is through prayer and your quiet times with God that you will be spiritually nourished and replenished. God will bless you with the tools you need to serve him, and he will give you the energy and strength to follow him and do his will. As followers of Christ, we are called to minister to those around us and to lead nonbelievers into a relationship with Jesus. If we have neglected our own spiritual nourishment by failing to pray, how can we expect to minister to others?

We *must* pray so that we are able to minister to others, but we *should* pray because we are in a fierce and constant battle. We are going to be constantly opposed by Satan and the sin that this earthly world has to offer us. The bible tells us in the book of Ephesians 6:12 that, *"Our struggle and battles is not against flesh and blood, but against the rulers, against the authorities, against the powers of this dark world and against the spiritual forces of evil in the heavenly realms."* We are in a battle, and we need the help of God. The enemy is ready to defeat us, so we cannot neglect prayer and go into battle unarmed.

The spiritual nourishment and protection that we can receive in this book through prayer does not come without a cost. God has made Himself, accessible to us any time of day or night, yet so few believers take advantage of this opportunity. One of the reasons for this is that prayer is costly, because it takes time and effort to converse with God through prayer. If you look at the life of any great minister, you will notice that they all spent a great deal of time on their knees in prayer, some for several hours every day. That's a lot of time!

Everything in our world today, fights against prayer. Our busy lives interfere with times of prayer. Our bodies resist it, our minds resist it, and Satan encourages us to resist it. But we must pray because it is our necessary lifeline to God.

Now there is no specific formula for how we should pray. One of the things that make prayer so great is that there is no right or wrong way to pray. However, in order for us not to become stagnant in our prayer life, and in order for us to be as spiritually nourished as possible, there are some guidelines I'd like to share with you about how to pray. You have probably heard of different prayer plans to follow, but I find the one I present to you in this book, the most well rounded. This plan utilizes five words to guide your prayer life.

The first is Confession. The bible says, in the book of 1 John 1:9 *"If we confess our sins, he is faithful and just and will forgive us our sins and purify us from all unrighteousness."* You should confess all known sin in your life when you start in prayer so that you can open the channel of communication between you and God. If you try to hide your sins from God or simply ignore it, you put up a roadblock in your communication with God. As you confess your sins to God, ask him to look into your heart and reveal sins to you that you may not be aware of. David gives us a great example in the book of Psalms 139:23-4 *"Search me, O God, and know my heart; test me and know my anxious thoughts. See if there is any offensive way in me, and lead me in the way everlasting."* As God searches your heart and reveals things that are displeasing to him, take the time to confess and ask for forgiveness. Confession also has to do with you declaring what the scripture says concerning your situation. A closed mouth is a closed destiny. The bible says in the book of Psalms 81:10 "open thy mouth wide, and I will fill it" there is not going to be any filling until there is an opening. The book of Romans 10:10 says, *"For with the heart man believeth unto righteousness; and with the mouth* confession *is made unto salvation."*

After confession comes **Praise**. 1 Chronicles 29:10–13.

The bible says, David praised the Lord in the presence of the whole assembly, saying, 'Praise be to you, O Lord, God of our father Israel, from everlasting to everlasting. Yours, O Lord, is the greatness and the power and the glory and the majesty and the splendor, for everything in heaven and earth is yours. Yours, O Lord, is the kingdom; you are exalted as head over all. Wealth and honor come from you; you are the ruler of all things. In your hands are strength and power to exalt and give strength to all. Now, our God, we give you thanks, and praise your glorious name.'

After you have been cleansed of your sin, it is a good time to give praise to God. Praise expresses our love and adoration for our heavenly father. As you praise God, focus your thoughts on his greatness, power, majesty, grace, mercy, and unending love for you and God will raise you.

After praises comes **Thanksgiving.** The book of 1 Thessalonians 5:18 says, *"Give thanks in all circumstances, for this is God's will for you in Christ Jesus."* Every day of our lives we have something for which we can be thankful. We can thank God for our health, safety, friends, family, church, joyful times, and of course for salvation. In the first chapter of Romans, Paul speaks of the sinfulness of mankind, and he includes thanklessness as one of those sins. The book of Romans 1:21 says, *"For although they knew God, they neither glorified him as God nor gave thanks to him, but their thinking became futile and their foolish hearts were darkened."* Don't allow yourself to fall into this same trap of thanklessness. God has blessed us abundantly, but he desires us to humble ourselves before him and give him thanks and glory for those blessings.

After thanksgiving comes **Intercession**. The book of 1 Timothy 2:1–4 says, *"I urge, then, first of all, that requests, prayers, intercession and thanksgiving be made for everyone, for kings and all those in authority, that we may live peaceful and quiet lives in all godliness and holiness. This is good, and pleases God our Savior, who wants all men to be saved and to come to knowledge of the truth."* This means that we are responsible to pray for others. How many of you have enthusiastically promised to pray for someone and then forgotten to do so? I have done it several times, and there's no excuse for it. We should pray regularly for our pastors, our government leaders, our missionaries, our friends, and our family members. We should especially pray for those who are in need because of physical or emotional problems. We should pray for others in the same way that we pray for ourselves. God will meet the needs of others if we pray for them, just as he meets our own needs.

The final point to our plan of prayer is **Petition**. The book of Mark 11:24 says, *"Therefore I tell you, whatever you ask for in prayer, believe that you have received it, and it will be yours."* We need to pray for ourselves and our personal needs. Whatever these may be, we can bring them to God and expect him to answer. We should pray for specific things for which we can expect specific answers. A faithful prayer is one you expect God to hear and to answer; it is also a prayer that is unselfish and seeks God's will and not your own. A prayer of petition is not meant for our own selfish needs, but to help us meet the needs that God desires and to do his will. In the book of Mark 14:36, Jesus provides a perfect example of the unselfish prayers we should offer: *"'Abba, Father,' he said, 'everything is possible for you. Take this cup from me. Yet not what I will, but what you will.'"* This is one of Jesus final prayers in the Garden of Gethsemane in which he asked God to spare him from having to die on the cross, yet he asked for it to be the will of the father and not his own. Ask God to provide for you, ask God to bless you, ask God for guidance in school and your career, ask God to protect your future mate and to reveal him or her to you if that is your desire, ask God for protection and for good health and for save travel and anything that you need.

Through all of these steps, reveal to God your requests and let them be made known to him, but do so with a humble heart and truly seek his will. God desperately desires to commune with us on a daily basis, but he can't do so if we

Apostle A.O. Solomon

don't talk to him or if we don't pause to listen to him. As you strive to model your prayer life after that of a faithful disciple for God, be ready for God to answer you. Be ready to submit unto God's will and unto the direction that he leads you. I see it becoming real to you as enjoy this book.

I want you to feel hungry for a greater prayer life, and I want you to long for a committed walk with God so that we can be his disciples giving him glory in everything that we do. I don't want to "beat you up"; I want to "stir you up." I want you to see prayer not as a duty but as a privilege. I want you to pray not just because of our battle with the devil, or just because of the pain of those around you. I want you to pray because of the sweetness that comes from spending time with the Father and from the glory that will be all God's if we do everything he desires from us.

Go from here being warriors in prayer. Stay focused on the commitment you have made to be God's army, and be ready for him to use you for great things. *Shalom!*

Yours in the School of Prayer,
Apostle Solomon Abiodun Odejayi
(The Shadow of the Almighty Prayer Line)
Telephone: 712-432-8813 / Access Code: 574018#

Daily Prophetic Decree

By the Blood of Jesus Christ! By the Blood of Jesus Christ! By the Blood of Jesus Christ! I knock on the door of this day [mention the date], I command the door of (date) to open for me now, in the name of Jesus.

I command the doors of favor, blessings, riches, good news, and testimonies to open for me today. I decree good doors to open for me today, in the name of Jesus.

It is written in the Word of God— Luke 11:9 *"And I say unto you, Ask, and it shall be given you; seek, and ye shall find; knock, and it shall be opened unto you."* Therefore, I knock and it shall be opened unto me, in the name of Jesus.

I have the keys to the house of David. The Word of God says in the book of Isaiah 22: 22 *"And the key of the house of David will I lay upon his shoulder; so he shall open and none shall shut; and he shall shut, and none shall open."* Therefore, I use the keys of the house of David to open every good door today, in the name of Jesus.

As I go forward today, the sun shall not smite me by day; neither shall the moon smite by night, in the name of Jesus. As I go forward today, I command the gates and everlasting doors of (date) to open to me on their own accord, in the name of Jesus.

I declare that Jesus Christ is the Lord over my going out and my coming in today in the name of Jesus. I release the blood of Jesus Christ to speak for me and bring better things to me today.

You, (date) hear the word of the Living God, It is written in the Word of God: Psalms 68:19 *"Blessed be the Lord, who daily loads us with benefits, even the God of our salvation."* Therefore, I command this day (date) to bring and release good things and good news to me in the name of Jesus.

I shall not suffer any loss of life and property today, in the name of Jesus. The Lord is my shepherd; the Lord is with me as a mighty and terrible One. I shall not suffer any loss today, both of lives and properties, in the name of Jesus. I am blessed and highly favored! It is well with me! Glory be to God! Jesus Christ is Lord. Amen.

Confession:

"Yea, though I walk through the valley of the shadow of death, I will fear no evil throughout this year: For God is with me; His rod and His staff comfort me" Psalms 23:4.

Wisdom for Today:

With so many expectations and desires within you, look forward into the year with faith and courage in God and a strong determination that all shall be well. God will fulfill his word in your life if you don't lose faith.

Read the Bible Today: Genesis 1 and 2

Prayer Points:

1. Almighty God, I thank you for making me see the first day in this New Year, and I thank you because I will see the end of the year by your special grace, in Jesus name.
2. Let the blood of Jesus go before and after me today, in Jesus name.
3. Let the presence of God be with me today, in Jesus name.
4. Almighty God let me prosper In all I shall do today, in the name of Jesus.
5. Let God arise on my behalf, and let all my enemies be scattered, in Jesus name.
6. Almighty God baptize me with your favor today, in the name of Jesus.
7. Almighty God make this year my year of blessings, favor, profit, breakthroughs, fulfillment, and perfection, in the name of Jesus.
8. Lord Jesus, pray for me today.
9. I shall not die young; I shall live a fulfilled live, in the name of Jesus.
10. Every day, let the time and appointment with death set for me and my family this year be canceled with the blood of Jesus.
11. I take over this day by the blood of Jesus Christ, in Jesus name.
12. Every god and goddess demanding worship or anything from me, perish and rise no more, in the name of Jesus.
13. Almighty God, breathe upon me and make me whole, in the name of Jesus Christ.

14. Almighty God, by your never failing power, stand beside me and defend me, in the name of Jesus.
15. Everything from my past that the devil and my enemies are using to torment and afflict my life, Almighty God, take it away, in the name of Jesus Christ.
16. I prophesy that new and wonderful things will manifest in my life this year, in the name of Jesus Christ.
17. Almighty God, have mercy upon me, and seal up all the holes in bags and pockets that might leak misery upon me, in the name of Jesus Christ.
18. Every evil tree planted by fear in my life, dry up from the roots, in the name of Jesus Christ.
19. All the curses, enchantments, and spells that are against me, I cancel you by the blood of Jesus Christ, in the name of Jesus.
20. Almighty God, by your power, let objects of ridicule that reflect on me be converted to sources of miracles, in the name of Jesus Christ.
21. I decree in the name of the Lord Jesus that every conspiracy of darkness and wickedness against me today shall not stand; neither shall it come to pass, in the name of Jesus Christ.
22. All shall be well with my family and me this year, in the name of Jesus.
23. I shall not suffer any loss of life or property this year, in the name of Jesus.
24. I decree that this year will be the best year of all the years I have lived in the name of Jesus.
25. I thank God, for he has all it takes for this year to be my best year in the name of Jesus.
26. Every hindering power and spirit to my glory this year be consumed by the fire of God, in the name of Jesus.
27. This year, God shall arise for my sake and turn my life around for his glory, in the name of Jesus.
28. Every problem prepared for me and my family this year, I command you to backfire, in the name of Jesus.
29. Every enemy of the manifestation of my glory be consumed by the fire of God, in the name of Jesus.
30. I cancel every evil dreams, visions, prophesy and prayers against my life and family in the name of Jesus.
31. Talk to God about your heart desires and your situation.
32. Thank God for answered prayers.

Confession:

"The Lord is my rock and my fortress, and my deliverer; my God, my strength in whom I will trust; my buckler, and the horn of my salvation, and my high tower. I will call upon the Lord, who is worthy to be praised: so shall I be saved from mine enemies" Psalms 18:2–3.

Wisdom for Today:

It is the light that comes out of darkness that eventually overcomes darkness. No evil can harm you if you are a follower of that which is good. Remember, you are the apple of God's eyes. So, stay in the light. Jesus Christ is Lord.

Read the Bible Today: *Genesis 3 and 4*

Prayer Points:

1. I thank God for the opportunity to see another beautiful day.
2. I refuse to answer the call of evil spirits, in the name of Jesus.
3. The hands of the enemy shall not prevail against me today, in Jesus name.
4. God is my strength; I will never be weary and tired, in Jesus name.
5. Let God be God in all my affairs today, in Jesus name.
6. I shall not see disaster this year, in the name of Jesus.
7. Almighty God anoint me for special favor today, in the name of Jesus.
8. Lord Jesus Christ, as you prayed for Peter and delivered him from the desire of satan, pray for me today in the mighty name of Jesus.
9. I shall not die young, in the name of Jesus.
10. Let the time and appointment with death set for me and my family this year be canceled with the blood of Jesus.
11. My going out and coming in today are blessed and preserved by God, in the name of Jesus.
12. I take over this day and this year by the blood of Jesus Christ, in the name of Jesus.
13. I commit my work, my business, and career unto God's hands in the name of Jesus.
14. I cover myself, my family, and my going out and coming in today with the blood of Jesus Christ in the name of Jesus.
15. The Lord is my Shepherd, I shall not want, in the name of Jesus.

16. I release myself from any power of witchcraft, by the blood of Jesus Christ in the name of Jesus.
17. Every problem in my life that originated from witchcraft, receive instant divine solution, in the name of Jesus Christ.
18. Every problem caused by sin and disobedience to God in my life, receive the blood of Jesus Christ and be terminated, in the name of Jesus Christ.
19. I confess all my sins to God today, and I declare myself forgiven and cleansed by the precious blood of Jesus Christ, in Jesus name.
20. All damages done to my life by witchcraft spirits, by familiar spirits, and marine spirits, be repaired now by the power of the Almighty God, in the name of Jesus Christ.
21. I give thanks to God for a blessed day; Jesus Christ is Lord!
22. Every power delaying my testimonies, perish and rise no more, in the name of Jesus.
23. Lord Jesus Christ, you are the light of the world; therefore, let your light arise and shine in my darkness in the name of Jesus.
24. You, the strongmen from both sides of my family who are attacking my career, destroy yourselves, in the mighty name of Jesus Christ.
25. I decree that my enemies shall not measure my movement; neither shall they determine my progress in life, in the name of Jesus Christ.
26. I cancel every evil dreams, visions, prophesy and prayers against my life and family in the name of Jesus.
27. Talk to God about your heart desires and your situation.
28. Thank God for answered prayers.

Confession:

"For God will not leave my soul in hell; neither will thou suffer me to see corruption" Psalms 16:10.

Wisdom for Today:

Christians are to live an exceptional life, devoted completely to God who has called them out of darkness into his marvelous light. Separation is the call of God, this end time. Decide to live a separate life today. Shalom.

Read the Bible Today: Genesis 5 and 6

Prayer Points:

1. I praise and thank God for allowing me to see yet another day by his grace in the name of Jesus.
2. I plead the blood of Jesus over my spirit, soul, and body, in the name of Jesus.
3. I give God the praise, for his mercy endures forever in the name of Jesus.
4. I appreciate him, the King of Kings and the Lord of Lords.
5. I lift up my voice and declare, "Jesus Christ is Lord!"
6. In thee Oh Lord do I put my trust let me not be ashamed in the name of Jesus.
7. Almighty God, bow your ear down to me, deliver me speedily, and save me, in Jesus name.
8. Every aggression directed against me and my destiny, backfire, in the name of Jesus.
9. Almighty God, for your name's sake, lead me and guide me, in the name of Jesus.
10. Almighty God, pull me out of every net that my enemies have secretly laid for me, in the name of Jesus.
11. Almighty God, I commit my spirit, soul, and body into your hands, in the name of Jesus.
12. Almighty God, consider my trouble of many years and deliver me speedily, in the name of Jesus.
13. Almighty God, have mercy upon me; do not shut me up in the hands of my enemies, in the name of Jesus.

14. Almighty God, my times are in your hands. Deliver me, Lord, from the hands of the enemy and the hands of those who persecute me, in the name of Jesus Christ.

15. Almighty God make your face shine upon me, in the name of Jesus.

16. Almighty God, arise and make my case simple, in the name of Jesus.

17. Every sign and symptom of reproach in my life, vanish, in the name of Jesus.

18. Let the presence of God overshadow my life, in the name of Jesus.

19. This is my month, the month the Lord has made for me, in the name of Jesus.

20. Let every evil hand and leg upon my destiny, blessing, and glory be broken, in the name of Jesus.

21. I break free and release myself from every evil family dedication, in the name of Jesus.

22. Every failure in my dreams, depart from my life and return no more, in the name of Jesus.

23. Father Lord, baptize me with your favor today, in the name of Jesus.

24. Lord Jesus, show up in all my affairs today in the name of Jesus.

25. I shall not die young; I shall not die in the midst of my days, in the name of Jesus.

26. I take over this day by the blood of Jesus Christ, in Jesus name.

27. I shall not fall into the trap of the enemies, in the name of Jesus.

28. Let the time and appointment with death set for me and my family this year be canceled by the blood of Jesus in the name of Jesus.

29. I claim my portion of blessing in this country, in the name of Jesus.

30. My glory, be released for manifestation, in the name of Jesus.

31. I cancel every evil dreams, visions, prophesy and prayers against my life and family in the name of Jesus.

32. Talk to God about your heart desires and your situation.

33. Thank God for answered prayers.

Confession:

"For in the time of trouble God shall hide me in his pavilion: in the secret of his tabernacle shall he hide me, he shall set me up upon a rock. And now shall my head be lifted up above mine enemies round about me" Psalms 27:5-6.

Wisdom for Today:

Your problems shall be your promotions. This can only happen when your eyes of understanding are opened ... when you begin to see your situations the way God sees them. Every Goliath before you is an invitation to the king's palace, so be strong and be courageous. Jesus Christ is Lord.

Read the Bible Today: Genesis 7 and 8

Prayer Points:

1. I praise and thank God for allowing me to see yet another day by his grace.
2. Success is my destiny; I refuse to be destitute, in the name of Jesus
3. Every stronghold of family failure in my life, I pull you down, in the name of Jesus.
4. By the blood of Jesus Christ, I break loose and break free from generational limitations, in the name of Jesus Christ.
5. By faith in Christ Jesus, I reclaim all that the devil has taken from me, in Jesus name.
6. I take over this day by the blood of Jesus Christ, in Jesus name.
7. I dismantle the anchor to every problem in my life, in the name of Jesus.
8. I shake off every element of sorrow from my life, in the name of Jesus.
9. Almighty God baptize me with your special favor today, in the name of Jesus.
10. Lord Jesus, pray for me today in the name of Jesus.
11. I shall not die young, in the name of Jesus.
12. Let the time and appointment with death set for me and my family this year be canceled by the blood of Jesus in the mighty name of Jesus.

13. God, please remove any curse you have placed on my life as a result of disobedience in the name of Jesus.
14. Almighty God, by your never-failing power, lead me in the way I should go in the name of Jesus Christ.
15. I take over this day by the blood of Jesus Christ, in Jesus name.
16. I speak to all creations through the spirit of prophesy: arise and assist me, in the name of Jesus.
17. All unprofitable broadcasters of my goodness, be silenced forever, in the name of Jesus.
18. Every witchcraft power assigned against my life, and the life of my loved ones, receive destruction, in the name of Jesus Christ.
19. Every power of witchcraft, familiar spirit, marine spirit, and herbalist, gathered against my prosperity, be swallowed by the blood of Jesus Christ.
20. Almighty God baptize me with your wisdom, knowledge, and understanding, in the name of Jesus.
21. I shall not become meat in the mouth of the enemy, in the name of Jesus.
22. I shall be blessed and be abundantly satisfied, in the name of Jesus Christ.
23. I retrieve my integrity from the hands of household witchcraft, in the name of Jesus Christ.
24. I shall not carry any evil burden, in the name of Jesus Christ.
25. I thank the Lord because he will arise and favor me, in the name of Jesus.
26. Divine anointing for great favor; overwhelm my life in the name of Jesus.
27. Almighty God, bless me with uncommon favor in the name of Jesus.
28. I prophesy that, wherever people are finding things difficult this year, I shall find things easy, in the name of Jesus.
29. I prophesy that, wherever there is famine this year, I shall experience abundance, in the name of Jesus.
30. I prophesy that, where people can find no way this year, I shall find a way, in the name of Jesus Christ.
31. I cancel every evil dreams, visions, prophesy and prayers against my life and family in the name of Jesus.
32. Talk to God about your heart desires and your situation.
33. Thank God for answered prayers.

Confession:

"The Lord hears me in the day of trouble; the name of the God of Jacob defends me" Psalms 20:1.

Wisdom for Today:

You serve a God who hears and answers prayer. What will God hear or answer when you refuse to pray? Don't give up in prayer. Pray until something happens, and when it happens, continue in prayer to make your victory, blessings, and deliverance last long. Shalom!

Read the Bible Today: *Genesis 9 and 10*

Prayer Points:

1. I praise and thank God for allowing me to see yet another day by his grace.
2. God's covenant is upon my life; I shall not be disgrace, in the name of Jesus.
3. Almighty God arise, fight against all those who fight against me, disgrace all those who disgrace me, and bless all those who bless me, In the name of Jesus.
4. I shall not vanish with this year, in the name of Jesus.
5. I command the days of affliction in my life and family to end now, in the name of Jesus.
6. Long life and prosperity is my portion with God; therefore, let every messenger of death go back to the sender, in the name of Jesus.
7. Almighty God rain your favor upon me today, in the name of Jesus.
8. Thou, Son of God, pray for me today in the name of Jesus.
9. I shall not die young, in the name of Jesus.
10. Let the time and appointment with death set for me and my family this year be canceled by the blood of Jesus.
11. Almighty God bless my life, in the name of Jesus.
12. I take authority over all curses issued against my life, in the name of Jesus.
13. I break and release myself from every curse of evil dedication, in the name of Jesus.
14. I take over this day by the blood of Jesus Christ, in Jesus name.

15. Almighty God baptize me with your love and desire for the things of heaven, in the name of Jesus.
16. I reverse every witchcraft burial fashioned against me, in the name of Jesus.
17. I reverse the evil effect of any witchcraft summons of my spirit, in the name of Jesus Christ.
18. Any witch who projects herself into the body of any animal in order to harm me, perish in the body of such animal, in the name of Jesus Christ.
19. By the power in the blood of Jesus Christ, I remove my hands and feet from any witchcraft bewitchment and bondage, in the name of Jesus.
20. Blood of Jesus Christ, wash away from my life every identification mark of witchcraft on me or on any of my property, in the name of Jesus.
21. I take over this day by the power in the blood of Jesus Christ.
22. Holy Spirit of God, have your way in my life in the name of Jesus.
23. Every evil assigned against my prayers be paralyzed, in the name of Jesus.
24. I declare Jesus Christ is Lord!
25. Almighty God, visit me in a new way, in the name of Jesus.
26. Almighty God, let this year, be my year of great increase, in the mighty name of Jesus Christ.
27. Almighty God, this year I refuse to harden my heart against you, in the name of Jesus Christ.
28. Almighty God, remove every mountain in the way of my breakthrough, in the name of Jesus.
29. Every mighty mountain that stands against my testimony be removed, in the name of Jesus.
30. Almighty God, fill my mouth with laughter and my lips with rejoicing, in the name of Jesus.
31. I cancel every evil dreams, visions, prophesy and prayers against my life and family in the name of Jesus.
32. Talk to God about your heart desires and your situation.
33. Thank God for answered prayers.

Confession:

"The Lord is my strength and my shield; my heart trusted in him, and I am helped" Psalms 28:7.

Wisdom for Today:

Most of what we are afraid we can't do, get, or accomplish often eventually comes easily for us, and we wonder where the fear came from in the first place. Step out with faith today. Be very optimistic that God's strength is available for you always, and you will come back home today rejoicing. Victory is surely yours today, in the name of Jesus. Jesus Christ is Lord!

Read the Bible Today: Genesis 11 and Exodus 3

Prayer Points:

1. I praise and thank God that I have seen yet another day by his grace.
2. I refuse to enter into any coffin this year, in the name of Jesus.
3. Almighty God direct my helpers to locate me, in the name of Jesus.
4. I stand under the covenant of God's mercy, and I obtain great grace, in the name of Jesus.
5. My eyes shall see good things, and my ears shall hear good news, in the name of Jesus.
6. I shall not fail; I shall not be disgraced, in the name of Jesus.
7. Let the favor of God fall upon me today, in the name of Jesus.
8. Lord Jesus, pray for me today in the name of Jesus.
9. I shall not die young, in the name of Jesus.
10. I take over this day by the blood of Jesus Christ, in Jesus name.
11. I decree in the mighty name of Jesus Christ that my life shall not be ruled by the fear of the harm that anyone can do to me in Jesus name.
12. Almighty God set me aside for yourself in the name of Jesus.
13. Let the time and appointment with death set for me and my family this year be canceled by the blood of Jesus.
14. Almighty God let your name be glorified in my life in the name of Jesus.
15. Almighty God let me be a channel of blessings to others, in the name of Jesus.

16. I bind the strongman who wants to harm my life and destiny, in the name of Jesus Christ.
17. I bind the strongman who wants to harm my family, in the name of Jesus Christ.
18. I bind the strongman who wants to harm my blessings, in the name of Jesus Christ.
19. I bind every satanic strongman that may want to harm my life, my work, business, and career, in the name of Jesus Christ.
20. Every evil power trying to imprison me, I crush you under my feet, in the name of Jesus Christ.
21. Every power that prevents the perfect will of God from being fulfilled in my life, receive failure and defeat, in the name of Jesus.
22. I declare Jesus Christ is Lord!
23. I declare that whatever was difficult for me to achieve in the past shall be easy for me from now on, in the name of Jesus.
24. I prophesy that this year shall be trouble and stress free year for me, in the name of Jesus Christ.
25. By the blood of Jesus Christ, I connect myself to the realm of possibility, in the name of Jesus.
26. I speak by the blood of Jesus Christ; this year shall be better for me in all areas of my life, in the name of Jesus Christ.
27. This year shall be a most blessed year for me, in the name of Jesus.
28. Let the kingdom of God be established in every area of my life, in the name of Jesus.
29. I decree that my ways shall be prosperous; my coming in and going out shall be greatly blessed, in the name of Jesus.
30. Throughout this year, I shall be divinely guided, in the name of Jesus Christ.
31. I cancel every evil dreams, visions, prophesy and prayers against my life and family in the name of Jesus.
32. Talk to God about your heart desires and your situation.
33. Thank God for answered prayers.

Confession:

"I will rejoice in thy salvation, and in the name of my God will I set up my banners" Psalms 20:5.

Wisdom for Today:

Lifting up banners is a sign of victory in warfare. Raise the banner of thanks, praise, and songs of victory to the Lord, and tell the devil to his face that he was defeated over two thousand years ago by the blood of the Lord Jesus Christ. Victory is sure for you today by the blood of Jesus. Amen.

Read the Bible Today: Genesis 11 and Revelation 12

Prayer Points:

1. I praise and thank God for allowing me to see yet another day by his grace.
2. My star shall not be cast down; my star shall continually shine, in the name of Jesus.
3. I redeem this month of January by the blood of Jesus; I shall be preserved with all my family, in the name of Jesus Christ.
4. Holy Spirit of God, revive me again today, in the name of Jesus.
5. This month of January is my month of glory and recovery, in the name of Jesus.
6. Good things shall prosper in my life throughout this month, in the name of Jesus.
7. Almighty God baptize me with your special favor, in the name of Jesus.
8. Lord Jesus, pray for me today in the name of Jesus.
9. I take over this day by the blood of Jesus Christ in the name of Jesus.
10. Almighty God, by your power, make me wise, in the name of Jesus.
11. I shall not die young, in the name of Jesus.
12. Let the time and appointment with death set for me and my family this year be canceled by the blood of Jesus in the name of Jesus.
13. I shall not live for nothing, in the name of Jesus.
14. Almighty God let my life celebrate your beauty, in the name of Jesus.

15. Almighty God let my life celebrate your glory, in the name of Jesus.
16. Anyone on any mission to block my way today, you shall not prosper, stumble and fall, in the name of Jesus Christ.
17. Anyone on any mission to hinder my glory, you shall not prosper, stumble and fall, in the name of Jesus Christ.
18. Anyone on any mission to disgrace me, you shall not prosper, be disgraced, in the name of Jesus Christ.
19. Anyone who has donated me as a sacrifice in any evil kingdom, take my position and die for me, in the name of Jesus Christ.
20. My blood shall not be the drink of my enemies, and my flesh shall not be meat in their mouths, in the name of Jesus Christ.
21. I declare that everything is turning around in my favor, in the name of Jesus.
22. Every evil dream, I forbid you in my life, die in the name of Jesus.
23. Throughout this year, I shall be blessed, and I shall be a blessing, in the name of Jesus Christ.
24. I declare that I am a blessed child of God; I am blessed and highly favored, in the name of Jesus.
25. I take over this day by the Holy Ghost and the blood of Jesus Christ in the name of Jesus.
26. I reject every evil in this day, in the name of Jesus Christ.
27. I connect myself to the favor of God, in the name of Jesus.
28. Throughout this year, I shall see the goodness of the Lord in the land of the living, in the name of Jesus Christ.
29. Because I am serving the way, throughout this year, there shall be way for me physically, spiritually, and financially in the name of Jesus Christ.
30. Because I am serving the truth; Jesus Christ the Son of God, therefore, no lie of the devil shall prevail over my life, in the name of Jesus.
31. I cancel every evil dreams, visions, prophesy and prayers against my life and family in the name of Jesus.
32. Talk to God about your heart desires and your situation.
33. Thank God for answered prayers.

Confession:

"The face of the Lord is against them that do evil, to cut off the re-membrance of them from the earth". Psalms 34:16.

Wisdom for Today:

Your character reflects the source of your being—whether you are a child of light or darkness ... whether you are born of God or of the devil. Promise yourself this: people shall glorify Jesus through me today, whether the devil likes it or not, in Jesus name.

Read the Bible Today: *Genesis 13 and 1 John 5*

Prayer Points:

1. I praise and thank God for letting me see yet another day by his grace.
2. I have a covenant of salt with God; I will always enjoy sweetness all the days of my life, in the name of Jesus.
3. As the grave could not hold Jesus Christ my Lord and Savior, no barrier will hinder my breakthroughs this year, in the name of Jesus.
4. As the brothers of Joseph bowed before him, so let the enemies of my entire household bow to me as from today, in the name of Jesus.
5. By the spirit of prophesy, I jump over every barrier to my promotion, in the name of Jesus.
6. Let the wind of God's fire clear away every personality that puts a barrier in my way, in Jesus name.
7. Almighty God favor me today, in the name of Jesus.
8. Lord Jesus, pray for me today in the name of Jesus.
9. Let the hand of God knock out every pillar that upholds evil in my life, in the name of Jesus.
10. I take over this day by the blood of Jesus Christ, in Jesus name.
11. I shall not die young, in the name of Jesus.
12. Let the time and appointment with death set for me and my family this year be canceled by the blood of Jesus.
13. There shall be no more poverty in my life, in the name of Jesus.
14. Almighty God, arise and break open every prison that holds me captive, in the name of Jesus.

15. I claim divine, unlimited favor today, in the name of Jesus.

16. Almighty God, send your angels to guide me out of the wilderness of frustration and confusion, in the name of Jesus.

17. Every act of warfare prepared against my peace, be scattered unto desolation by fire, in the name of Jesus Christ.

18. Every act of warfare prepared against my joy, be scattered unto desolation by fire, in the name of Jesus Christ.

19. Every act of warfare prepared against my success and progress in life, be scattered unto desolation by fire, in the name of Jesus Christ.

20. Every act of warfare prepared against my marriage and home, be scattered unto desolation by fire, in the name of Jesus Christ.

21. Almighty God let your grace be sufficient for me throughout my life, in the name of Jesus.

22. Almighty God let it please you to bless me this year, in the name of Jesus.

23. Lord Jesus Christ, it pleases the Father that in you all the fullness should dwell; therefore, let my full blessing, joy, testimony, and glory manifest, in the name of Jesus.

24. Through the blood of Jesus Christ, I obtain peace in all areas of my life, in the name of Jesus Christ.

25. Blood of Jesus Christ, reconcile me with my blessings, destiny, marriage, children, and parents this year, in the name of Jesus.

26. I give thanks to God for a blessed day.

27. Every evil imagination against my career, wither from the source, in the name of Jesus Christ.

28. I reject any demonic limitation on my progress, in the name of Jesus Christ.

29. All those circulating my name for evil, be disgraced, in the name of Jesus.

30. I release myself from every evil domination and control, in the name of Jesus.

31. I cancel every evil dreams, visions, prophesy and prayers against my life and family in the name of Jesus.

32. Talk to God about your heart desires and your situation.

33. Thank God for answered prayers.

Confession:

"The Lord brings the counsel of the heathen to naught: he makes the devices of the people of none effect" Psalms 30:10.

Wisdom for Today:

When you get to heaven, what shall be your reward? What have you done for God lately? Life is not all about money and pleasure alone, so be heaven conscious. There is a reward for good stewards. Jesus Christ is Lord!

Read the Bible Today: Genesis 15 and Psalms 58

Prayer Points:

1. I praise and thank God for allowing me to see yet another day by his grace.
2. Success is my portion; I refuse to be destitute, in the name of Jesus.
3. By the spirit of prophesy, I will affect my generation for good, in the name of Jesus.
4. I receive power today to pursue, overtake, and recover good things throughout this year, in the name of Jesus.
5. As Pharaoh perished in the Red Sea, so let all my stubborn pursuers perish today, in Jesus name.
6. Every unfriendly friend causing problems for me in my place of work, be arrested and be disgraced, in the name of Jesus.
7. Almighty God fill my life with special favor, in the name of Jesus.
8. Lord Jesus, pray for me as you prayed for Peter in the name of Jesus.
9. I shall not die young, in the name of Jesus.
10. I take over this day by the blood of Jesus Christ, in Jesus name.
11. Almighty God heal my every wound in the mighty name of Jesus.
12. Let the time and appointment with death set for me and family this year be canceled by the blood of Jesus.
13. Let all curses issued against me be converted to blessings, in the name of Jesus.
14. I apply the blood of Jesus Christ to break every curse, in the name of Jesus.
15. Frustration and disappointment shall not prosper in my life, in the name of Jesus Christ.

16. Any power or spirit that wants to transfer the problems of others onto me be consumed by fire, in the name of Jesus Christ.

17. The destroyer shall not destroy my life, the wasters shall not waste my life, and the emptiers, shall not empty my life, in the name of Jesus Christ.

18. I shall not be ruled by any Pharaoh, physically or spiritually, in the name of Jesus Christ.

19. Iniquity shall not prevail over my life, in the name of Jesus Christ.

20. Heavenly Father, breathe on me and give me uncommon favor, in the name of Jesus Christ.

21. I give thanks to God.

22. Anyone who wants to sacrifice me on any evil altar or at any evil meeting, die for me, in the name of Jesus Christ.

23. You devourers, vanish from my labor, in the name of Jesus Christ.

24. You wasters, vanish from my labor, in the name of Jesus Christ.

25. I thank God for a blessed day. Jesus Christ is Lord!

26. Every enemy of my open door this year be reduced to nothing, in the name of Jesus Christ.

27. Every evil dream, evil vision, evil prophesy against me, fail woefully, in the name of Jesus.

28. Every effort that shall be made this year to hinder my glory, shall increase the shining of my destiny, in the name of Jesus.

29. Almighty God, arise and reveal your glory in my life, in the name of Jesus Christ.

30. New door of opportunities shall continually be opened unto me, in the name of Jesus.

31. I cancel every evil dreams, visions, prophesy and prayers against my life and family in the name of Jesus.

32. Talk to God about your heart desires and your situation.

33. Thank God for answered prayers.

Confession:

"Evil shall slay the wicked: and they that hate the righteous shall be desolate. The Lord redeemed my soul, and I will not be desolate because I trust in him" .Psalms 34:21–22.

Wisdom for Today:

King David prayed in Psalms 19:13 that God would help him guard against evil. You can follow his example and ask God to make you strong in resisting and overcoming evil.

Read the Bible Today: Genesis 16 and John 1

Prayer Points:

1. I praise and thank God for allowing me to see yet another day by his grace.
2. God's covenant is upon my life, I shall not be disgraced, and I shall not be intimidated, in the name of Jesus.
3. Almighty God, arise and fight against all those who fight against me, disgrace all those who disgrace me, and bless all those who bless me, in the name of Jesus.
4. By the spirit of prophesy, this is my year of surplus and abundance, in Jesus name.
5. No more sorrow for and weeping for me in the name of Jesus.
6. Long life and prosperity is my portion with God; sudden or untimely death is not my portion or the portion of my family members, in the name of Jesus.
7. Almighty God, open the heaven of favor for me today, in the name of Jesus.
8. Lord Jesus, pray for me today in the name of Jesus.
9. I shall not die young, in the name of Jesus.
10. Let the time and appointment with death set for me and my family this year be canceled by the blood of Jesus.
11. As I step out today, I step into God's unlimited and unhindered blessings, in the name of Jesus.
12. I take over this day by the blood of Jesus Christ, in Jesus name.
13. Almighty God your name is a strong tower, I run to you for safety, in the name of Jesus.

14. I release my finances and my health from the control of evil spirits, in the name of Jesus Christ.
15. Every evil assigned against me, be judged by the fire of God today, in the name of Jesus Christ.
16. I say no to everything that keeps me from following the Lord, in the name of Jesus Christ.
17. I say yes to everything that brings me closer to the Lord, in the name of Jesus Christ.
18. Almighty God let your grace make way for me through this year, in the name of Jesus.
19. Every roadblock to the fulfillment of my life, dreams, and destiny be removed, in the name of Jesus.
20. Yoke of frustration, yoke of failure, yoke of un-fulfillment, be destroyed, in the name of Jesus.
21. Almighty God bring me together with those who will move my life forward, in the name of Jesus.
22. Almighty God separate me from those who will pull me down, in the name of Jesus.
23. Connect me, Lord, with friends and partners who will help me fulfill my destiny, in the name of Jesus.
24. Almighty God, by your great power, command the door of breakthroughs to open for me, in the name of Jesus.
25. Almighty God bless me with your increase, in the name of Jesus.
26. Almighty God, through your never-failing power, put an end to crises in my life, finances, and marriage, in the name of Jesus Christ.
27. Almighty God, force open every door that the enemy has shut forcefully against me in the name of Jesus.
28. Almighty God, baptize me with unusual favor, in the name of Jesus Christ.
29. Almighty God let the full time come for my blessing and miracle, in the name of Jesus.
30. Almighty God, have mercy upon me and roll away the reproach in my life, in the name of Jesus.
31. I cancel every evil dreams, visions, prophesy and prayers against my life and family in the name of Jesus.
32. Talk to God about your heart desires and your situation.
33. Thank God for answered prayers.

Confession:

"For evil doers shall be cut off: but I that wait upon the Lord shall inherit the earth" Psalms 37:9.

Wisdom for Today:

Having Jesus in your life should make an outstanding difference in the way you respond to temptation. When you make him your number-one priority, other things will take the back position.

Read the Bible Today: Psalm 26 and Ephesians 4

Prayer Points:

1. I praise and thank God for allowing me to see yet another day by his grace.
2. This year, all my helpers shall be blessed to bless me, in the name of Jesus.
3. This year, I will not miss good things, and good things shall not miss me, in Jesus name.
4. I have a seal of God's rest and peace upon my body; no demon is permitted to touch or harm me, in the name of Jesus.
5. My body is the body of Jesus; no sickness is permitted to dwell in my body, in Jesus name.
6. Almighty God perfect all that concerns me, in the name of Jesus.
7. Almighty God bless me with all-round favor, in the name of Jesus.
8. Lord Jesus, pray for me today in the name of Jesus.
9. I shall overcome every physical and spiritual evil set up against me today, by the blood of Jesus Christ.
10. Every enemy of my open heavens today, collapse and die, in the name of Jesus.
11. I step out today with the power of Jehovah God, and I declare that I shall return with blessings and testimonies, in the name of Jesus Christ.
12. "Surely, God's goodness and mercy shall follow me all the days of my life: and I will dwell in the house of the Lord forever" in the name of Jesus.
13. All is well with my going out and coming in today, in the name of Jesus.

14. I take over this day by the blood of Jesus Christ, in Jesus name.
15. Every battle at the edge of my success; be swallowed by the blood of Jesus Christ, in the name of Jesus.
16. Almighty God, empower me today to stand perfect and complete in all your will, in the name of Jesus.
17. Almighty God let me be filled with the knowledge of your will in all wisdom and spiritual understanding, in the name of Jesus.
18. Almighty God let me be fruitful in every good work, and let me increase in the knowledge of you, in the name of Jesus.
19. Almighty God, you are the Lord of peace; let your peace be with me always, in the name of Jesus.
20. I receive multiplied grace and peace, in the name of Jesus.
21. I am complete in Christ Jesus, in the name of Jesus.
22. I command every witchcraft power, spiritual wickedness, and household wickedness; remove your hands from my life, in the name of Jesus.
23. Fire of the Holy Ghost, possess my spirit, soul, and body and set me free, in Jesus name.
24. I decree that, throughout this year, there shall be no darkness in my way, no darkness on my path, in the name of Jesus.
25. Almighty God, open the double doors for me throughout this year, in the name of Christ.
26. Almighty God, don't let your work fail in my life, in the name of Jesus.
27. The spirit that robs God of tithes and offerings must not operate in my life, in the name of Jesus.
28. Almighty God let all your grace abound toward me, in the name of Jesus.
29. Almighty God, let the lines fall for me in pleasant places in all areas of life, in the name of Jesus.
30. I command every satanic agenda for me this year to fail, in the name of Jesus.
31. I cancel every evil dreams, visions, prophesy and prayers against my life and family in the name of Jesus.
32. Talk to God about your heart desires and your situation.
33. Thank God for answered prayers.

Confession:

"Let them be confounded and put to shame that seek after my soul: let them be turned back and brought to confusion that device my hurt. Let them be as chaff before the wind: and let the angel of the Lord chase them. Let their way be dark and slippery: and let the angel of the Lord persecute them" Psalms 35:4–6.

Wisdom for Today:

As long as the pot remains over the fire, the food will continue to cook. So, stay connected to Jesus. He is the source of true victory and lasting laughter. Shalom!

Read the Bible Today: John 14

Prayer Points:

1. I praise and thank God for allowing me to see yet another day by his grace.
2. Almighty God turn tears to laughter in my life, in the name of Jesus.
3. Tears over my health, turn to laughter, in the name of Jesus.
4. Tears over my marriage, turn to laughter, in the name of Jesus.
5. Tears over my livelihood, turn to laughter, in the name of Jesus.
6. Tears over my progress, turn to laughter, in the name of Jesus.
7. Almighty God anoint me today with your special favor, in the name of Jesus.
8. Lord Jesus, pray for me today as you prayed for Lazarus in the name of Jesus.
9. I claim God's blessings that makes one rich; I shall not see or experience poverty in the name of Jesus.
10. Almighty God bless those who bless me today, and curse those who curse me today, in the name of Jesus.
11. I take over this day by the blood of Jesus Christ, in Jesus name.
12. You, serpent and scorpion of darkness delegated against my victory, I trample upon you, in the name of Jesus.
13. Almighty God, by your never-failing power, let me experience unstoppable progress, in the name of Jesus.
14. Every familiar spirit reporting my activities in the spirit realm be consumed by the fire of God, in the name of Jesus.

15. I resist every counterattack of my enemies, in the name of Jesus Christ.
16. To God be all the glory for all areas of my life, in the name of Jesus.
17. The Lord is my light and my salvation; the Lord is the strength of my life, in the name of Jesus.
18. I declare all will be well with me throughout this year, in the name of Jesus Christ.
19. I shall not partake in the evil of this year, in the name of Jesus.
20. Every evil mark upon my life that attracts attack be wiped off by the blood of Jesus, in the name of Jesus.
21. Evil pronouncement for this year, my life and my family are not your candidates, in the name of Jesus.
22. I reject accident and tragedy, in the name of Jesus.
23. Blood of Jesus Christ, cover me and my family in the name of Jesus.
24. Almighty God, let there be answers and manifestations in response to the prayers I have been praying for a long time, in the name of Jesus.
25. Almighty God, take over my case and justify me, in the name of Jesus.
26. Almighty God let my testimony this year give birth to more testimonies, in the mighty name of Jesus.
27. Almighty God, make me fruitful and allow me to multiply, in the name of Jesus.
28. Almighty God, bless me with the blessings of Abraham, in the name of Jesus.
29. Almighty God, don't let me walk into the pit that the enemy dug for me, in the name of Jesus Christ.
30. Almighty God anoint me and give me grace to bear fruit for you, in the name of Jesus.
31. I cancel every evil dreams, visions, prophesy and prayers against my life and family in the name of Jesus.
32. Talk to God about your heart desires and your situation.
33. Thank God for answered prayers.

Confession:

"Let them be ashamed and brought to confusion together that rejoice at mine hurt: Let them be clothed with shame and dishonor that magnify themselves against me" Psalms 35:26.

Wisdom for Today:

You will soon overcome whatever you are going through presently. Endurance is evidence of salvation—it develops character; therefore pray for endurance. There is enough grace for you in God. Shalom! Hebrews 10:35–36

Read the Bible Today: Job 22

Prayer Points:

1. I praise and thank God for allowing me to see yet another day by his grace.
2. Every tear in my family, turn to laughter, in the name of Jesus.
3. Every tear in my daily job, turn to laughter, in the name of Jesus.
4. Let the trumpet of my glory reject every evil authority, in the name of Jesus.
5. Every enemy of my crown of glory, scatter, in the name of Jesus.
6. Father Lord, baptize me with your fresh fire, in the name of Jesus Christ.
7. Every tear in my finances, turn to laughter, in the name of Jesus.
8. Every tear in my promotion, turn to laughter, in the name of Jesus.
9. Almighty God baptize me with your favor today, in the name of Jesus.
10. Lord Jesus, pray for me today in the mighty name of Jesus.
11. Fire of the Holy Ghost; ignite the works of my hands, in the name of Jesus.
12. Anointing of profit, fall upon me today, in the name of Jesus.
13. I bind and paralyze every physical and spiritual attack on me today, in the name of Jesus.
14. I take over this day by the blood of Jesus Christ, in Jesus name.
15. I bind and paralyze every physical and spiritual robber today, in Jesus name.
16. I shall be blessed and highly favored today, in Jesus name.
17. I receive divine direction for my life, in the name of Jesus.

18. Almighty God, I humble myself under your mighty hand; may I decrease, and may Jesus increase in me, in Jesus name.
19. Almighty God I am grateful because you are the source of all my blessings, in Jesus precious name.
20. Almighty God I thank you, for my case shall not be impossible with you, in Jesus precious name.
21. Almighty God I thank you because this year shall be the best of all the years I have lived, in the name of Jesus.
22. Almighty God I thank you, because you will surely cause me to move from glory to glory, in the name of Jesus.
23. Almighty God, I thank you because your mercy, favor, and grace shall be upon me like a garment, in the name of Jesus.
24. Almighty God I thank you, because your banner over me is love, in the name of Jesus.
25. Almighty God, I thank you and I praise you because your glory shall cover my life as the waters cover the sea, in the name of Jesus.
26. I cancel every evil dreams, visions, prophesy and prayers against my life and family in the name of Jesus.
27. Talk to God about your heart desires and your situation.
28. Thank God for answered prayers.

Confession:

"Let them be ashamed and confounded together that seek after my soul to destroy it; let them be driven backward and put to shame that wish me evil" Psalms 40:14.

Wisdom for Today:

Are you passing through any difficulties now? Search the scriptures and find out what is written concerning your situation. It is the written word of God that can solve your problems. Remember, God's word resides forever in heaven, and it is the only one sure thing that can settle your case. Shalom!

Read the Bible Today: Psalm 119

Prayer Points:

1. I praise and thank God for allowing me to see yet another day by his grace.
2. Every tear in my foundation, turn to laughter, in the name of Jesus.
3. Every tear in the lives of my divine helpers, turn to laughter, in the name of Jesus.
4. Every tear in my family, turn to laughter, in the name of Jesus.
5. Every tear in the life and family of my pastor, turn to laughter, in Jesus name.
6. Every tear in my neighborhood, turn to laughter, in the name of Jesus.
7. Almighty God baptize me with your favor today, in the name of Jesus.
8. Lord Jesus, pray for me today in the name of Jesus.
9. Holy Spirit, ignite the works of my hand by fire, in the name of Jesus.
10. Every wall of failure at the edge of good things in my life, fall, in the name of Jesus.
11. Every wall of "almost there" built against my life, I pull you down by the power of God, in the name of Jesus.
12. I take over this day by the blood of Jesus Christ, in Jesus name.
13. I sanitize my dwelling place by the power in the blood of Jesus Christ in the name of Jesus in the name of Jesus.

14. Every power of waste that is hindering my prosperity, I overcome you today by the blood of Jesus Christ.
15. I reject every spirit of error and confusion today, in the name of Jesus.
16. Jesus Christ is Lord.
17. Holy Spirit of God, incubate me and give life to my dry bones, in the name of Jesus.
18. I claim victory by the blood of Jesus Christ throughout this year, in the name Jesus.
19. Almighty God, bless me with wisdom in all areas of my life, in the name of Jesus.
20. I reject struggle this year, in the name of Jesus.
21. I reject every dream of affliction in the name of Jesus Christ.
22. Almighty God, restore unto me the joy of your presence, in the name of a Jesus.
23. Every good thing that is happening in my life be lifted up in Jesus name.
24. Sickness and infirmity, I reject you be gone, in the name of Jesus.
25. I bind and cast out the spirit of slumber from my life, in the name of Jesus.
26. Almighty God, visit my life with your power, and remove every curse that is interfering with my blessings, in the name of Jesus.
27. I am blessed, curses cannot harm me, all is well with me, in the name of Jesus Christ.
28. Every satanic stronghold in my life, I break you down, I pull you down, in the name of Jesus.
29. I pull down the influence of any spirit wife or husband, in the name of Jesus.
30. I am redeemed from every curse through the blood of Jesus Christ in the name of Jesus .
31. I cancel every evil dreams, visions, prophesy and prayers against my life and family in the name of Jesus.
32. Talk to God about your heart desires and your situation.
33. Thank God for answered prayers.

Confession:

"God is my refuge and strength, a very present help in trouble"
Psalms 46:1.

Wisdom for Today:

The devil goes about trying to substitute nothing for something in people's lives. He started this with Eve in the Garden of Eden. Beloved, stand on guard! The devil has not changed his plan. He tried his deceit on Jesus, but the Lord resisted, and the devil left him. You too can do as your master by resisting the devil, and he will flee from you.

Read the Bible Today: Genesis 3 and Luke 4

Prayer Points:

1. I praise and thank God for allowing me to see yet another day by his grace.
2. Every covenant of failure in my life and family, break, in the name of Jesus.
3. Every door of failure in my life is closed so that the doors of success may open, in Jesus name.
4. Every power of failure upon my destiny is dethroned, in the name of Jesus.
5. Almighty God, dry up the stream of failure in my life and family, in the name of Jesus.
6. Every journey of failure is turned to a journey of success in my life, in Jesus name.
7. Every evil power laid upon my handiwork, be removed by fire, in the name of Jesus.
8. Every anointing of profitless efforts upon my life, I overcome you by the blood of Jesus in the name of Jesus.
9. I raise the blood of Jesus Christ against all witchcraft power that may want to work against me, and I overcome them, in the name of Jesus.
10. Every power of witchcraft in my life, fall down and die, in the name of Jesus.
11. I take over this day by the blood of Jesus Christ, in Jesus name.
12. Almighty God let me be at the right place at the right time, in the name of Jesus.

13. Every garment of poverty, I remove you from my life, and I set you on fire, in the name of Jesus.
14. From now on, every good thing I touch shall prosper, in the name of Jesus.
15. I prophesy unto the works of my hands: proper by the power in the blood of Jesus Christ.
16. I cover myself with the blood of Jesus Christ in the name of Jesus.
17. I place myself under the power of the cross of Jesus Christ in the name of Jesus.
18. I surround myself with the light of Jesus Christ in the name of Jesus.
19. I decree that the devil will not interfere with the work of God in my life, in the name of Jesus Christ.
20. I put on the whole amour of God, and I resist the devil, in the name of Jesus Christ.
21. Almighty God, have mercy upon me. Help my unbelief, in the name of Jesus.
22. Almighty God, regarding the situation in my life that is affecting my faith, arise, oh, Lord, and perform a miracle, in the name of Jesus.
23. Almighty God, lay your good hand upon my life and make me attractive to prosperity, in the name of Jesus.
24. By the power of the Holy Ghost, I claim back any territory of my life handed over to the devil, in the name of Jesus.
25. Almighty God, open doors for me that enemies cannot shut, in the name of Jesus.
26. Almighty God manifest your power and give me great deliverance, in the name of Jesus.
27. I give thanks to God.
28. Almighty God, by the power of your grace, keep all my bones in the name of Jesus.
29. I decree that the bones of my destiny, marriage, children, blessings, helpers, and business, shall not break, in the name of Jesus.
30. I thank God for a blessed day Jesus Christ is Lord.
31. I cancel every evil dreams, visions, prophesy and prayers against my life and family in the name of Jesus.
32. Talk to God about your heart desires and your situation.
33. Thank God for answered prayers.

Apostle A.O. Solomon

Confession:

"The Lord of hosts is with me; the God of Jacob is my refuge"
Psalms 46: 7.

Wisdom for Today:

The Lord's Prayer is more about living in a trusting and growing relationship with our heavenly Father than about getting what you want from him. Don't let your prayers always reflect only your wish-and-want list; instead, use prayer as an intimate conversation with God.

Read the Bible Today: Exodus 33 and Psalm 78

Prayer Points:

1. I praise and thank God for allowing me to see yet another day by his grace.
2. Every mark of failure upon my life, turn to success, in the name of Jesus.
3. Every failure in my business, turn to success, in the name of Jesus.
4. I declare that success will take over failure in my situation, in the name of Jesus.
5. Every power and personality that champions failure in my life, perish beyond remedy, in the name of Jesus.
6. I shall not lose focus on my Savior, in the name of Jesus.
7. I refuse to substitute my eternity for the vanities of this world, in the name of Jesus.
8. I take over this day by the blood of Jesus Christ, in Jesus name.
9. I prophesy good things upon my life, my destiny, my marriage, and my family in the name of Jesus.
10. I command every word of prophesy I utter to myself, begin to manifest, in the name of Jesus.
11. I come out of every slavery and chain, in the name of Jesus.
12. Arrows of the wicked be diverted away from my life and ways, in the name of Jesus.
13. Almighty God, breathe upon me your breath of life and revive my spirit, soul, and body, in the name of Jesus.
14. Almighty God, I commit this day into your hands ,bless my coming in and going out, in the name of Jesus

15. Almighty God let your favor answer to me, in the name of Jesus Christ.
16. Almighty God let me experience the wonder of your grace today, in the name of Jesus.
17. Almighty God, let your grace be sufficient for me today, and let it deliver me from shame and disgrace, in the name of Jesus.
18. Through the grace of Jesus Christ, I shall possess the gates of my enemies, in Jesus name.
19. I give thanks to God.
20. I break and release myself from all curses and negative words spoken against me, in the name of Jesus.
21. I drink the blood of Jesus Christ.
22. Let the miracle of God appear over every fear in my life, in the name of Jesus.
23. Every evil dream that is tormenting my life, the Lord rebuke you, in the name of Jesus.
24. Father Lord, place on my head the ornament of grace, in the name of Jesus.
25. I break away and release myself from the bondage and captivity of fake prophets and ministers, in the name of Jesus.
26. Every power that wants to eat my flesh or drink my blood, collapse and die, in the name of Jesus.
27. Let the healing power of Jesus flow into every department of my life, in the name of Jesus.
28. Let God arise, and all his enemies be scattered, in the name of Jesus.
29. I reject evil dreams and visions, in Jesus name.
30. I cancel every evil dreams, visions, prophesy and prayers against my life and family in the name of Jesus.
31. Talk to God about your heart desires and your situation.
32. Thank God for answered prayers.

Confession:

"Let death seize upon them, and let them go down quick into hell: for wickedness is in their dwelling, and among them. As for me, I will call upon God; and the Lord shall save me" Psalms 55:15–16.

Wisdom for Today:

God's will and word do work when they are understood and lived out every day. True prayer will do the following:
- build intimacy with God
- bring honor to his nature and character
- cause respect for his integrity
- enable and establish belief in his word
- cause a trust in his love
- affirm his purposes and will
- appropriate his promises

Ask God to teach you how to pray.

Read the Bible Today: Isaiah 58 and Revelation 2

Prayer Points:

1. I praise and thank God for allowing me to see yet another day by his grace.
2. I decree this day to yield joy, blessings, testimonies, abundance, success, money, breakthroughs, favors, and honor unto me, in the name of Jesus.
3. I am blessed and highly favored, in the name of Jesus.
4. Father Lord, let all those conspiring against me be disgraced openly, in Jesus name.
5. Let the angels of God clear the way for my blessings and breakthroughs today, in Jesus name.
6. I am secured under the shadow of the Almighty God, in Jesus name.
7. Father Lord, anoint me with your fresh fire for a new beginning, in the mighty name of Jesus.
8. You, my destiny, flesh, and blood, receive the fresh fire of God for deliverance, in the name of Jesus.
9. I take over this day by the blood of Jesus Christ, in Jesus name.

10. Every evil throne reigning against me be destroyed unto desolation, in the name of Jesus.

11. Every attack against my destiny, go back to sender, in the name of Jesus.

12. Every satanic agent assigned against me, be smitten, in the name of Jesus.

13. Every power assigned to put me on the sick bed, perish, in the name of Jesus.

14. Father Lord, set me free from debt, poverty, and lack, in the name of Jesus.

15. Father Lord, bless me today, in the name of Jesus.

16. Almighty God, remove everything that the devil is using to torment and afflict my life in the name of Jesus.

17. Every demon of my past, blocking my new blessings, I cast you out of my life, the Lord rebuke you, in the name of Jesus.

18. By the power of the Holy Ghost, I break and release myself from the powers of the past, in the name of Jesus.

19. Almighty God, heal me of every bitterness I harbor over my past ugly experiences, in the name of Jesus Christ.

20. Blood of Jesus Christ arise and erase the evil memory of my past in the name of Jesus.

21. Through the blood of Jesus Christ, satan you have lost the battle over my life in the name of Jesus.

22. I decree that the devil has lost the battle through the word of God, in the name of Jesus Christ.

23. Arise, Rock of Ages, and fall upon every power and spirit waging war against me in this land and against prosperity in my life, in the name of Jesus.

24. Almighty God, let all grace abound towards me, in the name of Jesus.

25. Any powers that want to cut the branches of my life, let fire consume them, in the name of Jesus Christ.

26. Father Lord, overwhelm my life with your glory and power, in the name of Jesus Christ.

27. I refuse to be stagnant in life; I receive power to move forward, in the name of Jesus.

28. Every power and spirit of stagnancy in my life, relinquish your hold over my life, in the name of Jesus.

29. Every character that is putting off my helpers be removed by the blood of Jesus, in the name of Jesus.
30. Almighty God, bless me and help me to be a blessing to others in the name of Jesus.
31. I cancel every evil dreams, visions, prophesy and prayers against my life and family in the name of Jesus.
32. Talk to God about your heart desires and your situation.
33. Thank God for answered prayers.

Confession:

"But those that seek my soul to destroy it, shall go into the lower part of the earth. They shall fall by the sword: they shall be a portion for foxes" Psalms 63:9–10.

Wisdom for Today:

Success does not come by human strength, but by the spirit and power of God. Hope in God, and all shall be well. Shalom!

Read the Bible Today: Exodus 8, 1 Samuel 2, and Zechariah 4

Prayer Points:

1. I praise and thank God for allowing me to see yet another day by his grace.
2. I thank God for his never failing power.
3. I thank God for making all things work together for good for me, in Jesus name.
4. I thank God for giving me the power to acquire wealth in the name of Jesus.
5. I thank God for making this my month of divine separation in the name of Jesus.
6. Let the blood of Jesus sanctify my spirit, soul, and body, in the name of Jesus.
7. Every seed of backsliding planted in my life, be removed by the power of God, in the name of Jesus.
8. I take over this day by the blood of Jesus Christ, in Jesus name.
9. I lift away every garment of sickness, in the name of Jesus.
10. I lift away every garment of shame, in the name of Jesus.
11. I lift away every garment of reproach, in the name of Jesus.
12. I shall not die before my restoration comes, in the name of Jesus.
13. Father Lord, open a new chapter of my life today, and I will live to give you the praise, in the name of Jesus.
14. Father Lord, let the heavens open for me and move to my direction, in the name of Jesus.
15. Arrows of the wicked be diverted away from me and my family in the name of Jesus.
16. I bind and cast away every trouble fashioned against me today, in the name of Jesus.

17. Father Lord, teach me the deep and secret things I need to know, in the name of Jesus.
18. Father Lord, silent every storm in my life, family, work, marriage, and business, in the name of Jesus.
19. Almighty God arise and silence every storm in my life in the name of Jesus.
20. Every giant occupying my Promised Land, I cast you out, in the name of Jesus.
21. Almighty God, bless me with the spirit of faith, help my unbelief, in the name of Jesus Christ.
22. Power and spirit of fulfillment, possess my life, in the name of Jesus.
23. I trample upon serpents and scorpions, in the mighty name of Jesus.
24. Let the angels of the living God manifest to bless and help me, in the name of Jesus Christ.
25. Almighty God, help me not to miss my time and chance, in the name of Jesus.
26. Almighty God let your hand be upon me and my family for good, in the name of Jesus.
27. Let the excellent oil of God fall upon me, in the name of Jesus.
28. Every garment prepared for me by the enemies this year, I refuse you, be consumed by fire, in the name of Jesus.
29. Almighty God, baptize me with your favor and the spirit of the Holy Ghost, in the name of Jesus.
30. I cancel every evil dreams, visions, prophesy and prayers against my life and family in the name of Jesus.
31. Talk to God about your heart desires and your situation.
32. Thank God for answered prayers.

Confession:

"Let God arise, let all my enemies be scattered". Psalms 68:1.

Wisdom for Today:

When the heavens move toward your direction, your mouth will be filled with testimony, a new chapter will be open for your life, and the old ones will be closed. There is nothing you can compare to the heavens opening for you. Pray for heaven to open for you and move to your direction.

Read the Bible Today: *1 Chronicles 4:1–9 and John 11*

Prayer Points:

1. I praise and thank God for allowing me to see yet another day by his grace.
2. Every spirit and power in the air, land, and sea against my prayers today, perish now, in Jesus name.
3. Every power supporting and strengthening my enemy, be paralyzed, in the name of Jesus.
4. I pull down every evil stronghold protecting my enemy today, in the name of Jesus.
5. Almighty God, open the book of remembrance for me today, in the name of Jesus.
6. Anything in my life blocking my breakthroughs, come out and enter no more, in the name of Jesus.
7. I refuse to go back to Egypt, in the name of Jesus.
8. Every spirit assigned to follow me about, be paralyzed now, in the name of Jesus.
9. I take over this day by the blood of Jesus Christ, in Jesus name.
10. Father Lord, open the heavens for me today, in the name of Jesus.
11. Every spirit assigned to hinder my progress and prosperity, be bound and paralyzed, in the name of Jesus.
12. I command the ground to swallow every death assigned against me and my family in the name of Jesus.
13. Every power and spirit stealing my blessings and promotions, perish and rise no more, in the name of Jesus.
14. Almighty God let my words matter in heaven today, in the name of Jesus.

15. Every darkness resisting my prayers, scatter unto desolation, in the name of Jesus.
16. Holy Spirit of God, overwhelm my life, in the name of Jesus Christ.
17. Holy Spirit of God, lead me in the way I should go, in the name of Jesus.
18. I take over this day by the blood of Jesus and the power of the Holy Ghost in the name of Jesus.
19. I receive divine direction for my life, in the name of Jesus Christ.
20. By the spirit of prophesy, I speak to all creation to arise and assist me, in the name of Jesus.
21. Almighty God, bless me with sufficient grace, in the name of Jesus.
22. Failure, frustration, and disappoint shall not prosper in my life this year, in the name of Jesus.
23. I release my money from the control of the enemy, in the name of Jesus.
24. I command the enemy of my breakthrough to go down in defeat, in the name of Jesus.
25. Every weapon of the enemy fashioned against me, backfire, in the name of Jesus.
26. Holy Spirit of God, rule over my life, in the name of Jesus.
27. Almighty God, open the heavens and let your angels begin to ascend and descend for my sake, in the name of Jesus.
28. Almighty God, place my feet on the ladder of divine breakthrough and accomplishment in life, in the name of Jesus.
29. Almighty God, stand above my life and speak solutions to my life today, in the name of Jesus.
30. Almighty God bless me and make me a blessing to others, in the name of Jesus.
31. I cancel every evil dreams, visions, prophesy and prayers against my life and family in the name of Jesus.
32. Talk to God about your heart desires and your situation.
33. Thank God for answered prayers.

Confession:

"When I cry unto thee, then shall mine enemies turn back; this I know; for God is for me" Psalms 56:9.

Wisdom for Today:

Don't feel small in your own eyes. 1 John 4:4 (ESV) tells us, "He who is in you is greater than he who is in the world." When God is in control, you have nothing to fear. You are precious!

Read the Bible Today: Isaiah 55 and Matthew 5

Prayer Points:

1. I praise and thank God for allowing me to see yet another day by his grace.
2. If I am my own enemy, Lord, deliver me today, in the name of Jesus.
3. I receive the fire of Elijah to disgrace my enemy, in the name of Jesus.
4. I receive the mantle of Elijah to cross over my Jordan today, in the name of Jesus.
5. By the power of the living God, let my rejection turn to divine selection, in Jesus name.
6. By the power of the living God, let my sorrow turn to joy, in the name of Jesus.
7. Let every secret plan of the devil against me and my family be exposed and be disgraced, in the name of Jesus Christ.
8. Every evil arrow sent to me and my family, back to the sender, in the name of Jesus.
9. Every evil queen in the heavens militating against my life and destiny, I overcome you today by the blood of Jesus Christ.
10. I take over this day by the blood of Jesus Christ, in Jesus name.
11. Almighty God, start your government upon every department of my life, in the name of Jesus.
12. Every satanic checkpoint erected in the heavens against my prosperity this year, I bulldoze you by the power of the living God, in the name of Jesus.
13. Every evil pursuer located in the high places of this state and country, be pulled down by the power of God, in the name of Jesus.

14. Father Lord, let your kingdom come into my life and your will be done in every area of my life, in the name of Jesus.
15. Holy Spirit, redefine my life to suit my divine destiny, in the name of Jesus.
16. Jesus Christ is Lord over every area of my life in the name of Jesus.
17. Almighty God, remember me for good today, be gracious unto me, and show me your great mercy, in Jesus name.
18. Lord Jesus Christ, I need your touch today, touch me and make me whole in the name of Jesus.
19. Almighty God, have your way in my life, in the name of Jesus Christ.
20. I hold the blood of Jesus against all evil dreams, and I decree they shall not stand; neither shall they come to pass, in the name of Jesus.
21. Almighty God, deliver my eyes from tears, in the name of Jesus.
22. Almighty God deliver me from all evil, in the name of Jesus Christ.
23. My imprisoned glory, receive deliverance now and blossom, in the name of Jesus.
24. Every goodness of my life that the enemies are covering be uncovered, in the name of Jesus.
25. I cancel every evil dreams, visions, prophesy and prayers against my life and family in the name of Jesus.
26. Talk to God about your heart desires and your situation.
27. Thank God for answered prayers.

Confession:

"In God I have put my trust: I will not be afraid what man can do unto me" Psalms 56:11.

Wisdom for Today:

As part of Christ's church today, you may get discouraged by resistance to the gospel. You need to remember that God's work is not done by your might or power, but by the Holy Spirit. Your responsibility is to speak out in faith in his name and leave the results to God. Rejoice; it's harvest season!

Read the Bible Today: *Acts 1–3*

Prayer Points:

1. I praise and thank God for allowing me to see yet another day by his grace.
2. Let my job receive deliverance now from every attack, in the name of Jesus.
3. This month shall yield blessings and abundance for me in all areas, in Jesus name.
4. I reject sorrow throughout this month, in the name of Jesus.
5. I refuse to weep throughout this month, in the name of Jesus.
6. I reject failure, frustration, and disappointment throughout this month, in Jesus name.
7. Let the heavens move against my enemies, in the name of Jesus.
8. Let the heavens move on my side for favor, in the name of Jesus.
9. Almighty God cast me not away from your presence, and take not your Holy Spirit from me, in the name of Jesus.
10. I shall see the goodness of the Lord in the land of the living, in the name of Jesus.
11. I take over this day by the blood of Jesus Christ, in Jesus name.
12. Every power broadcasting my goodness for evil be silenced, in the name of Jesus.
13. Almighty God, seal up all the holes in bags and pockets that might leak misery upon me, in the name of Jesus Christ.
14. All my blessings confiscated by witchcraft spirits, be released by the blood of Jesus Christ.
15. All my blessings confiscated by familiar spirits, be released by the blood of Jesus Christ.

16. Almighty God restore my lost chances and opportunities to me, in the name of Jesus Christ.
17. Almighty God let it be known that you are God in my life, in the name of Jesus.
18. Almighty God, arise and let every problem in my life vanish, in the name of Jesus.
19. Let God arise in my life, and let my family's bondage break asunder, in the name of Jesus.
20. Let God arise and every yoke in my life break, in the name of Jesus.
21. Let God arise in my life, and let poverty vanish from my life, in the name of Jesus.
22. Let God arise in my life, and let failure vanish from my life, in the name of Jesus.
23. Let God arise in my life, and let stubborn problems in my life vanish, in the name of Jesus.
24. Almighty God, be gracious unto me. Do not let me to spend this year the way I have spent my previous years, in the name of Jesus.
25. Almighty God, give me an outstanding breakthrough, in the name of Jesus.
26. Almighty God let me be celebrated and congratulated this year, in the name of Jesus Christ.
27. Every negative sign and feeling in my life, vanish, in the name of Jesus.
28. Every power swallowing my testimony, vomit them up now, in the name of Jesus Christ.
29. Every satanic power denying me my greatness be destroyed, in the name of Jesus.
30. Almighty God, rescue me today by great deliverance, in the name of Jesus.
31. I cancel every evil dreams, visions, prophesy and prayers against my life and family in the name of Jesus.
32. Talk to God about your heart desires and your situation.
33. Thank God for answered prayers.

Confession:

"My God of mercy shall come to meet me: God shall let me see my desire upon mine enemies" Psalms 59:10.

Wisdom for Today:

Decisions determine destiny. Many people have made wrong decisions in the past and are still suffering from the consequences today. So be careful not to make permanent decisions on temporary circumstances or situations. Shalom!

Read the Bible Today: Proverbs 1–4

Prayer Points:

1. I praise and thank God for allowing me to see yet another day by his grace.
2. I will not dance to the music of my enemies, in the name of Jesus.
3. Let the blood of Jesus go before and after me throughout the rest of my days, in Jesus name.
4. I shall not wander away from the presence of God, in the name of Jesus.
5. Every battle at the edge of my blessings and testimonies, I overcome you today, in Jesus name.
6. Almighty God baptize me with favor in my place of work, and promote me, in the name of Jesus.
7. I shall not move away from God, in the name of Jesus.
8. I shall be faithful in my tithes and offerings, in the name of Jesus.
9. I overcome every evil dream in my life by the blood of Jesus Christ in the name of Jesus.
10. Father Lord, let your presence melt away every mountain of problem in my life, in the name of Jesus Christ.
11. I take over this day by the blood of Jesus Christ, in Jesus name.
12. All my blessings confiscated by ancestral spirits, be released by the blood of Jesus Christ.
13. All my blessings swallowed by the enemies, be vomited now, in the name of Jesus Christ.
14. Whatever is hindering my progress, almighty God, locate and destroy it now, in the name of Jesus Christ.
15. I thank God for his faithfulness.
16. I declare Jesus Christ is Lord.

17. I declare the joy of the Lord is my strength, in the name of Jesus.

18. The Lord is the strength of my life; I will fear no one in the name of Jesus.

19. Every foundation of evil dreams in my life, be uprooted and be destroyed, in the name of Jesus.

20. Any evil planted in my life through dreams, come out and go back to your sender, in the name of Jesus.

21. I challenge my spirit, soul, and body with the fire of God, in the name of Jesus.

22. Every root of multiple failures in my life be uprooted, in the name of Jesus.

23. By the power of the Holy Ghost, I break and release myself from the grip of failure, in the name of Jesus.

24. Every stronghold of failure in my life, I pull you down in the name of Jesus.

25. Every foundation of delay in my life, be uprooted and be destroyed, in the name of Jesus.

26. Anything that is delaying my breakthrough, your time is up, die in the name of Jesus.

27. Almighty God, deliver me from every delay in my life [mention the delay], in the mighty name of Jesus Christ.

28. I pray for my country that all shall be well in the name of Jesus.

29. Almighty God deliver me and my country from mass destruction, in the name of Jesus.

30. Almighty God, establish, perfect, and settle me, in the name of Jesus.

31. I cancel every evil dreams, visions, prophesy and prayers against my life and family in the name of Jesus.

32. Talk to God about your heart desires and your situation.

33. Thank God for answered prayers.

Confession:

"All the horns of the wicked also will I cut off; but my horns shall be exalted" Psalms 75:10.

Wisdom for Today:

Divine guidance is your covenant from God and your gateway to supernatural breakthroughs.

Read the Bible Today: Psalms 23 and 91

Prayer Points:

1. I praise and thank God for allowing me to see yet another day by his grace.
2. I thank God in advance for the breakthrough and favor I am expecting in the name of Jesus.
3. I thank God for his faithfulness at all times to those who trust in him.
4. Father, I thank you because eyes have not seen and ears have not heard what you have in store for me in the name of Jesus.
5. Almighty God I thank you for giving me all things to enjoy in the name of Jesus.
6. Almighty God let me find favor for blessing in your sight, in the name of Jesus.
7. Almighty God, rend the heavens and come down to help me, in the name of Jesus.
8. I am God's anointed; no wickedness is permitted to touch me, in the name of Jesus.
9. Today my light shall break forth as the noonday sun, in the name of Jesus.
10. I take over this day by the blood of Jesus Christ, in Jesus name.
11. I call out to the star of my life from every thick darkness, in the name of Jesus.
12. I call out to the star of my destiny from every thick darkness, in the name of Jesus.
13. I call out to the star of my family from every thick darkness, in the name of Jesus.
14. I call out to the star of my finances from every thick darkness, in the name of Jesus.

15. Blood of Jesus Christ, manifest God's glory in my life, in Jesus name.
16. Almighty God, beautify and decorate me, in the name of Jesus.
17. Almighty God, rend the heavens and come down for my sake, in the name of Jesus.
18. Almighty God rend the heavens and help me to put my enemies to shame, in the name of Jesus.
19. I cancel every evil and its manifestation and consequence by the blood of Jesus, in the name of Jesus.
20. Almighty God give me my miracle today, in the name of Jesus.
21. Almighty God, deliver me from the hands of the wicked, in the name of Jesus.
22. I give thanks to God.
23. Almighty God, make this year my year, in the name of Jesus.
24. I shall not miss my chances this year; doors of goodness shall not be shut against me, in the name of Jesus.
25. Every power that has prepared shame for me this year, carry your hindrance away, in the name of Jesus.
26. I cancel every evil dreams, visions, prophesy and prayers against my life and family in the name of Jesus.
27. Talk to God about your heart desires and your situation.
28. Thank God for answered prayers.

Confession:

"Thou hast broken in pieces, as one that is slain; thou hast scattered thine enemies with thy strong arm" Psalms 89:10.

Wisdom for Today:

We are in the age of skill. Companies and employers are more interested in the skill you have than the certificate you possess. Some Christians in the labor market are unskilled. They use prayer and fasting as a substitute for skill. Your employer will not eat your fasting; he needs your input.

Read the Bible Today: Proverbs 18 and 22

Prayer Points:

1. I praise and thank God for allowing me to see yet another day by his grace.
2. Let the favor of God go with me everywhere I go, in the name of Jesus.
3. The favor of God shall manifest in my life, even in adverse places, as it did for Joseph, in the name of Jesus.
4. By faith, I receive the kind of favor God gave Israel to collect the goods of the Egyptians, in Jesus name.
5. I receive the favor of divine elevation in the sight of the enemy, in the name of Jesus.
6. I take over this day by the blood of Jesus Christ, in Jesus name.
7. Every evil written against me in the heavens, be blotted out by the blood of Jesus Christ, in Jesus name.
8. Every evil written against me on the earth, be blotted out by the blood of Jesus Christ, in Jesus name.
9. Every evil written against me under the earth, be blotted out by the blood of Jesus Christ, in Jesus name.
10. Almighty God, have mercy upon me by your never-failing power, return me to my glory, in the name of Jesus Christ.
11. Almighty God let your eyes go with me and cause me to stand before kings, in the name of Jesus.
12. Almighty God baptize me with your wisdom, knowledge, and understanding, in the name of Jesus.
13. This day shall be a pleasant day for me, in the name of Jesus.

14. I shall show forth the praises of the Lord my God today, in the name of Jesus.
15. By the anointing power of God, I throw out everything trouble the vessel of my life in the name of Jesus.
16. All the helpers attached to my success and greatness in life, be released from your captivity, in the name of Jesus.
17. Every negative information about my life in the hands of my helpers be consumed by fire, in the name of Jesus.
18. Every evil information about me in the heart of my helpers be erased by the blood of Jesus, in Jesus name.
19. Every strategy to chase my helpers away from me, fail woefully, in the name of Jesus.
20. Almighty God, whatever you need to do for my helpers to show up, do it now, in the name of Jesus Christ.
21. Every satanic stronghold erected in the heart of my helpers, I pull you down, in the name of Jesus.
22. Any character in me that is chasing my helpers away, fire of God consume them, in the name of Jesus.
23. Almighty God raise expected and unexpected help, for me, in the name of Jesus.
24. Almighty God, heal my soul and spirit, in the mighty name of Jesus Christ.
25. Every good door that has refused to open for me, almighty God, open it for me, in the name of Jesus Christ.
26. I cancel every evil dreams, visions, prophesy and prayers against my life and family in the name of Jesus.
27. Talk to God about your heart desires and your situation.
28. Thank God for answered prayers.

Confession:

"For the Lord is my defense; and the Holy one of Israel is my King"
Psalms 89:18.

Wisdom for Today:

Do not allow opportunities to promote Jesus pass you by. Even if you brought somebody who didn't stay, go and bring another. Keep bringing and bringing, and for every person you invite who stays with Jesus, you will be divinely rewarded.

Read the Bible Today: Revelation 2–5

Prayer Points:

1. I praise and thank God for allowing me to see yet another day by his grace.
2. By faith; I receive the kind of favor Moses found in the sight of God, in the name of Jesus.
3. Almighty God, lead me to those who will bless me and not to those who will destroy me, in the name of Jesus.
4. Almighty God order my steps to meet those who will believe in your ability in me, in Jesus name.
5. Almighty God give me breakthrough ideas that will open the door of favor to me, in the name of Jesus.
6. I confess by faith that I have the life and favor of God in the face of apparent danger, in Jesus name.
7. Anointing of God, overflow my life now, in the name of Jesus.
8. Let coals of fire rain on every evil gathering called for my sake, in the name of Jesus.
9. Let every evil cloud of frustration against me clear away, in the name of Jesus.
10. In the name of Jesus, I cover myself and my household with the shed blood of Jesus Christ in the name of Jesus.
11. I take over this day by the blood of Jesus Christ, in Jesus name.
12. I decree that I will no longer live a life of lack and uncertainty, in the name of Jesus Christ.
13. Contrary to the wishes of my enemies, my life shall not be stagnant, in the name of Jesus Christ.
14. Contrary to the wishes of my enemies, I shall fulfill my destiny, in the name of Jesus.

15. Almighty God bless me this day and make your face to shine upon me, in the name of Jesus Christ
16. Almighty God, heal my soul and spirit, in the mighty name of Jesus Christ.
17. Every good door, that has refused to open to me, almighty God, open it for me in the name of Jesus Christ.
18. Almighty God, do something great in my life, in the name of Jesus.
19. Almighty God, bless me and my family with peace in the mighty name of Jesus Christ.
20. Every snare prepared for my soul, be destroyed in the name of Jesus.
21. I give thanks to God; I am a blessed child in the name of Jesus.
22. Almighty God, help me to serve you better in spirit and in truth, in the name of Jesus Christ.
23. I cancel every evil dreams, visions, prophesy and prayers against my life and family in the name of Jesus.
24. Talk to God about your heart desires and your situation.
25. Thank God for answered prayers.

Confession:

"The enemy shall not exact upon me; nor the sons of wickedness afflict me. And God will beat all my foes before my face, and plague them that hate me..." Psalms 89:22–24.

Wisdom for Today:

Praying without planning is playing without knowing. Planning is as crucial as praying. It is not enough to have a word from God. You must have a plan to match the word; otherwise, the word will look like a word that never came. Planning is a nontransferable responsibility. God won't do the planning for you; he will only direct you to be sure you are on the right path.

Read the Bible Today: *Proverbs 24 and Hebrews 11*

Prayer Points:

1. I praise and thank God for allowing me to see yet another day by his grace.
2. I receive special favor today that will cause kings to seek after me, in the name of Jesus.
3. Almighty God let the blessing of your favor make me full of your blessing, in Jesus name.
4. I pull down every wall of resistance to my favor, in the name of Jesus.
5. I will always have cause to rejoice, in the name of Jesus.
6. The favor of God shall flow from me to those who are around me, in Jesus name.
7. By the reason of the shed blood of Jesus, let every evil wind blow away, in the name of Jesus.
8. I possess the keys to the gate of my hidden blessings, in the name of Jesus.
9. Almighty God, heal my soul and spirit, in the mighty name of Jesus Christ.
10. Every good door that has refused to open to me, almighty God, open it for me, in the name of Jesus Christ.
11. Almighty God, do something great in my life, in the name of Jesus.
12. Almighty God, bless me and my family with peace in the mighty name of Jesus Christ.

13. Almighty God, this year don't let me weep over my family, and don't let my family weep over me, in the name of Jesus Christ.
14. Every snare prepared for my soul, be destroyed in the name of Jesus.
15. I give thanks to God; I am a blessed child in the name of Jesus.
16. Almighty God, help me to serve you better in spirit and in truth, in the name of Jesus Christ.
17. Almighty God, do something great in my life, in the name of Jesus.
18. I cancel every evil dreams, visions, prophesy and prayers against my life and family in the name of Jesus.
19. Talk to God about your heart desires and your situation.
20. Thank God for answered prayers.

Confession:

"He that dwelleth in the secret place of the most high shall abide under the shadow of the Almighty" Psalms 91:1.

Wisdom for Today:

What many call problems are merely stepping-stones toward progress. You must stay focused like Nehemiah. Many have learned by experience that, when enemies perceive what God is doing in your life, they'll bring up a multitude of obstacles to discourage you and divert your focus.

Read the Bible Today: Nehemiah 6

Prayer Points:

1. I praise and thank God for allowing me to see yet another day by his grace.
2. I thank God that my appointed time of favor has come in the name of Jesus.
3. I give Praise to God because he will not let the enemy triumph over me, in the name of Jesus.
4. I confess that the favor of God will make me a lender not a borrower, in Jesus name.
5. Praise the Lord, for even in a strange land, I shall be a carrier of his favor in the name of Jesus.
6. I thank and praise God because his goodness and mercy will follow me all the days of my life in Jesus name.
7. Anyone who curses me shall carry the curse; anyone who blesses me shall be blessed, in Jesus name.
8. Every power programmed in to the heavenlies to manipulate my destiny, be captured, in the name of Jesus.
9. I plead the blood of Jesus Christ over all that I shall do today, in the name of Jesus.
10. Every power like Goliath that is trying to confound my life and destiny, receive the stones of fire and die, in the name of Jesus.
11. I shall not see the grave of my children, in the name of Jesus Christ.

12. Every devil after my blessings and testimonies be defeated by the blood of Jesus in the name of Jesus.

13. It is well with my going out and my coming in today, in Jesus name.

14. I overcome evil dreams by the blood of Jesus Christ in the name of Jesus.

15. I overcome every work of the enemy by the blood of Jesus Christ in the name of Jesus.

16. I sprinkle the blood of Jesus over this day in the name of Jesus.

17. Holy Spirit of God, move my life forward; I refuse to be moving in circles, in the name of Jesus.

18. Every power and spirit making me move in circles, physically and spiritually; release me by fire, in the name of Jesus.

19. Every mountain of failure, I refuse to move around you any longer; be removed and be cast into the sea in the name of Jesus.

20. Mountain of sickness and infirmity, I refuse to move around you any longer; Be removed and be cast into the sea in the name of Jesus.

21. Almighty God, bless me and multiply that blessing a thousand times in the name of Jesus.

22. Every giant occupying my promised land, pack your load and depart in the name of Jesus Christ.

23. I receive power to possess my promised land this year in the name of Jesus Christ.

24. Every evil king reigning in my promised land, I dethrone you in the name of Jesus.

25. Almighty God, remove every sickness from my life in the name of Jesus.

26. Let joy and peace in the Holy Spirit overwhelm my soul in the name of Jesus.

27. You, spirit of fear, I bind and cast you out of my life in the name of Jesus.

28. Let my heavens open, in the name of Jesus.

29. Every evil arrow fired into my heart, come out, in the name of Jesus Christ.

1. Heal me, O Lord, and I shall be healed, in the name of Jesus Christ.

2. Every perfected work of the enemies in my life, family, and my work, oh, God, arise and destroy them, in the name of Jesus.

3. Almighty God let your purpose for me this year come to pass, in the name of Jesus Christ.

4. Almighty God, I pray for a major breakthrough this year, in the name of Jesus Christ.

5. Almighty God; make me a major source of blessing this year, in the name of Jesus Christ.

6. Almighty God, do something great in my life, in the name of Jesus.

7. I cancel every evil dreams, visions, prophesy and prayers against my life and family in the name of Jesus.

8. Talk to God about your heart desires and your situation.

9. Thank God for answered prayers.

Confession:

"Lift up your heads, O ye gates; and be ye lifted up, ye everlasting doors; and the king of glory shall come in. Who is this king of glory? The Lord strong and mighty, the Lord mighty in battle. Lift up your heads, O ye gates; even lift them up, ye everlasting doors; and the king of glory shall come in. Who is this king of glory? The Lord of hosts, he is the king of glory" Psalms 24:7–10.

Wisdom for Today:

Whatever your situation, know that the Lord is standing near. Don't abandon the door. Keep on knocking; it will eventually be opened for you. Many doors open just after the person knocking gives up and leaves!

Read the Bible Today: Luke 7

Prayer Points:

1. I praise and thank God for allowing me to see yet another day by his grace.
2. I thank God for allowing me to see the end of this first month.
3. By the Blood of Jesus, I enter into a covenant of prosperity with God in the name of Jesus.
4. By the Blood of Jesus I enter into a covenant of abundance with God in Jesus name.
5. By faith in Christ Jesus I receive the winners'anointing over every situation in my life, in Jesus name.
6. Every power, spirit, and personality that wants me to fail, be disgraced, in the name of Jesus.
7. Lord Jesus, you are the rock of ages, let me hide myself in thee in Jesus name.
8. I prophesy that every blessing I have yet to experience this month shall manifest in the days ahead, in the name of Jesus.
9. My enemies shall rise up against themselves, in the name of Jesus.
10. Almighty God empower my prayer altar, in the name of Jesus.
11. I withdraw my blessings from the hands of the oppressors, in the name of Jesus.
12. I command that all the dark work done against my life in secret shall be undone by the blood of Jesus Christ in the name of Jesus.

13. Almighty God if my life is on the wrong course, correct me, in the name of Jesus.
14. I put on the garment of God's favor, in the name of Jesus.
15. Everyone who desires to carry an evil burden into my life, carry it away now, in the name of Jesus.
16. Almighty God change my destiny for the better, in the name of Jesus.
17. Every evil spiritual law that is against me be revoke by the blood of Jesus.
18. I thank God for keeping me through the month.
19. I cancel every evil dreams, visions, prophesy and prayers against my life and family in the name of Jesus.
20. Talk to God about your heart desires and your situation.
21. Thank God for answered prayers.

Confession:

"Nevertheless he saved them for his name's sake, that he might make his mighty power to be known" Psalms 106:8.

Wisdom for Today:

Be careful of your desire for pleasures; it leads to internal war in your life and extends to negative reactions toward others.

Read the Bible Today: James 4 and John 14

Prayer Points:

1. I praise and thank God for allowing me to see yet another day by his grace.
2. Almighty God, let the rest of the days in this year bring blessings and testimonies to me, in the name of Jesus.
3. Almighty God, let the rest of the days in this year bring shame and calamities to everyone seeking to hurt me, in the name of Jesus.
4. Shout this out twenty-one times: "I am a winner!" In the name of Jesus.
5. Let the power of God disgrace my oppressors, in the name of Jesus.
6. I am redeemed and will not be reduced; I am saved and will not be a slave, in Jesus name.
7. I destroy every satanic network fashioned against me today, in the name of Jesus.
8. I destroy every satanic network fashioned against my work and career today, in the name of Jesus.
9. I destroy every satanic network fashioned against my peace and joy today, in the name of Jesus.
10. I destroy every satanic network fashioned against my family today, in the name of Jesus.
11. Every element in this day, hear the word of God; favor me, and work contrary to my enemies, in the name of Jesus.
12. Almighty God, lead us by your Holy Spirit, in the name of Jesus.
13. Almighty God, have your way, in the name of Jesus Christ.
14. Almighty God, fill my life to overflowing with your blessing this year, in the name of Jesus.

15. Almighty God feed me with the bread of heaven again, in the name of Jesus.
16. Almighty God let your hand remain open unto me, in the name of Jesus.
17. By the blood of Jesus Christ, I claim my healing and deliverance, in the name of Jesus.
18. Declare: "I drink the blood of Jesus Christ." 7 times.
19. Family bondage, break and relinquish your hold over my life, in the name of Jesus Christ.
20. I break and release myself from every serpentine covenant, in the name of Jesus Christ.
21. Let the power in the blood of Jesus Christ deliver my destiny now, in the name of Jesus.
22. Let the power in the blood of Jesus Christ deliver my spirit, soul, and body now, in the name of Jesus.
23. By the blood of Jesus Christ, no evil dream, prophesy, or vision shall come to pass in my life, in the name of Jesus.
24. Almighty God, whatever is impossible for others to achieve this year, let your grace make it easy for me, in the name of Jesus Christ.
25. I give thanks to God for a blessed day. Jesus Christ is Lord!
26. I cancel every evil dreams, visions, prophesy and prayers against my life and family in the name of Jesus.
27. Talk to God about your heart desires and your situation.
28. Thank God for answered prayers.

Confession:

"God shall save me from the hand of him that hated me, and redeemed me from the hand of the enemy. And the waters shall cover mine enemies: none of them will be left "Psalms 106:10–11.

Wisdom for Today:

Who is wise and understanding among you? Let him show by good conduct that his works are done in the meekness of wisdom. But if you have bitter envy and self-seeking in your heart, do not boast and lie against the truth. This wisdom does not descend from above, but is earthly, sensual, and demonic. For where envy and self-seeking exist, there you will also find confusion and every evil thing. But the wisdom that is from above is first pure, then peaceable, gentle, willing to yield, full of mercy and good fruits, without partiality, and without hypocrisy.

Read the Bible Today: Proverbs 4

Prayer Points:

1. I praise and thank God for allowing me to see yet another day by his grace.
2. I shall arise above all the unbelievers around me, in the name of Jesus.
3. Arrows of demotion shall not prosper in my life, in the name of Jesus.
4. I will always rise and shine; I shall not be limited, in the name of Jesus.
5. I break every curse of satanic limitations upon my life, in the name of Jesus.
6. I receive divine wings to fly over every limitation, in the name of Jesus.
7. Almighty God order my spirit, and fashion my life in your will, in the name of Jesus.
8. Holy Spirit, breathe on me so that sin will no more find a place in me, in the name of Jesus.
9. Almighty God let your blessing have a foothold in my life, in the name of Jesus.
10. I reject any mistake of my parents and the mistake of my family members in my life, in the name of Jesus.

11. Almighty God, have your way in my life, in Jesus name.
12. Almighty God, arise and visit both sides of my family and consume anything that is affecting my life in a negative way in the name, of Jesus.
13. Evil pattern in my father's family and mother's family, manifesting in any area of my life, break asunder, in the name of Jesus.
14. In any way I have been marked for evil, blood of Jesus Christ cancel it in the name of Jesus.
15. Every death ritual projected against me and my family backfire against the sender, in the name of Jesus.
16. Almighty God, throughout this year, let me be chosen, in the name of Jesus.
17. I refuse to fall out of favor before my helpers, in the name of Jesus Christ.
18. Within twenty-four hours, oh, Lord, grant me a miracle, in the name of Jesus.
19. You, power of the coffin, I command you relinquish your hold over my life and family, in the name of Jesus.
20. Because I am serving the life, I shall not die, but shall live and declare the works of God, in the name of Jesus.
21. In the name of Jesus Christ, this year, this decade, I shall not be put to shame; I shall not experience disgrace, in the name of Jesus.
22. Almighty God, the hour has come, and this is the year; glorify Jesus Christ in my life, in the name of Jesus.
23. Almighty God I want to see you, Lord; Manifest yourself in my life, in the name of Jesus.
24. Almighty God, grant me life and favor, and let your visitation preserve my spirit, in the name of Jesus.
25. Almighty God, glorify Jesus in my life, in the name of Jesus.
26. I cancel every evil dreams, visions, prophesy and prayers against my life and family in the name of Jesus.
27. Talk to God about your heart desires and your situation.
28. Thank God for answered prayers.

Confession:

"Save us, O Lord our God, and gather us from among the heathen, to give thanks unto thy holy name, and to triumph in thy praise" Psalms 106:47.

Wisdom for Today:

It does not matter where you are if the Lord God is with you. He who is for you is a million times greater than all who can be against you. The Bible says, "the people who know their God will display strength and take action" (Daniel 11:32/ NAS). So, your problem is your lack of knowledge of your God.

Read the Bible Today: Daniel 11

Prayer Points:

1. I praise and thank God for allowing me to see yet another day by his grace.
2. Let every embargo on my way of progress be consumed by fire, in the name of Jesus.
3. I receive the anointing of the head; I reject the anointing of the tail, in the name of Jesus.
4. Let the blood of Jesus repairs all that sin has destroyed in my life in the name of Jesus.
5. Let the fresh fire of revival fall upon me today, in the name of Jesus.
6. Let the power of sin and iniquity be destroyed in my life, in the name of Jesus.
7. The enemy shall not convert my spirit, soul, and body to rag, in the name of Jesus.
8. Almighty God enlarge my horizons and bless me indeed, in the name of Jesus.
9. I shall not come to the world in vain, in the name of Jesus.
10. You, my spiritual life, be revived, in the name of Jesus.
11. Almighty God, please provide all that I need to serve you this year, in the name of Jesus.
12. Let this week take me to my next level, in the name of Jesus.
13. Anything that will challenge my healing, my good news, my prosperity, let the ground open up and swallow it, in the name of Jesus.

14. Almighty God let me end this week, this month, and this year shouting, "Hallelujah!" In the name of Jesus Christ.

15. Lord Jesus Christ, I lift you up in my life, work, family, ministry, my going out and coming in the name of Jesus.

16. Almighty God, every door I knock at this week, let it open unto me, in the name of Jesus.

17. Almighty God let me find every good thing I seek in the land of the living in the name of Jesus.

18. Almighty God, give me every good thing I ask, in the name of Jesus Christ.

19. Almighty God, answer me with your fire, in the name of Jesus.

20. Every mountain in my way this week, that hinders my helpers, remove yourself and be cast into the sea, in the name of Jesus Christ.

21. Almighty God, let your presence bring me unusual blessing, in the name of Jesus.

22. Almighty God, I lift up my children unto you, let your anointing rest upon them, in the name of Jesus.

23. Almighty God, manifest yourself in my life as Jehovah El-Shaddai this week, in the name of Jesus.

24. Almighty God, do not replace me, in the name of Jesus Christ.

25. Almighty God open the double doors for me, in the name of Jesus.

26. I cancel every evil dreams, visions, prophesy and prayers against my life and family in the name of Jesus.

27. Talk to God about your heart desires and your situation.

28. Thank God for answered prayers.

Confession:

"Then they cried unto the Lord in their trouble, and he saves them out of their distresses" Psalms 107; 19.

Wisdom for Today:

It takes vision to set out on a mission. Before you embark on any mission, be sure of a revelation from heaven. When the unexpected happens on your way to your mission, it is what God has told or showed you that will keep you on the move.

Read the Bible Today: Habakkuk 2

Prayer Points:

1. I give praise and thanks to God for allowing me to see yet another day by his grace.
2. I renounce my involvements with darkness, by the blood of Jesus in the name of Jesus.
3. I shake off every evil deposit from my system, in the name of Jesus.
4. Evil deposits in my dreams come out with all your roots, in the name of Jesus.
5. No man made me; no man will determine my destiny, in the name of Jesus.
6. Almighty God let your glory overshadow my life, in the name of Jesus.
7. Every power contending against my divine destiny, collapse and die, in the name of Jesus.
8. I break the curse of backwardness in every area of my life, in the name of Jesus.
9. I shall not be a victim of any evil prophesy, prayer, or vision, in the name of Jesus.
10. Let the wonders of the name of Jesus begin to manifest in every area of my life and in all that I lay my hands on today, in the name of Jesus.
11. Almighty God, I pray for a special visitation today, in the name of Jesus.
12. Almighty God, bless me today and surround me with favor as a shield, in the name of Jesus.

13. Blood of Jesus Christ, minister better things to me today, in the name of Jesus.
14. Almighty God, overwhelm my life with your mercy, in the name of Jesus.
15. Almighty God, instruct me and guide me in the way I should go, in the name of Jesus.
16. Almighty God let your blessing be upon the work of my hand, in the name of Jesus.
17. Almighty God, open my eyes to behold my blessing and grant me the power and strength to possess them, in the name of Jesus.
18. Angels of the living God, clothe me with garment of favor and glory, in the name of Jesus.
19. Every garment of ridicule and disfavor, I put you off now, in the name of Jesus.
20. Foundation of rejection in my life be uprooted, in the name of Jesus Christ.
21. Every evil register containing my name and that of my family, be consumed by fire, in the name of Jesus.
22. Every manifestation of death in my dreams be cancelled by the blood of Jesus in the name of Jesus.
23. Every manifestation of failure in my dreams be cancelled by the blood of Jesus in the name of Jesus.
24. Every manifestation of barrenness in my dreams be cancelled by the blood of Jesus in the name of Jesus.
25. Every manifestation of poverty and lack in my dreams be cancelled by the blood of Jesus in the name of Jesus.
26. Every manifestation of witchcraft in my dreams be cancelled by the blood of Jesus in the name of Jesus.
27. Every manifestation of a spirit wife or husband in my dreams be cancelled by the blood of Jesus Christ.
28. Every manifestation of accident and tragedy in my dreams, I cancel you, in the name of Jesus.
29. Almighty God, reverse evil dreams in my life, in the name of Jesus Christ.
30. I cancel every evil dreams, visions, prophesy and prayers against my life and family in the name of Jesus.
31. Talk to God about your heart desires and your situation.
32. Thank God for answered prayers.

Confession:

"For God has broken the gates of brass, and cut the bars of iron in sunder" your Psalms 107:16.

Wisdom for Today:

Bring your thought into captivity. Every thought can be brought into captivity to the obedience of Christ. Tackle them with the sword of the Spirit, which is the word of God. Take passages of scripture that are the God-given solution and fight against your thought.

Read the Bible Today: 2 Corinthians and 10, John 1

Prayer Points:

1. I praise and thank God for allowing me to see yet another day by his grace.
2. Fire of the Holy Ghost; defeat every power that attacks God's glory in my life, in the name of Jesus.
3. I put off every garment of shame and reproach, and I put on the garment of glory, in the name of Jesus.
4. Let every shame waiting for me in this year be buried now, in the name of Jesus.
5. Let honor and glory be my portion at all times, in the name of Jesus.
6. Let all my disappointments be converted to divine appointments, in the name of Jesus.
7. Every deeply entrenched problem in my life and marriage, dry to the root, in the name of Jesus.
8. I prophesy that my days of favor and plenty shall begin today, in the name of Jesus.
9. My destiny shall not be swallowed by household enemies, in the name of Jesus.
10. Power of unlimited breakthroughs, fall upon me now, in the name of Jesus.
11. Almighty God, let there be a positive turn of events in my life, in the name of Jesus.
12. Almighty God, by your never-failing power, let there be a positive turn of events in this state and country, in the name of Jesus.

13. Almighty God, let there be a positive turn of events for me in my marriage, in the name of Jesus.
14. Almighty God, by the greatness of your power, let there be a positive turn of events for every student, in the name of Jesus.
15. Almighty God, let there be a positive turn of events financially from lack to prosperity, in the name of Jesus.
16. I thank God, for I know there will be positive turns of events in my life, in the name of Jesus.
17. Almighty God, by the greatness of your power, let me experience positive turns of events today, this week, this month, and this year, in the name of Jesus.
18. Almighty God put upon my head the ornament of grace and the crown of glory, in the name of Jesus.
19. Almighty God, order my steps toward outstanding success, in the name of Jesus.
20. Almighty God, let every valley in my life be exalted and every mountain and hill be brought low, in the name of Jesus.
21. Almighty God make every crooked area of my life straight in the name of Jesus.
22. Almighty God let every rough place in my life become smooth, in the name of Jesus.
23. Almighty God let your glory be revealed in every area of my life, in the name of Jesus Christ.
24. I cancel every evil dreams, visions, prophesy and prayers against my life and family in the name of Jesus.
25. Talk to God about your heart desires and your situation.
26. Thank God for answered prayers.

Confession:

"Let them curse, but bless thou, when they arise, let them be ashamed, but let thy servant rejoice. Let mine adversaries be clothed with shame, and let them cover themselves with their own confusion, as with a mantle" Psalms 109:28–29.

Wisdom for Today:

Your attitude reflects who you are: the son or daughter of God or the son or daughter of the devil. Determine within yourself not to show any negative attitude for the next seven days; it may eventually become your lifestyle.

Read the Bible Today: Ruth 1–4

Prayer Points:

1. I praise and thank God for allowing me to see yet another day by his grace.
2. I shall be a wonder to my generation to the glory of God, in the name of Jesus.
3. I reject the struggles of my father in my life, in the name of Jesus.
4. I reject the struggles of my mother in my life, in the name of Jesus.
5. I reject the failures of my parents in my life, in the name of Jesus.
6. I refuse to bear the sins and iniquities of my parents, in the name of Jesus.
7. Let the spirit of excellence fall upon me today, in the name of Jesus.
8. I withdraw from my progress every evil regulation and domination, in the name of Jesus.
9. I refuse to follow any evil pattern today, in the name of Jesus.
10. I declare that Jesus Christ is lord over my spirit, soul, and body in the name of Jesus.
11. I plead the blood of Jesus Christ over my life in the name of Jesus.
12. Almighty God, arise and deliver me from every confusion and minister peace to my life, in the name of Jesus.

13. Almighty God let this day stand out for me for good. It is written: *"This is the day that the Lord has made; I will rejoice and be glad in it"* in the name of Jesus. Psalms 118:24

14. Every written ordinance against my life be wiped off by the blood of Jesus Christ.

15. Let the blood of Jesus Christ cleanse me now from every evil mark, in the name of Jesus.

16. Blood of Jesus Christ, blot out from my life every evil mark, mark of witchcraft, envy, failure, rejection, enemy, in the name of Jesus.

17. Almighty God, I commit my life and my ways to you, lead me, Lord, in the way I should go in the name of Jesus.

18. I reject every evil in this day; it is written that there shall be no evil before me, in the name of Jesus.

19. Lift up your voice and begin to declare: the Lord God is my refuge and my fortress, in Jesus precious name.

20. Declare, "I dwell in the secret place of the Most High."

21. Almighty God, deliver me and my family from the snare of the fowler and from every pestilence, in the mighty name of Jesus Christ.

22. Almighty God, cover me and my family with your feather and let us take refuge under your wings, in the name of Jesus.

23. You, terror of the night, lose your hold over my life, in the name of Jesus.

24. Every arrow that flies by day, I am not your candidate; my family members are not your candidates, I reject you in my life and the life of my family; we are covered by the blood of Jesus in the name of Jesus.

25. Every destruction that lays waste at noonday; I am not your candidate; my family are not your candidate, we overcome you by the blood of Jesus in the name of Jesus.

26. It is written that no evil shall befall me and my family in the name of Jesus.

27. Almighty God let no evil befall me and my family in the name of Jesus.

28. Almighty God, give your angels charge over me and my family to keep us in all our ways, in the name of Jesus Christ.

29. I thank the Lord for turning everything in my favor, in Jesus precious name.

30. Almighty God, don't let this week and month go without manifesting my blessings and breakthroughs, in Jesus precious name.

31. Almighty God, overwhelm my life with your mercy, in the name of Jesus Christ.

32. Almighty God, surround me with your favor, in Jesus precious name.

33. I cancel every evil dreams, visions, prophesy and prayers against my life and family in the name of Jesus.

34. Talk to God about your heart desires and your situation.

35. Thank God for answered prayers.

Confession:

"The Lord is on my side; I will not fear: what can man do unto me. The Lord takes my part with them that help me: therefore shall I see my desire upon them that hate me" Psalms 118:7.

Wisdom for Today:

Growing in grace raises a person more and more above the world. The growing saint regards less and less either the good or ill opinions of men. A tree either grows or dies; you must decide to grow and not die spiritually. Remember, you are a tree of righteousness, the planting of the Lord.

Read the Bible Today: Isaiah 60 and 61 √

Prayer Points:

1. I praise and thank God for allowing me to see yet another day by his grace.
2. I break away and release myself from every evil family covenant, in the name of Jesus.
3. Let the Lion of Judah destroy every evil family strongman attached to my life in the name of Jesus.
4. I will rise and shine, and prosper above all my family members, in the name of Jesus.
5. My Joseph shall not die in prison, in the name of Jesus.
6. I move from prison to palace, in the name of Jesus.
7. I reject every form of decay, in the name of Jesus Christ.
8. I rebuke every evil manifestation in my life by the blood of Jesus Christ in the name of Jesus.
9. I rebuke every evil manifestation in my career by the blood of Jesus Christ in the name of Jesus.
10. I rebuke every evil manifestation in my marriage and family by the blood of Jesus Christ in the name of Jesus.
11. Lord Jesus Christ, lay your hand upon me and lift me up in Jesus name.
12. I command infirmities, sickness, diseases, and failure to leave me alone, in the name of Jesus.
13. I command every demon troubling my life to hold its peace and come out of my life, in the name of Jesus Christ.
14. Almighty God heal me in the mighty name of Jesus.

15. You, spirit of error, I bind you and cast you out of my life, in the name of Jesus.
16. Any hold of the wicked on my life, to attract evil unto my life, be paralyzed, in the name of Jesus Christ.
17. By the blood of Jesus Christ, I reject and refuse to listen to strange and uncertain voices, in the name of Jesus Christ.
18. Blood of Jesus Christ, bless my dream life in the name of Jesus.
19. Almighty God, make me hear you and grant me the grace to follow you in the name of Jesus.
20. Almighty God grant us and our children the grace to follow you in the mighty name of Jesus.
21. Lord Jesus, increase your goodness in every area of my life in Jesus name.
22. Almighty God take over my thought life, and reign in my wandering thoughts, in the name of Jesus.
23. Almighty God, deliver me from every negative assumption, in the name of Jesus Christ.
24. Almighty God, deliver us from every satanic incident, in the name of Jesus.
25. Almighty God bless me with eyes that see and ears that hear, in the name of Jesus Christ.
26. I Command every problem that comes into my life through the hours of the night to depart, in the name of Jesus.
27. I drink the blood of Jesus in the name of Jesus.
28. Almighty God, surprise me before the end of this week in Jesus name.
29. I cancel every evil dreams, visions, prophesy and prayers against my life and family in the name of Jesus.
30. Talk to God about your heart desires and your situation.
31. Thank God for answered prayers.

Confession:

"The Lord is my strength and song, and is become my salvation". Psalm 118:14 this day shall bring glory, honor, favor and glory to my family and me, in the name of Jesus.

Wisdom for Today:

The person who grows in grace has less relish for the world. He has less and less desire for its wealth, its honors, and its pleasures. A desire for these has less and less influence, and is less a motive in his mind. He seeks wealth and honor only as instruments for glorifying God and of doing good to men. What is the motive behind your pursuit?

Read the Bible Today: 2 Chronicles 6 and 7 √

Prayer Points:

1. I praise and thank God for allowing me to see yet another day by his grace.
2. Almighty God, let favor always meet favor in my life, and let prosperity meet prosperity in my life, in the name of Jesus.
3. I shall have opportunities more than my colleagues, in the name of Jesus.
4. I shall be favored above all my colleagues, in the name of Jesus.
5. I shall be blessed above all my colleagues, in the name of Jesus.
6. Let every Goliath boasting against my destiny receive divine judgment, in the name of Jesus.
7. Almighty God deliver me from every carnal desire, in the name of Jesus.
8. I refuse to share glory with my God, in the name of Jesus Christ.
9. I refuse to seek after my own glory; I seek only for God's glory, in the name of Jesus.
10. Every seed of pride and selfishness in me come out and enter no more, in the name of Jesus.
11. Every blessing that is due unto me; be gathered and come back to me, in the name of Jesus.

12. Every blessing that I have missed, turn back and locate me, in the name of Jesus.

13. Almighty God, the world awaits your manifestation in my life, in the name of Jesus.

14. Blood of Jesus Christ, anoint me for special favor, in the name of Jesus.

15. Blood of Jesus Christ, anoint me for success in every area of my life, in the name of Jesus.

16. Blood of Jesus Christ, anoint me for greatness, in the name of Jesus.

17. Wherever I have fallen out of favor, blood of Jesus undertake and speak for me, in the name of Jesus.

18. Blood of Jesus Christ arise and remove my name from all evil family records, in the name of Jesus.

19. Jesus Christ is Lord over my spirit, soul, and body; witchcraft powers release me and let me go, in the name of Jesus Christ.

20. Jesus Christ is Lord over my spirit, soul, and body; marine spirits release me and let me go, in the name of Jesus.

21. Jesus Christ is Lord over my destiny and career; therefore, spirit of failure, release me, in the name of Jesus.

22. Every failure and hardship programmed into this land against me be frustrated, in the name of Jesus.

23. I anoint this land with the blood of Jesus, and I decree that I shall prosper and be blessed, in the name of Jesus.

24. I plead the blood of Jesus over the land, and I decree it must not harbor any bewitchment against me, in the name of Jesus.

25. By covenant, I am a child of the living God; therefore, you, land of (country), yield your increase to me, in the name of Jesus.

26. Oh, land of (country) hear the word of the Lord; you shall not record any defeat against me, in the name of Jesus.

27. "The heavens were opened and I saw visions of God" Ezekiel 1:1. Every satanic vision and dream, vanish from my life, in the name of Jesus.

28. Every power behind evil dreams in my life, fire of the Holy Ghost, consume them, in the name of Jesus.

29. Almighty God, by the greatness of your power, let there be a glorious and positive turnaround for me, in the name of Jesus.

30. Almighty God, let the glory of your throne and presence be released upon me, in the name of Jesus.
31. Oh, heavens open unto me your good treasure, in the name of Jesus.
32. Almighty God, before the end of this month, surprise me, in the name of Jesus.
33. I cancel every evil dreams, visions, prophesy and prayers against my life and family in the name of Jesus.
34. Talk to God about your heart desires and your situation.
35. Thank God for answered prayers.

Confession:

"I shall not die, but live, and declare the works of the Lord"Psalms 118:17.

Wisdom for Today:

Growing weary of being asked to give for promoting the kingdom of Christ is evidence of spiritual decline. Never think you have given God enough. He gave you all you have and will ever possess in life, mostly the breath that keeps you alive.

Read the Bible Today: Psalm 24 and Luke 6

Prayer Points:

1. I praise and thank God for allowing me to see yet another day by his grace.
2. Anywhere I appear after today, failure shall disappear, in the name of Jesus.
3. Almighty God direct my feet to the place of prosperity, in the name of Jesus.
4. Almighty God give me the power to acquire wealth, in the name of Jesus.
5. Almighty God give me power to enjoy your wealth, in the name of Jesus.
6. Whatever must happen for me to have breakthroughs, happen now, in the name of Jesus.
7. Almighty God, baptize me with the spirit of Christ Jesus in the name of Jesus.
8. Power to yield my all to God; fall upon me now, in the name of Jesus.
9. I receive power to live beyond my limits, in the name of Jesus.
10. I send the blood of Jesus to go ahead of me today and make way for my blessings and favor, in the name of Jesus.
11. Almighty God; I submit myself to you, in the name of Jesus.
12. I surrender everything to Jesus in the mighty name of Jesus.
13. By the blood of Jesus Christ, I resist the devil in every area of my life, in the name of Jesus.
14. Almighty God set my spirit man free wherever it is tied down in the name of Jesus.

15. Every arrow fired into my spirit, soul, and body, come out by fire and go back to your sender, in the name of Jesus.
16. Satanic arrow fired into my body, come out and enter no more, in the name of Jesus.
17. Let blood the of Jesus Christ and the fire of God minister deliverance to my body now, in the name of Jesus.
18. Blood of Jesus Christ, heal my wounded spirit and my broken heart, in the name of Jesus.
19. Every satanic poison circulating in my system be flushed out by the blood of Jesus in the name of Jesus.
20. Any satanic strongman attached to any area of my life, I bind you and command you; relinquish your hold, in the name of Jesus.
21. By the power of the Holy Ghost, I enter into the house of the strongman and collect all my blessings, in the name of Jesus.
22. Every arrow fired to trouble me and my family; go back to your sender, in the name of Jesus.
23. Let the favor of God answer for me anywhere I go, in the name of Jesus.
24. Anything standing between me and my testimony, I tear you down, in the name of Jesus.
25. Heavenly Father, give me this day my daily bread, in the name of Jesus.
26. Almighty God, lead me not into temptation, in the name of Jesus.
27. I cancel every evil dreams, visions, prophesy and prayers against my life and family in the name of Jesus.
28. Talk to God about your heart desires and your situation.
29. Thank God for answered prayers.

Confession:

"Let the proud be ashamed; for they dealt perversely with me without a cause: but I will meditate in thy precepts" Psalms 119:78.

Wisdom for Today:

Living a life full of joy leaves you with a responsibility. You have to know what to do to live a life of joy and praise. Your clothes do not just jump onto you; you must put them on yourself. Likewise, the Bible says you are to put on the garment of praise. You must determine that whatever comes your way in your life, you're not going to allow anything to break you down or develop a negative attitude.

Read the Bible Today: Isaiah 61 and Philippians 4

Prayer Points:

1. I praise and thank God for allowing me to see yet another day by his grace.
2. Lord, give me divine wisdom to defeat all satanic wisdom, in the name of Jesus.
3. Blood of Jesus, destroy every curse affecting my life, marriage, and destiny, in the name of Jesus.
4. Almighty God, perfect every good work you have begun in my life, in the name of Jesus.
5. I recover every good thing I have lost through dreams, in the name of Jesus.
6. I recover every good thing I have lost to the enemies, in the name of Jesus.
7. Every work of the wicked in my life, the Lord disapproves of you, in the name of Jesus.
8. Almighty God, let this day be a blessed day for me, in the name of Jesus.
9. I take over this day by the blood of Jesus Christ in the name of Jesus.
10. Every satanic intervention on the affairs of my life, become desolate, in the name of Jesus.
11. Every satanic decree against me, I cancel you by the blood of Jesus in the name of Jesus.
12. The enemy shall not eat my flesh and shall not drink my blood, in the name of Jesus.

13. Almighty God, give answer to my prayers today, in the name of Jesus.

14. Almighty God give me strength and power to pray, strengthen me to prevail in prayer in the name of Jesus.

15. I pray against every satanic retaliation on the nation in the name of Jesus.

16. Almighty God be gracious unto this country, bless and preserve this country in the name of Jesus.

17. Almighty God we commit all the citizens of the United State of America into your hands, preserve them wherever they may be under the surface of the earth, deliver them from every satanic retaliation; we release the mark of the blood of Jesus upon them all in the name of Jesus.

18. Almighty God return every satanic retaliation against me and the United States of America back to the sender in the name of Jesus.

19. Anyone that may be of retaliation against me, my children, and my family, almighty God, let their retaliation fall back upon their head in the name of Jesus.

20. Almighty God let your name defend me throughout this month, this year and all the days of my life, I run into your name defend and preserve me, my family, my marriage and job in Jesus name.

21. Every attack of the enemies, of evil dreams, vision, attack, arrow of declaration over me, my family, my marriage, my job, thus saith the Lord by the same way you came in by the same way you shall return in Jesus name.

22. You failure, poverty, lack, death, fear, rejection ,bad news, bad luck disease, pain, infirmity trouble, crisis, shame, the same way you came in shall you return in Jesus name.

23. Power of God set me free from fear and uncertainty in Jesus name.

24. Almighty God bless me with unbeatable results and victory, in all areas of my life in the name of Jesus.

25. Almighty God lead me and my family in the path of righteousness, let us be at the right place at the right time, lead us in the way that we should go in the name of Jesus.

26. Almighty God deliver me and my family, your church from natural disaster in Jesus name.

27. I cancel every evil dreams, visions, prophesy and prayers against my life and family in the name of Jesus.

28. Talk to God about your heart desires and your situation.

29. Thank God for answered prayers.

Apostle A.O. Solomon

Confession:

"Be surety for thy servant for good; let not the proud oppress me"
Psalms 119:122.

Wisdom for Today:

You can have a new start despite all the mistakes in your past. Don't listen to the voice of the devil telling you that it's over. It is not over! God can still open a new chapter for you. He said in Isaiah 43:19 that he will do a new thing for you. David made a lot of blunders. He committed adultery and even ordered the husband of the woman to be killed. But when he repented and sought the Lord for mercy and forgiveness, God forgave him and gave him a new start. You too can do the same today and now.

Read the Bible Today: 2 Samuel 11–12 and Psalm 51

Prayer Points:

1. I praise and thank God for allowing me to see yet another day by his grace.
2. Almighty God restore back to me all my wasted years and opportunities, in the name of Jesus.
3. The devil shall not waste my life and destiny, in the name of Jesus.
4. Let all my good dreams, visions, and prophesies begin to manifest in my life now, in the name of Jesus.
5. Almighty God is my refuge at all times, I am the apple of his eye, I shall enter into the new year with glory, honor, power, and prosperity, in the name of Jesus.
6. Almighty God disgrace the pride of the enemies against me, in Jesus name.
7. Let the power of God's anointing destroy the yoke of sin and evil desire in my life, in the name of Jesus.
8. Almighty God have your way in my life and the life of my family in the name of Jesus.
9. Almighty God, thank you for another opportunity to call on your name.
10. Almighty God, as you redesigned the earth that is without form, redesign my life, in the name of Jesus.

11. Almighty God let your favor overwhelm my life, in the name of Jesus.

12. You, spirit and power of wastage operating in my life, I bind and cast you out, in the name of Jesus.

13. You, spirit of back to square one, my life is not your candidate, be gone from my life, in the name of Jesus.

14. Almighty God forgive me for any sin I have committed in the name of Jesus.

15. Almighty God, deliver me from the hands of the enemy, in the name of Jesus.

16. Almighty God, arise against every harvest destroyer in my life, in the name of Jesus.

17. By the blood of Jesus Christ, I forbid and reject any circumstance or situation that will lead to shame and sorrow, in the name of Jesus.

18. Almighty God, let there be a positive turn of events for me, in the name of Jesus.

19. This year I shall harvest what has been delayed in my life, in the name of Jesus.

20. Any power prolonging my stay in the wilderness, your time is up, die, in the name of Jesus.

21. Every power delaying my blessing, I command you to die, in the name of Jesus.

22. Every power making me moves about in a circle, die, in the name of Jesus.

23. Almighty God break me free from every evil cycle, in the name of Jesus.

24. Almighty God let your grace and your mercy take me beyond my limitations, in the name of Jesus.

25. Almighty God let every seed I sow grow to financial fulfillment, in the name of Jesus.

26. I cancel every evil dreams, visions, prophesy and prayers against my life and family in the name of Jesus.

27. Talk to God about your heart desires and your situation.

28. Thank God for answered prayers.

Confession:

"My soul is escaped as a bird out of the snare of the fowlers: the snare is broken, and we are escaped. My help is in the name of the Lord, who made the heaven and earth" Psalms 124:7–8.

Wisdom for Today:

"Reputation is what men and women think of us; character is what God and the angels know of us." —Thomas Paine

Read the Bible Today: Revelation 1–3 ✓

Prayer Points:

1. I praise and thank God for allowing me to see yet another day by his grace.
2. Almighty God I thank you for your life-changing power, in the name of Jesus.
3. I plead the blood of Jesus against every voice speaking against my destiny, in the name of Jesus.
4. I plead the blood of Jesus against everything the devil is holding against me, in the name of Jesus.
5. I plead the blood of Jesus against every weapon of the enemy fashioned against me and my family in the name of Jesus.
6. Let God arise, and let all my enemies scatter unto desolation, in the name of Jesus.
7. I call the blood of Jesus Christ over every situation in my life in the name of Jesus.
8. I approach the throne of mercy with the blood of Jesus in the name of Jesus.
9. Let the spirit and anointing of Zion rest upon me, in the name of Jesus.
10. Almighty God, fulfill your promises in my life, in the name of Jesus.
11. I bury every evil dream in the blood of Jesus, and I command each one to be canceled in the name of Jesus.
12. May all evil desires fashioned against me and my family backfire, in the name of Jesus.
13. I put the mark of Jesus upon my life and family in the name of Jesus.

14. Any problem in my life that I have prayed and fasted over and yet remains, I command it to clear away now, in Jesus name.
15. Almighty God remove whatever is standing as a reproach in my life in the name of Jesus.
16. Almighty God destroy every evil kingdom contesting against the kingdom of God in my life in the name of Jesus.
17. Every power and spirit diverting good blessings from my life be consumed by the Holy Ghost fire, in Jesus name.
18. All my diverted blessings, hear the word of the living God, gather yourself together, and come back to me, in the name of Jesus.
19. Almighty God reduce to nothing every problem I am having with my job, business, or school in Jesus name.
20. Almighty God let your mercy heal me, deliver me and bless my life, in the name of Jesus.
21. Almighty God, by your mercy answer all my past prayers, in the name of Jesus.
22. God of Abraham, Isaac, and Jacob, manifest your power in my life and let me experience your blessings, in the name of Jesus.
23. Almighty God, deliver me from the hands of my oppressors, in the name of Jesus.
24. Almighty God, deliver our children from the hand of wasters, in the name of Jesus.
25. Almighty God, anoint all our children to succeed in the name of Jesus.
26. Any power that wants to use my children to make me cry, die, in the name of Jesus.
27. Any power attacking my children because of me, die, in the name of Jesus.
28. Almighty God, give me rest of mind, in the name of Jesus.
29. I cancel every evil dreams, visions, prophesy and prayers against my life and family in the name of Jesus.
30. Talk to God about your heart desires and your situation.
31. Thank God for answered prayers.

Confession:

"Surely thou will slay the wicked, O, God: depart from me therefore, ye bloody men" Psalms 139:19.

Wisdom for Today:

Love your neighbor for God's sake, and love God for your own sake.

Read the Bible Today: Exodus 20–22 ✓

Prayer Points:

1. I praise and thank God for allowing me to see yet another day by his grace.
1. Every arrow of death fired against me and my family, return to your sender, in the name of Jesus.
2. Everyone who carries an evil burden into my life, carry your burden away now, in the name of Jesus.
3. Anyone fighting against my blessing and promotion, sleep to death, in Jesus name.
4. Every incantation and enchantment against me and my family, relinquish your power and die, in the name of Jesus.
5. Let all those planning to drink my blood collapse and die, in the name of Jesus.
6. Almighty God, empower me today to stand perfect and complete in all your will, in the name of Jesus.
7. Almighty God let me be filled with the knowledge of your will in all wisdom and spiritual understanding, in the name of Jesus.
8. Almighty God let me be fruitful in every good work and let me increase in the knowledge of you, in the name of Jesus.
9. Almighty God, you are the God of peace, Let me have peace always in the name of Jesus.
10. I receive multiplied grace and peace, in the name of Jesus.
11. I am complete in Christ Jesus in the name of Jesus.
12. I command every witchcraft power, spiritual wickedness, and household wickedness to remove its hands from my life, in the name of Jesus.
13. Fire of the Holy Ghost, possess my spirit, soul, and body and set me free, in Jesus name.

14. Almighty God; Let this month be productive for me in all areas in the name of Jesus.
15. Almighty God, cover my nakedness in all areas of life in the name of Jesus.
16. Almighty God let my life reflect your glory in the name of Jesus.
17. Almighty God do not let me lack any good thing in the name of Jesus.
18. Almighty God, don't let me spend this month like the previous one; bless me and give me financial breakthrough, with open heaven in the name of Jesus.
19. This month, I reject bad news in the name of Jesus.
20. Anyone mandated by the enemy to destroy my joy, angels of the living God bury them in the name of Jesus.
21. This month, I shall not suffer any loss of life or property in the name of Jesus.
22. Almighty God, in every area of my life throughout this month, let it be known that you are greater than man in the name of Jesus.
23. I cancel every evil dreams, visions, prophesy and prayers against my life and family in the name of Jesus.
24. Talk to God about your heart desires and your situation.
25. Thank God for answered prayers.

Confession:

"Though I walk in the midst of trouble, thou wilt revive me: thou shall stretch forth thine hand against the wrath of mine enemies, and thy right hand shall save me" Psalms 138:7.

Wisdom for Today:

The study of God's Word, for the purpose of discovering God's will, is the secret discipline which has formed the greatest characters.

Read the Bible Today: Joshua 1–2

Prayer Points:

1. I praise and thank God for allowing me to see yet another day by his grace.
2. Let all those making me run up and down be destroyed by fire, in Jesus name.
3. Every power that says I will not rise and shine be crushed to pieces, in the name of Jesus.
4. Every power that says I will have no peace, die with your word, in the name of Jesus.
5. Almighty God, gather my broken life together by your power, in the name of Jesus.
6. Almighty God let my situations be rearranged to favor me, in Jesus name.
7. Almighty God, make me an eternal excellence, the joy of many generations, in the name of Jesus.
8. Almighty God, throughout this year, bring me honor instead of disgrace in the name of Jesus.
9. Almighty God, by the greatness of your power, bring me good success instead of failure in the mighty name of Jesus.
10. Almighty God, fulfill your never-failing promise in my life in Jesus name.
11. Almighty God put an end to violence in my land, in the name of Jesus Christ.
12. Almighty God, I decree by the power of your word that my sun shall not go down; and my moon shall not withdraw, in the name of Jesus.

13. Almighty God, from this moment be my everlasting light in the name of Jesus.
14. Almighty God, by the power of your word, I decree that the days of affliction in my life shall be ended, in the name of Jesus.
15. Almighty God, have mercy upon me don't let me spend this year the way I have spent the previous years, in the name of Jesus.
16. Every stubborn problem in my life, I command you to drop dead in the name of Jesus.
17. Every work of the enemy against me and family back fire in the name of Jesus.
18. Almighty God; make me shine in the name of Jesus.
19. Almighty God; bring an end to every problem in my life in the name of Jesus Christ.
20. Almighty God; let every evil season in my life expire in the name of Jesus.
21. Almighty God; connect me to my new season in the name of Jesus.
22. I cancel every evil dreams, visions, prophesy and prayers against my life and family in the name of Jesus.
23. Talk to God about your heart desires and your situation.
24. Thank God for answered prayers.

Confession:

"Keep me, O Lord, from the hands of the wicked; preserve me from the violent men; who have purposed to overthrow my goings" *Psalms 140:4.*

Wisdom for Today:

Love your neighbor for God's sake, and God for your own sake.

Read the Bible Today: Joshua 3–4 ✓

Prayer Points:

1. I praise and thank God for allowing me to see yet another day by his grace.
2. With the sword of fire, I cut off every hand of darkness from my spirit, soul, and body, in the name of Jesus.
3. I refuse to go about in debt this year in the name of Jesus.
4. I refuse to go about in sorrow this year in Jesus name.
5. I refuse to go about with sickness and infirmity this year in Jesus name.
6. The enemies shall not laugh last over my life, marriage, and family, in Jesus name.
7. It is written that I shall be the head and not the tail, in the name of Jesus.
8. My beauty and my glory shall not be destroyed, in the name of Jesus.
9. I reject natural disaster; I shall not be a victim of any disaster, in the name of Jesus.
10. Almighty God have your way in our lives and situation in Jesus name.
11. Almighty God, visit me specially, meet me at the point of my need in Jesus name.
12. Almighty God give me uncommon victory this month and all through this year, what others have been pursuing for so long and could not get, God do for me with ease in Jesus name.
13. Almighty God bring all my good dreams, expectations and visions to pass and let all my good expectation turn to manifestation for your own sake in Jesus name.

14. God use me to shock the world, give me outstanding results in this month and for the rest of this year that will silence, shake and shock the world and those who have written me off, counted me out and have looked down on me in Jesus name.

15. Lord give me a result that will make me the world hero, give me the grace of breaking records, almighty God give me great achievements that will break records in my father's house, my mother's house, in my place of work ,among my competitors, and in my nation in Jesus name.

16. Almighty God make me an international hero in the mighty name of Jesus, let the world gather to celebrate and rejoice with me because of your work in my life in the name of Jesus.

17. God give me cheap and sweat less victory in every area of my life and in all that I do in Jesus name.

18. Almighty God have your way in our lives and situation in Jesus name.

19. Almighty God, visit me specially, meet me at the point of my need in Jesus name.

20. Almighty God give me uncommon victory this month and all through this year, what others have been pursuing for so long and could not get, do for me with ease in Jesus name.

21. Almighty God bring all my good dreams, expectations and visions to pass in Jesus name, let all my good expectation turn to manifestation in Jesus name.

22. God use me to shock the world , give me outstanding results in this month and for the rest of this year that will silence those who have written me off , counted me out and have looked down on me, give me outstanding results that will silence them up, shake and shock the world in Jesus name.

23. Lord give me a result that will make me the world hero, give me the grace of breaking records, almighty God give me great achievements that will break records in my father's house, my mother's house, in my place of work ,among my competitors, and in my nation in Jesus name.

24. Almighty God make me an international hero let the world gather to celebrate and rejoice with me because of your work in my life in the name of Jesus.

25. God give me cheap and sweat less victory in every area of my life and in all that I do in Jesus name.

26. Lord arise for my sake tonight and let all my enemies be scattered in Jesus name.

27. Almighty God let it be known that you are God in my life, my family, marriage and my situation in Jesus name.
28. I cancel every evil dreams, visions, prophesy and prayers against my life and family in the name of Jesus.
29. Talk to God about your heart desires and your situation.
30. Thank God for answered prayers.

Confession:

"But mine eyes are unto thee, O God the Lord: in thee is my trust; leave not my soul destitute. Keep me from the snares which they have laid for me" Psalms 141:8–10.

Wisdom for Today:

The study of God's Word, for the purpose of discovering God's will, is the secret discipline which has formed the greatest characters.

Read the Bible Today: Zephaniah 1–2 ✓

Prayer Points:

1. I praise and thank God for allowing me to see yet another day by his grace.
2. By fire and by force, let my enemies enter into the grave they have dug for me and my family, in the name of Jesus.
3. I cancel every dream of death against me and my family, by the blood of Jesus in the name of Jesus.
4. I break the power of death over my life and family, by the blood of Jesus in the name of Jesus.
5. Let all those planning my shame be put to eternal shame, in the name of Jesus.
6. Let the blood of Jesus begin to speak on my behalf, in the name of Jesus.
7. I disagree with every satanic agenda for my life, my family, my children and spouse in the name of Jesus.
8. Almighty God, I decree that I shall not cry or weep concerning every area of my life in the name of Jesus.
9. Almighty God I know you are in control of my life, let no man prevail over my life, my family, my career, my job, my business and in my home in Jesus name.
10. My destiny jump out by fire from every witchcraft cage in Jesus name.
11. By fire by force I move away from every satanic bus stop in Jesus name.
12. I move my career, my job, my marriage, family, home and finances away from every satanic bus stop in Jesus name.

13. 11. Almighty God arise and fight for me with jealousy in the name of Jesus.
14. 12. Almighty God I thank you because I will not see trouble throughout this month in the name of Jesus.
15. 13. Every storm prepared for me and my family be diverted away in the name of Jesus.
16. 14. Every mark of bewitchment upon my life; lose your power and be erased in the name of Jesus.
17. 15. Every evil hand writing upon my life; be erased in the name of Jesus.
18. I cancel every evil dreams, visions, prophesy and prayers against my life and family in the name of Jesus.
19. Talk to God about your heart desires and your situation.
20. Thank God for answered prayers.

Confession:

"Quicken me O Lord, for thy name's sake: for thy righteousness' sake bring my soul out of trouble. And of thy mercy cut off mine enemies, and destroy all them that afflict my soul: for I am thy servant" Psalms 143:11–12.

Wisdom for Today:

Prayer is a shield to the soul, a sacrifice to God, and a scourge for Satan.

Read the Bible Today: Zephaniah 3

Prayer Points:

1. I praise and thank God for allowing me to see yet another day by his grace.
2. Almighty God sanctify me unto yourself in the name of Jesus.
3. Almighty God heal every wounded area of my life, destiny, and marriage, in Jesus name.
4. I take authority over every spirit and power of affliction targeted against me and my family in the name of Jesus.
5. I refuse to be divided against myself, in the name of Jesus.
6. Every power of satanic limitation upon my life, die now, in the name of Jesus.
7. Every witchcraft operation in my life, family, and church; die in the name of Jesus.
8. Every power attacking me from the land of the dead; die the second time in the name of Jesus.
9. Almighty God; use my life to confuse the enemy in the name of Jesus.
10. Every appointment with death in this month; I reject you in the name of Jesus.
11. Every pillar of sorrow in my life; I pull you down in the name of Jesus.
12. Anything standing as a pillar of sorrow in this country in my life; I pull you down in the name of Jesus.
13. O thou that troubled my Israel be pulled down now in the name of Jesus.
14. I reject tragedy and calamity throughout this month in the name of Jesus.

15. Sorrow shall not branch in my dwelling place throughout this month in the name of Jesus.
16. I shall not carry any evil load throughout this month in the name of Jesus.
17. Every maturity day of affliction; be nullified by the blood of Jesus in the name of Jesus.
18. Every incantation against me be cancelled, in the name of Jesus.
19. Every owner of evil load in my life, appear and carry your load in the name of Jesus.
20. Every perfected work of the enemy over my life; die in the name of Jesus.
21. I cancel every evil dreams, visions, prophesy and prayers against my life and family in the name of Jesus.
22. Talk to God about your heart desires and your situation.
23. Thank God for answered prayers.

Confession:

"Blessed be the Lord my strength, which teacheth my hands to war and my fingers to fight" Psalms 144:1.

Wisdom for Today:

In all trouble you should seek God. You should not set him over against your troubles, but within them. God can relieve your troubles only if you, in your anxiety, cling to him. Trouble should not really be thought of as this thing or that in particular, for our whole life on earth involves trouble; and through the troubles of our earthly pilgrimage, we find God.

Read the Bible Today: Ezekiel 12 and Mark 4

Prayer Points:

1. I praise and thank God for allowing me to see yet another day by his grace.
2. Almighty God, encircle me and my family with your wall of fire, in Jesus name.
3. Almighty God, encircle me and my family with the wall of your blood, in Jesus name.
4. Almighty God, encircle me and my family with the wall of your angels, in Jesus name.
5. Almighty God bless me indeed, in the name of Jesus.
6. Almighty God you are the God of promotion, promote me from minimum to maximum, in the name of Jesus.
7. Almighty God, deliver me from delay, in the name of Jesus.
8. By the Blood of Jesus, I receive freedom from every financial bondage in the name of Jesus.
9. You spirit of frustration I reject you in my life in the name of Jesus.
10. I refuse to be wasted; any power that wants to waste my life be wasted in the name of Jesus.
11. Every waster of my prosperity wherever you are; be arrested in the name of Jesus.
12. Every aggression of the enemy against my prosperity; be paralyzed in the name of Jesus.
13. Shout 21 Halleluiah.

14. My life you shall not be stagnant; move forward in the name of Jesus.
15. Every clever and hidden devourer, working in my life collapse and die in the name of Jesus.
16. Every poverty that came into my life through evil handshake come out with all root in the name of Jesus.
17. Every witchcraft inspired problem in my life come out; go back to your sender and destroy them in the name of Jesus.
18. I cancel every evil dreams, visions, prophesy and prayers against my life and family in the name of Jesus.
19. Talk to God about your heart desires and your situation.
20. Thank God for answered prayers.

Confession:

"The Lord preserves all them that love him: but all the wicked will he destroy" Psalms 145:20.

Wisdom for Today:

"That which does not kill us makes us stronger." —Friedrich Nietzsche

Read the Bible Today: Ezekiel 13–14

Prayer Points:

1. I praise and thank God for allowing me to see yet another day by his grace.
2. God of perfection, perfect everything that concerns me and my family in Jesus name.
3. Almighty God arise and blow away every wicked power working against me and my family in the name of Jesus.
4. Let my enemies enter their own traps in the mighty name of Jesus.
5. All eaters of flesh and drinkers of blood fashioned against me and my family eat your own flesh and drink your own blood, in Jesus name.
6. I disagree with every evil decision over my life, marriage, and family, in Jesus name.
7. By the Blood of Jesus, I rise above every limitation and *shine*, in Jesus name.
8. 8. I will prosper and be in good health in this country in the name of Jesus.
9. 9. This country is not complete without me; I shall possess my possession in the name of Jesus.
10. 10. I prophesy, I will not cry again in this county in Jesus name.
11. 11. Every power that does not want me to see the days of joy; die in the name of Jesus.
12. 12. I refuse to lose in the name of Jesus.
13. I cancel every evil dreams, visions, prophesy and prayers against my life and family in the name of Jesus.
14. Talk to God about your heart desires and your situation.
15. Thank God for answered prayers.

Confession:

"The Lord lifteth me up: he casteth the wicked down to the ground"
Psalms 147:6.

Wisdom for Today:

They gave our Master a crown of thorns. Why do we hope for a crown of roses?

Read the Bible Today: Ezekiel 15–16

Prayer Points:

1. I praise and thank God for allowing me to see yet another day by his grace.
2. Every evil agreement against me and my family scatter unto desolation, in Jesus name.
3. Any tree harboring anything against me, dry to the root, in the name of Jesus.
4. Every witchcraft gathering against me and my family be uprooted by fire, in the name of Jesus.
5. I break every witchcraft plot with the cross of Jesus Christ, in Jesus name.
6. Let the fire of God expose and disgrace every witch in my family, in the name of Jesus.
7. Every defeat that I have ever suffered in the dream be converted to victory in the name of Jesus.
8. Fresh power of God, over shadow my life in the name of Jesus.
9. Almighty God, open my spiritual ears and let me hear what you want me to hear in the name of Jesus.
10. Every internal failure in my life, come out in the name of Jesus.
11. Every seed of sorrow in my life come out in the name of Jesus.
12. Anything standing as problem in my life; fall down and die in the name of Jesus.
13. I bind and render to knot every evil counsel and imagination against my life, marriage and family in the name of Jesus.
14. Let the entrance door of poverty into my life be closed now in the name of Jesus.
15. Every power adding problem to my problem, what are you waiting for? die in the name of Jesus.
16. You doors of my prosperity, open now in the name of Jesus.

17. Let my enemies bow before me and congratulate me in the name of Jesus.
18. Almighty God remove from my life every garment of suffering, like you did for Joseph in the name of Jesus.
19. Any power that wants me to die; die for my sake in the name of Jesus.
20. Every owner of evil load; in my life, I command you to carry your load in the name of Jesus.

Confession:

"They that hate me shall be clothed with shame; and the dwelling place of the wicked shall come to nought" Job 8:22.

Wisdom for Today:

"The man who does not learn to wait upon the Lord and have his thoughts molded by him will never possess that steady purpose and calm trust, which is essential to the exercise of wise influence upon others, in times of crisis and difficulty." —Dixon Edward Hoste

Read the Bible Today: Ezekiel 17–18

Prayer Points:

1. I praise and thank God for allowing me to see yet another day by his grace.
2. Anyone who has entered into witchcraft because of me and my family die with your power, in the name of Jesus.
3. I command a change for better in my life by the blood of Jesus, in Jesus name.
4. Every power working against my better living, die, in the name of Jesus.
5. Any power that wants me to die in bad condition, die now, in the name of Jesus.
6. Let all those who entered into any evil covenant in order to kill or destroy me, die with their evil covenant, in the name of Jesus.
7. Witchcraft covenant upon my life, I command you to break in the name of Jesus.
8. Every general curse working against my life; break and release me in the name of Jesus.
9. Family evil strongman or woman; release my life by fire in the name of Jesus.
10. Water spirit I belong to Jesus release me by fire, in the name of Jesus.
11. Any covenant binding me with marine spirit, break by the blood of Jesus in the name of Jesus.
12. Every curse upon my life as a result of the wickedness of my ancestors break and release me in the name of Jesus.

13. Every curse standing in the way of my children's blessing, break in the name of Jesus.
14. I forbid every storm in my life this year in the name of Jesus.
15. Every power destroying good things in my life; be destroyed by fire in the name of Jesus.
16. Every covenant of late blessing, break and release my life in the name of Jesus.
17. I cancel every evil dreams, visions, prophesy and prayers against my life and family in the name of Jesus.
18. Talk to God about your heart desires and your situation.
19. Thank God for answered prayers.

Confession:

"He shall deliver me in six troubles: yea, in the seven there shall no evil touch me" Job 5:19.

Wisdom for Today:

"Blessed is he who bears affliction with thankfulness." —Saint Abba Copres

Read the Bible Today: Ezekiel 19–20

Prayer Points:

1. I praise and thank God for allowing me to see yet another day by his grace.
2. I shall not eat the bread of sorrow, in the name of Jesus.
3. I shall not drink the water of affliction, in the name of Jesus.
4. Any power that will not let me go die, in the name of Jesus.
5. Every anti-prayer power working in my life, come out and die, in the name of Jesus.
6. Let my prayer life receive deliverance by fire, in the name of Jesus.
7. I am that I am, arise and manifest your power in my life in the name of Jesus.
8. I am that I am, arise and destroy my poverty in the name of Jesus.
9. I am that I am, arise and destroy the bondage in my family in the name of Jesus.
10. Blood of Jesus Christ speak better things to my life in the name of Jesus.
11. Anything that will take me away from divine protection, come out of my life and enter no more in the name of Jesus.
12. Almighty God hold me up for I put my hope in you in the name of Jesus.
13. Almighty God empower me for victory tonight in the name of Jesus.
14. Every operation of the enemies in my dreams; fail woefully in the name of Jesus.
15. Any manifestation of the enemy in my dream, I command you to be consumed by the fire of God in the name of Jesus.

16. Every appointment with weeping, I reject you in the name of Jesus.
17. I refuse to weep for the enemies to rejoice in the name of Jesus.
18. I cancel every evil dreams, visions, prophesy and prayers against my life and family in the name of Jesus.
19. Talk to God about your heart desires and your situation.
20. Thank God for answered prayers.

Confession:

"But I will deliver thee in that day, saith the lord: and thou shall not be given into the hand of the men of whom thou art afraid. For I will surely deliver thee, and thou shall not fall by the sword, but thy life shall be for a prey unto thee: because thou hast put thy trust in me, saith the Lord" Jeremiah 39:17–18.

Wisdom for Today:

"God grant me the serenity to accept the things I cannot change, the courage to change the things I can; and the wisdom to know the difference." —Reinhold Niebuhr

Read the Bible Today: Ezekiel 21 and 1 Kings 19

Prayer Points:

1. I praise and thank God for allowing me to see yet another day by his grace.
2. I refuse to die physically and spiritually, in the name of Jesus.
3. Let the angels of God pursue every evil power pursuing me from my father's house, in the name of Jesus.
4. Let the angels of God pursue all evil powers pursuing me from my mother's house, in the name of Jesus.
5. The voice of the enemy shall not prevail over my life and marriage, in Jesus name.
6. I declare as from today, life shall be easy for me, in the name of Jesus.
7. Any area of secret tears in my life, receive the touch of God's miracle in the name of Jesus.
8. Almighty God, go back to every second of my past, and remove anything that is causing problem in my life in the name of Jesus.
9. Almighty God arise and nullify every word of human being that is manifesting in my life in the name of Jesus.
10. Almighty God, remove every reproach in my life, and the life of my family, in the name of Jesus.
11. I cancel every evil dream by the blood of Jesus in the name of Jesus.
12. All my good dreams; be empowered for speedy manifestation in the name of Jesus.

13. Every power fuelling problems in my life your time is up; die in the name of Jesus.
14. I release myself from every curse working in my family in the name of Jesus.
15. Every spiritual evil dedication against me and my family; receive the stones of fire and die in the name of Jesus.
16. You messenger of death assigned against me and my family, go back to your sender in the name of Jesus.
17. Every evil gathering against me and my family be scattered in the name of Jesus.
18. Every evil wisdom working against, my breakthroughs; be disgraced in the name of Jesus.
19. I put every evil under my feet in the name of Jesus.
20. Thou power of sin and iniquity in my life, die in the name of Jesus.
21. Every evil desire in my life; the Lord rebuke you in the name of Jesus.
22. I cancel every evil dreams, visions, prophesy and prayers against my life and family in the name of Jesus.
23. Talk to God about your heart desires and your situation.
24. Thank God for answered prayers.

Confession:

"God shall deliver the island of the innocent: and it is delivered by the pureness of thine hands" Job 22:30.

Wisdom for Today:

If we walk one step toward God, God will run ten steps toward us. "I am the vine, you are the branches. Whoever remains in me and I in him will bear much fruit, because without me you can do nothing" John 15:5. "With God all things are possible" Matthew 19:26.

Read the Bible Today: Ezekiel 22–23

Prayer Points:

1. I praise and thank God for allowing me to see yet another day by his grace.
2. Almighty God, send your fire of deliverance into the foundation of my life, in the name of Jesus.
3. I lay hold on the divine sword of fire and cut off every power holding me in bondage, in the name of Jesus.
4. I command internal bondages in my life to be broken by the blood of Jesus in the name of Jesus.
5. I release myself from parental and family bondage, in the name of Jesus.
6. Almighty God deliver me from every conscious and unconscious bondage, in the name of Jesus.
7. I am seated with Christ in the heavenly places, far above principalities and powers in the name of Jesus.
8. Anointing of deliverance fall upon me now in the name of Jesus.
9. Every power that pursued my parents and now pursuing me, what are you waiting for, die in the name of Jesus.
10. Every problem in the life of my parents that is now appearing in my life; vanish in the name of Jesus.
11. Every pillar of disgrace in my life, I pull you down in the name of Jesus.
12. Every evil preparation to disgrace me; be destroyed by fire in the name of Jesus.
13. Every power that has singled me out for affliction, Holy Ghost fire, locate and destroy them in the name of Jesus.

14. Every evil mark upon my body, wherever you are vanish in the name of Jesus.
15. Almighty God restore all my wasted years in the name of Jesus Christ.
16. Every power covering my glory, fall down and die in the name of Jesus.
17. You my glory arise and shine in the name of Jesus.
18. I cancel every evil dreams, visions, prophesy and prayers against my life and family in the name of Jesus.
19. Talk to God about your heart desires and your situation.
20. Thank God for answered prayers.

Confession:

"God will deliver my soul from going into the pit and my life shall see the light" (Job 33:28.

Wisdom for Today:

The safest place to be is within the will of God.

Read the Bible Today: Ezekiel 24–25

Prayer Points:

1. I praise and thank God for allowing me to see yet another day by his grace.
1. I break every covenant with bondage, in the name of Jesus.
2. Any evil material buried for my sake, be exhumed, be roasted, and relinquish your power, in the name of Jesus.
3. I walk out of bondage into God's perfect deliverance, in the name of Jesus.
4. Almighty deliver me from any form of bondage, in the name of Jesus.
5. Almighty God, separate me from every evil attachment by your power, in the name of Jesus.
6. Every seed of the enemy in my life come out by fire in the name of Jesus.
7. Every seed of poverty in my life come out by fire in the name of Jesus.
8. Every dream of poverty, I cancel you by the blood of Jesus in the name of Jesus.
9. Every evil burial for my sake, be destroyed by fire in the name of Jesus.
10. I break the power of death over my life in the name of Jesus.
11. Every hold of the enemy over my blood break by fire in the name of Jesus.
12. Every messenger of death on assignment against me and my family, die in the name of Jesus.
13. Good dreams in my life, hear the word of God, come alive and manifest in the name of Jesus.
14. Every weapon of demotion fashioned against my life, scatter in the name of Jesus.

15. By the spirit of the prophet, I send back every evil arrow fired against my life, go back to sender in the name of Jesus.

16. Anything packaged to destroy my joy in this country be destroyed by fire in the name of Jesus.

17. Foundation of sorrow in my life; be broken to pieces in the name of Jesus.

18. I proclaim that my joy shall last forever in the name of Jesus.

19. Evil deposit in my life and body your time is up, come out in the name of Jesus.

20. I cancel every evil dreams, visions, prophesy and prayers against my life and family in the name of Jesus.

21. Talk to God about your heart desires and your situation.

22. Thank God for answered prayers.

Confession:

"He delivers the poor in his affliction, and openeth their ears in oppression" Job 36:15.

Wisdom for Today:

"Anyone who kneels before God can stand before anyone"

Read the Bible Today: Ezekiel 26 and Psalm 68

Prayer Points:

1. I praise and thank God for allowing me to see yet another day by his grace.
2. I command deliverance upon every department of my life, in the name of Jesus.
3. I break every curse of bondage issued against my life, in the name of Jesus.
4. I declare that no power shall be able to put my life in bondage, in the name of Jesus.
5. I live upon Mount Zion; therefore, I am delivered, in the name of Jesus.
6. I shall not end my life in shame, in the name of Jesus.
7. Every attempt to cover my glory; be frustrated in the name of Jesus.
8. Every evil power monitoring the gates of my prosperity why are you still alive, I command you to die in Jesus name.
9. Every evil arrow fired to useless my life, come out and go back to your sender in the name of Jesus.
10. Spirit of poverty come out of my life and enter no more in the name of Jesus.
11. Any power that is making my family to suffer your time is up, die in the name of Jesus.
12. I shall not answer the call of any evil spirit in the name of Jesus Christ.
13. Every power hired to curse me, my destiny, what are you waiting for, die in the name of Jesus.
14. Any power or covenant of my father's house that wants to waste my life and calling, die in the name of Jesus.

15. Stubborn pursuers of my life die in the name of Jesus.
16. Every evil stamp of the enemy; be removed in the name of Jesus.
17. Almighty God; turn my failures to success in the name of Jesus.
18. I cancel every dreams, visions, prophesy and prayers against my life and family in the name of Jesus.
19. Talk to God about your heart desires and your situation.
20. Thank God for answered prayers.

Confession:

"Therefore I shall see no more vanity, nor divine divination: for God will deliver his people out of the hand of the wicked: and ye shall know that I am the Lord" Ezekiel 13:23.

Wisdom for Today:

"To be a Christian without prayer is no more possible than to be alive without breathing." —Martin Luther King, Jr.

Read the Bible Today: Ezekiel 27 and Luke 18

Prayer Points:

1. I praise and thank God for allowing me to see yet another day by his grace.
2. I shall not weep over what has been giving me joy, in the name of Jesus.
3. I shall not wear rags; I shall not wear the garment of shame, in the name of Jesus.
4. I shall not turn into a beggar, in the name of Jesus.
5. Almighty God baptize me with your divine favor, in the name of Jesus.
6. Every gate in this nation shot against me, open now in the name of Jesus.
7. Every curse that is delaying good things in my life; break and release me in the name of Jesus.
8. Every spirit of this world attached to my mind, I cut you off in the name of Jesus.
9. Spirit of God, reign in my life in the name of Jesus.
10. Almighty God, teach my hand to war in the name of Jesus.
11. Almighty God arise and prevail over my enemies in the name of Jesus.
12. Let the wicked and their wickedness be destroyed by fire in the name of Jesus.
13. Let every stubborn enemy that has risen against me; be defeated now in the name of Jesus.
14. By the power of the Holy Ghost, I destroy the enemies and their work in my life in the name of Jesus.

15. Let the dwelling place of my enemies come to nothing, and let those who hate me be put to shame in the name of Jesus.
16. Let every weapon of my enemies back fire and destroy them in the name of Jesus.
17. Almighty God; turn my failures to success in the name of Jesus.
18. I cancel every dreams, visions, prophesy and prayers against my life and family in the name of Jesus.
19. Talk to God about your heart desires and your situation.
20. Thank God for answered prayers.

Confession:

"And it shall come to pass, that whosoever shall call on the name of the Lord shall be delivered: for in Mount Zion and in Jerusalem shall be deliverance, as the Lord hath said, and in the remnant whom the Lord shall call" Joel 2:32.

Wisdom for Today:

Take a stand for Christ, or you may fall for anything. If we should abide in Christ, we shall abound in Christ!

Read the Bible Today: Ezekiel 28–29

Prayer Points:

1. I praise and thank God for allowing me to see yet another day by his grace.
2. Let every instance of internal and external warfare in my life and family be quenched, in the name of Jesus.
3. I command the weapons of my enemies to turn against them, in the name of Jesus.
4. Every instance of satanic warfare arranged against me in the heavenly places and on earth, be dismantled by thunder, in the name of Jesus.
5. I command the weapons of war, which my enemies depend on, to disappoint them, in the name of Jesus.
6. Almighty God prove yourself as a man of war over my enemies, in the name of Jesus.
7. Every evil power that is holding me down, die in the name of Jesus.
8. I move from nothing to something good in the name of Jesus.
9. In this country I shall not be disgraced in the name of Jesus.
10. In this country I shall not be put to shame, or disgraced in the name of Jesus.
11. Every attack in my dream that is now affecting my life be reversed in the name of Jesus.
12. Evil arrows from my dream come out and go back to sender in the name of Jesus.
13. Powers from my father's house, mother's house begin to attack yourself in Jesus name.

14. Almighty God, I need a break in this country in the name of Jesus.
15. Almighty God, heal every area that I have been wounded in the name of Jesus.
16. Every power bent on seeing my destiny destroyed, Holy Ghost fire locate and destroy them in the name of Jesus.
17. My ears shall hear good news, my eyes shall see good things, and my hands shall possess good things in the name of Jesus.
18. Almighty God, arise quickly and deliver me from shame in the name of Jesus.
19. Evil arrows my body is not for you in the name of Jesus.
20. Every owner of evil load in my life, carry your load in the name of Jesus.
21. I shall not be wasted; I shall not be useless in the name of Jesus.
22. Every power affecting my joy, lose your power and die in the name of Jesus.
23. Almighty God; turn my failures to success in the name of Jesus.
24. I cancel every dreams, visions, prophesy and prayers against my life and family in the name of Jesus.
25. Talk to God about your heart desires and your situation.
26. Thank God for answered prayers.

Confession:

"But upon Mount Zion shall be deliverance, and there shall be holiness; and the house of Jacob shall possess their possessions" Obadiah 1:17.

Wisdom for Today:

Satan subtracts and divides; God adds and multiplies. "God can draw a straight line with a crooked stick." —Martin Luther

Read the Bible Today: Ezekiel 30 and Isaiah 40

Prayer Points:

1. I praise and thank God for allowing me to see yet another day by his grace.
2. I declare no weapon fashioned against me shall prosper in the name of Jesus.
3. I remove the protection of the enemy going to war against me, and I expose him to the danger of death, in the name of Jesus.
4. Every power constantly challenging me to battle and making me live my life in a warzone receive double destruction by fire, in the name of Jesus.
5. Any power wanting to replace my peace with war, die suddenly, in the name of Jesus.
6. I release discord into the camp of the enemies planning war against me, and I command them to fight themselves to death, in the name of Jesus.
7. I shall not bury my children in the name of Jesus.
8. Every dry bone in my life, receive the touch of resurrection and life in the name of Jesus.
9. Every good door that has been closed against me, lift up your heads and let the King of glory come in in Jesus name.
10. Almighty God arise in your mercy and close the old chapter in my life in the name of Jesus.
11. Every word of the enemy waiting for manifestation in my life, die in the name of Jesus.
12. Every maturity date of evil words and prophesies in my life, be nullified in the name of Jesus.

13. I fire back, every arrow of evil prophecy that is pursuing my life; in the name of Jesus.
14. Every satanic assignment, I reject you in my life in the name of Jesus.
15. Every power demanding tears from my eyes before receiving my blessings, die in the name of Jesus.
16. Every power sponsoring weeping in my family; carry your load and die in the name of Jesus.
17. Almighty God; turn my failures to success in the name of Jesus.
18. I cancel every dreams, visions, prophesy and prayers against my life and family in the name of Jesus.
19. Talk to God about your heart desires and your situation.
20. Thank God for answered prayers.

Confession:

"Christ hath redeemed me from the curse of the law, being made a curse for me: for it is written, cursed is every one that hangeth on a tree" Galatians 3:13.

Wisdom for Today:

"What we are is God's gift to us. What we become is our gift to God." —Eleanor Powell

Read the Bible Today: Ezekiel 31 and Luke 11

Prayer Points:

1. I praise and thank God for allowing me to see yet another day by his grace.
2. Almighty God fight my battles for me, in the name of Jesus.
3. I go with the Lord Jesus into every battle of my life, and I come out victorious, in the name of Jesus.
4. It is well with my spirit, soul, and body, in Jesus name.
5. Let every curse issued against me turn to blessing now, in the name of Jesus.
6. My head shall not be bewitched, in Jesus name.
7. Every witchcraft cage caging my destiny, break by thunder fire of God.
8. Almighty God, deliver me from the strife of tongue in the name of Jesus.
9. Evil arrows go back to your sender in the name of Jesus.
10. Every attack of eaters of flesh and drinkers of blood, back fire in the name of Jesus.
11. I withdraw my blood from witchcraft altar in the name of Jesus.
12. Anything representing me in any kingdom of darkness, I withdraw you by fire in the name of Jesus.
13. I walk out of the prison of evil dreams in the name of Jesus.
14. Every dream of backwardness in my life die in the name of Jesus.
15. Any power using anything in my past to torment me, die in the name of Jesus.
16. By the blood of Jesus, I register my name for solution today in the name of Jesus.

17. I shall not serve my enemies and I shall not serve my friend in the name of Jesus.
18. I disagree with every satanic decision over my life in the name of Jesus.
19. Almighty God; turn my failures to success in the name of Jesus.
20. I cancel every dreams, visions, prophesy and prayers against my life and family in the name of Jesus.
21. Talk to God about your heart desires and your situation.
22. Thank God for answered prayers.

Confession:

"That he would grant unto us, that we being delivered out of the hand of our enemies might serve God without fear" Luke 1:74.

Wisdom for Today:

There is no room for fear in your life. Even if you have messed up, God can turn your mess into miracles.

Read the Bible Today: Psalm 118

Prayer Points:

1. I praise and thank God for allowing me to see yet another day by his grace.
2. Every evil dream against my destiny, lose your power and die, in the name of Jesus.
3. No sickness shall come near my dwelling place, in the name of Jesus.
4. I shake sickness and infirmity out of my body; I declare that I am strong, in the name of Jesus.
5. I claim divine health upon my life, in the name of Jesus.
6. Every evil challenge against my destiny be disgraced, in the name of Jesus.
7. I shall not answer the call of evil spirits, in the name of Jesus.
8. I cancel every former and present agreement with the spirit of Egypt in the name of Jesus.
9. Every agreement with the power of the air, I command you to break in the name of Jesus.
10. I recover every blessing I have lost to spirit of Egypt in the name of Jesus.
11. Almighty God deliver me from every problem I have brought upon myself in the name of Jesus.
12. I reject every invitation to bondage in the name of Jesus.
13. Almighty God give me power to overcome pressures in life in the name of Jesus.
14. Almighty God, make me a good sign and use me for your glory in the name of Jesus.
15. By the anointing of the Holy Ghost, I leap over every negative situation surrounding me in the name of Jesus.

16. My soul hopes and wait on the Lord, for you God is gracious In the name of Jesus.
17. I shall not fail God in the name of Jesus.
18. Almighty God I commit my life to you; organize my scattered life in the name of Jesus.
19. Almighty God, change my story as you did Jabez in the name of Jesus.
20. I reject automatic failure in my life in the name of Jesus.
21. Every enemy of divine presence in my life, I command you to die in the name of Jesus.
22. Anointing to excel above all my family members fall upon me now in the name of Jesus.
23. I shall experience divine favor throughout the days of my life in Jesus name.
24. Holy Spirit; coordinate me in the name of Jesus.
25. Arrows of the enemy you shall not locate me, go back to your sender in the name of Jesus.
26. Almighty God; turn my failures to success in the name of Jesus.
27. I cancel every dreams, visions, prophesy and prayers against my life and family in the name of Jesus.
28. Talk to God about your heart desires and your situation.
29. Thank God for answered prayers.

Confession:

"For now will I break his yoke from off thee, and will burst thy bonds in sunder" Nahum 1:13.

Wisdom for Today:

Just see yourself delivered from whatever you are going through. There may be scars, yet you are healed in the name of Jesus.

Read the Bible Today: *Isaiah 53:1–5*

Prayer Points:

1. Every seed of sickness growing in the foundation of my life die by fire, in the name of Jesus.
2. I detach myself from every inherited sickness, in the name of Jesus.
3. Oh, great physician, heal me with your healing balm, in the name of Jesus.
4. Oh, great healer let your healing power flow through my body, in the name of Jesus.
5. I command every terminal and seasonal illness to get out of my life with all its roots, in the name of Jesus.
6. Power to sin no more, fall upon me now in the name of Jesus.
7. I put the yoke of Jesus Christ upon myself in the name of Jesus.
8. God shall help me and fight for me in the name of Jesus.
9. I shall not lose my job in the name of Jesus.
10. My source of money shall not be blocked this month in the name of Jesus.
11. Throughout this month I shall be blessed and highly favored in the name of Jesus.
12. Where there is no way for others, there shall be way for me this month in the name of Jesus.
13. I reject any death in my family and church in the name of Jesus.
14. O Lord, let your hand be upon me for good throughout this month in the name of Jesus.
15. Father Lord, do not give me up to the desires of my enemies in the name of Jesus.
16. Evil shall not prevail against me and my family in the name of Jesus.

17. Sin shall not rule over me in the name of Jesus.
18. Every good thing my hands have started, my hands shall complete, and I shall enjoy them in the name of Jesus.
19. My head hear the word of the Lord; you shall not be bewitched in the name of Jesus.
20. I shall not become what the enemies want me to be in the name of Jesus.
21. O God of Abraham, Isaac, and Jacob rearrange this country to favor me in the name of Jesus.
22. Every completed work of my enemies over my life; be destroyed with all your effects in the name of Jesus.

Confession:

"Blotting out the handwriting of ordinances that was against me, which was contrary to me, and took it out of the way, nailing it to his cross; and having spoiled principalities and powers, he made a show of them openly, triumphing over them in it" Colossians 2:14–15.

Wisdom for Today:

Whatever affairs you had with the devil in the past have been erased by the precious blood of Jesus. You are no longer bound to sin; in fact, Jesus Christ the Son of God has given you victory. Take your burden to the cross and drop it there.

Read the Bible Today: Ephesians 1 ✓

Prayer Points:

1. You, the spirit of poverty assigned against my life, I cut off your head, in the name of Jesus.
2. I render every spirit of fruitless effort and profitless handwork working against my life powerless, in the name of Jesus.
3. I destroy by the blood of Jesus every power binding me to poverty, failure, and disappointment, in the name of Jesus.
4. I refuse to wear the garment of poverty, lack, or debt, in the name of Jesus.
5. I refuse to follow the poverty pattern of my ancestors, in the name of Jesus.
6. I break and lose myself from the stronghold of darkness in the name of Jesus.
7. Any power that wants to replace my peace with war, die suddenly in the name of Jesus.
8. By the blood of Jesus Christ, I rise above all limitation in life in the name of Jesus.
9. Almighty God reign supreme in my life in the name of Jesus.
10. Almighty God set me free from poverty in the name of Jesus.
11. By the power in the word of God, I command every darkness in my life to vanish in the name of Jesus.
12. Every step by step work of the enemy in my life tonight be destroyed in the name of Jesus.

13. Every perfected works of the enemy in my life be over turned by the blood of Jesus.
14. Every evil altar in my family working against my glory; be consumed by fire in the name of Jesus.
15. Every good thing the enemy scattered in my life, come together in the name of Jesus.
16. Every power and spirit that has set my life for affliction, I bind you in the name of Jesus.
17. In the name of Jesus, my life shall not follow satanic agenda in the name of Jesus.
18. Almighty God, it is time give me rest, comfort me, and prosper me in the name of Jesus.
19. By the blood of Jesus, I register my name for solution today in the name of Jesus.
20. Almighty God; turn my failures to success in the name of Jesus.
21. I cancel every dreams, visions, prophesy and prayers against my life and family in the name of Jesus.
22. Talk to God about your heart desires and your situation.
23. Thank God for answered prayers.

Confession:

"And the Lord shall deliver me from every evil work, and will preserve me unto his heavenly kingdom: to whom be glory forever and ever. Amen" 2 Timothy 4: 18.

Wisdom for Today:

"God, who foresaw your tribulation, has specially armed you to go through it, not without pain but without stain." —C.S. Lewis

Read the Bible Today: Ruth 1–2 ✓

Prayer Points:

1. Every power attacking my source of income be destroy beyond remedy, in the name of Jesus.
2. Let all those who do not want to see me prosper be destroyed by fire, in the name of Jesus.
3. You, the spirit of poverty, failure, and backwardness, I am not your candidate; therefore, relinquish your hold upon my life, in the name of Jesus.
4. I repossess my destiny, benefits, and potentials stolen by anybody dead or alive, by the blood of Jesus, in Jesus name.
5. Almighty God soak me in your favor, success, and breakthrough, in the name of Jesus.
6. I connect myself with the power of God in the name of Jesus.
7. Every pillar of witchcraft in my family, what are you waiting for? I pull you down in the name of Jesus.
8. Witchcraft powers why are you pursuing my life? die in the name of Jesus.
9. It is suffer not a witch to live, therefore any witchcraft pursuing my life, I command you to die in the name of Jesus.
10. 10. I disagree with failure in the name of Jesus.
11. 11. Failure at the edge of good things, depart from my life by the blood of Jesus in the name of Jesus.
12. 12. Witchcraft battle at the edge of my success return to your sender in the name of Jesus.
13. 13. Every evil seed planted by the enemy in my life, be uprooted by fire in the name of Jesus.

14. 14. Every plantation of darkness in my life, come out with all your roots in the name of Jesus.
15. 15. Every evil seed planted into my life through dreams, be uprooted by fire in the name of Jesus.
16. 16. I challenge my system with the fire of God, in the name of Jesus.
17. 17. Every instrument of satanic control in my life, wherever you are be destroyed by fire in the name of Jesus.
18. 18. Arrows of darkness in my life come out of your hiding places and go back to your sender in the name of Jesus.
19. 19. As from today, life shall be easy for me in the name of Jesus.
20. 20. By the blood of Jesus, I stand in gap for every member of my family in the name of Jesus.
21. 21. Every of my family that is appointed for death, be redeemed by the blood of Jesus in the name of Jesus.
22. 22. Any power that wants to attack me, Holy Ghost fire attack and destroy them in the name of Jesus.
23. 23. Arrows of madness fired against me and any member of my family, gather yourself together and go back to your sender in the name of Jesus.
24. 24. All those in the system of this country that will not favor me, o Lord replace them with people that will favor me in the name of Jesus.
25. 25. All those who are boasting to fire me in my place of work, let the Holy Ghost fire, fire them in the name of Jesus.
26. 26 Almighty God; turn my failures to success in the name of Jesus.
27. I cancel every dreams, visions, prophesy and prayers against my life and family in the name of Jesus.
28. Talk to God about your heart desires and your situation.
29. Thank God for answered prayers.

Apostle A.O. Solomon

Confession:

"Who hath delivered me from the power of darkness, and hath translated me into the kingdom of his dear son" Colossians 1:13.

Wisdom for Today:

With God all things are possible. Impossible only means that you haven't found the solution yet.

Read the Bible Today: Ruth 3–4

Prayer Points:

1. Almighty God rend the heavens for my sake and pour your unlimited blessings upon me, in the name of Jesus.
2. From the east, west, north, and south, I possess all my possessions, in the name of Jesus.
3. I shall receive expected and unexpected financial breakthroughs today, in the name of Jesus.
4. Almighty God of heaven and earth; make haste to connect me with my divine helpers, in the name of Jesus.
5. I command the sun, moon, and stars to begin to favor me, in the name of Jesus.
6. Every evil register containing my name, Holy Ghost fire consume them in the name of Jesus.
7. Every broom of darkness sweeping good things away from my life, catch fire in the name of Jesus.
8. Angel of the living God; begin to sweep back all my blessings in the name of Jesus.
9. Every spirit of laboring without achievement; be destroyed in the name of Jesus.
10. I hold the hammer of the word of God and command every padlock ministering evil against my life; break in the name of Jesus.
11. With the garment of fire and power of Jesus, I enter the strong room of the enemy and collect all my blessing in the name of Jesus.
12. I go with the Lord Jesus and the Holy Ghost fire into every witchcraft coven, and collect my blessings in the name of Jesus.
13. Any man or woman, attending witchcraft meeting because of me, you shall not return in the name of Jesus.

14. Anyone calling my name for evil in the night, angel of God; slap them in the name of Jesus.
15. Every night captivity in my life, break in the name of Jesus.
16. Anything done against me in the night; be destroyed by fire in the name of Jesus.
17. Every satanic power appearing in my dream, the Lord rebuke you perish in the name of Jesus.
18. Any fire that the enemy has lighted against me and my family be quenched by the blood of Jesus.
19. Every evil pot caging anything good in my life, break by thunder in the name of Jesus.
20. Almighty God put upon me now your garment of mercy and favor in the name of Jesus.
21. My spirit man, my body, my soul hear the word of the Lord; you shall not answer the call of the enemy day or night in the name of Jesus.
22. Let the voice of God thunder against my enemies and divide them in the name of Jesus.
23. Let the voice of God, divide the fire of my enemy and destroy them in the name of Jesus.
24. Let the voice of God, shake down the camp of my enemies in the name of Jesus
25. Almighty God, clothe me with mercy and compassion in the name of Jesus.
26. Almighty God; turn my failures to success in the name of Jesus.
27. I cancel every dreams, visions, prophesy and prayers against my life and family in the name of Jesus.
28. Talk to God about your heart desires and your situation.
29. Thank God for answered prayers.

Confession:

"But God will redeem my soul from the power of the grave: for he shall receive me" Psalms 49:15.

Wisdom for Today:

God promised to set you above in praise, name and honor. (Deuteronomy 26:19) "Try not to become a man of success but a man of value." —Albert Einstein

Read the Bible Today: 1 Samuel 1–2

Prayer Points:

1. Almighty God give me the power to prosper in all I do, in the name of Jesus.
2. I rise above every limitation in life, in the name of Jesus.
3. This year shall be year of all-round comfort for me and my family in Jesus name.
4. Failure shall not be my portion this year, in Jesus name.
5. Sorrow, sighing, and weeping shall not be my portion this year, in Jesus name.
6. Accident, tragedy, and death shall not be my portion this year, in Jesus name.
7. Almighty God, empower my hands for profit in the name of Jesus.
8. Every attack against my labor, break and release me in the name of Jesus.
9. Every curse of the enemy against the works of my hands, break by the blood of Jesus in the name of Jesus.
10. Every physical and spiritual chain upon my hands, break in the name of Jesus.
11. Thou son of David use your key, and set me free from hand cuffs and chains in the name of Jesus.
12. Jesus set me free; I am free indeed in the name of Jesus.
13. I drink the blood of Jesus, and I cover myself with the blood of Jesus in the name of Jesus.
14. Any power that wants to destroy the works of God in my life, Holy Ghost fire; destroy them in the name of Jesus.
15. Every satanic bondage from evil dreams programmed into my life; break and release me in the name of Jesus.

16. Every sickness introduced into my life as a result of evil dreams die now in the name of Jesus.
17. Every dream of failure in my past be reversed in the name of Jesus.
18. Every witchcraft agent pursuing me in the dream fall down and die in the name of Jesus.
19. Almighty God, make me holy by your power in the name of Jesus.
20. Every satanic dream attached to my progress, die in the name of Jesus.
21. I come out of every dream prison by the power of the Holy Ghost in the name of Jesus.
22. I fire back every witchcraft arrow fired into my dream in the name of Jesus.
23. Every evil dream of the past affecting my life now, die in the name of Jesus.
24. Every witchcraft serpent attacking me in the dream, return to your sender and destroy them in the name of Jesus.
25. Every dream affecting my life, marriage, and career lose your power and die in the name of Jesus.
26. Every good thing I have lost in the dream I repossess you back in Jesus name.
27. Every agent of darkness in my dream life, I command you to die in the name of Jesus.
28. Almighty God; turn my failures to success in the name of Jesus.
29. I cancel every dreams, visions, prophesy and prayers against my life and family in the name of Jesus.
30. Talk to God about your heart desires and your situation.
31. Thank God for answered prayers.

Confession:

"Lord my God, in thee do I put my trust: save me from all them that persecute me, and deliver me" Psalms 7:1.

Wisdom for Today:

To find what you seek in the road of life, heed the advice of these wise men:
"Leave no stone unturned." — Edward Bulwer Lytton
"If you would create something, you must be something." — Johann Wolfgang von Goethe
Read the Bible Today: 1 Samuel 3–4 ✓

Prayer Points:

1. I command all the enemies of success and prosperity in my business to turn back now; for God is for me, in the name of Jesus.
2. As negative influences turn back, let the doors of breakthroughs open for me now, in the name of Jesus.
3. Let the angels of God connect me with all those who will move my business forward, in the name of Jesus.
4. Let the name of my business attract favor anywhere it appears, in the name of Jesus.
5. Almighty God, release your favor and prosperity upon my life and business today, in the name of Jesus.
6. Every evil pronouncement against me in the dream shall not stand, and it shall not come to pass in the name of Jesus.
7. My resting time shall not be a trouble time in the name of Jesus.
8. Any power, spirit, personality that wants to trouble me, my God shall trouble you in the name of Jesus.
9. Life shall not be difficult for me in the name of Jesus.
10. I reject every form of nakedness physically and spiritually in the name of Jesus.
11. I reject every form of disorder in the name of Jesus.
12. Me and my family shall be for good signs and wonders in the name of Jesus.
13. As the Lord God lives, people will see the good work of God in my life in Jesus name.
14. 14. Almighty God, let all those that will bless me be blessed, and let all those that curse me; be cursed in Jesus name.

15. 15. Every completed work of the enemy over my life be destroyed with all your power in the name of Jesus.
16. 16. I plead the blood of Jesus against every voice speaking against my destiny in the name of Jesus.
17. 17. Every owner of evil load in my life, wherever you are appear and carry your load in Jesus name.
18. 18. I plead the blood of Jesus over everything the devil is holding against me in the name of Jesus.
19. 19. Jesus I belong to you, I disconnect from the iniquity of my ancestors in the name of Jesus.
20. 20. Every ancestral oat that is affecting my life now; break by the blood of Jesus in the name of Jesus.
21. 21. Every evil word that is pursuing my destiny, the Lord rebuke you, turn back in the name of Jesus.
22. 22. Every prophecy demoting my life lose your hold and die in the name of Jesus.
23. 23. Evil family pattern, break and release me by fire in the name of Jesus.
24. 24. Every evil water flowing in my family, dry up by fire in the name of Jesus.
25. 25. Family bondage affecting my life, break in the name of Jesus.
26. 26. Ancestral evil covenant, I separate myself from you now in the name of Jesus.
27. 27. Every evil register containing my name, be roasted by fire in the name of Jesus.
28. 28. Almighty God; turn my failures to success in the name of Jesus.
29. 29. I cancel every dreams, visions, prophesy and prayers against my life and family in the name of Jesus.
30. 30. Talk to God about your heart desires and your situation.
31. 31. Thank God for answered prayers.

Confession:

"God delivereth me from my strong enemy, and from them which hated me: for they were too strong for me" Psalms 18:19.

Wisdom for Today:

"The more difficulties one has to encounter, within and without, the more significant and the higher in inspiration his life will be." —Horace Bushnell

Read the Bible Today: 1 Samuel 5–6

Prayer Points:

1. I break any curse operating in my life and business, in the name of Jesus.
2. Every good thing presently eluding my business, I possess you back, in Jesus name.
3. Let anything buried against my business be exhumed now, in the name of Jesus.
4. I reject failure in my business, in the name of Jesus.
5. I ask God for ideas that will move my business forward in the name of Jesus.
6. Almighty God, arise and fight for me with jealousy in the name of Jesus.
7. Almighty God I thank you because I will not see trouble throughout this month in the name of Jesus.
8. Every storm prepared for me and my family; be diverted away in the name of Jesus.
9. Every mark of bewitchment upon my life; lose your power and be erased in the name of Jesus.
10. Every evil hand writing upon my life; be erased in the name of Jesus.
11. Every witchcraft operation in my life, family, and church; die in the name of Jesus.
12. Every power attacking me from the land of the dead; die the second time in the name of Jesus.
13. Almighty God, use my life to confuse the enemy in the name of Jesus.
14. Every appointment with death in this month; I reject you in the name of Jesus.

15. Every pillar of sorrow in my life; I pull you down in the name of Jesus.

16. Anything standing as a pillar of sorrow in this country in my life; I pull you down in the name of Jesus.

17. O thou that troubled my Israel be pulled down now in the name of Jesus.

18. I reject tragedy and calamity throughout this month in the name of Jesus.

19. Sorrow shall not branch in my dwelling place throughout this month in the name of Jesus.

20. I shall not carry any evil load throughout this month in the name of Jesus.

21. Every maturity day of affliction; be nullified by the blood of Jesus in the name of Jesus.

22. Every incantation against me; be cancelled, in the name of Jesus.

23. Every owner of evil load in my life, appear and carry your load in the name of Jesus.

24. Every perfected work of the enemy over my life; die in the name of Jesus.

25. I cancel every dreams, visions, prophesy and prayers against my life and family in the name of Jesus.

26. Talk to God about your heart desires and your situation.

27. Thank God for answered prayers.

Confession:

"Many are the afflictions of the righteous: but the Lord delivereth him out of them all. He keepeth all his bones; not one of them is broken" Psalms 34:19–20.

Wisdom for Today:

"Experience is the child of thought, and thought is the child of action."
—Benjamin Disraeli
"Our God even weighs our actions, so be careful". 1 Samuel 2:3)

Read the Bible Today: 1 Samuel 7–8

Prayer Points:

1. I thank God for making my body a dwelling place of the Holy Spirit.
2. I thank God for sending another comforter to live with me.
3. Let the rain of God's power fall upon my life now, in the name of Jesus.
4. Almighty God, open the heaven above my head as of the day of Pentecost and release your power and fire upon me, in the name of Jesus.
5. Let the power of the carnal mind die, and let the spirit of God take control, in the name of Jesus.
6. Let every anti–Holy Ghost revival in my life die now, in the name of Jesus.
7. Let anything standing between me and the power of God die now, in the name of Jesus.
8. By the Blood of Jesus, I receive freedom from every financial bondage in the name of Jesus.
9. You spirit of frustration I reject you in my life in the name of Jesus.
10. I refuse to be wasted, any power that wants to waste my life be wasted in the name of Jesus.
11. Every waster of my prosperity wherever you are; be arrested in the name of Jesus.
12. Every aggression of the enemy against my prosperity; be paralyzed in the name of Jesus.
13. Shout 21 hallelujah.

14. All shall be well with me today in the name of Jesus.
15. My blessings you shall not be stagnant; move and locate me in the name of Jesus.
16. Every clever and hidden devourer, working in my life collapse and die in the name of Jesus.
17. Every handshake of poverty, come out with all your roots in the name of Jesus.
18. Every witchcraft problem in my life come out and go back to your sender and destroy them in the name of Jesus.
19. I cancel every dreams, visions, prophesy and prayers against my life and family in the name of Jesus.
20. Talk to God about your heart desires and your situation.
21. Thank God for answered prayers.

Confession:

"Thou art my king, O God; command deliverance for Jacob" Psalms 44: 4.

Wisdom for Today:

Happy are those who dream dreams and are ready to pay the price to make them come true. — Leon Joseph Cardinal Suenens

Read the Bible Today: 1 Samuel 9–10

Prayer Points:

1. I pull down every stronghold of weakness in my life, in the name of Jesus.
2. Let the fire of God and the blood of Jesus purge me of all spiritual impurities and fill me with power, in Jesus name.
3. Let self-die in me, and let the power of God fill me, in Jesus name.
4. I bind and cast out the spirit of slumber from my life, in the name of Jesus.
5. Every weakness in my flesh that has been holding me back; be destroyed in the name of Jesus.
6. Every lack of interest in spiritual things and studying the word of God; be crucified to the cross of Jesus, in Jesus name.
7. Every defeat that I have ever suffered in the dream be converted to victory in the name of Jesus.
8. Fresh power of God, over shadow my life in the name of Jesus.
9. O Lord, open my spiritual ears and let me hear what you want me to hear in the name of Jesus.
10. Every internal failure in my life, come out in the name of Jesus.
11. Every seed of sorrow in my life come out in the name of Jesus.
12. Anything standing as problem in my life; fall down and die in the name of Jesus.
13. I bind and render to knot every evil counsel and imagination against my life, marriage and family in the name of Jesus.
14. Let the entrance door of poverty into my life be closed now in the name of Jesus.
15. Every power adding problem to my problem, what are you waiting for? die in the name of Jesus.

16. You doors of my prosperity, open now in the name of Jesus.
17. Let my enemies bow before me and congratulate me in the name of Jesus.
18. Father Lord, remove from my life every garment of suffering like you did for Joseph in the name of Jesus.
19. Any power that wants me to die; die for my sake in the name of Jesus.
20. Every owner of evil load; in my life, I command you to carry your load in the name of Jesus.
21. I will prosper and be in good health in this country in the name of Jesus.
22. This country is not complete without me; I shall possess my possession in the name of Jesus.
23. I prophesy I will not cry in this country again in Jesus name.
24. Every power that does not want me to see the days of joy; die in the name of Jesus.
25. I refuse to lose in the name of Jesus.

I will prosper and be in good health in this country in the name of Jesus.

26. This country is not complete without me; I shall possess my possession in the name of Jesus.
27. I prophesy I will not cry in this country again in Jesus name.
28. I refuse to lose in the name of Jesus.
29. I cancel every evil dreams, visions, prophesy and prayers against my life and family in the name of Jesus.
30. Talk to God about your heart desires and your situation.

Thank God for answered prayers.

Apostle A.O. Solomon

Confession:

"He dissappointeth the devices of the crafty, so that their hands cannot perform their enterprise" Job 5:12.

Wisdom for Today:

You cannot avoid criticism but you can learn to live with it.

Read the Bible Today: 1 Samuel 11–12

Prayer Points:

1. I refuse to fall into satanic error, in the name of Jesus.
2. Evil arrows will not prosper in my life today, in Jesus name.
3. Father Lord, order my steps today, in Jesus name.
4. Father Lord, correct every error in my life and marriage, in Jesus name.
5. Let the mercy and favor of God prevail in my life today, in Jesus name.
6. Witchcraft covenant upon my life, I command you to break in the name of Jesus.
7. Every general curse working against my life; break and release me in the name of Jesus.
8. Family evil strongman or woman; release my life by fire in the name of Jesus.
9. Water spirit release me by fire, I belong to Jesus in the name of Jesus.
10. Any covenant binding me with marine spirit, break by the blood of Jesus in the name of Jesus.
11. Every curse upon my life as a result of the wickedness of my ancestors, break and release me in the name of Jesus.
12. Every curse standing in the way of my children's blessing, break in the name of Jesus.
13. I forbid every storm in my life this year in the name of Jesus.
14. Every power destroying good things in my life; be destroyed by fire in the name of Jesus.
15. Every covenant of late blessing, break and release my life in the name of Jesus.
16. I cancel every dreams, visions, prophesy and prayers against my life and family in the name of Jesus.
17. Talk to God about your heart desires and your situation.
18. Thank God for answered prayers.

Confession:

"He shall break in pieces mighty men without number, and set others in their stead. There he knoweth their works, and he overturneth them in the night, so that they are destroyed" Job 34:24–25.

Wisdom for Today:

"The true measure of life is not length, but honesty." —John Lyly

Read the Bible Today: 1 Samuel 13–14

Prayer Points:

1. O Lord, make me your oracle for miracles, signs, and wonders, in Jesus name.
2. I receive fire and power to do exploit for God and for my generation, in Jesus name.
3. O giant of powerlessness in my life, die, in the name of Jesus.
4. Holy Ghost, connect me with your fire, in the name of Jesus.
5. I refuse to become what my enemies want me to be; I am what God says I am, in the name of Jesus.
6. I am that I am, arise manifest your power in my life in the name of Jesus.
7. I am that I am, arise and destroy my poverty in the name of Jesus.
8. I am that I am, arise destroy the bondage in my family in the name of Jesus.
9. Blood of Jesus Christ speak better things to my life in the name of Jesus.
10. Anything that will take me away from divine protection; come out of my life and enter no more in the name of Jesus.
11. O Lord hold me up for I put my hope in you in the name of Jesus.
12. O Lord, empower me for victory tonight in the name of Jesus.
13. Every operation of the enemies in my dreams; fail woefully in the name of Jesus.
14. Any manifestation of the enemy in my dream be consumed by the fire of God in the name of Jesus.
15. Every appointment with weeping, I reject you in the name of Jesus.
16. I refuse to weep for the enemies to rejoice in the name of Jesus.

17. Any area of secret tears in my life, receive the touch of God's miracle in the name of Jesus.
18. Almighty God, go back to every second of my past and remove anything that is causing problem in my life in the name of Jesus.
19. Almighty God, arise and nullify every word of human being that is manifesting in my life in the name of Jesus.
20. Almighty God, enough of reproach in my life, family, and ministry in the name of Jesus.
21. I cancel every evil dream with by the blood of Jesus in the name of Jesus.
22. All my good dreams; be empowered for speedy manifestation in the name of Jesus.
23. I cancel every dreams, visions, prophesy and prayers against my life and family in the name of Jesus.
24. Talk to God about your heart desires and your situation.
25. Thank God for answered prayers.

Confession:

"Behold, God is mighty, and despieth not any: he is mighty in strength and wisdom. He preserveth not the life of the wicked: but giveth right to the poor" Job 36:5–6.

Wisdom for Today:

"Welcome every problem as an opportunity." —Grace Spear

What you are going through now is not how your story will end. Ecclesiastes 3:1–11

Read the Bible Today: 1 Samuel 15–16

Prayer Points:

1. I confess every sexual sin that may want to keep me in bondage, and I ask for forgiveness, in the name of Jesus.
2. As I go into this prayer session, I surround myself with the fire of God, and cover myself with the blood of Jesus, in Jesus name.
3. Every foundational covenant with spirit husband and wife be destroyed by the blood of Jesus.
4. Every spirit husband and wife from my foundation be consumed by the fire of God, in the name of Jesus.
5. I receive divine wisdom to escape satanic conspiracy, in Jesus name.
6. Every power fuelling problems in my life your time is up; die in the name of Jesus.
7. I release myself from every curse working in my family in the name of Jesus.
8. Every spiritual gathering against me and my family; receive the stones of fire and die in the name of Jesus.
9. You messenger of death assigned against me and my family, go back to your sender in the name of Jesus.
10. Every evil plantation in my life; be uprooted by fire in the name of Jesus.
11. Every evil wisdom working against, my breakthroughs; be disgraced in the name of Jesus.
12. By the power of the Holy Ghost, I put every evil under my feet in the name of Jesus.

13. Thou power of sin and iniquity in my life, the Lord rebuke you, die in the name of Jesus.
14. Every evil desire in my life; the Lord rebuke you, die in the name of Jesus.
15. I am seated with Christ in the heavenly places, far above principalities and powers in the name of Jesus.
16. Anointing of deliverance fall upon me now in the name of Jesus.
17. Every power that pursued my parents and now pursuing me, what are you waiting for, die in the name of Jesus.
18. Every problem in the life of my parents that is now appearing in my life; vanish in the name of Jesus.
19. Every pillar of disgrace in my life, I pull you down in the name of Jesus.
20. Every evil preparation to disgrace me; be destroyed by fire in the name of Jesus.
21. Every power that has singled me out for affliction, Holy Ghost fire, locate and destroy them in the name of Jesus.
22. Every evil mark upon my body, wherever you are vanish in the name of Jesus.
23. Father Lord, restore all my wasted years in the name of Jesus Christ.
24. Every power covering my glory, fall down and die in the name of Jesus.
25. You my glory arise and shine in the name of Jesus.
26. I cancel every dreams, visions, prophesy and prayers against my life and family in the name of Jesus.
27. Talk to God about your heart desires and your situation.
28. Thank God for answered prayers.

Confession:

"Associate yourselves, o ye people, and ye shall be broken in pieces; and give ear, all ye of far countries: gird yourselves, and ye shall be broken in pieces: gird yourselves, and ye shall be broken in pieces. Take counsel together and it shall come to nought; speak the word, and it shall not stand: for God is with us." Isaiah 8:9–10.

Wisdom for Today:

"In order to experience everyday spirituality, we need to remember that we are spiritual beings spending some time in a human body." — Barbara de Angelis

Read the Bible Today: 1 Samuel 17–18

Prayer Points:

1. Every evil power in the air, land, and sea against my prayers; I bind you all with chains that cannot be broken, in the name of Jesus.
2. I cover myself with the blood of Jesus.
3. O Lord, let your angels assist me to prevail today, in the name of Jesus.
4. I release myself from any inherited bondage, in the name of Jesus.
5. I release myself from any evil limitations, in the name of Jesus.
6. O Lord, send your fire of deliverance to my foundation, in the name of Jesus.
7. I release myself from the grip of problems transferred into my life from the womb, in the name of Jesus.
8. Every seed of the enemy in my life come out by fire in the name of Jesus.
9. Every seed of poverty in my life come out by fire in the name of Jesus.
10. Every dream of poverty, I cancel you by the blood of Jesus in the name of Jesus.
11. Every evil burial for my sake, be destroyed by fire in the name of Jesus.
12. I break the power of death over my life in the name of Jesus.
13. Every hold of the enemy over my blood break by fire in the name of Jesus.
14. Every messenger of death on assignment against me and my family, die in the name of Jesus.

15. Good dreams in my life, hear the word of God, come alive and manifest in the name of Jesus.
16. Every weapon of demotion fashioned against my life, scatter in the name of Jesus.
17. I send back every evil arrow fired against my life; I command you to go back to your sender in the name of Jesus.
18. Anything packaged to destroy my joy in this country be destroyed by fire in the name of Jesus.
19. Foundation of sorrow in my life; be broken to pieces in the name of Jesus.
20. I proclaim that my joy shall last forever in the name of Jesus.
21. Evil deposit in my life and body your time is up, come out in the name of Jesus.
22. Every attempt to cover my glory; be frustrated in the name of Jesus.
23. Every evil power monitoring the gates of my prosperity why are you still alive, I command you to die in Jesus name.
24. Every evil arrow fired to useless my life, come out and go back to your sender in the name of Jesus.
25. Spirit of poverty come out of my life and enter no more in the name of Jesus.
26. Any power that is making my family to suffer your time is up, die in the name of Jesus.
27. I shall not answer the call of any evil spirit in the name of Jesus Christ.
28. Every power hired to curse me, my destiny, what are you waiting for, die in the name of Jesus.
29. Any power or covenant of my father's house that wants to waste my life and calling, die in the name of Jesus.
30. Stubborn pursuers of my life hear the word of the Lord; die in the name of Jesus.
31. Every evil stamp of the enemy in my life; be removed in the name of Jesus.
32. Almighty God; turn my failures to success in the name of Jesus.
33. I cancel every dreams, visions, prophesy and prayers against my life and family in the name of Jesus.
34. Talk to God about your heart desires and your situation.
35. Thank God for answered prayers.

Confession:

"Behold, God is my salvation; I will trust, and not be afraid: for the Lord Jehovah is my strength and my song; he also is become my salvation". Isaiah 12:2

Wisdom for Today:

"Take the attitude of a student, never be too big to ask questions, never know too much to learn something new." — Og Mandino

Read the Bible Today: 1 Samuel 19–20

Prayer Points:

1. Fire of the Holy Ghost; purge every organ in my body, in the name of Jesus.
2. Let the blood of Jesus cleanse every organ in my body, in the name of Jesus.
3. I revoke every evil covenant from my foundation by the blood of Jesus Christ in the name of Jesus.
4. Let the blood of Jesus arise and deliver me from every evil dedication, in the name of Jesus.
5. I revoke all curses hanging upon my head and turn them to blessing, in the name of Jesus.
6. I refuse to carry the physical and spiritual failures of my father, in the name of Jesus.
7. I refuse to carry the physical and spiritual failures of my mother, in the name of Jesus.
8. Every gate in this nation shot against me, open now in the name of Jesus.
9. Every curse that is delaying good things in my life; break and release me in the name of Jesus.
10. Every spirit of this world attached to my mind, I cut you off in the name of Jesus.
11. Spirit of God, reign in my life in the name of Jesus.
12. O Lord, teach my hand to war tonight in the name of Jesus.
13. Arise O God and prevail over my enemies in Jesus name.
14. Let the wicked and their wickedness melt by fire in the name of Jesus.

15. Let every stubborn enemy that has risen against me; be defeated now in the name of Jesus.
16. By the power of the Holy Ghost, I destroy the enemies and their work in my life in the name of Jesus.
17. Let the dwelling place of my enemies come to nothing, and let those who hate me be put to shame in the name of Jesus.
18. Let every weapon of my enemies back fire and destroy them in the name of Jesus.
19. Almighty God, reveal to me the secret of becoming a winner in life in the name of Jesus.
20. Blood of Jesus, make way for me tonight in the name of Jesus.
21. Let the power of God clear way for my prayers tonight in the name of Jesus.
22. Let the angels of God come to my aid, support me tonight in the name of Jesus.
23. Holy Ghost, arise in your power and deliver me from my tight places in the name of Jesus.
24. I cancel every dreams, visions, prophesy and prayers against my life and family in the name of Jesus.
25. Talk to God about your heart desires and your situation.
26. Thank God for answered prayers.

Confession:

"By the way that he came, by the same shall he return, and shall not come into this city, saith the Lord". Isaiah 37:34.

Wisdom for Today:

"Joy is the simplest form of gratitude." — Karl Barth
The joy of the Lord is your strength if you allow it. Nehemiah 8:9–12

Read the Bible Today: *1 Samuel 21–22*

Prayer Points:

1. By the blood of Jesus, I undo every evil done to me by any witch doctors, in the name of Jesus.
2. By faith, I vomit every evil food I have eaten from the devil's table, in the name of Jesus.
3. Evil plantings in my life be uprooted by fire, in the name of Jesus.
4. I destroy the power and influence of bewitchment upon my life, in the name of Jesus.
5. I release myself from every evil domination and control, in the name of Jesus.
6. Lord Jesus, walk back to every second of my life and deliver me where I need delivering, heal me where I need healing, and transform me where I need transforming in the name of Jesus.
7. Evil dreams depart from my life in the name of Jesus.
8. Every power of darkness polluting and attacking my dreams; be arrested by fire in the name of Jesus.
9. By the blood of Jesus, I cancel every effect of evil dreams in my life in the name of Jesus.
10. Every messenger of death in my church; depart and enter no more in the name of Jesus.
11. Every evil power that is holding me down, die in the name of Jesus.
12. I move from nothing to something good in the name of Jesus.
13. In this country I shall not be disgraced in the name of Jesus.
14. In this country I shall not be put to shame in the name of Jesus.
15. Every attack in my dream that is now affecting my life be reversed in the name of Jesus.

Apostle A.O. Solomon

16. Evil arrows from my dream come out and go back to sender in the name of Jesus.
17. Powers from my father's house and my mother's house begin to attack yourself in Jesus name.
18. Almighty God, I need a break in this country in the name of Jesus.
19. Lord, heal me from every area that I have been wounded in the name of Jesus.
20. I cancel every dreams, visions, prophesy and prayers against my life and family in the name of Jesus.
21. Talk to God about your heart desires and your situation.
22. Thank God for answered prayers.

Confession:

"And it shall be said in that day, lo, this is our God; we have waited for him, we will be glad and rejoice in his salvation" Isaiah 25:9.

Wisdom for Today:

"Reversing your treatment of the man you have wronged is better than asking his forgiveness."— Elbert Hubbard

Not everyone who asked for forgiveness has really changed.

Read the Bible Today: 1 Samuel 23–24

Prayer Points:

1. Holy Ghost, purge every impurity from my heart with your fire, in the name of Jesus.
2. O Lord, create in me a clean heart, in the name of Jesus.
3. O Lord, renew a right spirit within me in the name of Jesus.
4. O Lord, purge my eyes that I may always see what you want me to see, in Jesus name.
5. O Lord, purge my ears that I may always hear you and you alone, in the name of Jesus.
6. Every power bent on destroying my destiny; Holy Ghost fire locate and destroy them in the name of Jesus.
7. My ears shall hear good news, my eyes shall see good things, my hands shall possess good things in the name of Jesus.
8. O Lord, arise quickly and deliver me from shame in the name of Jesus.
9. Evil arrows my body is not for you in the name of Jesus.
10. Every owner of evil load in my life, carry your load in the name of Jesus.
11. I shall not be wasted; I shall not be useless in the name of Jesus.
12. Every power affecting my joy, lose your power and die in the name of Jesus.
13. I shall not bury my children in the name of Jesus.
14. Every dry bone in my life, receive the touch of resurrection and life in the name of Jesus.
15. Every good door that has been closed, lift up your heads and let the King of glory come in in Jesus name.

Apostle A.O. Solomon

16. O Lord, arise in your mercy close the old chapter in my life in the name of Jesus.
17. Every evil word waiting for manifestation in my life, be canceled in the name of Jesus.
18. Every maturity date of evil words and prophesies in my life, be nullified in the name of Jesus.
19. I fire back, every arrow of evil prophecy that is pursuing my life; I fire you back in Jesus name.
20. Every satanic assignment, I reject you in my life in the name of Jesus.
21. Every power demanding tears from my eyes before receiving my blessings, die in the name of Jesus.
22. Every power sponsoring weeping in my family; carry your load and die in the name of Jesus.
23. I cancel every dreams, visions, prophesy and prayers against my life and family in the name of Jesus.
24. Talk to God about your heart desires and your situation.
25. Thank God for answered prayers.

Confession:

"The lord hath broken the staff of the wicked, and the scepter of the rulers" Isaiah 14:5.

Wisdom for Today:

"The state of your life is nothing more than a reflection of your state of mind." — Dr. Wayne W. Dyer

Read the Bible Today: 1 Samuel 25–26

Prayer Points:

1. O Lord, establish me in your righteousness, in Jesus name.
2. O Lord, establish me as a holy person unto you, in the name of Jesus.
3. Let every evil character in me die, in the name of Jesus.
4. Fire of God's revival; fall upon me now, in the name of Jesus.
5. I reject a life of mediocrity; I shall always be on fire for my God, in the name of Jesus.
6. I will not disappoint God; I will not fail my generation, in the name of Jesus.
7. Every witchcraft cage caging my destiny, break by the fire of God in the name of Jesus.
8. Almighty God, deliver me from the strife of tongue in the name of Jesus.
9. Evil arrows go back to your sender in the name of Jesus.
10. Every attack of eaters of flesh and drinkers of blood, back fire in the name of Jesus.
11. I withdraw my blood from witchcraft altar in the name of Jesus.
12. Anything representing me in any kingdom of darkness, I withdraw you by fire in the name of Jesus.
13. I walk out of the prison of evil dreams in the name of Jesus.
14. Every dream of backwardness in my life die in the name of Jesus.
15. Any power using anything in my past to torment me, die in the name of Jesus.
16. By the blood of Jesus, I register my name for solution today in the name of Jesus.

17. I shall not serve my enemies and I shall not serve my friend in the name of Jesus.
18. I disagree with every satanic decision over my life in the name of Jesus.
19. I cancel every dreams, visions, prophesy and prayers against my life and family in the name of Jesus.
20. Talk to God about your heart desires and your situation.
21. Thank God for answered prayers.

Confession:

"For the Lord is our judge, the Lord is our lawgiver, the Lord is our king; he will save us" Isaiah 33:22.

Wisdom for Today:

"Success is that feeling that comes after overcoming a failure, you will not feel it as long as you are not failing, so be proud of your failures, they are the path to your success." — Mina Tadros

Read the Bible Today: 1 Samuel 27–28

Prayer Points:

1. I thank God for making my body a dwelling place of the Holy Spirit.
2. I thank God for sending another comforter to live with me.
3. Let the rain of God's power fall upon my life now, in the name of Jesus.
4. O God, open the heaven above my head as of the day of Pentecost and release your power and fire upon me, in the name of Jesus.
5. Let the power of the carnal mind die, and let the spirit of God take control, in the name of Jesus.
6. I recover every blessing I have lost to spirit of Egypt in the name of Jesus.
7. O Lord, deliver me from every problem I have brought upon myself in the name of Jesus.
8. I reject every invitation to bondage in the name of Jesus.
9. O Lord, give me power to overcome pressures in life in the name of Jesus.
10. O Lord, make me a good sign and use me for your glory in the name of Jesus.
11. By the anointing of the Holy Ghost, I leap over every negative situation surrounding me in the name of Jesus.
12. I shall not fail God in the name of Jesus.
13. O God, I commit my life to you; organize my scattered life in the name of Jesus.
14. Almighty God, change my story as you did Jabez in the name of Jesus.
15. I reject automatic failure in my life in the name of Jesus.

16. Every enemy of divine presence in my life, I command you to die in the name of Jesus.
17. Anointing to excel above all my family members fall upon me now in the name of Jesus.
18. I shall experience divine favor throughout the days of my life in Jesus name.
19. Holy Spirit; coordinate me in the name of Jesus.
20. Arrows of the enemy you shall not locate me, go back to your sender in the name of Jesus.
21. Power to sin no more, fall upon me now in the name of Jesus.
22. I put the yoke of Jesus Christ upon myself in the name of Jesus.
23. God shall help me and fight for me in the name of Jesus.
24. I shall not lose my job in the name of Jesus.
25. My source of money shall not be blocked this month in the name of Jesus.
26. I cancel every dreams, visions, prophesy and prayers against my life and family in the name of Jesus.
27. Talk to God about your heart desires and your situation.
28. Thank God for answered prayers.

Confession:

"Trust ye in the Lord forever: for in the Lord Jehovah is everlasting strength". Isaiah 26:4.

Wisdom for Today:

"Always look on the bright side of life." -Eric Idle

Read the Bible Today: 1 Samuel 29–31

Prayer Points:

1. Let every anti–Holy Ghost revival in my life die now, in the name of Jesus.
2. Let anything standing between me and the power of God die now, in the name of Jesus.
3. I pull down every stronghold of weakness in my life, in the name of Jesus.
4. Let the fire of God and the blood of Jesus purge me of all spiritual impurities and fill me with power, in Jesus name.
5. Let self-die in me, and let the power of God fill me, in Jesus name.
6. I bind and cast out the spirit of slumber from my life, in the name of Jesus.
7. Throughout this month I shall be blessed and highly favored in the name of Jesus.
8. Where there is no way for others, there shall be way for me this month in the name of Jesus.
9. I reject death in my family and church in the name of Jesus.
10. O Lord, let your hand be upon me for good throughout this month in the name of Jesus.
11. Father Lord, do not give me up to the desires of my enemies in the name of Jesus.
12. Evil shall not prevail against me and my family in the name of Jesus.
13. Sin shall not rule over me in the name of Jesus.
14. Every good thing my hands have started, my hands shall complete; and I shall enjoy them in the name of Jesus.
15. My head hear the word of the Lord; you shall not be bewitched in the name of Jesus.

Apostle A.O. Solomon

16. I shall not become what my enemies want me to be in the name of Jesus.

17. O God of Abraham, Isaac, and Jacob rearrange this country to favor me in the name of Jesus.

18. Every completed work of my enemies over my life; be destroyed with all your effects in the name of Jesus.

19. I break and lose myself from the stronghold of darkness in the name of Jesus.

20. Any power that wants to replace my peace with war, die suddenly in the name of Jesus.

21. By the blood of Jesus Christ, I rise above limitation in life in the name of Jesus.

22. I cancel every dreams, visions, prophesy and prayers against my life and family in the name of Jesus.

23. Talk to God about your heart desires and your situation.

24. Thank God for answered prayers.

Confession:

"Fear thou not; for I am with thee: be not dismayed". Isaiah 41:10.

Wisdom for Today:

When a friend is in trouble, don't annoy him by asking if there is anything you can do. Think up something appropriate—and do it!

Read the Bible Today: 2 Samuel 1–2

Prayer Points:

1. Almighty God; destroy every weakness in my flesh that has been holding me back, in the name of Jesus.
2. Every lack of interest in spiritual things, and studying the word of God be crucified to the cross of Jesus, in Jesus name.
3. Almighty God, make me your oracle for miracles, signs, and wonders, in Jesus name.
4. I receive fire and power to do exploit for God and for my generation, in Jesus name.
5. Almighty God render the giant powerless in my life, in the name of Jesus.
6. Almighty God reign supreme in my life in the name of Jesus.
7. Almighty God set me free from poverty in the name of Jesus.
8. By the power in the word of God, I command every darkness in my life to vanish in the name of Jesus.
9. Every step by step work of the enemy in my life tonight be destroyed in the name of Jesus.
10. Every perfected works of the enemy in my life be over turned by the blood of Jesus.
11. Every evil altar in my family working against my glory, be consumed by fire in the name of Jesus.
12. Every good thing the enemy scattered in my life, come together in the name of Jesus.
13. Every power and spirit that has set my life for affliction, I bind you in the name of Jesus.
14. In the name of Jesus, my life shall not follow satanic agenda in the name of Jesus.

15. Almighty God, it is time give me rest and comfort me, prosper me in the name of Jesus.
16. By the blood of Jesus, I register my name for solution to night in the name of Jesus.
17. I cancel every dreams, visions, prophesy and prayers against my life and family in the name of Jesus.
18. Talk to God about your heart desires and your situation.
19. Thank God for answered prayers.

Confession:

"As for our redeemer, the Lord of hosts is his name, the holy one of Israel" Isaiah 47:4.

Wisdom for Today:

The woman in the Bible had the issue of blood, but the truth is this: we all have our different issues in life. People deal with issues of failure, poverty, debt, foreclosure, bankruptcy, sickness, and much more. Don't leave your own issue and be a busybody in other people's issues.

Read the Bible Today: 2 Samuel 3–4

Prayer Points:

1. Holy Ghost, connect me with your fire, in the name of Jesus.
2. I refuse to become what my enemies want me to be; I am what God says I am, in the name of Jesus.
3. By your creative power, oh, Lord, touch my life, in Jesus name.
4. Let people seek me and favor me today, in Jesus name.
5. Almighty God, dash every witchcraft caldron prepared against me to pieces, in the name of Jesus.
6. I connect myself with the power of God in the name of Jesus.
7. Every pillar of witchcraft in my family, what are you waiting for? I pull you down in the name of Jesus.
8. Witchcraft powers why are you pursuing my life? die in the name of Jesus.
9. It is written suffer not a witch to live, therefore any witchcraft pursuing my life, I command you to die in the name of Jesus.
10. I disagree with failure in the name of Jesus.
11. Failure at the edge of good things, depart from my life by the blood of Jesus in the name of Jesus.
12. Witchcraft battle at the edge of my success return to your sender in the name of Jesus.
13. Every evil seed planted by the enemy in my life, be uprooted by fire in the name of Jesus.
14. Every plantation of darkness in my life, come out with all your roots in the name of Jesus.
15. Every evil seed planted into my life through dreams, be uprooted by fire in the name of Jesus.

16. I challenge my system with the fire of God, in the name of Jesus.
17. Every instrument of satanic control in my life, wherever you are be destroyed by fire in the name of Jesus.
18. Arrows of darkness in my life come out of your hiding places and go back to your sender in the name of Jesus.
19. As from today, life shall be easy for me in the name of Jesus.
20. By the blood of Jesus, I stand in gap for every member of my family in the name of Jesus.
21. Every of my family that is appointed for death, be redeemed by the blood of Jesus.
22. Any power that wants to attack me, Holy Ghost fire attack and destroy them in the name of Jesus.
23. Arrows of madness fired against me and any member of my family, gather yourself together and go back to your sender in the name of Jesus.
24. All those in the system of this country that will not favor me, o Lord replace them with people that will favor me in the name of Jesus.
25. All those who are boasting to fire me in my place of work, let the Holy Ghost fire; fire them in the name of Jesus.
26. I cancel every dreams, visions, prophesy and prayers against my life and family in the name of Jesus.
27. Talk to God about your heart desires and your situation.
28. Thank God for answered prayers.

Confession:

"Thus saith the Lord the king of Israel, and his redeemer the Lord of hosts; I am the first, and I am the last; and beside me there is no God" Isaiah 44:6.

Wisdom for Today:

Dreams get you into the future and add excitement to the present. Without goals, and plans to reach them, you are like a ship that has set sail with no destination.

Read the Bible Today: 2 Samuel 5–6

Prayer Points:

1. Every failure in my dreams, go and return no more, in the name of Jesus.
2. I have a destiny of prosperity; I refuse to be destitute, in the name of Jesus.
3. Every stronghold of family failure in my life, I pull you down, in the name of Jesus.
4. By faith in Christ Jesus, I take back all that the devil has taken from me, in Jesus name.
5. I dismantle every problem that serves as an anchor in my life, in the name of Jesus.
6. Every evil register containing my name, Holy Ghost fire consume them in the name of Jesus.
7. Every broom of darkness sweeping good things away from my life, catch fire in the name of Jesus.
8. Angel of the living God; begin to sweep back all my blessings in the name of Jesus.
9. Every spirit of laboring without achievement; be destroyed in the name of Jesus.
10. I hold the hammer of the word of God and command every padlock ministering evil against my life, break in the name of Jesus.
11. With the garment of fire and power of Jesus, I enter the strong room of the enemy and collect all my blessing in the name of Jesus.
12. I go with the Lord Jesus and the Holy Ghost fire into every witchcraft coven and collect my blessings in the name of Jesus.

13. Any man or woman, attending witchcraft meeting because of me, you shall not return in the name of Jesus.
14. Anyone calling my name for evil in the night, angel of God; slap them in the name of Jesus.
15. Every night captivity in my life, break in the name of Jesus.
16. Anything done against me in the night; be destroyed by fire in the name of Jesus.
17. Every satanic power appearing in my dream, the Lord rebuke you perish in the name of Jesus.
18. Any fire that the enemy has lighted against me and my family be quenched by the blood of Jesus.
19. Every evil pot caging anything good in my life, break by thunder in the name of Jesus.
20. Almighty God put upon me now your garment of mercy and favor in the name of Jesus.
21. My spirit man, my body, my soul hear the word of the Lord you shall not answer the call of the enemy day or night in the name of Jesus.
22. Let the voice of God thunder against my enemies and divide them in the name of Jesus.
23. Let the voice of God, divide the fire of my enemy and destroy them in the name of Jesus.
24. Let the voice of God, shake down the camp of my enemies in the name of Jesus.
25. Almighty God, clothe me with mercy and compassion in the name of Jesus.
26. I cancel every dreams, visions, prophesy and prayers against my life and family in the name of Jesus.
27. Talk to God about your heart desires and your situation.
28. Thank God for answered prayers.

Confession:

"For the nation and kingdom that will not serve thee shall perish; yea, those nations shall be utterly wasted" Isaiah 60:12.

Wisdom for Today:

"No matter how qualified or deserving we are, we will never reach a better life until we can imagine it for ourselves and allow ourselves to have it".

Read the Bible Today: 2 Samuel 7–8

Prayer Points:

1. I shake off every magnet of sorrow from my life, in the name of Jesus.
2. God's covenant is upon my life; I shall not be disgraced, in the name of Jesus.
3. O God, arise; and fight against all those who fight against me, disgrace all those who disgrace me, and bless all those who bless me, in the name of Jesus.
4. I shall not vanish with this year, in the name of Jesus.
5. I command the days of affliction in my life and family to end now, in the name of Jesus.
6. Long life and prosperity is my portion with God; therefore, let every messenger of death go back to the sender, in the name of Jesus.
7. Almighty God, empower my hands for profit in the name of Jesus.
8. Every attack against my labor, break and release me in the name of Jesus.
9. Every curse of the enemy against the works of my hands, break by the blood of Jesus in the name of Jesus.
10. Every physical and spiritual chain upon my hands, break in the name of Jesus.
11. Thou son of David use your key, and set me free from hand cuffs and chains in the name of Jesus.
12. Jesus set me free; I am free indeed in the name of Jesus.
13. I drink the blood of Jesus, and I cover myself with the blood of Jesus in the name of Jesus.
14. Any power that wants to destroy the works of God in my life, Holy Ghost fire; destroy them in the name of Jesus.

15. Every satanic bondage from evil dreams programmed into my life; break and release me in the name of Jesus.
16. Every sickness introduced into my life as a result of evil dreams die now in the name of Jesus.
17. Every dream of failure in my past be reversed in the name of Jesus.
18. Every witchcraft power pursuing me in the dream fall down and die in the name of Jesus.
19. Almighty God, make me holy by your power in the name of Jesus.
20. Every satanic dream attached to my progress, die in the name of Jesus.
21. I cancel every dreams, visions, prophesy and prayers against my life and family in the name of Jesus.
22. Talk to God about your heart desires and your situation.
23. Thank God for answered prayers.

Confession:

"There is no peace, saith my God, to the wicked". Isaiah 57:21.

Wisdom for Today:

"Love begins by taking care of the closest ones—the ones at home".

Read the Bible Today: 2 Samuel 9–10

Prayer Points:

1. I refuse to enter into any coffin this year, in the name of Jesus.
2. Lord, direct my helpers to locate me, in the name of Jesus.
3. I stand under the covenant of God's mercy, and I obtain great grace, in the name of Jesus.
4. My eyes shall see good things, and my ears shall hear good news, in the name of Jesus.
5. I shall not fail; I shall not be disgraced, in the name of Jesus.
6. My star shall not be cast down; my star shall continually be shining, in the name of Jesus.
7. Any power, spirit, personality that wants to trouble me, my God shall trouble you in the name of Jesus.
8. Life shall not be difficult for me in the name of Jesus.
9. I reject every form of nakedness physically and spiritually in the name of Jesus.
10. I reject every form of disorder in the name of Jesus.
11. Me and my family shall be for good signs and wonders in the name of Jesus.
12. As the Lord God lives, people will see the good work of God in my life in Jesus name.
13. Almighty God let all those that will bless me, be blessed, and let all those that curse me b cursed in Jesus name.
14. Every completed work of the enemy over my life be destroyed with all your power in the name of Jesus.
15. I plead the blood of Jesus against every voice speaking against my destiny in the name of Jesus.
16. Every owner of evil load in my life, wherever you are appear and carry your load in Jesus name.
17. I plead the blood of Jesus over everything the devil is holding against me in the name of Jesus.

18. I belong to Jesus; therefore I disconnect from the iniquity of my ancestors in the name of Jesus.
19. Every ancestral oat that is affecting my life now be canceled by the blood of Jesus in the name of Jesus.
20. Every evil word that is pursuing my destiny, the Lord rebuke you, turn back in the name of Jesus.
21. Every prophecy demoting my life lose your hold and die in the name of Jesus.
22. Evil family pattern, break and release me by fire in the name of Jesus.
23. Every evil water flowing in my family, dry up by fire in the name of Jesus.
24. Family bondage affecting my life, break in the name of Jesus.
25. Ancestral evil covenant, I separate myself from you now in the name of Jesus.
26. Every evil register containing my name, be roasted by fire in the name of Jesus.
27. I cancel every dreams, visions, prophesy and prayers against my life and family in the name of Jesus.
28. Talk to God about your heart desires and your situation.
29. Thank God for answered prayers.

Confession:

"The sons of them that afflicted thee shall come bending unto thee; and all they that despised thee shall bow themselves down at the soles of thy feet; and they shall call thee, the city of the Lord, the Zion of the Holy one of Israel" Isaiah 60:14.

Wisdom for Today:

If a man or woman deserts you, pick yourself up and move forward. Your destiny is not tied to anyone who left you. 1 John 2:19

Read the Bible Today: 2 Samuel 11–12

Prayer Points:

1. I shall not fail; I shall not be disgraced, in the name of Jesus.
2. My star shall not be cast down; my star shall continually shine, in the name of Jesus.
3. I redeem this day by the blood of Jesus; I shall be preserve with all my families in the name of Jesus.
4. Holy Spirit of God, revive me again, in the name of Jesus.
5. This day is my day of glory and recovery, in the name of Jesus.
6. Good things shall prosper in my life throughout the days of my life, in the name of Jesus.
7. Jesus Christ is Lord.
8. Every evil stronghold erected against me in this country, I pull you down in the name of Jesus.
9. By the power of the Holy Ghost, I come out of every slavery life in the name of Jesus.
10. Father, deliver me from every limitation in the name of Jesus.
11. By the power of the Holy Ghost, I remove every garment of darkness in the name of Jesus.
12. Almighty God solve my financial need in the name of Jesus.
13. Almighty God give me financial miracle and deliverance in the name of Jesus Christ.
14. My hands are blessed in the name of Jesus.
15. Almighty God heal my heart and spirit in the name of Jesus Christ.
16. Almighty God; open my eyes to the mystery of the kingdom of heaven in the name of Jesus.

17. Almighty God bless me with your knowledge, wisdom and understanding in the name of Jesus Christ.
18. Almighty God; reveal to me the secret of giving and sowing in the name of Jesus.
19. Almighty God; give me the result of my seed in the name of Jesus Christ.
20. Every power destroying my harvest be destroyed in the name of Jesus.
21. Every power swallowing my money die in the name of Jesus.
22. Every Power assigned to put me on the sick bed; you shall not prosper in the name of Jesus.
23. I cancel every dreams, visions, prophesy and prayers against my life and family in the name of Jesus.
24. Talk to God about your heart desires and your situation.
25. Thank God for answered prayers.

Confession:

"Behold, the Lord God will help me; who is he that shall condemn me? Lo, they all shall wax old as a garment; the moth shall eat them up" Isaiah 50:9.

Wisdom for Today:

"Whenever you're in conflict with someone, there is one factor that can make the difference between damaging your relationship and deepening it. That factor is attitude".

Read the Bible Today: 2 Samuel 13–14

Prayer Points:

1. I have a covenant of salt with God; I will always enjoy sweetness all the days of my life, in the name of Jesus.
2. As the grave could not hold Jesus, no barrier will hinder my breakthroughs this year, in the name of Jesus.
3. As the brothers of Joseph bowed before him, so let my entire household enemies bow to me as from today, in the name of Jesus.
4. By the spirit of prophesy, I jump over every barrier to my promotion, in the name of Jesus.
5. Let the wind of God's fire clear away every personality-putting barrier on my way, in Jesus name.
6. Begin to give thanks unto the Lord.
7. Declare Jesus Christ is Lord.
8. Every satanic strategy to block my blessings fail woefully in the name of Jesus Christ.
9. Almighty God; arise for my sake and fight for me in the name of Jesus.
10. I plead the blood of Jesus Christ over my spirit, soul and body in the name of Jesus.
11. Almighty God; send your angels to help me today in the name of Jesus Christ.
12. Almighty God; send your angels to the north, south, east, and west to bring in my blessings in the name of Jesus.
13. Anywhere my blessings has been hiding, I command the angels of God to release them in the name of Jesus.

14. Let my helpers be released from captivity in the name of Jesus.
15. Every attack against my helpers, backfire in the name of Jesus.
16. I speak unto this day, favor me and work against my enemies in the name of Jesus Christ.
17. I refuse my destiny and blessings to be sabotaged in the name of Jesus.
18. Every power sabotaging any area of my life; be destroyed in the name of Jesus.
19. Almighty God; it is written: ask and It shall be given to you, therefore by faith in Christ Jesus; I ask for my blessings in the name of Jesus.
20. Almighty God; as you deliver the Israelites out of their tight corner, Lord; deliver me in the name of Jesus.
21. Almighty God; make way for me where there seems to be no way in the name of Jesus.
22. Almighty God; show me your great mercy, and deliver me from sadness and sorrow in the name of Jesus.
23. Almighty God; I commit my children to your hand in the name of Jesus.
24. Blood of Jesus Christ come upon our lives; mark us for safety and favor in the name of Jesus.
25. I cancel every dreams, visions, prophesy and prayers against my life and family in the name of Jesus.
26. Talk to God about your heart desires and your situation.
27. Thank God for answered prayers.

Confession:

"And I will utter my judgments against them touching all their wickedness, who have forsaken me, and have burned incense unto other gods, and worshipped the works of their own hands". Jeremiah 1:16.

Wisdom for Today:

"Wisdom is knowing what to do next; virtue is doing it". - David Starr Jordan

Read the Bible Today: 2 Samuel 15–16

Prayer Points:

1. I receive power today to pursue, overtake, and recover good things throughout this year, in the name of Jesus.
2. As Pharaoh perished in the Red Sea, so let all my stubborn pursuers perish today, in Jesus name.
3. Every unfriendly person causing problems for me in my place of work, be arrested and be disgraced, in the name of Jesus.
4. God's covenant is upon my life; I shall not be disgraced, and I shall not be intimidated, in the name of Jesus.
5. Almighty God arise and fight against all those who fight against me, disgrace all those who disgrace me, and bless all those who bless me, in the name of Jesus.
6. Declare Jesus Christ is Lord.
7. Almighty God; have mercy upon me and remember me in the name of Jesus.
8. You spirit of fear and doubt keeping me in the wilderness of life, I bind and cast out in the name of Jesus.
9. Every confusion holding me captive, break away in the name of Jesus.
10. Every past sin and error that is keeping me down physically, spiritually, financially be removed by the blood of Jesus Christ in the name of Jesus.
11. Almighty God; deliver me from the captivity of wrong counsel in the name of Jesus Christ.
12. Almighty God; deliver from any human being blocking my success in the name of Jesus.

13. Let the way make way for me in all areas of life in the name of Jesus.
14. Thank the Lord for blessing the works of your hands.
15. Declare Jesus Christ is Lord.
16. Almighty God, I give you all the glory in the name of Jesus.
17. Almighty God; I commit my job, school, ministry, business into your hands in the name of Jesus.
18. Almighty God, connect me to that one man that will make the difference in my life in the name of Jesus.
19. Almighty God, connect me with my burden bearer in the name of Jesus.
20. Almighty God, show me your great mercy, breath on me in the name of Jesus.
21. Every witchcraft power attacking the works of my hands, die in the name of Jesus.
22. Almighty God, deliver me from every witchcraft coven in the name of Jesus.
23. Almighty God, show me your great mercy and don't allow the wicked to determine my progress in the name of Jesus.
24. I reject unprofitable hard labor in the name of Jesus.
25. Every witchcraft power urinating on my life, business, place of blessing, and destiny die in the name of Jesus.
26. You my labor receive deliverance in the name of Jesus Christ.
27. I cancel every dreams, visions, prophesy and prayers against my life and family in the name of Jesus.
28. Talk to God about your heart desires and your situation.
29. Thank God for answered prayers.

Confession:

"Israel was holiness unto the Lord, and the first-fruits of his increase: all that devour him shall offend; evil shall come upon them, saith the Lord" Jeremiah 2:3.

Wisdom for Today:

The thoughts we choose to think are the tools we use to paint the canvas of our lives".
"To believe a thing is impossible is to make it so.

Read the Bible Today: 2 Samuel 17–18

Prayer Points:

1. No more sorrow for me, and no more weeping, in the name of Jesus.
2. Long life and prosperity are my portion with God; no sudden or untimely death for me and my family in the name of Jesus.
3. This year, all my helpers shall be blessed to bless me, in the name of Jesus.
4. In this year, I will not miss good things, and good things shall not miss me, in Jesus name.
5. I have a seal of God's rest and peace upon my body; no demon is permitted to touch or harm me, in the name of Jesus.
6. My body is the body of Jesus; no sickness is permitted to dwell in my body, in Jesus name.
7. O Lord, perfect all that concerns me and my family today, in the name of Jesus.
8. Declare Jesus Christ is Lord.
9. God of new beginnings visit my life in the name of Jesus Christ.
10. Almighty God; you are my God; I put my trust in you, manifest in the name of Jesus.
11. Almighty God; let heaven release blessing for me in the name of Jesus.
12. Anything in my environment that is limiting my life, I command you to break away in the name of Jesus.
13. Almighty God; I commit my environment into your hands; revive it in the name of Jesus.

14. Everything I need in life let heaven begin to supply in the name of Jesus.
15. Open to me your good treasure in the name of Jesus.
16. Almighty God; Let the heavens give rain to my land in its season in the name of Jesus.
17. Almighty God; Show me your great mercy, let me lend; to many nations in the name of Jesus.
18. I reject demotion in every area of life; I claim promotion in the name of Jesus.
19. Almighty God; arise and take me to my promised land in the name of Jesus.
20. Almighty God; let the victory of the cross of Jesus Christ manifest in all areas of my life in the name of Jesus.
21. I cancel every dreams, visions, prophesy and prayers against my life and family in the name of Jesus.
22. Talk to God about your heart desires and your situation.
23. Thank God for answered prayers.

Confession:

"In righteousness shall I be established: I shall be far from oppression; for I shall not fear: and from terror; for it shall not come near me. Behold, they shall surely gather together, but not by me, whosoever shall gather together against me shall fall for my sake, says the Lord of hosts" Isaiah 54:14–15.

Wisdom for Today:

"Your life is your message to the world. Make it inspiring".

Read the Bible Today: 2 Samuel 19–20

Prayer Points:

1. I thank God for his faithfulness and righteousness.
2. Almighty God, sanctify me by your truth, your word is truth, in Jesus name.
3. Let the blood of Jesus speak on my behalf, in the name of Jesus.
4. I take authority and power over every power and spirit of affliction targeted against my life, in the name of Jesus.
5. Every power programming evil into the day against me and my family carry your affliction away, in the name of Jesus.
6. Give God all the praise.
7. Declare Jesus Christ is Lord.
8. I plead the blood of Jesus against every evil dream, be cancelled in the name of Jesus.
9. Almighty God, empower my dreams and visions for my life to come to pass in the name of Jesus Christ.
10. Almighty God; deliver me from every affliction following me about as a result of negative thinking in the name of Jesus.
11. I reject every satanic inspiration in the name of Jesus.
12. Every good door that I have shut against myself, great mercy of God; open them in the name of Jesus.
13. By the blood of Jesus Christ, you failure in my life fall and I command success to arise in the name of Jesus.
14. Every kingdom of failure, barrenness, I command you to fall and rise no more in the name of Jesus.
15. Almighty God; supply all that I need in the name of Jesus.
16. You the spirit of pride, get thee behind me in Jesus name.

17. Almighty God, I humble myself under your mighty power, exalt me in due season in the name of Jesus.
18. I cancel every dreams, visions, prophesy and prayers against my life and family in the name of Jesus.
19. Talk to God about your heart desires and your situation.
20. Thank God for answered prayers.

Confession:

"No weapon that is formed against me shall prosper; and every tongue that shall rise against me in judgment I shall condemn, This is my heritage as a servant of the Lord, and my righteousness is of God, says the Lord". Isaiah 54:17.

Wisdom for Today:

Your title is only a label, we all have our struggles and things we don't want people to know about us.

Read the Bible Today: 2 Samuel 21–22

Prayer Points:

1. I attack every evil prophesy against my life, destiny, and marriage with the blood of Jesus.
2. I cancel every evil word pursuing my life by the blood of Jesus in the name of Jesus.
3. Almighty God profit and prosper my life, in the name of Jesus.
4. Almighty God promote my life, in the name of Jesus.
5. Almighty God you are the man of war fight my battles for me by fire, in the name of Jesus.
6. God of signs and wonders, manifest your wonders in my life, in Jesus name.
7. Declare Jesus Christ is Lord.
8. Almighty God, manifest your great power in the name of Jesus.
9. Almighty God; by your power subdue my enemies and problems in the name of Jesus.
10. Almighty God; let your great power change my story tonight in the name of Jesus.
11. Great power of the living God, subdue every opposition to my glory in the name of Jesus.
12. Great power of the living God, make new ways for me in the name of Jesus.
13. By the power of the living God, I decree no opposition shall prevail over my life and destiny in the name of Jesus.
14. Almighty God, help me to identify and operate in my territory in the name of Jesus.
15. I prevail over every opposition in the name of Jesus.

Apostle A.O. Solomon

16. Every stranger occupying my God given territory I cast you out in the name of Jesus Christ.
17. Almighty God show me your great mercy in the name of Jesus.
18. By the stripes of Jesus I am healed in the name of Jesus.
19. I am complete in Christ Jesus in the name of Jesus.
20. I cancel every dreams, visions, prophesy and prayers against my life and family in the name of Jesus.
21. Talk to God about your heart desires and your situation.
22. Thank God for answered prayers.

Confession:

"So shall they fear the name of the Lord from the west and his glory from the rising of the sun. When the enemy shall come in as a flood, the spirit of the Lord shall lift up a standard against them" Isaiah 59:19.

Wisdom for Today:

"Where you begin doesn't matter. Your willingness to start is what counts.

Read the Bible Today: 2 Samuel 23–24

Prayer Points:

1. Fire of the Holy Ghost; attack all my attackers, in the name of Jesus.
2. The rod of the wicked shall not rest upon me and my family, in the name of Jesus.
3. Let all those who are working full time to demote my life, receive double disgrace, in the name of Jesus.
4. Let all the efforts of the enemies over me and my family be destroyed, in the name of Jesus.
5. Almighty God revive my life and my church, in the name of Jesus.
6. I come out of every dream prison by the power of the Holy Ghost in the name of Jesus.
7. I fire back every witchcraft arrow fired into my dream in the name of Jesus.
8. Every evil dream of the past affecting my life now, die in the name of Jesus.
9. Every witchcraft serpent attacking me in the dream, return to your sender and destroy them in the name of Jesus.
10. Every dream affecting my life, marriage, and career lose your power and die in the name of Jesus.
11. Every good thing I have lost in the dream I repossess you back in Jesus name.
12. Every agent of darkness in my dream life, I command you to die in the name of Jesus.
13. Every evil pronouncement against me in the dream shall not stand, and neither shall it not come to pass in the name of Jesus.

Apostle A.O. Solomon

14. My resting time shall not be a trouble time in the name of Jesus.
15. I cancel every dreams, visions, prophesy and prayers against my life and family in the name of Jesus.
16. Talk to God about your heart desires and your situation.
17. Thank God for answered prayers.

Confession:

"Behold, the Lord God will help me; who is he that shall condemn me? Lo, they all shall wax old as a garment; the moth shall eat them up" Isaiah 50:9.

Wisdom for Today:

Your failures are no surprise to God. He knows your limitation and will always help you if you are willing to try again and again. 1 Kings 19.

Read the Bible Today: 1 Kings 1–2

Prayer Points:

1. Almighty God, arise and advertise your power in my life, in the name of Jesus.
2. Almighty God arise and advertise your glory in my life, in the name of Jesus.
3. Almighty God give me the testimonies that cannot be covered, in the name of Jesus.
4. Almighty God, give me the blessing that will speak for itself, in the name of Jesus.
5. I reject sickness and infirmities in every department of my life, in Jesus name.
6. Declare Jesus Christ is Lord.
7. Almighty God; help me not to fight useless battles in the name of Jesus.
8. Help me Lord, to fight the good fight of faith in the name of Jesus.
9. Almighty God; give me a heart that perceive, an eye that sees and ear that hears in the name of Jesus.
10. Almighty God help me to recognize your voice in the name of Jesus.
11. I shall not die in the battle field in the name of Jesus.
12. You spirit of stubbornness, I bind and cast you out of my life in the name of Jesus.
13. Almighty God; hide me in your secret place, from the plots of men in the name of Jesus.
14. Almighty God; arise destroy and divide the tongues of my enemies in the name of Jesus.

15. Almighty God; lift me up before those who are pulling me down in the name of Jesus.

16. Almighty God lead me to prosperity and success in the name of Jesus Christ.

17. I prevail over my enemies in all areas of life in the name of Jesus.

18. I triumph over sickness, failure, poverty, dream attack, family crisis, in the name of Jesus.

19. Every waster in the garden of my life, depart in the name of Jesus.

20. Every destroyer in the garden of my life, I cast you out in the name of Jesus.

21. Every emptier, in the garden of my life, I cast you out depart in the name of Jesus.

22. I refuse to labor for my enemies in the name of Jesus.

23. I reject wasted efforts in the name of Jesus.

24. Every power attacking my labor and my profit; you shall not prevail in the name of Jesus.

25. Almighty God; show me your mercy and grace and promote me by your signs and wonders in the name of Jesus.

26. I cancel every dreams, visions, prophesy and prayers against my life and family in the name of Jesus.

27. Talk to God about your heart desires and your situation.

28. Thank God for answered prayers.

Confession:

"And he hath made my mouth like a sharp sword; in the shadow of his hand hath he hid me, and made me a polished shaft; in his quiver hath he hid me; and said unto me, thou art my servant, in whom I will be glorified" Isaiah 49:2–3.

Wisdom for Today:

A friend is one that knows you as you are, understands where you have been, accepts what you have become, and still, gently allow you to grow.

Read the Bible Today: 1 Kings 3–4

Prayer Points:

1. Almighty God I thank you for your protection and for the daily provisions for me and my family in Jesus name.
2. Almighty God I thank you for not giving me unto the desires of my enemies, in the name of Jesus.
3. Almighty God I thank you for last month, and I thank you for this new month, in Jesus name.
4. Almighty God let me always see you alone in all areas of my life, in Jesus name.
5. Almighty God let this month be the beginning of new things in my life and marriage, in Jesus name.
6. Angels of the living God; guide me to my promised land in the name of Jesus.
7. Every good door I closed against myself, I open you now by fire, by force in the name of Jesus.
8. Holy Spirit, arise and control the affairs of my life in the name of Jesus.
9. Holy Spirit of God, breathe upon my dry bones and make me fruitful in the name of Jesus.
10. Holy Spirit of God spread your wings over my life and cover me with your shadow in the name of Jesus.
11. I shall not pray in vain, I shall see the result of prayers in the name of Jesus.
12. I shall not pray when it is too late in the name of Jesus.
13. Almighty God, encourage me to pray in the name of Jesus.

14. Holy Spirit of God, possess me now and let me mount with wings as eagles in the name of Jesus.
15. My prayer life receive deliverance in the name of Jesus.
16. My prayer life receive revival in the name of Jesus.
17. Result of my prayers wherever you are manifest in the name of Jesus.
18. Frustration at the hour of prayer my life is not your candidate, die and rise no more in the name of Jesus.
19. Distraction and confusion at the hour of prayers my life is not your candidate, die and rise no more in the name of Jesus.
20. Almighty God I thank you because I will have progress and I will prosper, in the name of Jesus Christ.
21. Almighty God, I thank you for bringing me out of every tight corner, in the name of Jesus.
22. Almighty God, bless me with abundant grace, all abounding grace, all sufficient grace, physically, spiritually, financially, and in all areas of life, in the name of Jesus Christ.
23. Almighty God let your grace arise and raise profitable helpers for me, in the name of Jesus Christ.
24. I break and release myself from the negative forces of worry, fear, and self-pity, in the name of Jesus.
25. I cancel every dreams, visions, prophesy and prayers against my life and family in the name of Jesus.
26. Talk to God about your heart desires and your situation.
27. Thank God for answered prayers.

Confession:

"But thus saith the Lord, even the captives of the mighty shall be taken away, and the prey of the terrible shall be delivered: for I will contend with him that contendeth with thee, and I will save thy children. And I will feed them that oppress thee with their own flesh; and they shall be drunken with their own blood, as with sweet wine: and all flesh shall know that I the Lord am thy saviour and thy redeemer, the mighty one of Jacob" Isaiah 49:25–26.

Wisdom for Today:

Turn your wounds into wisdom.

There isn't a person anywhere who isn't capable of doing more than he thinks he can.

Read the Bible Today: 1 Kings 5–6

Prayer Points:

1. I wipe off the handwriting that predicts my impossibilities, by the blood of Jesus.
2. You, gates of my life, be lifted up, and let the King of Glory come in, in the name of Jesus.
3. King of Glory, establish your kingdom in every area of my life, in the name of Jesus.
4. I reject evil arrows and bullets from every area of my life, and I send them back to sender, in the name of Jesus.
5. Anything programmed into this month against me and my family relinquish your power and die, in the name of Jesus.
6. Declare Jesus Christ is Lord.
7. Lord Jesus let your blood bring positive change and good result to my prayers in the name of Jesus.
8. Every enemy of my prayer be consumed by the fire of God in the name of Jesus.
9. I claim my divine benefits today in the name of Jesus.
10. Almighty God; have mercy upon me; show me your great mercy and uncommon mercy in the name of Jesus.
11. I break and lose myself from every satanic control and domination in the name of Jesus.
12. I cancel every evil dream in the name of Jesus.

Apostle A.O. Solomon

13. I shall not be afraid for the Lord God is with me in the name of Jesus.
14. I refuse to limit God in my life in the name of Jesus Christ.
15. Almighty God undertake for me in the name of Jesus.
16. I refuse to fight another man's battle in the mighty name of Jesus Christ.
17. I refuse to carry another man's load and problem in the name of Jesus.
18. You powers hijacking my blessings, you shall not hijack my blessings in the name of Jesus.
19. Almighty God; help me to keep your covenant in the name of Jesus.
20. Anyone that is saying that certain things cannot be possible in my life, you are not God, be disappointed in the name of Jesus.
21. Whatever has been declared impossible in my life, father Lord make it possible in the name of Jesus.
22. I shall not die but live and declare the works of God in the name of Jesus.
23. Almighty God; redeem my spirit, soul and body from death in the name of Jesus.
24. I cancel every dreams, visions, prophesy and prayers against my life and family in the name of Jesus.
25. Talk to God about your heart desires and your situation.
26. Thank God for answered prayers.

Confession:

"But the wicked shall be cut off from the earth, and the transgressors shall be rooted out of it" Proverbs 2:22.

Wisdom for Today:

Focus more on your desire than on your doubt, and the dream will take care of itself. You may be surprised at how easily this happens. Your doubts are not as powerful as your desires, unless you make them so.

Read the Bible Today: 1 Kings 7–8

Prayer Points:

1. Let all my blessings locked up in any prison be released to me now, in the name of Jesus.
2. Let all my blessings locked up in any evil pot be released unto me now, in the name of Jesus.
3. I dismantle every evil pot that holds any of my goodness, in the name of Jesus.
4. Let the fire of God's deliverance continually burn in my system, in the name of Jesus.
5. I command my blood to reject every stranger of darkness, in the name of Jesus.
6. Declare Jesus Christ is Lord.
7. I claim the life in the blood of Jesus in the name of Jesus.
8. I claim the victory of the blood of Jesus over death in my life and family in the name of Jesus.
9. I overcome the spirit of death operating in any area of my life in the name of Jesus.
10. Let the power that raised Jesus from the dead rest on any of my document or certificate that is not bringing profit to my life and cause them to bring profit and blessing to my life in the name of Jesus.
11. Every dead marriage; come alive in the name of Jesus.
12. Every spirit and power killing people before their time in my family and around me, die in the name of Jesus Christ.
13. Every attack of death upon me and my family back fire in the name of Jesus.
14. Declare Jesus Christ is Lord.

15. Blood of Jesus Christ flow like a destroying flood and sweep the enemies of my life in the name of Jesus.
16. Almighty God you are the great deliverer come down and deliver me from death in the name of Jesus.
17. Almighty God; let the deliverance that cannot be forgotten come upon me in the name of Jesus.
18. The anointing that rejects insult; come upon my life in the name of Jesus.
19. Every evil yoke affecting my life, break by the anointing of God in the name of Jesus.
20. Every satanic register containing my life span and the life span of my family catch fire in the name of Jesus.
21. I cancel every dreams, visions, prophesy and prayers against my life and family in the name of Jesus.
22. Talk to God about your heart desires and your situation.
23. Thank God for answered prayers.

Confession:

"Then shall I walk in my way safely, and my foot shall not stumble. When I lie down, I shall not be afraid" Proverbs 3:23.

Wisdom for Today:

"I can be changed by what happens to me. But I refuse to be reduced by it".

Read the Bible Today: 1 Kings 9–10

Prayer Points:

1. I reject the spirit and anointing of satanic struggles in this land, in the name of Jesus.
2. I refuse to be in a tight corner in this land, in the name of Jesus.
3. The cows producing the milk of the land will not knock me down, in the name of Jesus.
4. The bees producing the honey of this land will not attack me, in the name of Jesus.
5. This land will be a better land for me and not a bitter land against me, in the name of Jesus.
6. Let every law in this land contrary to God's plan be abolished by the blood of Jesus, in the name of Jesus.
7. Whatever is killing people in my family, I am not your candidate; die in the name of Jesus.
8. Every mark of death upon me and my family be cancelled by the blood of Jesus in the name of Jesus.
9. Almighty God; in the battle of my destiny, I need total deliverance in the name of Jesus.
10. The spirit of the Lord God is in charge of my life; therefore satan; get thee behind me in the name of Jesus.
11. You evil powers controlling people in my family; release me in the name of Jesus.
12. The deliverance that will change failure to success, sorrow to joy and poverty to prosperity let it fall upon me in the name of Jesus.
13. The deliverance that will restore my lost glory, possess my life in the name of Jesus.
14. Lord I thank you for not allowing trouble to swallow me up in the name of Jesus.

15. Almighty God, I thank you for you derive pleasure in my wellbeing in the name of Jesus.
16. Thank you Lord for preserving and keeping my soul from evil in the name of Jesus.
17. Almighty God I thank you for subduing my enemies in the name of Jesus.
18. Declare Jesus Christ is Lord.
19. I refuse to be a living dead in the name of Jesus.
20. Almighty God, help me to always be at the right place at the right time in the name of Jesus.
21. Almighty God; bless the works of my hands, and deliver my labor from debt in the name of Jesus.
22. I cancel every dreams, visions, prophesy and prayers against my life and family in the name of Jesus.
23. Talk to God about your heart desires and your situation.
24. Thank God for answered prayers.

Confession:

"The curses of the Lord is in the house of the wicked: but he blesseth the habitation of the just. Surely he scorneth the scorners: but he giveth grace unto the lowly" Proverbs 3:33–34.

Wisdom for Today:

"Life is like a mirror. Smile at it and it smiles back at you".

***Read the Bible Today:** 1 Kings 11–12*

Prayer Points:

1. Let all the efforts of satanic conspirators against me be frustrated, in the name of Jesus.
2. Let the magnet of sorrow in my life be destroyed by the fire of God, in Jesus name.
3. Every anti-progressive arrow fired into my life, come out now and go back to your sender, in the name of Jesus.
4. Let the God that parted the Red Sea separate my life from failure, in the name of Jesus.
5. Almighty God perfect everything that concerns me and my family in the name of Jesus.
6. Almighty God help me to always appreciate you and to give you all the glory due unto you throughout the rest of my life in the name of Jesus.
7. Every arrow of death fired against me and my family, you shall not prosper in the name of Jesus.
8. Almighty God, send your angels to deliver my children from death and calamity in the name of Jesus.
9. I reject untimely death In the name of Jesus.
10. Every good thing that is dead or at the point of death in my life, come alive by the blood of Jesus in the name of Jesus.
11. Every power suffocating and killing good things in my life, the Lord rebuke you, be destroyed in the name of Jesus.
12. I come out of the grave by the power of the Holy Ghost in the name of Jesus.
13. Every death on my way, clear away in the name of Jesus.
14. Every sentence of death over my life and family, I reverse you in the name of Jesus.

15. I cancel every evil decision against my life in the name of Jesus.
16. Every stubborn power pursuing my life; turn back and perish in the name of Jesus.
17. Every untimely death hovering over me and my family, catch fire in the name of Jesus.
18. Almighty God according to the greatness of your power, preserve anyone appointed to die in the name of Jesus Christ.
19. This year I reject the loss of life and property in the name of Jesus.
20. I shall not die but live, the number of my days shall be fulfilled in the name of Jesus.
21. Almighty God, answer me speedily and show me your great mercy in the name of Jesus Christ.
22. Almighty God cause me to know your loving kindness in the name of Jesus.
23. I cancel every dreams, visions, prophesy and prayers against my life and family in the name of Jesus.
24. Talk to God about your heart desires and your situation.
25. Thank God for answered prayers.

Confession:

"His own iniquities shall take the wicked himself, and he shall be holden with the cords of his sin. He shall die without instruction; and in the greatness of his folly he shall go astray" Proverbs 5:22–23.

Wisdom for Today:

All of us do not have equal talents, but all of us should have an equal opportunity to develop our talents.

Read the Bible Today: 1 Kings13–14

Prayer Points:

1. Almighty God let all my enemies fall into the pit they dug for me and my family in Jesus name.
2. Almighty God disgrace the pride of the enemies in my life, in Jesus name.
3. Almighty God let the wickedness of the wicked against me destroy the wicked, in Jesus name.
4. I reject every form of pride in my life, in Jesus name.
5. Almighty God teach me the way of salvation, in the name of Jesus.
6. Almighty God arise and fight for me with jealousy in the mighty name of Jesus.
7. Almighty God I thank you because I will not see trouble throughout this month in the name of Jesus.
8. Every storm prepared for me and my family be diverted away in the name of Jesus.
9. Thank the Lord for all he has done.
10. Every mark of bewitchment upon my life; lose your power and be erased in the name of Jesus.
11. Every evil hand writing upon my life; be erased in the name of Jesus.
12. Every witchcraft operation in my life, family, and church; die in the name of Jesus.
13. Every power attacking me from the land of the dead; die the second time in the name of Jesus.
14. Almighty God use my life to confuse the enemy in the name of Jesus.

15. Every appointment with death in this month; I reject you in the name of Jesus.
16. Every pillar of sorrow in my life; I pull you down in the name of Jesus.
17. Anything standing as a pillar of sorrow in this country in my life; I pull you down in the name of Jesus.
18. O thou that troubled my Israel be pulled down now in the name of Jesus.
19. I cancel every dreams, visions, prophesy and prayers against my life and family in the name of Jesus.
20. Talk to God about your heart desires and your situation.
21. Thank God for answered prayers.

Confession:

"Therefore shall his calamity come suddenly; suddenly shall he be broken without remedy" Proverbs 6:15.

Wisdom for Today:

"Faith is the substance of things hoped for, the evidence of things not seen".

Read the Bible Today: 1 John 1–2

Prayer Points:

1. Almighty God I thank you for the life given to me through the precious blood of Jesus.
2. The blood of Jesus is my refuge; therefore, no sudden death shall locate my habitation, in the name of Jesus.
3. The name of the Lord is my strong tower; I am already in it, and I am saved with my family, in the name of Jesus.
4. I refuse to answer the call of the enemy, in the name of Jesus.
5. I am not ready to die now any power that wants me to die, die for me, in Jesus name.
6. I cancel every death ordained for me and my family by the blood of Jesus in the name of Jesus.
7. I reject tragedy and calamity throughout this month in the name of Jesus.
8. Sorrow shall not branch in my dwelling place throughout this month in the name of Jesus.
9. I shall not carry any evil load throughout this month in the name of Jesus.
10. Every maturity day of affliction; be nullified by the blood of Jesus in the name of Jesus.
11. Every incantation against me; be cancelled, in the name of Jesus.
12. Every owner of evil load in my life, appear and carry your load in the name of Jesus.
13. Every perfected work of the enemy over my life; die in the name of Jesus.
14. By the blood of Jesus, I receive freedom from every financial bondage in the name of Jesus.
15. You spirit of frustration I reject you in my life in the name of Jesus.

Apostle A.O. Solomon

16. I refuse to be wasted, any power that wants to waste my life be wasted in the name of Jesus.
17. Every waster of my prosperity wherever you are; be arrested in the name of Jesus.
18. Every aggression of the enemy against my prosperity; be paralyzed in the name of Jesus.
19. Shout 21 Halleluiah.
20. My blessings shall not be stagnant, move and locate me in the name of Jesus.
21. Every clever and hidden devourer, working in my life collapse and die in the name of Jesus.
22. Every handshake of poverty, come out with all your roots in the name of Jesus.
23. Every power that does not want me to see the days of joy die in the name of Jesus.
24. I cancel every dreams, visions, prophesy and prayers against my life and family in the name of Jesus.
25. Talk to God about your heart desires and your situation.
26. Thank God for answered prayers.

Confession:

"The memory of the just is blessed: but the name of the wicked shall rot" Proverbs 10:7.

Wisdom for Today:

"No matter how good you get, there's always something further out there".

Read the Bible Today: Job 20

Prayer Points:

1. Let all those preparing a burial ceremony for me and my family enter into their own coffins, in the name of Jesus.
2. Jesus died young so that I may live long; therefore, any power assigned to kill me while I am young, go back to your sender, in the name of Jesus.
3. I raise the blood of Jesus against every death in my dreams, and I cancel them, in the name of Jesus.
4. Every dream of death, calamity, and destruction, relinquish your power and die, in Jesus name.
5. Every power that has converted my dreams to battlegrounds, relinquish your power and die, in the name of Jesus.
6. Every defeat that I have ever suffered in the dream be converted to victory in the name of Jesus.
7. Fresh power of God, over shadow my life in the name of Jesus.
8. Almighty God open my spiritual ears and let me hear what you want me to hear in the name of Jesus.
9. Every internal failure in my life, come out in the name of Jesus.
10. Every seed of sorrow in my life come out in the name of Jesus.
11. Anything standing as problem in my life; fall down and die in the name of Jesus.
12. I bind and render to knot every evil counsel and imagination against my life, marriage and family in the name of Jesus.
13. Let the entrance door of poverty into my life be closed now in the name of Jesus.
14. Every power adding problem to my problem, what are you waiting for? die in the name of Jesus.
15. You doors of my prosperity, open now in the name of Jesus.

Apostle A.O. Solomon

16. Let my enemies bow before me and congratulate me in the name of Jesus.
17. Almighty God remove from my life every garment of suffering as you did for Joseph in the name of Jesus.
18. Any power that wants me to die, die for my sake in the name of Jesus.
19. Every owner of evil load; in my life, I command you to carry your load in the name of Jesus.
20. I will prosper and be in good health in this country in the name of Jesus.
21. This country is not complete without me; I shall possess my possession in the name of Jesus.
22. I will not cry again in this country in Jesus name.
23. Every power that does not want me to see the days of joy die in the name of Jesus.
24. I refuse to lose in the name of Jesus.
25. Witchcraft covenant upon my life, I command you to break in the name of Jesus.
26. Every general curse working against my life; break and release me in the name of Jesus.
27. Family evil strongman or woman; release my life by fire in the mighty name of Jesus.
28. Water spirits I belong to Jesus release me by fire, in the name of Jesus.
29. Any covenant binding me with marine spirit, break by the blood of Jesus in the name of Jesus.
30. I cancel every dreams, visions, prophesy and prayers against my life and family in the name of Jesus.
31. Talk to God about your heart desires and your situation.
32. Thank God for answered prayers.

Confession:

"The fear of the wicked, it shall come upon him: but the desire of the righteous shall be granted. As the whirlwind passeth, so is the wicked no more: but the righteous is an everlasting foundation" Proverbs 10:24–25.

Wisdom for Today:

"It's easy to have faith in yourself when you're a winner, when you're number one. What you've got to have is faith in yourself when you're not a winner".

Read the Bible Today: Revelation 1–2

Prayer Points:

1. Let everything programmed to trouble my peace and joy be destroyed by the fire of God, in the name of Jesus.
2. You, the spirit of death and hell, I am not your candidate, in the name of Jesus.
3. Let all those calling my name for evil carry their evil, in the name of Jesus.
4. Let all those who want to eat my flesh and drink my blood, eat their own flesh and drink their own blood, in the name of Jesus.
5. I fire back every arrow of death fired against me and my family in the name of Jesus.
6. Every curse upon my life as a result of the wickedness of my ancestors break and release me in Jesus name.
7. Every curse standing in the way of my children's blessing, break in the name of Jesus.
8. I forbid every storm in my life this year in the name of Jesus.
9. Every power destroying good things in my life; be destroyed by fire in the name of Jesus.
10. Every covenant of late blessing, break and release my life in the name of Jesus.
11. I am that I am, arise and manifest your power in my life in the name of Jesus.
12. I am that I am, arise and destroy my poverty in the name of Jesus.
13. I am that I am, arise and destroy the bondage in my family in the name of Jesus.

Apostle A.O. Solomon

14. Blood of Jesus Christ speak better things to my life in the name of Jesus.

15. Anything that will take me away from my divine protection, come out of my life and enter no more in the name of Jesus.

16. O Lord hold me up for I put my hope in you in the name of Jesus.

17. O Lord, empower me for victory tonight in the name of Jesus.

18. Every operation of the enemies in my dreams; fail woefully in the name of Jesus.

19. Any manifestation of the enemy in my dream, I command you to be consumed by the fire of God in the name of Jesus.

20. Every appointment with weeping, I reject you in the name of Jesus.

21. I refuse to weep for the enemies to rejoice in the name of Jesus.

22. Any area of secret tears in my life, receive the touch of God's miracle in the name of Jesus.

23. Almighty God, go back to every second of my past and remove anything that is causing problem in my life in the name of Jesus.

24. Almighty God arise and nullify every word of human being that is manifesting in my life in the name of Jesus.

25. Almighty God enough of reproach in my life, family, and ministry in the name of Jesus.

26. I cancel every evil dream by the blood of Jesus in the name of Jesus.

27. All my good dreams; be empowered for speedy manifestation in the name of Jesus.

28. Every power fuelling problems in my life your time is up; die in the name of Jesus.

29. I release myself from every curse working in my family in the name of Jesus.

30. Every spiritual dedication against me and my family; receive the stones of fire and die in the name of Jesus.

31. You messenger of death assigned against me and my family, go back to your sender in the name of Jesus.

32. Every evil seed planted in the life of my helpers, be uprooted by fire in the name of Jesus.

33. I cancel every dreams, visions, prophesy and prayers against my life and family in the name of Jesus.

34. Talk to God about your heart desires and your situation.

35. Thank God for answered prayers.

Confession:

"The righteous shall never be removed: but the wicked shall not inhabit the earth" Proverbs 10:30.

Wisdom for Today:

"If you can find a path with no obstacles, it probably doesn't lead anywhere".

Read the Bible Today: Luke 1

Prayer Points:

1. I throw back every stone of death thrown at me and my family in the name of Jesus.
2. Every register of death containing my name and the names of my family be destroyed by the fire of God in the name of Jesus.
3. Shout this out loud twenty-one times: "I refuse to die now!" In the name of Jesus.
4. Almighty God turn me into a hot coal of fire that my enemies cannot handle, in Jesus name.
5. Almighty God preserve my going out and my coming in, in the name of Jesus.
6. Every evil wisdom working against, my breakthroughs; be disgraced in the name of Jesus.
7. By the power of the Holy Ghost, I put every evil under my feet in the name of Jesus.
8. Thou power of sin and iniquity in my life, the Lord rebuke you, die in the name of Jesus.
9. Every evil desire in my life; the Lord rebuke you in the name of Jesus.
10. I am seated with Christ in the heavenly places, far above principalities and powers in the name of Jesus.
11. Anointing of deliverance fall upon me now in the name of Jesus.
12. Every power that pursued my parents and are now pursuing me, what are you waiting for, die in the name of Jesus.
13. Every problem in the life of my parents that is now appearing in my life; vanish in the name of Jesus.
14. Every pillar of disgrace in my life, I pull you down in the name of Jesus.

Apostle A.O. Solomon

15. Every evil preparation to disgrace me; be destroyed by fire in the name of Jesus.
16. Every power that has singled me out for affliction, Holy Ghost fire, locate and destroy them in the name of Jesus.
17. Every evil mark upon my body, wherever you are vanish in the name of Jesus.
18. Almighty God restore all my wasted years in the name of Jesus Christ.
19. Every power covering my glory, fall down and die in the name of Jesus.
20. I cancel every dreams, visions, prophesy and prayers against my life and family in the name of Jesus.
21. Talk to God about your heart desires and your situation.
22. Thank God for answered prayers.

Confession:

"Though hand join in hand, the wicked shall not be unpunished: but the seed of the righteous shall be delivered" Proverbs 11:21.

Wisdom for Today:

"Obstacles are like wild animals. They are cowards but they will bluff you if they can. If they see you are afraid of them, they are liable to spring upon you; but if you look at them squarely in the eye, they will slink out of sight".

Read the Bible Today: Luke 2–3

Prayer Points:

1. Evil beings shall not gather in my dwelling place, in the name of Jesus.
2. I reject satanic sympathy, in the name of Jesus.
3. If it is a must for somebody to die this year, it shall not be me or any member of my family, in the name of Jesus.
4. I dwell in the secret place of the most high God, and I abide under the shadow of the Almighty; death cannot swallow me there, in the name of Jesus.
5. I thank God for divine protection in the name of Jesus.
6. You my glory arise and shine in the name of Jesus.
7. Every seed of the enemy in my life come out by fire in the name of Jesus.
8. Every seed of poverty in my life come out by fire in the mighty name of Jesus.
9. Every dream of poverty, I cancel you by the blood of Jesus in the name of Jesus.
10. Every evil burial for my sake, be destroyed by fire in the name of Jesus.
11. I break the power of death over my life in the name of Jesus.
12. Every hold of the enemy over my blood break by fire in the name of Jesus.
13. Every messenger of death on assignment against me and my family, die in the name of Jesus.
14. Good dreams in my life, hear the word of God, come alive and manifest in the name of Jesus.

Apostle A.O. Solomon

15. Every weapon of demotion fashioned against my life, scatter in the name of Jesus.
16. By the spirit of ; I send back every evil arrow fired against my life, go back to sender in the name of Jesus.
17. Anything packaged to destroy my joy in this country be destroyed by fire in the name of Jesus.
18. Foundation of sorrow in my life; be broken to pieces in the name of Jesus.
19. I proclaim that my joy shall last forever in the name of Jesus.
20. Evil deposit in my life and body your time is up, come out in the name of Jesus.
21. Every attempt to cover my glory; be frustrated in the name of Jesus.
22. Every evil power monitoring the gates of my prosperity why are you still alive, I command you to die in Jesus name.
23. Every evil arrow fired to useless my life, come out and go back to your sender in the name of Jesus.
24. Spirit of poverty come out of my life and enter no more in the name of Jesus.
25. Any power that is making my family to suffer your time is up, die in the name of Jesus.
26. I shall not answer the call of any evil spirit in the name of Jesus Christ.
27. Every power hired to curse me and my destiny, what are you waiting for, die in the name of Jesus.
28. Any power or covenant of my father's house that wants to waste my life and calling, die in the name of Jesus.
29. Stubborn pursuers of my life, hear the word of the Lord, die in the name of Jesus.
30. Every evil stamp of the enemy; be removed in the name of Jesus.
31. Almighty God; turn my failures to success in the name of Jesus.
32. I cancel every dreams, visions, prophesy and prayers against my life and family in the name of Jesus.
33. Talk to God about your heart desires and your situation.
34. Thank God for answered prayers.

APRIL 16

Confession:

"A good man obtaineth favor of the Lord: but a man of wicked devices will be condemned" Proverbs 12:2.

Wisdom for Today:

If you love life, don't waste time, for time is what life is made up of.

Read the Bible Today: Luke 4–5

Prayer Points:

1. I thank God for his never-failing promises.
2. I cover my spirit, soul, and body with the blood of Jesus in the name of Jesus.
3. I bind and paralyze every enemy of my prayer, in the name of Jesus.
4. Almighty God let my prayers become too hot for the enemies to handle, in Jesus name.
5. My joy in this country shall not vanish, in the name of Jesus.
6. Every gate in this nation shot against me, open now in the name of Jesus.
7. Every curse that is delaying good things in my life; break and release me in the name of Jesus.
8. Every spirit of this world attached to my mind, I cut you off in the name of Jesus.
9. Spirit of God, reign in my life in the name of Jesus.
10. Almighty God teach my hand to war in the name of Jesus.
11. Almighty God arise and prevail over my enemies in Jesus name.
12. Let the wicked and their wickedness be consumed by fire in the name of Jesus.
13. Let every stubborn enemy that has risen against me; be defeated now in the name of Jesus.
14. By the power of the Holy Ghost, I destroy the enemies and their work in my life in the name of Jesus.
15. Let the dwelling place of my enemies come to nothing, and let those who hate me be put to shame in the name of Jesus.
16. Let every weapon of my enemies back fire and destroy them in the name of Jesus.

Apostle A.O. Solomon

17. Almighty God reveal to me the secret of becoming a winner in life in the name of Jesus.
18. Blood of Jesus, make way for me tonight in the name of Jesus.
19. Let the power of God clear way for my prayers tonight in the name of Jesus.
20. Let the angels of God come to my aid, support me tonight in the name of Jesus.
21. Holy Ghost, arise in your power and deliver me from my tight places in the name of Jesus.
22. I cancel every dreams, visions, prophesy and prayers against my life and family in the name of Jesus.
23. Talk to God about your heart desires and your situation.
24. Thank God for answered prayers.

Confession:

"The wicked are overthrown, and are not: but the house of the righteous shall stand" Proverbs 12:7.

Wisdom for Today:

"Don't let life discourage you; everyone who got where he is had to begin where he was. Live the life you've dreamed".

Read the Bible Today: Luke 6–7

Prayer Points:

1. My testimonies shall not disappear, in the name of Jesus.
2. My laughter in this country shall not turn to weeping, in Jesus name.
3. My dancing in this country shall not turn to mourning, in Jesus name.
4. My success in this country shall not turn to failure, in Jesus name.
5. I will not weep over what I have rejoiced over, in this country in the name of Jesus.
6. Shout fire of deliverance fall on me... 7 times
7. Evil dreams depart from my life in the name of Jesus.
8. Every power of darkness polluting and attacking my dreams; be arrested by fire in the name of Jesus.
9. By the blood of Jesus, I cancel every effect of evil dreams in my life in the name of Jesus.
10. Every messenger of death in my church; depart and enter no more in the name of Jesus.
11. Every evil power that is holding me down, die in the name of Jesus.
12. I move from nothing to something good in the name of Jesus.
13. In this country I shall not be disgraced in the name of Jesus.
14. Every attack in my dream that is now affecting my life be reversed in the name of Jesus.
15. Evil arrows from my dream come out and go back to sender in the name of Jesus.
16. Powers from my father's house and my mother's house begin to attack yourself in Jesus name.

17. Almighty God I need a break in this country in the name of Jesus.
18. Almighty God heal me from every area that I have been wounded in the name of Jesus.
19. Holy Ghost fire locate and destroy every power bent on seeing my destiny destroyed, in the name of Jesus.
20. My ears shall hear good news, my eyes shall see good things, and my hands shall possess good things in the name of Jesus.
21. Almighty God arise quickly and deliver me from shame in the name of Jesus.
22. Evil arrows my body is not for you in the name of Jesus.
23. Every owner of evil load in my life, carry your load in the name of Jesus.
24. I shall not be wasted; I shall not be useless in the name of Jesus.
25. I cancel every dreams, visions, prophesy and prayers against my life and family in the name of Jesus.
26. Talk to God about your heart desires and your situation.
27. Thank God for answered prayers.

Confession:

"The wicked is snared by the transgression of his lips: but the just shall come out of trouble" Proverbs 12:13.

Wisdom for Today:

I will! I am! I can! I will actualize my dream. I will press ahead. I will settle down and see it through. I will solve the problems. I will pay the price. I will never walk away from my dream until I see my dream walk away: Alert! Alive! Achieved!

Read the Bible Today: Luke 8–9

Prayer Points:

1. Every attack against my destiny in this land, go back to your sender, in Jesus name.
2. Instability shall not be my portion in this country, in the name of Jesus.
3. Evil wind shall not blow against me and my family in this land, in Jesus name.
4. Good doors shall not be shut against me in this country, in the name of Jesus.
5. I refuse to be in a tight corner in this country, in the name of Jesus.
6. Every power affecting my joy, lose your power and die in the name of Jesus.
7. I shall not bury my children in the name of Jesus.
8. Every dry bone in my life, receive the touch of resurrection and live in the name of Jesus.
9. Every good door that has been closed against me, lift up your heads and let the King of glory come in Jesus name.
10. Almighty God arise in your mercy close the old chapter in my life in the name of Jesus.
11. Every word of the wicked waiting for manifestation in my life, die in the name of Jesus.
12. Every maturity date of evil words and prophesies in my life, be nullified in the name of Jesus.
13. I fire back, every arrow of evil prophecy that is pursuing my life in Jesus name.

14. Every satanic assignment, I reject you in my life in the name of Jesus.
15. Every power demanding tears from my eyes before receiving my blessings, die in the name of Jesus.
16. Every power sponsoring weeping in my family; carry your load and die in the name of Jesus.
17. Every witchcraft cage caging my destiny, break by the fire of God in the name of Jesus.
18. Almighty God deliver me from the strife of tongue in the name of Jesus.
19. Evil arrows go back to your sender in the name of Jesus.
20. Every attack of eaters of flesh and drinkers of blood, back fire in the name of Jesus.
21. I withdraw my blood from witchcraft altar in the name of Jesus.
22. Anything representing me in any kingdom of darkness, I withdraw you by fire in the name of Jesus.
23. I walk out of the prison of evil dreams in the name of Jesus.
24. Every dream of backwardness in my life die in the name of Jesus.
25. Any power using anything in my past to torment me, die in the name of Jesus.
26. By the blood of Jesus, I register my name for solution today in the name of Jesus.
27. I shall not serve my enemies and I shall not serve my friend in the name of Jesus.
28. I disagree with every satanic decision over my life in the name of Jesus.
29. I cancel every dreams, visions, prophesy and prayers against my life and family in the name of Jesus.
30. Talk to God about your heart desires and your situation.
31. Thank God for answered prayers.

Confession:

"There shall no evil happen to the just: but the wicked shall be filled with mischief" Proverbs 12:21.

Wisdom for Today:

There is no self-made man. You will reach your goals only with the help of others.

Read the Bible Today: Luke 10–11

Prayer Points:

1. I will not regret staying in this country, in the name of Jesus.
2. I shall not be useless; I shall not be wasted, in the name of Jesus.
3. Almighty God fill me with the power to get things easily in life, in the name of Jesus.
4. I receive power to prosper above all unbelievers around me, in the name of Jesus.
5. Angels of good news, locate my dwelling place, in the name of Jesus.
6. I cancel every former and present agreement with the spirit of Egypt in the name of Jesus.
7. Every agreement with the power of the air, I command you to break in the name of Jesus.
8. I recover every blessing I have lost to spirit of Egypt in the name of Jesus.
9. Almighty God deliver me from every problem I have brought upon myself in the name of Jesus.
10. I reject every invitation to bondage in the name of Jesus.
11. Almighty God give me power to overcome pressures in life in the name of Jesus.
12. Almighty use me for your glory in the name of Jesus.
13. By the anointing of the Holy Ghost, I leap over every negative situation surrounding me in the name of Jesus.
14. Almighty God my soul hopes and wait on you, be gracious in my situation in the name of Jesus.
15. I shall not fail in the mighty name of Jesus.
16. Almighty God, I commit my life to you; organize my scattered life in the name of Jesus.

17. Almighty God change my story as you did Jabez in the name of Jesus.

18. I reject automatic failure in my life in the name of Jesus.

19. Every enemy of divine presence in my life, I command you to die in the name of Jesus.

20. Anointing to excel above all my family members fall upon me now in the name of Jesus.

21. I shall experience divine favor throughout the days of my life in Jesus name.

22. Holy Spirit; coordinate me in the name of Jesus.

23. Arrows of the enemy you shall not locate me, go back to your sender in the name of Jesus.

24. I cancel every dreams, visions, prophesy and prayers against my life and family in the name of Jesus.

25. Talk to God about your heart desires and your situation.

26. Thank God for answered prayers.

Confession:

"The light of the righteous rejoiceth: but the lamp of the wicked shall be put out" Proverbs 13:9.

Wisdom for Today:

Faith in something greater than ourselves enables us to do what we have said we'll do, to press forward when we are tired or hurt or afraid, and to keep going when the challenge seems overwhelming and the course is entirely uncertain.

Read the Bible Today: Luke 11–13

Prayer Points:

1. I refuse to tell evil stories in this country; I shall always give testimonies, in the name of Jesus.
2. My better life in this country shall not become a bitter life, in the name of Jesus.
3. Every power working against my better life in this country, die, in Jesus name.
4. Every power working against my better life from both sides of my family, die, in the name of Jesus.
5. The source of my income shall not dry up, in the name of Jesus.
6. Power to sin no more, fall upon me now in the name of Jesus.
7. I put the yoke of Jesus Christ upon myself in the name of Jesus.
8. God shall help me and fight for me in the name of Jesus.
9. I shall not lose my job, and business in the name of Jesus.
10. My source of money shall not be blocked in the name of Jesus.
11. Throughout this month I shall be blessed and highly favored in the name of Jesus.
12. Where there is no way for others, there shall be way for me this month in the name of Jesus.
13. I reject death in my family and church in the name of Jesus.
14. Almighty God let your hand be upon me for good throughout this month in the name of Jesus.
15. Almighty God do not give me up to the desires of my enemies in the name of Jesus.
16. Evil shall not prevail against me and my family in the name of Jesus.
17. Sin shall not rule over me in the name of Jesus.

18. Every good thing my hands have started, my hands shall complete, and I shall enjoy them in the name of Jesus.
19. My head hear the word of the Lord; you shall not be bewitched in the name of Jesus.
20. I shall not become what my enemies want me to be in the name of Jesus.
21. Almighty God of Abraham, Isaac, and Jacob rearrange this country to favor me in the name of Jesus.
22. Every completed work of my enemies over my life; be destroyed with all your effects in the name of Jesus.
23. I break and lose myself from the stronghold of darkness in the name of Jesus.
24. Any power that wants to replace my peace with war, die suddenly in the name of Jesus.
25. By the blood of Jesus Christ, I rise above limitation in life in the name of Jesus.
26. I cancel every dreams, visions, prophesy and prayers against my life and family in the name of Jesus.
27. Talk to God about your heart desires and your situation.
28. Thank God for answered prayers.

Confession:

"The house of the wicked shall be overthrown: but the tabernacle of the upright shall flourish" Proverbs 14:11.

Wisdom for Today:

"When you make a mistake, don't look back at it long. Take the reason of the thing into your mind, and then look forward. Mistakes are lessons of wisdom. The past cannot be changed. The future is yet in your power".

Read the Bible Today: Luke 14–15

Prayer Points:

1. This country shall not fight against me; it shall comfort and favor me, in the name of Jesus.
2. My testimonies in this country shall not become evil stories, in the name of Jesus.
3. God has given me this land; I shall prosper in it, and nothing shall hinder me, in the name of Jesus.
4. I will flourish in every good thing I lay my hands on, in the name of Jesus.
5. My eagle will fly high; the enemies shall not bring me down, in Jesus name.
6. Almighty God reign supreme in my life in the name of Jesus.
7. Almighty God set me free from poverty in the name of Jesus.
8. By the power in the word of God, I command every darkness in my life to vanish in the name of Jesus.
9. Every step by step work of the enemy in my life be destroyed in the name of Jesus.
10. Every perfected works of the enemy in my life be over turned by the blood of Jesus in the name of Jesus.
11. Every evil alter in my family working against my glory, be consumed by fire in the name of Jesus.
12. Every good thing the enemy has scattered in my life, come together in the name of Jesus.
13. Every power and spirit that has set my life for affliction, I bind you in the name of Jesus.
14. In the name of Jesus, my life shall not follow satanic agenda in the name of Jesus.

Apostle A.O. Solomon

15. Almighty God it is time, give me rest and comfort me, prosper me in the name of Jesus.

16. By the blood of Jesus, I register my name for solution today in the name of Jesus.

17. I connect myself with the power of God in the name of Jesus.

18. Every pillar of witchcraft in my family, what are you waiting for? die in the name of Jesus.

19. Witchcraft powers why are you pursuing my life? die in the name of Jesus.

20. It is suffer not a witch to live, therefore any witchcraft pursuing my life, I command you to die in the name of Jesus.

21. I disagree with failure in the name of Jesus.

22. Failure at the edge of good things, depart from my life by the blood of Jesus in the name of Jesus.

23. I cancel every dreams, visions, prophesy and prayers against my life and family in the name of Jesus.

24. Talk to God about your heart desires and your situation.

25. Thank God for answered prayers.

↱ *Confession:*

"The Lord hath made all things for himself: yea, even the wicked for the day of evil" Proverbs 16:4.

Wisdom for Today:

"Take the first step in faith. You don't have to see the whole staircase, just take the first step".

Read the Bible Today: Luke 16–18

Prayer Points:

1. Almighty God I thank you for delivering me from all evil, in Jesus name.
2. I shall break through; I shall not break down, in the name of Jesus.
3. I have life by the blood of Jesus, and in my pathway there is no death, in Jesus name.
4. I decree that the world shall read of my rising and not of my falling, in Jesus name.
5. What is difficult for others will not be difficult for me, in the name of Jesus.
6. Witchcraft battle at the edge of my success return to your sender in the name of Jesus.
7. Every evil seed planted by the enemy in my life, be uprooted by fire in the name of Jesus.
8. Every plantation of darkness in my life, come out with all your roots in the name of Jesus.
9. Every evil seed planted into my life through dreams, be uprooted by fire in the name of Jesus.
10. I challenge my system with the fire of God, in the name of Jesus.
11. Every instrument of satanic control in my life, wherever you are be destroyed by fire in the name of Jesus.
12. Arrows of darkness in my life come out of your hiding places and go back to your sender in the name of Jesus.
13. As from today, life shall be easy for me in the name of Jesus.
14. By the blood of Jesus, I stand in gap for every member of my family in the name of Jesus.

15. Any of my family member that is appointed for death, be redeemed by the blood of Jesus in the name of Jesus.
16. Any power that wants to attack me, Holy Ghost fire attack and destroy them in the name of Jesus.
17. Arrows of madness fired against me and any member of my family, gather yourself together and go back to your sender in the name of Jesus.
18. All those in the system of this country that will not favor me, o Lord replace them with people that will favor me in the name of Jesus.
19. All those who are boasting to fire me in my place of work, let the Holy Ghost fire, fire them in the name of Jesus.
20. Every evil register containing my name, Holy Ghost fire consume them in the name of Jesus.
21. Every broom of darkness sweeping good things away from my life, catch fire in the name of Jesus.
22. Angel of the living God; begin to sweep back all my blessings in the name of Jesus.
23. Every spirit of laboring without achievement; be destroyed in the name of Jesus.
24. I hold the hammer of the word of God and command every padlock ministering evil against my life; break in the name of Jesus.
25. With the garment of fire and power of Jesus, I enter the strong room of the enemy and collect all my blessing in the name of Jesus.
26. Holy Ghost fire go into every witchcraft coven and collect my blessings in the name of Jesus.
27. Any man or woman, attending witchcraft meeting because of me, you shall not return in the name of Jesus.
28. Anyone calling my name for evil in the night, angel of God; slap them in the name of Jesus.
29. Every night captivity in my life, break in the name of Jesus.
30. I cancel every dreams, visions, prophesy and prayers against my life and family in the name of Jesus.
31. Talk to God about your heart desires and your situation.
32. Thank God for answered prayers.

Confession:

"And I shall be like a tree planted by the side of water, that bringeth forth his fruits in his season; my leaf also shall not wither; and whatsoever I doeth shall prosper" Psalms 1:3.

Wisdom for Today:

"We are what we repeatedly do. Excellence, then, is not an act, but a habit".

Read the Bible Today: Luke 19–20

Prayer Points:

1. I decree that, as the heavens rule, so I rule in the affairs of men, in Jesus name.
2. As the stars shine above, so I shine among my colleagues and rise above them, in Jesus name.
3. What is impossible for others will be possible for me with God, in the name of Jesus.
4. People will find me in the height that others cannot reach, in the name of Jesus.
5. By the power and favor of God, I will rule from the position that others cannot occupy, in Jesus name.
6. I command every fear of the future in my life to die, in the name of Jesus.
7. Anything done against me in the night; be destroyed by fire in the name of Jesus.
8. Every satanic power appearing in my dream, the Lord rebuke you perish in the name of Jesus.
9. Any fire that the enemy has lighted against me and my family be quenched by the blood of Jesus.
10. Every evil pot caging anything good in my life, break by thunder in the name of Jesus.
11. Almighty God put upon me your garment of mercy and favor in the name of Jesus.
12. My spirit man, my body, my soul hear the word of the Lord you shall not answer the call of the enemy day or night in the name of Jesus.
13. Let the voice of God thunder against my enemies and divide them in the name of Jesus.

14. Let the voice of God, divide the fire of my enemy and destroy them in the name of Jesus.
15. Let the voice of God; shake down the camp of my enemies in the name of Jesus.
16. Almighty clothe me with mercy and compassion in the name of Jesus.
17. Almighty God, empower my hands to profit in the name of Jesus.
18. Every attack against my labor, break and release me in the name of Jesus.
19. Every curse of the enemy against the works of my hands, break by the blood of Jesus.
20. Every physical and spiritual chain upon my hands, break in the name of Jesus.
21. Thou son of David use your key, and set me free from hand cuffs and chains in the name of Jesus.
22. Jesus set me free; I am free indeed in the name of Jesus.
23. I drink the blood of Jesus, and I cover myself with the blood of Jesus in the name of Jesus.
24. Any power that wants to destroy the work of God in my life, Holy Ghost fire; destroy them in the name of Jesus.
25. Every satanic bondage from evil dreams programmed into my life; break and release me in the name of Jesus.
26. I cancel every dreams, visions, prophesy and prayers against my life and family in the name of Jesus.
27. Talk to God about your heart desires and your situation.
28. Thank God for answered prayers.

Confession:

"Ask of me, and I shall give thee the heathen for thine inheritance, and the uttermost parts of the earth for thy possession" Psalms 2:8.

Wisdom for Today:

"Don't judge each day by the harvest you reap, but by the seeds you plant".

Read the Bible Today: *Luke 21–22*

Prayer Points:

1. My future is secure, because I trust in Jesus in the name of Jesus.
2. I refuse to be poor; Jesus Christ has redeemed me from the curse of poverty, in Jesus name.
3. I decree by the power in the blood of Jesus, I shall not experience any dry season in my finances again, in Jesus name.
4. Almighty God feed me with the food of champions, in the name of Jesus.
5. I will be favored in every department of my life, in the name of Jesus.
6. Every sickness introduced into my life as a result of evil dreams die now in the name of Jesus.
7. Every dream of failure in my past be reversed in the name of Jesus.
8. Every witchcraft power pursuing me in the dream fall down and die in the name of Jesus.
9. Almighty God make me holy by your power in the name of Jesus.
10. Every satanic dream attached to my progress, die in the name of Jesus.
11. I come out of every dream prison by the power of the Holy Ghost in the name of Jesus.
12. I fire back every witchcraft arrow fired into my dream in the name of Jesus.
13. Every evil dream of the past affecting my life now, die in the name of Jesus.
14. Every witchcraft serpent attacking me in the dream, back to sender in the mighty name of Jesus.

Apostle A.O. Solomon

15. Every dream affecting my life, marriage, and career lose your power and die in the name of Jesus.
16. Every good thing I have lost in the dream I repossess you back in Jesus name.
17. Every agent of darkness in my dream life, I command you to die in the name of Jesus.
18. Every evil pronouncement against me in the dream they shall not stand, and shall not come to pass in the name of Jesus.
19. My resting time shall not be a trouble time in the name of Jesus.
20. I cancel every dreams, visions, prophesy and prayers against my life and family in the name of Jesus.
21. Talk to God about your heart desires and your situation.
22. Thank God for answered prayers.

Confession:

"Being justified freely by his grace through the redemption that is in Christ Jesus" Romans 3:24.

Wisdom for Today:

"There are no secrets to success. It is the result of preparation, hard work, learning from failure".

Read the Bible Today: Luke 23–24

Prayer Points:

1. The people whom others cannot meet will be my friends to the glory of God, in Jesus name.
2. The miracle that is difficult for others to receive will be my daily experience, in Jesus name.
3. All those expecting my shame shall be disgraced without remedy, in the name of Jesus.
4. All those expecting my failure shall be disgraced without remedy, in Jesus name.
5. Every power of evil against me and family die by the blood of Jesus, in Jesus name.
6. Any power, spirit, personality that wants to trouble me, my God shall trouble you in the name of Jesus.
7. Life shall not be difficult for me in the name of Jesus.
8. I reject every form of nakedness physically and spiritually in the name of Jesus.
9. I reject every form of disorder in the name of Jesus.
10. Me and my family shall be for good signs and wonders in the name of Jesus.
11. As the Lord God lives, people will see the good work of God in my life in Jesus name.
12. Almighty God let all those that will bless me, be blessed, and let all those that will curse me be cursed in Jesus name.
13. Every completed work of the enemy over my life be destroyed with all your power in the name of Jesus.
14. I plead the blood of Jesus against every voice speaking against my destiny in the name of Jesus.

15. Every owner of evil load in my life, wherever you are appear and carry your load in Jesus name.
16. I plead the blood of Jesus over everything the devil is holding against me in the name of Jesus.
17. Almighty God I belong to you, I disconnect from the iniquity of my ancestors in the name of Jesus.
18. Every ancestral oat that is affecting my life break now by the blood of Jesus in the name of Jesus.
19. Every evil word that is pursuing my destiny, the Lord rebuke you; turn back in the name of Jesus.
20. Every prophecy demoting my life lose your hold and die in the name of Jesus.
21. Evil family pattern, break and release me by fire in the name of Jesus.
22. Every evil water flowing in my family, dry up by fire in the name of Jesus.
23. Family bondage affecting my life, break in the name of Jesus.
24. Ancestral evil covenant, I separate myself from you now in the name of Jesus.
25. Every evil register containing my name, be roasted by fire in the name of Jesus.
26. I cancel every dreams, visions, prophesy and prayers against my life and family in the name of Jesus.
27. Talk to God about your heart desires and your situation.
28. Thank God for answered prayers.

Confession:

"For in him (Christ Jesus) we live and move and have!" Acts 17:28.

Wisdom for Today:

"Painful as it may be, a significant emotional event can be the catalyst for choosing a direction that serves us—and those around us—more effectively. Look for the learning".

Read the Bible Today: *Zechariah 1–2*

Prayer Points:

1. The horn of the wicked shall not harm me, in the name of Jesus.
2. Almighty God let my handwork prosper, in the name of Jesus.
3. Jesus became poor for me to become rich; therefore, I shall prosper and be in good health, in the name of Jesus.
4. I pursue my enemies, I overtake them, and I recover all my blessings from them, in Jesus name.
5. Anywhere the soles of my feet shall tread, the Lord has given it unto me, in Jesus name.
6. I release the power in the blood of Jesus to my situation in the name of Jesus.
7. Every dry bone in my life, receive the blood of Jesus and live in the name of Jesus.
8. I cover my door post with the blood of Jesus in the name of Jesus.
9. Blood of Jesus arise in your power and fight for me in the name of Jesus.
10. I am made perfect through the blood of the everlasting covenant in the name of Jesus.
11. I have redemption through the blood of Jesus in the name of Jesus.
12. Every spirit of fear operating in my life, I rebuke you in the name of Jesus.
13. I receive healing through the blood of Jesus in the name of Jesus.
14. I receive deliverance through the blood of Jesus in the name of Jesus.

15. Every evil yoke upon my life break in the name of Jesus.
16. I cancel every dreams, visions, prophesy and prayers against my life and family in the name of Jesus.
17. Talk to God about your heart desires and your situation.
18. Thank God for answered prayers.

Confession:

"Every good gift and perfect gifts is from above" James 1:17.

Wisdom for Today:

"We'll never know the worth of water till the well goes dry."

"Trying is a part of failing. If you are afraid to fail then you're afraid to try".

Read the Bible Today: *Zechariah 3–4*

Prayer Points:

1. I have the peace of God that surpasses all understanding, in Jesus in the name of Jesus.
2. I will walk into the upcoming year with favor, honor, peace, power, strength, glory, blessings, and abundance, in the name of Jesus.
3. I cover myself and my family with the blood of Jesus in the name of Jesus.
4. Lord I come into your presence by the blood of Jesus Christ in the name of Jesus.
5. Almighty God, shine your light to every department of our lives in the name of Jesus.
6. Jesus Christ is Lord over my life therefore; I refuse to live in darkness in the name of Jesus.
7. Blood of Jesus open up all the doors and gates short against me in the name of Jesus.
8. Every evil dream in my life be cancelled in the name of Jesus.
9. Every good dream and vision in my life; receive the power of God and manifest in the name of Jesus.
10. Any evil dream programmed for manifestation in my life this week, this month, and this year; I cancel you by the blood of Jesus in the name of Jesus.
11. I plead the blood of Jesus over every dream in my life in the name of Jesus.
12. Holy Ghost; baptize our children in the name of Jesus.
13. Let the Spirit of God rest upon the life of my children in the name of Jesus.
14. Almighty God, arise and deliver my children from affliction in the name of Jesus.

Apostle A.O. Solomon

15. Almighty God; give me and my family a new beginning in the name of Jesus.
16. By the blood of Jesus Christ I cancel every appointment with death in the name of Jesus.
17. Almighty God enlarge my coast and bless me indeed in the name of Jesus.
18. Almighty God, command deliverance and blessing upon my life in the name of Jesus.
19. Almighty God visit my life, let my failure, pain, and shortcoming disappear in the name of Jesus.
20. Almighty God, arise and rebuild the damage walls of my life in the name of Jesus.
21. Every satanic whisperer be silenced in the name of Jesus.
22. Every bewitchment upon my life be destroyed in the name of Jesus.
23. Almighty God, deliver me from failure at the edge of success in the name of Jesus.
24. Every power, every spirit, any agent arranging battle for me at the edge of my breakthrough in all areas of my life, let fire go before God and consume them in the name of Jesus Christ.
25. Almighty God wherever I have failed, give me a miracle in the name of Jesus.
26. I cancel every dreams, visions, prophesy and prayers against my life and family in the name of Jesus.
27. Talk to God about your heart desires and your situation.
28. Thank God for answered prayers.

Confession:

"He which rose up the lord Jesus shall raise me up also by Jesus"
2 Corinthians 4:14.

Wisdom for Today:

Fire goes out without wood, and quarrels disappear when gossip stops.

Read the Bible Today: Zechariah 5–6

Prayer Points:

1. I shall not be cited as a bad example, in Jesus name.
2. Let all dry bones in my life and marriage come alive now, by the blood of Jesus in the name of Jesus.
3. I shall not be wasted, in the name of Jesus.
4. Any power delegated to waste my life, be wasted, in the name of Jesus.
5. This is my time of surplus and favor I must shine, in the name of Jesus.
6. Lord I come into your presence by the blood of Jesus Christ in the name of Jesus.
7. Almighty God, shine your light to every department of my life in the name of Jesus.
8. Blood of Jesus open up all the doors and gates short against me in the name of Jesus.
9. Every evil dream in my life be cancelled in the name of Jesus.
10. Every good dream and vision in my life; receive the power of God and manifest in the name of Jesus.
11. Any evil dream programmed for manifestation in my life this week, month, this year I cancel you by the blood of Jesus in the name of Jesus.
12. I plead the blood of Jesus over every dream in my life in the name of Jesus.
13. Holy Ghost; baptize our children in the name of Jesus.
14. Let the Spirit of God rest upon the life of my children in the name of Jesus.
15. Almighty God, arise and deliver my children from affliction in the name of Jesus.

16. Almighty God; give me and my family a new beginning in the name of Jesus.
17. By the blood of Jesus Christ we cancel every appointment with death in the name of Jesus.
18. Almighty God enlarge my coast and bless me indeed in the name of Jesus.
19. Almighty God, command deliverance and blessing upon my life in the name of Jesus.
20. Almighty God visit my life, let my failure, pain, and shortcoming disappear in the name of Jesus.
21. Almighty God, arise and rebuild the damage walls of my life in the name of Jesus.
22. Every satanic whisperer be silenced in the name of Jesus.
23. Every bewitchment upon my life be destroyed in the name of Jesus.
24. Almighty God, deliver me from failure at the edge of success in the name of Jesus.
25. Every power, every spirit, any agent arranging battle for me at the edge of my breakthrough in all areas of my life, let fire go before God and consume them in the name of Jesus Christ.
26. Almighty God wherever I have failed, God give me a miracle in the name of Jesus.
27. I cancel every dreams, visions, prophesy and prayers against my life and family in the name of Jesus.
28. Talk to God about your heart desires and your situation.
29. Thank God for answered prayers.

Confession:

"Thou shall increase my greatness, and comfort me on every side".
Psalms 71:21.

Wisdom for Today:

"The key to change is to let go of fear".

Read the Bible Today: *Zechariah 7–8* ✓

Prayer Points:

1. Almighty God disgrace every enemy of my greatness, in the name of Jesus.
2. O Lord, extend my horizons by your power, in Jesus name.
3. I shall not know pain, I shall not suffer, I shall be comforted on every side, in Jesus name.
4. Instead of shame, Father Lord, give me double honor, in Jesus name.
5. I declare my promotion from minimum to maximum, in Jesus name.
6. I plead the blood of Jesus Christ over your prayers in the name of Jesus.
7. Declare Jesus Christ is Lord.
8. Declare, I know that my redeemer lives.
9. Father manifest your presence in my life in the name of Jesus.
10. Almighty God show me your kindness in the name of Jesus Christ.
11. Any power that wants to attack me in my dream, perish in the name of Jesus.
12. By the ordinances that establish day and night, I reject every evil dream and attacks in the name of Jesus.
13. By the ordinances that establish day and night, let all those seeking my life, die in the name of Jesus.
14. Every battle in my life, father Lord shift them to my enemies in the name of Jesus.
15. Almighty God, deliver me from harvest eaters and destroyers in the name of Jesus.
16. Every power pushing me away from the road of success and progress be consumed by the anger of God in the name of Jesus.

17. Almighty God if I have been forced away from the road of success and progress, father take me back, and establish me Lord in the name of Jesus.
18. Almighty God locate and destroy any power, and spirit that want to force me into hiding in the name of Jesus.
19. I cancel every dreams, visions, prophesy and prayers against my life and family in the name of Jesus.
20. Talk to God about your heart desires and your situation.
21. Thank God for answered prayers.

Confession:

"Deliver the poor and needy: rid them out of the hand of the wicked". Psalms 72:12.

Wisdom for Today:

"Exert your talents, and distinguish yourself, and don't think of retiring from the world, until the world will be sorry that you retire".

Read the Bible Today: Zechariah 9–10 ✓

Prayer Points:

1. Angels of God, fight for me today, in the name of Jesus.
2. Let the blood of Jesus clear the way for me today, in Jesus name.
3. Holy Spirit, clear the way for me today, in Jesus name.
4. I shall reign in life, because I am born to reign, in Jesus name.
5. I shall prosper in life, because I am born to prosper, in Jesus name.
6. Declare Jesus Christ is Lord.
7. I reject frustration today in the name of Jesus.
8. I take over this day by the blood of Jesus Christ in the name of Jesus.
9. Almighty God, give me wisdom, knowledge and understanding to excel in all areas of life in the name of Jesus Christ.
10. I bring me and my family under the coverage of the blood of Jesus Christ in the name of Jesus.
11. By the blood of Jesus Christ, I reject every evil in this day in the name of Jesus.
12. I withdraw the secret of my life from the hands of the enemy in the name of Jesus Christ.
13. Almighty God, show me your kindness in the name of Jesus.
14. Almighty God, forgive my iniquity and remember my sin no more in the name of Jesus.
15. Almighty God; make a new covenant with me in the name of Jesus.
16. Almighty God, perform the good things which you have promised me in the name of Jesus.
17. By the ordinances that establish day and night, I command every good door closed against me to open in the name of Jesus.

Apostle A.O. Solomon

18. By the ordinances that establish day and night, I command the pipeline of prosperity to open into my life in the name of Jesus.

19. By the ordinances that establish day and night, I command every evil dream to die in the name of Jesus.

20. By the ordinances that establish day and night, I command every power blocking my way in this country; perish in the name of Jesus.

21. I cancel every dreams, visions, prophesy and prayers against my life and family in the name of Jesus.

22. Talk to God about your heart desires and your situation.

23. Thank God for answered prayers.

Confession:

"Bless my family and me forever!" 2 Samuel 7:29

Wisdom for Today:

"Never part without loving words to think of during your absence. It may be that you will not meet again in this life".

Read the Bible Today: Zechariah 11–12

Prayer Points:

1. Almighty God, remove whatever the devil is using against me and my family in the name of Jesus.
2. From this moment, I step into my success zone, in Jesus name.
3. I declare this month my month of double miracles, in the name of Jesus.
4. Every evil law operating in my family, I cancel you by the blood of Jesus, in Jesus name.
5. Almighty God let me and my family eat in plenty from now on, in Jesus name.
6. Declare Jesus Christ is Lord.
7. Blood of Jesus Christ begin to flow in my system in the name of Jesus.
8. Almighty God, show me great mercy in the name of Jesus.
9. Let impossibility become possible in my life in the name of Jesus.
10. Almighty God, show me your great mercy and make way for me where there seems to be no way in the name of Jesus.
11. Almighty God; show me the kind of mercy that you showed to David in the name of Jesus.
12. Almighty God; show me the kind of mercy that you showed to Elizabeth in the name of Jesus.
13. Almighty God Let your great mercy begin to defend my life in the name of Jesus.
14. Almighty God I trust in your mercy let my heart rejoice in your salvation in the name of Jesus.
15. Every power and spirit rebelling against my life; be consumed by the fire of God in the name of Jesus.
16. I cancel every dreams, visions, prophesy and prayers against my life and family in the name of Jesus.
17. Talk to God about your heart desires and your situation.
18. Thank God for answered prayers.

MAY 2

Confession:

"With everlasting kindness will I have mercy on thee, saith the Lord thy Redeemer" Isaiah 54:8.

Wisdom for Today:

"They that sow in tears shall reap joy".

Read the Bible Today: Zechariah 13 and Psalm 126

Prayer Points:

1. Almighty God, open my eyes to see opportunities you have placed before me, in Jesus name.
2. I oppose every opposition, I pursue every pursuer, and I oppress every oppressor, in the name of Jesus.
3. Power to prosper without struggles in life, fall upon me now, in the name of Jesus.
4. Every power supervising evil in my life, go permanently blind, in Jesus name.
5. Every dry bone in my finances, come alive now, in the name of Jesus.
6. Declare Jesus Christ is Lord.
7. Almighty God; Let this month be productive for me in all areas of life in the name of Jesus.
8. Almighty God, cover my nakedness in all areas of life in the name of Jesus
9. Almighty God let my life reflect your glory in the name of Jesus.
10. Almighty God, do not let me lack any good thing in the name of Jesus.
11. Almighty God, do not let me spend this month like the previous one; bless me, and give me financial breakthrough, with open heaven in the name of Jesus.
12. I reject bad news this month in the name of Jesus.
13. Anyone mandated by the enemy to destroy my joy, angels of the living God bury them in the name of Jesus.
14. This month, I shall not suffer any loss of life or property in the name of Jesus.
15. Almighty God, in every area of my life throughout this month, let it be known that you are greater than man in the name of Jesus.

16. Every stubborn problem in my life, I command you to drop dead in the name of Jesus.
17. Every work of the enemy against me and my family back fire in the name of Jesus.
18. Almighty God; make me shine in the name of Jesus.
19. Almighty God; bring an end to every problem in my life in the name of Jesus Christ.
20. Almighty God; let every evil season in my life expire in the name of Jesus.
21. Almighty God; connect me to my new season in the name of Jesus.
22. I cancel every dreams, visions, prophesy and prayers against my life and family in the name of Jesus.
23. Talk to God about your heart desires and your situation.
24. Thank God for answered prayers.

Confession:

"The Lord is my shepherd; I shall not want" Psalms 23:1.

Wisdom for Today:

"Vision without action is a daydream. Action without vision is a nightmare".

Read the Bible Today: Zechariah 14 and Psalm 149

Prayer Points:

1. Almighty God, pump your blood into my blood, in Jesus name.
2. Let impossibilities in my life become possible, in Jesus name.
3. I break every family curse upon my life, in Jesus name.
4. Power to prevail in prayer; fall upon me now, in Jesus name.
5. Almighty God, replace everything that needs replacement in my life, in Jesus name.
6. Almighty God, have your way in our lives and situation in Jesus name.
7. Almighty God, visit me specially and meet me at the point of my need in Jesus name.
8. Almighty God give me uncommon victory this month throughout this year, what others have been pursuing for so long and could not get, God do for me with ease in Jesus name.
9. Almighty God, bring all my good dreams, expectations and visions to pass and let my good expectation turn to manifestation in Jesus name.
10. God use me to shock and shake the world, give me outstanding results this month and for the rest of this year that will silence those who have written me off, counted me out and have looked down on me in the name of Jesus.
11. Lord give me a result that will make me the world hero, give me the grace of great achievements and breaking records, in my father's house, my mother's house, in my place of work ,among my competitors, and in my nation in Jesus name.
12. Almighty God make me an international hero in the mighty name of Jesus, let the world gather to celebrate and rejoice with me because of your work in my life in the name of Jesus.
13. God give me cheap and sweat less victory in every area of my life and in all that I do in Jesus name.

14. O Lord, arise for my sake today and let all my enemies be scattered in Jesus name.
15. Almighty God let it be known that you are God in my life, my family, marriage and my situation in the name of Jesus.
16. God give me strength and power to pray, strengthen me to prevail in prayer in the name of Jesus.
17. We pray against every satanic retaliation on the nation in the name of Jesus.
18. Almighty God be gracious unto this country, bless and preserve this country in the name of Jesus.
19. Almighty God we commit all the citizens of the United State of America into your hands, preserve them wherever they may be under the surface of the earth deliver them from every satanic retaliation; we release the mark of the blood of Jesus upon them all in the name of Jesus.
20. Almighty God, return every satanic retaliation against me and the United States of America back to sender in the name of Jesus.
21. Anyone that may be of retaliation against me, my children, my family; almighty God let their retaliation fall back upon their head in the name of Jesus.
22. I cancel every dreams, visions, prophesy and prayers against my life and family in the name of Jesus.
23. Talk to God about your heart desires and your situation.
24. Thank God for answered prayers.

Confession:

"The meek shall eat and be satisfied: they shall praise the Lord that seek him: mine heart shall live forever" Psalms 22:26.

Wisdom for Today:

"To the question of your life you are the answer, and to the problems of your life God is the solution".

Read the Bible Today: John 1–2

Prayer Points:

1. Let the blood of Jesus cleanse me of every evil mark from head to toe, in Jesus name.
2. I regain my balance today, in all areas of life, in the name of Jesus.
3. I refuse to be shaken by the enemy, in Jesus name.
4. I claim abundance in every area of my life, in Jesus name.
5. Almighty God let your name defend me throughout this month, this year and all the days of my life, I run into your name defend and preserve me, my family, my marriage and job in Jesus name.
6. Every attack of the enemies, against me, my family, my marriage, my job; thus saith the Lord by the same way you came in by the same way you shall return in Jesus name.
7. You failure, poverty, lack, death, fear, rejection ,bad news, bad luck disease, pain, infirmity trouble, crisis and shame, the same way you came in shall you return in Jesus name.
8. Power of God set me free from fear and uncertainty in Jesus name.
9. Almighty God bless me with unbeatable results and victory, in all areas of my life, give me unbeatable results and victory in my family, finances, spiritual life, my business and in my job in Jesus name.
10. Almighty God, lead me and my family in the path of righteousness, lead us in the way that we should go and let us be at the right place at the right time in the name of Jesus.
11. Almighty God, deliver me, my family, and my church from natural disaster in Jesus name.
12. Anyone on any retaliation mission against my life, my children, and my job be destroyed in the name of Jesus.

13. Almighty God, deliver the citizens of this country from every satanic retaliation wherever they may be in Jesus name.

14. Almighty God undertake for me, my family, my business, my marriage against the marks of the enemies, the destroyer, failure, poverty, witchcraft attack limitation, frustration, depression, spirit of error, rejection, aimlessness, calamity and condemnation in Jesus name.

15. Almighty God for your own sake be my surety and undertake for me against all those who are praying against me in Jesus name.

16. I plead the blood of Jesus over my spirit soul and body, over my life, my home, and my ways in Jesus name.

17. Blood of Jesus Christ arise in your power and begin to speak and minister better things to my life, my home, job, marriage and all that concerns me speak to me and speak for me in Jesus name.

18. Almighty God, move me from strength to strength, empower me all the days of my life financially, maritally, physically and in every areas of my life in the name of Jesus.

19. Almighty God, help me to walk uprightly in all areas of my life and do not withhold any good things from my life in Jesus name.

20. Almighty God, baptize me with the spirit of the fear of God and protect me in Jesus name.

21. Almighty God let your kingdom come into my life, my home, my job, my family and every department of my life and let your will be done in my life in Jesus name.

22. Almighty God, be the sun and shield in my life, my home, my marriage and in every area of my life and all the days of my life in Jesus name.

23. Almighty God let all your grace abound toward me and my family in Jesus name.

24. Almighty God do not with hold any good things from my life and family, have mercy upon me, my family and all that concerns me, be gracious unto us in every area of life in Jesus name.

25. Almighty God manifests yourself in my life, remove every evil mark upon my life, my home, marriage and consume them by your fire in Jesus name.

26. Every covenant with death and hell over my life and family break by the blood of Jesus in the name of Jesus.

27. Almighty God let my ways prosper financially, spiritually, maritally and in every area of life in Jesus name.

28. Whatever the enemies have declared impossible in my life financially, spiritually, maritally, almighty God do it and make them possible in Jesus name.
29. Almighty God, do what only you can do in my life, my family, my finances, and my marriage this month in Jesus name.
30. I cancel every dreams, visions, prophesy and prayers against my life and family in the name of Jesus.
31. Talk to God about your heart desires and your situation.
32. Thank God for answered prayers.

Confession:

"Thou will show me the path of life: in thy presence is fullness of joy; at thy right hand there are pleasures for evermore" Psalms 16:11.

Wisdom for Today:

"He that respects himself is safe from others; he wears a coat of mail that none can pierce." —Henry Wadsworth Longfellow

Read the Bible Today: John 3–4

Prayer Points:

1. I reverse all damages done to my life from the womb, in Jesus name.
2. Almighty God, give me power to overcome all the challenges of the enemy, in Jesus name.
3. Let the blood of Jesus remove every curse placed upon my family, in Jesus name.
4. Let my breakthroughs find me and bring me success, in Jesus name.
5. Almighty God please let it please you to bless my life, my job, my home, my marriage, business, career, my ministry and every area of my life in this country and wherever I go in Jesus name.
6. Almighty God have mercy upon me give me financial miracle, tackle all my financial need, meet me at the point of my needs, supply all my financial needs in Jesus name.
7. Almighty God, deliver me from unprofitable hard labor, don't let me labor in vain in your house and in every area of my life in Jesus name.
8. Almighty God according to your word bless me and give me financial recovery in the name of Jesus.
9. Almighty God I commit the works of my hand to your hands, take control over my struggle and work for me in Jesus name.
10. Almighty God, erase my name, and the name of my family members from the register of the poor in the name of Jesus.
11. Almighty God let the reign of poverty in my life, my family, in my business and in my home come to an end in Jesus name.
12. Poverty I forbid you, no parking for you in my life in Jesus name.

13. In the name of Jesus I destroy every yoke of sickness in my health, finances, career, marriage and every area of my life in Jesus name.

14. Almighty God, as from today make life easy for me in all areas of my life; deliver me from struggle, pains, non-achievement, and hard labor in the name of Jesus.

15. Almighty God let your blessing manifest in my life in Jesus name.

16. Every agent of shame be paralyzed, in Jesus name.

17. I disagree with every satanic agenda for my life, my family, my children and spouse in Jesus name.

18. I decree that I shall cry and weep no more concerning every area of my life in the name of Jesus.

19. Almighty God I know you are in control of my life, let no man prevail over my life, my family, my career, my job, my business and in my home in Jesus name.

20. My destiny, jump out by fire from every witch craft cage in Jesus name.

21. By fire by force I move away from every satanic bus stop in Jesus name.

22. I move my career, my job, my marriage, family, home and finances away from every satanic bus stop in Jesus name.

23. I cancel every dreams, visions, prophesy and prayers against my life and family in the name of Jesus.

24. Talk to God about your heart desires and your situation.

25. Thank God for answered prayers.

Confession:

"As for me, I will behold thy face in righteousness: I shall be satisfied, when I awake, with thy likeness" Psalms 17:15.

Wisdom for Today:

"I believe that any man's life will be filled with constant and unexpected encouragement, if he makes up his mind to do his level best each day, and as nearly as possible reaching the high water mark of pure and useful living".

Read the Bible Today: John 5–6

Prayer Points:

1. Every demonic resistance to my prayers be broken by fire, in Jesus name.
2. I claim my freedom from the consequences of attitude problems, in Jesus name.
3. I claim my freedom from the consequences of idolatry, in Jesus name.
4. I claim my freedom from the consequences of sins by the blood of Jesus, in Jesus name.
5. Let the healing power of God flow into every damaged part of my body, in Jesus name.
6. Arise O Lord and fight for me with jealousy in the name of Jesus.
7. Almighty God I thank you because I will not see trouble throughout this month in the name of Jesus.
8. Every storm prepared for me and my family be diverted away in the name of Jesus.
9. Thank the Lord for the month that the Lord has made.
10. Every mark of bewitchment upon my life; lose your power and be erased in the name of Jesus.
11. Every evil hand writing upon my life; be erased in the name of Jesus.
12. Every witchcraft operation in my life, family, and church; die in the name of Jesus.
13. Every power attacking me from the land of the dead; die the second time in the name of Jesus.
14. Almighty God, use my life to confuse the enemy in the name of Jesus.

15. Every appointment with death in this month; I reject you in the name of Jesus.
16. Every pillar of sorrow in my life; I pull you down in the name of Jesus.
17. Anything standing as a pillar of sorrow in this country in my life; I pull you down in the name of Jesus.
18. O thou that troubled my Israel be pulled down now in the name of Jesus.
19. I reject tragedy and calamity throughout this month in the name of Jesus.
20. Sorrow shall not branch in my dwelling place throughout this month in the name of Jesus.
21. I shall not carry any evil load throughout this month in the name of Jesus.
22. Every maturity day of affliction; be nullified by the blood of Jesus in the name of Jesus.
23. Every incantation against me, the Lord rebuke you; be cancelled in the name of Jesus.
24. Every owner of evil load in my life, appear and carry your load in the name of Jesus.
25. Every perfected work of the enemy over my life; die in the name of Jesus.
26. I cancel every dreams, visions, prophesy and prayers against my life and family in the name of Jesus.
27. Talk to God about your heart desires and your situation.
28. Thank God for answered prayers.

Confession:

"The earth is the Lord's and the fullness thereof; the world, and they that dwell therein" Psalms 24:1.

Wisdom for Today:

"Be the change you want to see in the world".

Read the Bible Today: John 7–8

Prayer Points:

1. I release the creative miracle of God into every department of my life and marriage, in Jesus name.
2. Almighty God, restore me fully, in Jesus name.
3. Almighty God, empower my life with your authority over every demonic force that sets itself against my life, in Jesus name.
4. Almighty God, take me from where I am to where you want me to be, in Jesus name.
5. I refuse to be in any tight corner in life, in the name of Jesus.
6. By the Blood of Jesus, I receive freedom from every financial bondage in the name of Jesus.
7. You spirit of frustration I reject you in my life in the name of Jesus.
8. I refuse to be wasted, any power that wants to waste my life be wasted in the name of Jesus.
9. Every waster of my prosperity wherever you are; be arrested in the name of Jesus.
10. Every aggression of the enemy against my prosperity; be paralyzed in the name of Jesus.
11. Shout 21 Halleluiah.
12. Every clever and hidden devourer, working in my life collapse and die in the name of Jesus.
13. Every witchcraft problem in my life come out and go back to your sender and destroy them in the name of Jesus.
14. Every defeat that I have ever suffered in the dream be converted to victory in the name of Jesus.
15. Fresh power of God, over shadow my life in the name of Jesus.
16. Almighty God open my spiritual ears and let me hear what you want me to hear in the name of Jesus.

17. Every internal failure in my life, come out in the name of Jesus.
18. Every seed of sorrow in my life come out in the name of Jesus.
19. Anything standing as problem in my life; fall down and die in the name of Jesus.
20. I bind and render to knot every evil counsel and imagination against my life, marriage and family in the name of Jesus.
21. Let the entrance door of poverty into my life be closed now in the name of Jesus.
22. I cancel every dreams, visions, prophesy and prayers against my life and family in the name of Jesus.
23. Talk to God about your heart desires and your situation.
24. Thank God for answered prayers.

Confession:

"The young lions do lack, and suffer hunger: but they that seek the Lord shall not want any good thing" Psalms 34:10.

Wisdom for Today:

"You are never too old to set another goal or to dream a new dream".

Read the Bible Today: John 9–10

Prayer Points:

1. Almighty God, break me and remold me, in Jesus name.
2. Almighty God, give me breakthroughs and miracles in all areas of my life, in Jesus name.
3. Almighty God by your power, I break out of every obstacle on my way to progress, in Jesus name.
4. Almighty God add flavor to my life, work, and marriage, in Jesus name.
5. Every witchcraft battle at the edge of my breakthroughs be defeated by the blood of Jesus.
6. Every power adding problem to my problem, what are you waiting for? die in the name of Jesus.
7. You doors of my prosperity, open now in the name of Jesus.
8. Let my enemies bow before me and congratulate me in the name of Jesus.
9. Almighty God, remove from my life every garment of suffering like you did for Joseph in the name of Jesus.
10. Any power that wants me to die, die for my sake in the name of Jesus.
11. Every owner of evil load; in my life, I command you to carry your load in the name of Jesus.
12. I will prosper and be in good health in this country in the name of Jesus.
13. This country is not complete without me; I shall possess my possession in the name of Jesus.
14. I will not cry in this country again in Jesus name.
15. Every power that does not want me to see the days of joy die in the name of Jesus.
16. I refuse to lose in the name of Jesus.

17. Witchcraft covenant upon my life, I command you to break in the name of Jesus.
18. Every general curse working against my life; break and release me in the name of Jesus.
19. Family evil strongman or woman; release my life by fire in the name of Jesus.
20. Water spirit I belong to Jesus, release me by fire, in the name of Jesus.
21. I cancel every dreams, visions, prophesy and prayers against my life and family in the name of Jesus.
22. Talk to God about your heart desires and your situation.
23. Thank God for answered prayers.

Confession:

"I have been young, and now am old; yet have not seen the righteous forsaken, nor his seed begging bread" Psalms 37:25.

Wisdom for Today:

"Where there is great love there are always miracles. Love does not claim possession, but gives freedom. Life without love is like a tree without blossoms or fruit".

Read the Bible Today: John 11–12

Prayer Points:

1. Almighty God, turn my weaknesses into strengths, in the name of Jesus.
2. Almighty God, confront my evil confronters and disgrace them, in the name of Jesus.
3. Almighty God, make me an instrument of blessings, in Jesus name.
4. I refuse to labor under any curse, in the name of Jesus.
5. I revoke every curse under which I labor, in Jesus name.
6. Any covenant binding me with marine spirit, break by the blood of Jesus in the name of Jesus.
7. Every curse upon my life as a result of the wickedness of my ancestors break and release me in the name of Jesus.
8. I forbid every storm in my life this year in the name of Jesus.
9. Every power destroying good things in my life; be destroyed by fire in the name of Jesus.
10. Every covenant of late blessing, break and release my life in the name of Jesus.
11. I am that I am, arise and manifest your power in my life in the name of Jesus.
12. I am that I am, arise and destroy my poverty in the name of Jesus.
13. I am that I am, arise and destroy the bondage in my family in the name of Jesus.
14. Blood of Jesus Christ speak better things to my life in the name of Jesus.
15. Anything that will take me away from divine protection, come out of my life and enter no more in the name of Jesus.

16. Almighty God, hold me up for I put my hope in you in the name of Jesus.
17. Almighty God, empower me for victory tonight in the name of Jesus.
18. Every operation of the enemies in my dreams; fail woefully in the name of Jesus.
19. Any manifestation of the enemy in my dream, I command you to be consumed by the fire of God in the name of Jesus.
20. Every appointment with weeping, I reject you in the name of Jesus.
21. I refuse to weep for the enemies to rejoice in the name of Jesus.
22. Any area of secret tears in my life, receive the touch of God's miracle in the name of Jesus.
23. I cancel every dreams, visions, prophesy and prayers against my life and family in the name of Jesus.
24. Talk to God about your heart desires and your situation.
25. Thank God for answered prayers.

Confession:

"When God bringeth back the captivity of his people, Jacob shall rejoice, and Israel shall be glad" Psalms 53:6.

Wisdom for Today:

"Courage doesn't always roar. Sometimes courage is the quiet voice at the end of the day saying, I will try again tomorrow".

Read the Bible Today: John 13–14

Prayer Points:

1. Every power that is causing warfare at the edge of my breakthroughs be defeated permanently by fire, in Jesus name.
2. Holy Ghost, connect me to my breakthroughs, in Jesus name.
3. No one shall pluck my stars out of my hands, in Jesus name.
4. No one shall pluck my stars out of my head, in Jesus name.
5. My glory shall not sink, in the name of Jesus.
6. Almighty God, go back to every second of my past and destroy anything that is causing problem in my life in the name of Jesus.
7. Almighty God, arise and nullify every word of human being that is manifesting in my life in the name of Jesus.
8. Almighty God enough of reproach in my life, my family, and ministry in the name of Jesus.
9. I cancel every evil dream by the blood of Jesus in the name of Jesus.
10. All my good dreams; be empowered for speedy manifestation in the name of Jesus.
11. Every power fuelling problems in my life your time is up; die in the name of Jesus.
12. I release myself from every curse working in my family in the name of Jesus.
13. Every spiritual dedication against me and my family; receive the stones of fire and die in the name of Jesus.
14. You messenger of death assigned against me and my family, go back to your sender in the name of Jesus.
15. Every evil wisdom working against, my breakthroughs; be disgraced in the name of Jesus.
16. I put every evil under my feet in the name of Jesus.

17. Thou power of sin and iniquity in my life, the Lord rebuke you, die in the name of Jesus.
18. Every evil desire in my life; the Lord rebuke you in the name of Jesus.
19. I cancel every dreams, visions, prophesy and prayers against my life and family in the name of Jesus.
20. Talk to God about your heart desires and your situation.
21. Thank God for answered prayers.

MAY 11

Confession:

"For God shall deliver the needy when he crieth; the poor also, and him that hath no helper" Psalms 72:12.

Wisdom for Today:

"Life is a succession of lessons which must be lived to be understood".

Read the Bible Today: John 15–16

Prayer Points:

1. Let the angels of God take evil attackers down to the grave, in the name of Jesus.
2. Let the rain of fire fall upon every army of wickedness against me, in Jesus name.
3. I close the entrance doors of problems; and I open the exit doors of blessings, in Jesus name.
4. I neutralize every satanic attention on my destiny, goodness, and marriage, in Jesus name.
5. I use the blood of Jesus to cancel every report brought against me in the kingdom of darkness, in Jesus name.
6. I am seated with Christ in the heavenly places, far above principalities and powers in the name of Jesus.
7. Anointing of deliverance fall upon me now in the name of Jesus.
8. Every power that pursued my parents and now pursuing me, what are you waiting for, die in the name of Jesus.
9. Every problem in the life of my parents that is now appearing in my life; vanish in the name of Jesus.
10. Every pillar of disgrace in my life, I pull you down in the name of Jesus.
11. Every evil preparation to disgrace me; be destroyed by fire in the name of Jesus.
12. Every power that has singled me out for affliction, Holy Ghost fire, locate and destroy them in the name of Jesus.
13. Every evil mark upon my body, wherever you are vanish in the name of Jesus.
14. Almighty God restore all my wasted years in the name of Jesus Christ.

15. Every power covering my glory, fall down and die in the name of Jesus.
16. You my glory arise and shine in the name of Jesus.
17. Every seed of the enemy in my life come out by fire in the name of Jesus.
18. Every seed of poverty in my life come out by fire in the name of Jesus.
19. I cancel every dreams, visions, prophesy and prayers against my life and family in the name of Jesus.
20. Talk to God about your heart desires and your situation.
21. Thank God for answered prayers.

Confession:

"For the Lord is a sun and shield: the Lord will give grace and glory: no good thing will he withhold from them that walk uprightly"
Psalms 84:11.

Wisdom for Today:

"As far as we can discern, the sole purpose of human existence is to kindle a light in the darkness of mere being".

Read the Bible Today: John 17–18

Prayer Points:

1. I claim unending favor, in Jesus name.
2. I claim encompassing favor, in Jesus name.
3. I refuse to turn into a beggar, in Jesus name.
4. I shall not run mad, in Jesus name.
5. I shall not walk naked, in Jesus name.
6. Every evil burial for my sake, be destroyed by fire in the name of Jesus.
7. I break the power of death over my life in the name of Jesus.
8. Every hold of the enemy over my blood break by fire in the name of Jesus.
9. Every messenger of death on assignment against me and my family, die in the name of Jesus.
10. Good dreams in my life, hear the word of God, come alive and manifest in the name of Jesus.
11. Every weapon of demotion fashioned against my life, scatter in the name of Jesus.
12. By the spirit of prophecy, I send back every evil arrow fired against my life, go back to your sender in the name of Jesus.
13. Anything packaged to destroy my joy in this country be destroyed by fire in the name of Jesus.
14. Foundation of sorrow in my life; be broken to pieces in the name of Jesus.
15. I proclaim that my joy shall last forever in the name of Jesus.
16. Evil deposit in my life, and body your time is up, come out in the name of Jesus.

17. Every attempt to cover my glory; be frustrated in the name of Jesus.
18. I cancel every dreams, visions, prophesy and prayers against my life and family in the name of Jesus.
19. Talk to God about your heart desires and your situation.
20. Thank God for answered prayers.

Confession:

"The Lord is a man of war: the Lord is his name" Exodus 15:3.

Wisdom for Today:

"Begin each day as if it were on purpose".

Read the Bible Today: John 19–20

Prayer Points:

1. I cancel every accusation brought against me in the kingdom of darkness, in the name of Jesus.
2. I revoke and nullify every negative judgment passed upon me and my marriage, in Jesus name.
3. I forbid evil hands to perform their work upon my destiny, in Jesus name.
4. I cut off the power supplying my enemies with energy, in Jesus name.
5. You workers of iniquity depart from my destiny, in the name of Jesus.
6. Every evil power monitoring the gates of my prosperity why are you still alive, I command you to die in Jesus name.
7. Every evil arrow fired to useless my life, come out and go back to your sender in the name of Jesus.
8. Spirit of poverty come out of my life and enter no more in the name of Jesus.
9. Any power that is making my family to suffer your time is up, die in the name of Jesus.
10. I shall not answer the call of any evil spirit in the name of Jesus Christ.
11. Every power hired to curse me, curse my destiny, what are you waiting for, die in the name of Jesus.
12. Any power or covenant of my father's house that wants to waste my life and calling, die in the name of Jesus.
13. Stubborn pursuers of my life hear the word of the Lord; die in the name of Jesus.
14. Every evil stamp of the enemy; be removed in the name of Jesus.
15. Almighty God; turn my failures to success in the name of Jesus.

16. Every gate in this nation shot against me, open now in the name of Jesus.
17. Every curse that is delaying good things in my life; break and release me in the name of Jesus.
18. Every evil spirit of this world attached to my life, I cut you off in the name of Jesus.
19. Spirit of God, reign in my life in the name of Jesus.
20. I cancel every dreams, visions, prophesy and prayers against my life and family in the name of Jesus.
21. Talk to God about your heart desires and your situation.
22. Thank God for answered prayers.

Confession:

"Yea, the Lord shall give that which is good; and our land shall yield her increase" Psalms 85:12.

Wisdom for Today:

"At the end of a matter ask, 'what will I learn from this to make me better?'.

Read the Bible Today: John 21

Prayer Points:

1. I am a winner; I shall never be a loser, in Jesus name.
2. I will always go up; I shall not go down, in Jesus name.
3. I throw my problems into the fire of God, in Jesus name.
4. Let every opposition against me be turned to favor, in Jesus name.
5. I refuse to live an unfulfilled life, in the name of Jesus.
6. Almighty God, teach my hand to war in the name of Jesus.
7. Almighty God, arise and prevail over my enemies in Jesus name.
8. Let the wicked and their wickedness be consumed by fire in the name of Jesus.
9. Let every stubborn enemy that has risen against me; be defeated now in the name of Jesus.
10. By the power of the Holy Ghost, I destroy the enemies and their work in my life in the name of Jesus.
11. Let the dwelling place of my enemies come to nothing, and let those who hate me be put to shame in the name of Jesus.
12. Let every weapon of my enemies back fire and destroy them in the name of Jesus.
13. Almighty God, reveal to me the secret of becoming a winner in life in the name of Jesus.
14. Blood of Jesus, make way for me today in the name of Jesus.
15. Let the power of God clear way for my prayers today in the name of Jesus.
16. Let the angels of God come to my aid, support me tonight in the name of Jesus.
17. Holy Ghost, arise in your power deliver me from my tight places in the name of Jesus.
18. Shout fire of deliverance fall on me... 7 times.
19. Evil dreams depart from my life in the name of Jesus.

20. Every power of darkness polluting and attacking my dreams; be arrested by fire in the name of Jesus.
21. By the blood of Jesus, I cancel every effect of evil dreams in my life in the name of Jesus.
22. Every messenger of death in this church; depart and enter no more in the name of Jesus.
23. I cancel every dreams, visions, prophesy and prayers against my life and family in the name of Jesus.
24. Talk to God about your heart desires and your situation.
25. Thank God for answered prayers.

Confession:

"Thou shall arise, and have mercy upon Zion: for the time to favor her, yea, the set time, is come" Psalms 102:13.

Wisdom for Today:

"Consider calling it a challenge rather than calling it a crisis or problem".

Read the Bible Today: Psalm 34

Prayer Points:

1. I shall not spend my life in lack and want, in the name of Jesus.
2. Almighty God you are the God of performance, perform wonders in my life, in the name of Jesus.
3. Almighty God, perform my expectations, in Jesus name.
4. Let my enemies bow and submit that which is mine unto me, in the name of Jesus.
5. I shall dwell in a fertile land where the blessings of the Lord abound, in Jesus name.
6. Every evil power that is holding me down, die in the name of Jesus.
7. I move from nothing to something good in the name of Jesus.
8. In this country I shall not be disgraced in the name of Jesus.
9. In this country I shall not be put to shame, I shall not be disgraced in the name of Jesus.
10. Every attack in my dream that is now affecting my life be reversed in the name of Jesus.
11. Evil arrows from my dream come out and go back to sender in the name of Jesus.
12. Powers from my father's house and mother's house begin to attack yourself in Jesus name.
13. Almighty God, I need a break in this country in the name of Jesus.
14. Almighty God, heal me from every area that I have been wounded in the name of Jesus.
15. Every power bent on seeing my destiny destroyed, Holy Ghost fire locate and destroy them in the name of Jesus.
16. My ears shall hear good news, my eyes shall see good things, and my hands shall possess good things in the name of Jesus.

Apostle A.O. Solomon

17. Almighty God, arise quickly and deliver me from shame in the name of Jesus.
18. Evil arrows my body is not for you in the name of Jesus.
19. Every owner of evil load in my life, carry your load in the name of Jesus.
20. I shall not be wasted; I shall not be useless in the name of Jesus.
21. Every power affecting my joy, lose your power and die in the name of Jesus.
22. I shall not bury my children in the name of Jesus.
23. Every dry bone in my life, receive the touch of resurrection and live in the name of Jesus.
24. I cancel every dreams, visions, prophesy and prayers against my life and family in the name of Jesus.
25. Talk to God about your heart desires and your situation.
26. Thank God for answered prayers.

Confession:

"The bows of the mighty men are broken, and they that stumbled are girded with strength" 1 Samuel 2:4.

Wisdom for Today:

"We must be willing to get rid of the life we've planned, so as to have the life that is waiting for us".

Read the Bible Today: Jeremiah 1–2

Prayer Points:

1. Almighty God I turn my heart to you completely, in Jesus name.
2. Almighty God let me love what you love, and hate what you hate, in Jesus name.
3. Almighty God, deliver me from the will of the enemies, in Jesus name.
4. I bind and destroy every controlling power of lack, in Jesus name.
5. Almighty God, teach me how to spend my money, in Jesus name.
6. Every good door that has been closed, lift up your heads and let the King of glory come in, in Jesus name.
7. Almighty God, arise in your mercy and close the old chapter in my life in the name of Jesus.
8. Every word of the enemy waiting for manifestation in my life, die in the name of Jesus.
9. Every maturity date of evil words and prophesies in my life, be nullified in the name of Jesus.
10. I fire back, every arrow of evil prophecy that is pursuing my life in Jesus name.
11. Every satanic assignment, I reject you in my life in the name of Jesus.
12. Every power demanding tears from my eyes before receiving my blessings, die in the name of Jesus.
13. Every power sponsoring weeping in my family; carry your load and die in the name of Jesus.
14. Every witchcraft cage caging my destiny, break by the fire of God in the name of Jesus.
15. Almighty God, deliver me from the strife of tongue in the name of Jesus.

16. I cancel every dreams, visions, prophesy and prayers against my life and family in the name of Jesus.
17. Talk to God about your heart desires and your situation.
18. Thank God for answered prayers.

Confession:

"Who satisfieth thy mouth with good things; so that thy youth is renewed like the eagles" Psalms 103:5.

Wisdom for Today:

"The old skin has to be shed before the new one can come".

Read the Bible Today: Isaiah 43

Prayer Points:

1. My divine daily allocation will not miss me, in the name of Jesus.
2. I receive my angelic distribution and portion, in Jesus name.
3. Almighty God, make me a positive wonder unto my generation, in the name of Jesus.
4. By the power of God, I command the day to favor me, in Jesus name.
5. Dark places shall not oppress me, in the name of Jesus.
6. Evil arrows go back to your sender in the name of Jesus.
7. Every attack of eaters of flesh and drinkers of blood, back fire in the name of Jesus.
8. I withdraw my blood from witchcraft altar in the name of Jesus.
9. Anything representing me in any kingdom of darkness, I withdraw you by fire in the name of Jesus.
10. I walk out of the prison of evil dreams in the name of Jesus.
11. Every dream of backwardness in my life die in the name of Jesus.
12. Any power using anything in my past to torment me, die in the name of Jesus.
13. By the blood of Jesus, I register my name for solution today in the name of Jesus.
14. I shall not serve my enemies and I shall not serve my friends in the name of Jesus.
15. I disagree with every satanic decision over my life in the name of Jesus.
16. I cancel every former and present agreement with the spirit of Egypt in the name of Jesus.
17. Every agreement with the power of the air, I command you to break in the name of Jesus.

18. I recover every blessing I have lost to spirit of Egypt in the name of Jesus.
19. Almighty God, deliver me from every problem I have brought upon myself in the name of Jesus.
20. I reject every invitation to bondage in the name of Jesus.
21. I cancel every dreams, visions, prophesy and prayers against my life and family in the name of Jesus.
22. Talk to God about your heart desires and your situation.
23. Thank God for answered prayers.

Confession:

"Save now, I beseech thee, O Lord: O Lord, I beseech thee, send now prosperity" Psalms 118:25.

Wisdom for Today:

"Use the power of your word in the direction of truth and love".

Read the Bible Today: Jeremiah 3–4

Prayer Points:

1. Almighty God, empower me to tap into your limitless power, in Jesus name.
2. Almighty God, empower me to tap into your limitless blessings, in Jesus name.
3. I cancel every satanic appointment, in the name of Jesus.
4. As I go out today, I shall not enter into bondage, in the name of Jesus.
5. As I go out today, I shall not encounter any problem, in Jesus name.
6. Almighty God, give me power to overcome pressures in life in the name of Jesus.
7. Almighty God, make me a good sign and use me for your glory in the name of Jesus.
8. By the anointing of the Holy Ghost, I leap over every negative situation surrounding me in the name of Jesus.
9. My soul hopes and wait on the Lord, for you God is gracious in the name of Jesus.
10. I shall not fail in the name of Jesus.
11. Almighty God I commit my life to you; organize my scattered life in the name of Jesus.
12. Almighty God, change my story as you did Jabez in the name of Jesus.
13. I reject automatic failure in my life in the name of Jesus.
14. Every enemy of divine presence in my life, I command you to die in the name of Jesus.
15. Anointing to excel above all my family members fall upon me now in the name of Jesus.

16. I shall experience divine favor throughout the days of my life in Jesus name.
17. Holy Spirit; coordinate me in the name of Jesus.
18. Arrows of the enemy you shall not locate me, go back to your sender in the name of Jesus.
19. Power to sin no more, fall upon me now in the name of Jesus.
20. I put the yoke of Jesus Christ upon myself in the name of Jesus.
21. God shall help me and fight for me in the name of Jesus.
22. I shall not lose my job in the name of Jesus.
23. My source of money shall not be blocked in the name of Jesus.
24. Throughout this month I shall be blessed and highly favored in the name of Jesus.
25. I cancel every dreams, visions, prophesy and prayers against my life and family in the name of Jesus.
26. Talk to God about your heart desires and your situation.
27. Thank God for answered prayers.

Confession:

"He will keep the feet of the saints, and the wicked shall be silent in darkness; for by strength shall no man prevail" 1 Samuel 2:9.

Wisdom for Today:

"Your worst enemy cannot harm you as much as your own unguarded thoughts".

Read the Bible Today: Jeremiah 5–6

Prayer Points:

1. As I go out today, I shall not see or experience evil, in Jesus name.
2. As I go out today, I shall not experience accident or tragedy, in Jesus name.
3. As I go out today, I will not fall into any evil trap, in the name of Jesus.
4. Almighty God, make me a living oracle for signs and wonders in this generation, in the name of Jesus.
5. I overthrow disappointment, in the name of Jesus.
6. Where there is no way for others, there shall be way for me this month in the name of Jesus.
7. I reject death in my family and church in the name of Jesus.
8. Almighty God let your hand be upon me for good throughout this month in the name of Jesus.
9. Almighty God, do not give me up to the desires of my enemies in the name of Jesus.
10. Evil shall not prevail against me and my family in the name of Jesus.
11. Sin shall not rule over me in the name of Jesus.
12. Every good thing my hands have started, my hands shall complete in the name of Jesus.
13. My head hear the word of the Lord; you shall not be bewitched in the name of Jesus.
14. I shall not become what my enemies want me to be in the name of Jesus.
15. O God of Abraham, Isaac, and Jacobl rearrange this country to favor me in the name of Jesus.

16. Every completed work of my enemies over my life; be destroyed with all your effects in the name of Jesus.
17. I cancel every dreams, visions, prophesy and prayers against my life and family in the name of Jesus.
18. Talk to God about your heart desires and your situation.
19. Thank God for answered prayers.

Confession:

"From henceforth, let no man trouble me: for I bear in my body the marks of the Lord Jesus" Galatians 6:17.

Wisdom for Today:

"Discover the tools to build your own vision".

Read the Bible Today: *Jeremiah 7–8*

Prayer Points:

1. Let all arranged and sudden death targeted at me backfire, in Jesus name.
2. I position myself to receive blessings, in the name of Jesus.
3. Let God be instrumental in my affairs, in the name of Jesus.
4. The devil shall not prosper over my spirit, soul, and body, in Jesus name.
5. The devil shall not prosper over my finances, in Jesus name.
6. I break and lose myself from the stronghold of darkness in the name of Jesus.
7. Any power that wants to replace my peace with war, die suddenly in the name of Jesus.
8. By the blood of Jesus Christ, I rise above all limitation in life in the name of Jesus.
9. Almighty God reign supreme in my life in the name of Jesus.
10. Almighty God set me free from poverty in the name of Jesus.
11. By the power in the word of God, I command every darkness in my life to vanish in the name of Jesus.
12. Every step by step work of the enemy in my life; be destroyed in the name of Jesus.
13. Every perfected works of the enemy in my life; be over turned by the blood of Jesus in the name of Jesus.
14. Every evil altar in my family working against my glory be consumed by fire in the name of Jesus.
15. Every good thing the enemy scattered in my life, come together in the name of Jesus.
16. Every power and spirit that has set my life for affliction, I bind you in the name of Jesus.

17. I cancel every dreams, visions, prophesy and prayers against my life and family in the name of Jesus.
18. Talk to God about your heart desires and your situation.
19. Thank God for answered prayers.

Confession:

"The Lord hath been mindful of us: he will bless us; he will bless the house of Israel; he will bless the house of Aaron. He will bless them that fear the Lord, both small and old. The Lord shall increase me more and more, I and my children. We are blessed of the Lord which made heaven and earth" Psalms 115:12–15.

Wisdom for Today:

"Believe that life is worth living and your belief will help create the fact".

Read the Bible Today: Jeremiah 9–10

Prayer Points:

1. I reverse all curses released against my prosperity, in Jesus name.
2. Almighty God, empower me to rise and shine, in the name of Jesus.
3. Financial bankruptcy is not my portion, in Jesus name.
4. Let every evil pillar supporting my problems crumble now, in Jesus name.
5. My hands shall not befriend poverty, in the name of Jesus.
6. In the name of Jesus, my life shall not follow satanic agenda in the name of Jesus.
7. Almighty God, it is time, give me rest comfort me, and prosper me in the name of Jesus.
8. By the blood of Jesus, I register my name for solution today in the name of Jesus.
9. I connect myself with the power of God in the name of Jesus.
10. Every pillar of witchcraft in my family, what are you waiting for? I pull you down in the name of Jesus.
11. Witchcraft powers why are you pursuing my life? die in the name of Jesus.
12. It is suffer not a witch to live, therefore any witchcraft pursuing my life, I command you to die in the name of Jesus.
13. I disagree with failure in the name of Jesus.
14. Failure at the edge of good things, depart from my life by the blood of Jesus in the name of Jesus.
15. Witchcraft battle at the edge of my success return to your sender in the name of Jesus.

16. Every evil seed planted by the enemy in my life, be uprooted by fire in the name of Jesus.
17. Every plantation of darkness in my life, come out with all your roots in the name of Jesus.
18. Every evil seed planted into my life through dreams, be uprooted by fire in the name of Jesus.
19. I challenge my system with the fire of God, in the name of Jesus.
20. Every instrument of satanic control in my life, wherever you are, be destroyed by fire in the name of Jesus.
21. Arrows of darkness in my life come out of your hiding places and go back to your sender in the name of Jesus.
22. I cancel every dreams, visions, prophesy and prayers against my life and family in the name of Jesus.
23. Talk to God about your heart desires and your situation.
24. Thank God for answered prayers.

Confession:

"The Lord God is my strength, and he will make my feet like hinds' feet, and he will make me to walk upon my high places" Habakkuk 3:19.

Wisdom for Today:

"Holding on to anger is like grasping a hot coal with the intent of throwing it at someone else; you are the one who gets burned".

Read the Bible Today: Jeremiah 11–12

Prayer Points:

1. The devil shall not prosper over my marriage, in Jesus name.
2. The devil shall not prosper over my destiny, career, and education, in Jesus name.
3. The devil shall not prosper over my thoughts, in Jesus name.
4. The devil shall not prosper over my children, in Jesus name.
5. I refuse to follow an evil cycle, in the name of Jesus.
6. As from today, life shall be easy for me in the name of Jesus.
7. By the blood of Jesus, I stand in gap for every member of my family in the name of Jesus.
8. Every member of my family that is appointed for death be redeemed by the blood of Jesus in the name of Jesus.
9. Any power that wants to attack me, Holy Ghost fire attack and destroy them in the name of Jesus.
10. Arrows of madness fired against me and any member of my family, gather yourself together and go back to your sender in the name of Jesus.
11. All those in the system of this country that will not favor me, O Lord replace them with people that will favor me in the name of Jesus.
12. All those who are boasting to fire me in my place of work, let the Holy Ghost fire, fire them in the name of Jesus.
13. Every evil register containing my name, Holy Ghost fire consume them in the name of Jesus.
14. Every broom of darkness sweeping good things away from my life, catch fire in the name of Jesus.

15. Angel of the living God; begin to sweep back all my blessings in the name of Jesus.
16. Every spirit of laboring without achievement; be destroyed in the name of Jesus.
17. I hold the hammer of the word of God and command every padlock ministering evil against my life, break in the name of Jesus.
18. With the garment of fire and power in the blood of Jesus, I enter the strong room of the enemy and collect all my blessing in the name of Jesus.
19. I cancel every dreams, visions, prophesy and prayers against my life and family in the name of Jesus.
20. Talk to God about your heart desires and your situation.
21. Thank God for answered prayers.

Confession:

"That we should be saved from our enemies, and from the hand of all that hate us" Luke 1:71.

Wisdom for Today:

"You will not be punished for your anger; you will be punished by your anger".

Read the Bible Today: *Jeremiah 13–14*

Prayer Points:

1. I reject the spirit of disobedience to God's word, in the name of Jesus.
2. I refuse to be a victim of an evil altar, in the name of Jesus.
3. I refuse to follow evil advice, in the name of Jesus.
4. I conquer the power and forces of the night, in the name of Jesus.
5. I reverse all curses released against my prosperity, in Jesus name.
6. I go with the Lord Jesus and the Holy Ghost fire into every witchcraft coven and collect my blessings in the name of Jesus.
7. Any man or woman, attending witchcraft meeting because of me, you shall not return in the name of Jesus.
8. Anyone calling my name for evil in the night, angel of God; slap them in the name of Jesus.
9. Every night captivity in my life, break in the name of Jesus.
10. Anything done against me in the night; be destroyed by fire in the name of Jesus.
11. Every satanic power appearing in my dream, the Lord rebuke you perish in the name of Jesus.
12. Any fire that the enemy has lighted against me and my family be quenched by the blood of Jesus.
13. Every evil pot caging anything good in my life, break by thunder in the name of Jesus.
14. Almighty God put upon me now your garment of mercy, and favor me in the name of Jesus.
15. My spirit man, my body, my soul hear the word of the Lord you shall not answer the call of the enemy day or night in the name of Jesus.
16. Let the voice of God thunder against my enemies and divide them in the name of Jesus.

17. Let the voice of God, divide the fire of my enemy and destroy them in the name of Jesus.
18. Let the voice of God, shake down the camp of my enemies in the name of Jesus
19. Almighty God cloth me with mercy and compassion in the name of Jesus.
20. I cancel every dreams, visions, prophesy and prayers against my life and family in the name of Jesus.
21. Talk to God about your heart desires and your situation.
22. Thank God for answered prayers.

Confession:

"For I shall eat the labor of mine hands; happy shall I be, and it shall be well with me" Psalms 128:2.

Wisdom for Today:

"If the only prayer you ever say in your entire life is thank you, it will be enough".

Read the Bible Today: *Jeremiah 15–16*

Prayer Points:

1. Wherever I appear, let failure disappear, in Jesus name.
2. Wherever I appear, let oppression disappear, in Jesus name.
3. I will not weep so that my enemies can rejoice, in the name of Jesus.
4. I will not bow to any storm in life in Jesus name.
5. I receive an arrow-proof jacket against the arrows of the enemy, in Jesus name.
6. Almighty God, empower my hands to profit in the name of Jesus.
7. Every attack against my labor, break and release me in the name of Jesus.
8. Every curse of the enemy against the works of my hands, break by the blood of Jesus in the name of Jesus.
9. Every physical and spiritual chain upon my hands, break in the name of Jesus.
10. Thou son of David use your key, and set me free from hand cuffs and chains in the name of Jesus.
11. Jesus set me free; I am free indeed in the name of Jesus.
12. I drink the blood of Jesus, and cover myself with the blood of Jesus in the name of Jesus.
13. Any power that wants to destroy the works of God in my life, Holy Ghost fire; destroy them in the name of Jesus.
14. Every satanic bondage from evil dreams programmed into my life; break and release me in the name of Jesus.
15. Every sickness introduced into my life as a result of evil dreams die now in the name of Jesus.
16. Every dream of failure in my past be reversed in the name of Jesus.

17. Every witchcraft power pursuing me in the dream fall down and die in the name of Jesus.
18. Almighty, God make me holy by your power in the name of Jesus.
19. Every satanic dream attached to my progress, die in the name of Jesus.
20. I come out of every dream prison by the power of the Holy Ghost in the name of Jesus.
21. I fire back every witchcraft arrow fired into my dream in the name of Jesus.
22. Every evil dream of the past affecting my life now, die in the name of Jesus.
23. I cancel every dreams, visions, prophesy and prayers against my life and family in the name of Jesus.
24. Talk to God about your heart desires and your situation.
25. Thank God for answered prayers.

Confession:

"I will lift up mine eyes unto the hills, from whence cometh my help. My help cometh from the Lord which made heaven and earth" Psalms 121:1–2.

Wisdom for Today:

"Life is not about waiting for the storms to pass, it's about learning how to dance in the rain." —Author Unknown

Read the Bible Today: Jeremiah 17–18

Prayer Points:

1. I receive bullet-proof jacket against the bullets of the enemy, in Jesus name.
2. Let my presence confuse my opponents, in Jesus name.
3. Almighty God rearrange this country to favor me, in the name of Jesus.
4. Any evil tree harboring my virtue, dry up to the root, in the name of Jesus.
5. I silence every oracle speaking against my destiny, in Jesus name.
6. Every witchcraft serpent attacking me in the dream, return to your sender and destroy them in the name of Jesus.
7. Every dream affecting my life, marriage, and career lose your power and die in the name of Jesus.
8. Every good thing I have lost in the dream I repossess you back in Jesus name.
9. Every agent of darkness in my dream life, I command you to die in the name of Jesus.
10. Every evil pronouncement against me in the dream it shall not stand, and neither shall it come to pass in the name of Jesus.
11. My resting time shall not be a trouble time in the name of Jesus.
12. Any power, spirit, and personality that wants to trouble me, my God shall trouble you in the name of Jesus.
13. Life shall not be difficult for me in the name of Jesus.
14. I reject every form of nakedness physically and spiritually in the name of Jesus.
15. I reject every form of disorder in the name of Jesus.

16. My family and I shall be for signs and wonders in the name of Jesus.
17. As the Lord God lives, people will see the good work of God in my life in Jesus name.
18. Almighty God, bless all those that will bless me, and for those that curse me let their curse return unto them in Jesus name.
19. Every completed work of the enemy over my life; be destroyed with all your power in the name of Jesus.
20. I plead the blood of Jesus against every voice speaking against my destiny in the name of Jesus.
21. I cancel every dreams, visions, prophesy and prayers against my life and family in the name of Jesus.
22. Talk to God about your heart desires and your situation.
23. Thank God for answered prayers.

Confession:

"The Lord shall bless me out of Zion: and I shall see the good of Jerusalem all the days of my life" Psalms 128:5.

Wisdom for Today:

"Life may not be the party we hoped for, but while we are here we might as well dance".

Read the Bible Today: Jeremiah 19–20

Prayer Points:

1. Every entrance of satanic influence on my life; be closed by the blood of Jesus in the name of Jesus.
2. Let the blood of Jesus redeem all my lost ground, in the name of Jesus.
3. Almighty God awake to my plight today, in the name of Jesus.
4. Almighty God, rebuke the devourer of my finances, in the name of Jesus.
5. Almighty God; help me to be faithful in tithes and in offerings, in Jesus name.
6. Every owner of evil load in my life, wherever you are appear and carry your load in Jesus name.
7. I plead the blood of Jesus over everything the devil is holding against me in the name of Jesus.
8. Jesus Christ of Nazareth I belong to you, I disconnect from the iniquity of my ancestors in the name of Jesus.
9. Every ancestral oat that is affecting my life, break now by the blood of Jesus in the name of Jesus.
10. Every evil word that is pursuing my destiny, the Lord rebuke you; turn back in the name of Jesus.
11. Every prophecy demoting my life; lose your hold and die in the name of Jesus.
12. Evil family pattern, break and release me by fire in the name Jesus.
13. Every evil water flowing in my family, dry up by fire in the name of Jesus.
14. Family bondage affecting my life, break in the name of Jesus.

Apostle A.O. Solomon

15. Ancestral evil covenant, I separate myself from you now in the name of Jesus.
16. Every evil register containing my name, be roasted by fire in the name of Jesus.
17. I cancel every dreams, visions, prophesy and prayers against my life and family in the name of Jesus.
18. Talk to God about your heart desires and your situation.
19. Thank God for answered prayers.

Confession:

"And the God of peace shall bruise Satan under my feet shortly. The grace of our Lord Jesus Christ be with me. Amen!" Romans 16:20

Wisdom for Today:

"In the end, it's not the years in your life that count. It's the life in your years."

Read the Bible Today: *Jeremiah 21–22*

Prayer Points:

1. Anything that does not work with the heavenly programs in my life, come out and enter no more, in Jesus name.
2. Almighty God, turn my frustrations into fulfillment, in the name of Jesus.
3. I refuse to carry any evil burden, in the name of Jesus.
4. Anyone who carried an evil burden into my life, carry your burden away now, in the name of Jesus.
5. Almighty God, plant your fear and honor into me, in the name of Jesus.
6. Almighty God, arise and fight for me with jealousy in the name of Jesus.
7. Almighty God I thank you because I will not see trouble throughout this month in the name of Jesus.
8. Every storm prepared for me and my family; be diverted away in the name of Jesus.
9. Every mark of bewitchment upon my life; lose your power and be erased in the name of Jesus.
10. Every evil hand writing upon my life; be erased in the name of Jesus.
11. Every witchcraft operation in my life, family, and church; die in the name of Jesus.
12. Every power attacking me from the land of the dead; die the second time in the name of Jesus.
13. Almighty God, use my life to confuse the enemy in the name of Jesus.
14. Every appointment with death this month; I reject you in the name of Jesus.

Apostle A.O. Solomon

15. Every pillar of sorrow in my life; I pull you down in the name of Jesus.
16. Anything standing as a pillar of sorrow in this country in my life; I pull you down in the name of Jesus.
17. O thou that troubled my Israel be pulled down now in the name of Jesus.
18. I cancel every dreams, visions, prophesy and prayers against my life and family in the name of Jesus.
19. Talk to God about your heart desires and your situation.
20. Thank God for answered prayers.

Confession:

"When the lord turned again the captivity of Zion, we were like them that dream" Psalms 126:1.

Wisdom for Today:

"Life is a sum of all your choices. Our joy comes from living our own lives simply and gratefully—never from making any demands whatsoever upon others".

Read the Bible Today: Jeremiah 23–24

Prayer Points:

1. I must fulfill my divine agenda, in the name of Jesus.
2. Almighty God, turn my weakness into strength, in Jesus name.
3. My Israel will not bow for Pharaoh, in the name of Jesus.
4. I cancel every evil dream from coming to pass in my life, in Jesus name.
5. My name shall not be removed from the mind of my helpers, in the name of Jesus.
6. Almighty God, bless all my helpers, favor them, and let them remember me for good today, in the name of Jesus.
7. I reject tragedy and calamity throughout this month in the name of Jesus.
8. Sorrow shall not branch in my dwelling place throughout this month in the name of Jesus.
9. I shall not carry any evil load throughout this month in the name of Jesus.
10. Every maturity day of affliction; be nullified by the blood of Jesus.
11. Every incantation against me; be cancelled in the name of Jesus.
12. Every owner of evil load in my life, appear and carry your load in the name of Jesus.
13. Every perfected work of the enemy over my life; die in the name of Jesus.
14. By the Blood of Jesus, I receive freedom from every financial bondage in the name of Jesus.
15. You spirit of frustration I reject you in my life in the name of Jesus.
16. I refuse to be wasted, any power that wants to waste my life be wasted in the name of Jesus.

17. Every waster of my prosperity wherever you are; be arrested in the name of Jesus.
18. Every aggression of the enemy against my prosperity; be paralyzed in the name of Jesus.
19. Shout 21 Halleluiah.
20. I cancel every dreams, visions, prophesy and prayers against my life and family in the name of Jesus.
21. Talk to God about your heart desires and your situation.
22. Thank God for answered prayers.

Confession:

"For I, saith the Lord, will be unto her a wall of fire round about and I will be the glory in the midst of her" Zechariah 3:19".

Wisdom for Today:

"You don't have the power to make life 'fair,' but you do have the power to make life joyful".

Read the Bible Today: *Jeremiah 25–26*

Prayer Points:

1. Let every Jericho fall before me today, in the name of Jesus.
2. Almighty God let me hear from you in specific details, in Jesus name.
3. Every word I hear from you, Lord, will empower me, in the name of Jesus.
4. No weapon formed against my destiny shall prosper, in Jesus name.
5. Almighty God you who began a good work in me, will complete it, in the name of Jesus.
6. My blessings you shall not be stagnant locate me in the name of Jesus.
7. Every clever and hidden devourer, working in my life collapse and die in the name of Jesus.
8. Every evil handshake of poverty, I reject you in the name of Jesus.
9. Every witchcraft problem in my life come out, go back to your sender and destroy them in the name of Jesus.
10. Every defeat that I have ever suffered in the dream; be converted to victory in the name of Jesus.
11. Fresh power of God, over shadow my life in the name of Jesus.
12. Almighty God open my spiritual ears and let me hear what you want me to hear in the name of Jesus.
13. Every internal failure in my life, come out in the name of Jesus.
14. Every seed of sorrow in my life come out in the name of Jesus.
15. Anything standing as problem in my life; fall down and die in the name of Jesus.
16. I bind and render to knot every evil counsel and imagination against my life, marriage and family in the name of Jesus.

Apostle A.O. Solomon

17. Let the entrance door of poverty into my life be closed now in the name of Jesus.
18. Every power adding problem to my problem, what are you waiting for? die in the name of Jesus.
19. I cancel every dreams, visions, prophesy and prayers against my life and family in the name of Jesus.
20. Talk to God about your heart desires and your situation.
21. Thank God for answered prayers.

Confession:

"For the Lord my God brings me into a good land, a land of brooks of water" Deuteronomy 8:9.

Wisdom for Today:

"Joy increases and suffering decreases as one masters the distinction between events and one's feelings about those events".

Read the Bible Today: Jeremiah 27–28

Prayer Points:

1. I will accomplish that which the Lord has ordained for my life, in Jesus name.
2. Almighty God I declare that it shall be unto me according to your word in Psalms 68:19 today, in the name of Jesus.
3. As one redeemed by the Lord, I will reign in the kingdom of men, in the name of Jesus.
4. I command every right of satanic harassment to break now, in Jesus name.
5. Almighty God , baptize me with your power today, in Jesus name.
6. You doors of my prosperity, open now in the name of Jesus.
7. Let my enemies bow before me and congratulate me in the name of Jesus.
8. Almighty God, remove from my life every garment of suffering like you did for Joseph in the name of Jesus.
9. Any power that wants me to die, die for my sake in the name of Jesus.
10. Every owner of evil load; in my life, I command you to carry your load in the name of Jesus.
11. I will prosper and be in good health in this country in the name of Jesus.
12. This country is not complete without me; I shall possess my possession in the name of Jesus.
13. I prophesy I will not cry in this country again in Jesus name.
14. Every power that does not want me to see the days of joy; die in the name of Jesus.
15. I refuse to lose in the name of Jesus.

Apostle A.O. Solomon

16. Witchcraft covenant upon my life, I command you to break in the name of Jesus.
17. Every general curse working against my life; break and release me in the name of Jesus.
18. Family evil strongman or woman; release my life by fire in the name of Jesus.
19. Water spirit release me by fire, I belong to Jesus in the name of Jesus.
20. Any covenant binding me with marine spirit, break by the blood of Jesus in the name of Jesus.
21. Every curse upon my life as a result of the wickedness of my ancestors; break and release me in the name of Jesus.
22. I cancel every dreams, visions, prophesy and prayers against my life and family in the name of Jesus.
23. Talk to God about your heart desires and your situation.
24. Thank God for answered prayers.

Confession:

"He hath swallowed down riches, and he shall vomit them up again. God shall cast them out of his belly" Job 20:15.

Wisdom for Today:

"Be a passionate Observer of Life. See the events, feel the emotions, and recognize the difference".

Read the Bible Today: Jeremiah 29–30

Prayer Points:

1. Almighty God, baptize me with your fire today, in the name of Jesus.
2. Almighty God, go to the foundation of any problem in my life, and defeat it, in Jesus name.
3. Every problem attached to my family name, be neutralized, in the name of Jesus.
4. Every power that has swallowed my blessings, vomit my blessings now, in the name of Jesus.
5. Every problem that stands as Pharaoh in my life be defeated by the power of God, in the name of Jesus.
6. Let the enemies vomit all my blessings today, in the name of Jesus.
7. Every curse standing in the way of my children's blessing, break in the name of Jesus.
8. I forbid every storm in my life this year in the name of Jesus.
9. Every power destroying good things in my life; be destroyed by fire in the name of Jesus.
10. Every covenant of late blessing, break and release my life in the name of Jesus.
11. I am that I am, arise and manifest your power in my life in the name of Jesus.
12. I am that I am, arise and destroy my poverty in the name of Jesus.
13. I am that I am, arise and destroy the bondage in my family in the name of Jesus.
14. Blood of Jesus Christ speak better things to my life in the name of Jesus.

Apostle A.O. Solomon

15. Anything that will take me away from divine protection, come out of my life and enter no more in the name of Jesus.
16. Almighty God, hold me up for I put my hope in you in the name of Jesus.
17. Almighty God, empower me for victory tonight in the name of Jesus.
18. Every operation of the enemies in my dreams; fail woefully in the name of Jesus.
19. Any manifestation of the enemy in my dream, I command you to be consumed by fire in the name of Jesus.
20. Every appointment with weeping, I reject you in the name of Jesus.
21. I refuse to weep for the enemies to rejoice in the name of Jesus.
22. I cancel every dreams, visions, prophesy and prayers against my life and family in the name of Jesus.
23. Talk to God about your heart desires and your situation.
24. Thank God for answered prayers.

Confession:

"And it shall come to pass, that whosoever shall call on the name of the Lord shall be delivered: for in Mount Zion and in Jerusalem shall be deliverance, as the Lord hath said, and in the remnant whom the Lord shall call" Joel 2:32.

Wisdom for Today:

"Honor your being, release each and every struggle, gather strength from life's storms, relax into the arms of the Holy Spirit. All shall be well".

Read the Bible Today: Jeremiah 31–32

Prayer Points:

1. I come against the spirit of spiritual slumber, in the name of Jesus.
2. I break the cycle of poverty and lack that has been in my family for generations, in the name of Jesus.
3. I reverse the curse of dissatisfaction in all the things I do, in the name of Jesus.
4. I command the evil pronouncements of those who are envious of me to turn to my blessings, in the name of Jesus.
5. Almighty God, open my eyes to that which can provoke your curse on my work, and help me to prevent it, in the name of Jesus.
6. Any area of secret tears in my life, receive the touch of God's miracle in the name of Jesus.
7. Almighty God, go back to every second of my past and remove anything that is causing problem in my life in the name of Jesus.
8. Almighty God, arise and nullify every word of human being that is manifesting in my life in the name of Jesus.
9. Almighty God enough of reproach in my life, family, and ministry in the name of Jesus.
10. I cancel every evil dream by the blood of Jesus in the name of Jesus.
11. All my good dreams; be empowered for speedy manifestation in the name of Jesus.
12. Every power fuelling problems in my life your time is up; die in the name of Jesus.

Apostle A.O. Solomon

13. I release myself from every curse working in my family in the name of Jesus.
14. Every spiritual dedication against me and my family; receive the stones of fire and die in the name of Jesus.
15. You messenger of death assigned against me and my family, go back to your sender in the name of Jesus.
16. Every evil wisdom working against, my breakthroughs; be disgraced in the name of Jesus.
17. By the power of the Holy Ghost, I put every evil under my feet in the name of Jesus.
18. Thou power of sin and iniquity in my life, the Lord rebuke you, die in the name of Jesus.
19. I cancel every dreams, visions, prophesy and prayers against my life and family in the name of Jesus.
20. Talk to God about your heart desires and your situation.
21. Thank God for answered prayers.

Confession:

"Israel was holiness unto the Lord, and the first-fruits of his increase: all that devour him shall offend; evil shall come upon them, saith the Lord" Jeremiah 2:3.

Wisdom for Today:

"I forgive everyone for every 'wrong' that I believe they have ever inflicted upon me. I forgive them for my own sake, that I may release the venom—the anger and resentment within myself—and regain my joy and serenity." — Jonathan Lockwood Huie

Read the Bible Today: Jeremiah 33–34

Prayer Points:

1. Lord, deliver me from the emotional bondage I inherited from my parents in the name of Jesus.
2. I break the curse of worshipping any ungodly image in my family in the past, in Jesus name.
3. I break the curse of disrespect of my family militating against my life in the name of Jesus.
4. I break the curse of offence committed against my neighbors dating back generations in the name of Jesus.
5. I break the curse that comes as a result of misleading others, in Jesus name.
6. Every evil desire in my life; the Lord rebuke you in the name of Jesus.
7. I am seated with Christ in the heavenly places, far above principalities and powers in the name of Jesus.
8. Anointing of deliverance fall upon me now in the name of Jesus.
9. Every power that pursued my parents and now pursuing me, what are you waiting for, die in the name of Jesus.
10. Every problem in the life of my parents that is now appearing in my life; vanish in the name of Jesus.
11. Every pillar of disgrace in my life, I pull you down in the name of Jesus.
12. Every evil preparation to disgrace me; be destroyed by fire in the name of Jesus.

13. Every power that has singled me out for affliction, Holy Ghost fire, locate and destroy them in the name of Jesus.
14. Every evil mark upon my body, wherever you are vanish in the name of Jesus.
15. Almighty God, restore all my wasted years in the name of Jesus Christ.
16. Every power covering my glory, fall down and die in the name of Jesus.
17. You my glory arise and shine in the name of Jesus.
18. I cancel every dreams, visions, prophesy and prayers against my life and family in the name of Jesus.
19. Talk to God about your heart desires and your situation.
20. Thank God for answered prayers.

Confession:

"Verily I say unto you, whatsoever ye shall bind on earth shall be bound in heaven: and whatsoever ye shall loose on earth shall be loosed in heaven" Matthew 18:18.

Wisdom for Today:

"Powerful Dreams Inspire Powerful Action. Any dream without action will only lead to frustration".

Read the Bible Today: Jeremiah 35–36

Prayer Points:

1. Thus says the Lord; I (your name) am a child of the covenant, in the name of Jesus.
2. Thus says the Lord, I shall be the head and not the tail, in the name of Jesus.
3. Any ritual or fetish power fashioned against me, turn against your owner, in the name of Jesus.
4. This day, I cut off the head of the spirit of poverty, in the name of Jesus.
5. Let the angels of goodness and mercies follow me from now on, in Jesus name.
6. Every seed of the enemy in my life come out by fire in the name of Jesus.
7. Every seed of poverty in my life come out by fire in the name of Jesus.
8. Every dream of poverty, I cancel you by the blood of Jesus in the name of Jesus.
9. Every evil burial for my sake, be destroyed by fire in the name of Jesus.
10. I break the power of death over my life in the name of Jesus.
11. Every hold of the enemy over my blood break by fire in the name of Jesus.
12. Every messenger of death on assignment against me and my family, die in the name of Jesus.
13. Good dreams in my life, hear the word of God, come alive and manifest in the name of Jesus.

14. Every weapon of demotion fashioned against my life, scatter in the name of Jesus.
15. By the blood of Jesus, I send back every evil arrow fired against my life, to sender in the name of Jesus.
16. Anything packaged to destroy my joy in this country be destroyed by fire in the name of Jesus.
17. Foundation of sorrow in my life; be broken to pieces in the name of Jesus.
18. I proclaim that my joy shall last forever in the name of Jesus.
19. Evil deposit in my life, in my body your time is up, come out in the name of Jesus.
20. Every attempt to cover my glory; be frustrated in the name of Jesus.
21. Every evil power monitoring the gates of my prosperity why are you still alive, I command you to die in Jesus name.
22. Every evil arrow fired to useless my life, come out and go back to your sender in the name of Jesus.
23. Spirit of poverty come out of my life and enter no more in the name of Jesus.
24. Any power that is making my family to suffer your time is up, die in the name of Jesus.
25. I shall not answer the call of any evil spirit in the name of Jesus Christ.
26. I cancel every dreams, visions, prophesy and prayers against my life and family in the name of Jesus.
27. Talk to God about your heart desires and your situation.
28. Thank God for answered prayers.

Confession:

"The Lord will be awesome to them; for he will reduce to nothing all the gods of the earth; and men shall worship him, every one from his place, even all the isles of the heathen" Zephaniah 2:11.

Wisdom for Today:

"When you can taste, smell, and touch your dream, you can enroll the world".

Read the Bible Today: Jeremiah 37–38

Prayer Points:

1. I break the power of the curse that comes as a result of damaging my neighbors behind their backs, in the name of Jesus.
2. I break the generational curse that follows destroying the innocent without reason, in Jesus name.
3. I break the curse that follows disobedience to the word of God in the name of Jesus.
4. I break the curse that may have come on my business and my income, in Jesus name.
5. I reverse every curse pronounced against me and my family in the name of Jesus.
6. Almighty God, reduce all my enemies and problems to nothing, in the name of Jesus.
7. Every power hired to curse me, and my destiny, what are you waiting for, die in the name of Jesus.
8. Any power or covenant of my father's house that wants to waste my life and calling, die in the name of Jesus.
9. Stubborn pursuers of my life hear the word of the Lord; die in the name of Jesus.
10. Every evil stamp of the enemy; be removed in the name of Jesus.
11. Almighty God; turn my failures to success in the name of Jesus.
12. Every gate in this nation shot against me, open now in the name of Jesus.
13. Every curse that is delaying good things in my life; break and release me in the name of Jesus.
14. Every spirit of this world attached to my mind, I cut you off in the name of Jesus.
15. Spirit of God, reign in my life in the name of Jesus.

Apostle A.O. Solomon

16. Almighty God, teach my hand to war tonight in the name of Jesus.
17. Arise O God and prevail over my enemies in Jesus name.
18. Let the wicked and their wickedness be consumed by fire in the name of Jesus.
19. I cancel every dreams, visions, prophesy and prayers against my life and family in the name of Jesus.
20. Talk to God about your heart desires and your situation.
21. Thank God for answered prayers.

Confession:

"But I will deliver thee in that day, saith the lord: and thou shall not be given into the hand of the men of whom thou art afraid. For I will surely deliver thee, and thou shall not fall by the sword, but thy life shall be for a prey unto thee: because thou hast put thy trust in me, saith the Lord" Jeremiah 39:17–18.

Wisdom for Today:

God does not promise us a life without storm.

"The word 'happiness' would lose its meaning if it were not balanced by sadness."
—Carl Jung

"Happiness is not the absence of problems, but the willingness to deal with them joyfully." — H. Jackson (Jack) Brown Jr.

"Your greatest gift to others is to be happy and to radiate your happiness to the entire world."— Jonathan Lockwood Huie

Read the Bible Today: Psalm 34

Prayer Points:

1. I cancel the curse of restlessness and the bondage of fear in my life, in Jesus name.
2. I break the curse that the shedding of the blood of the innocent has brought upon me, in the name of Jesus.
3. I break the impact of the curse of sexual impurity, in the name of Jesus.
4. I cancel the curse that may have caused spiritual barrenness, in the name of the Jesus.
5. I cancel the curse that may have alighted through disrespect for God's anointed, in the name of Jesus.
6. Let every stubborn enemy that has risen against me; be defeated now in the name of Jesus.
7. By the power of the Holy Ghost, I destroy the enemies and their work in my life in the name of Jesus.
8. Let the dwelling place of my enemies come to nothing, and let those who hate me be put to shame in the name of Jesus.
9. Let every weapon of my enemies back fire and destroy them in the name of Jesus.

Apostle A.O. Solomon

10. Almighty God, reveal to me the secret of becoming a winner in life in the name of Jesus.
11. Blood of Jesus, make way for me in the name of Jesus.
12. Let the power of God clear way for my prayers tonight in the name of Jesus.
13. Let the angels of God come to my aid, support me in the name of Jesus.
14. Holy Ghost, arise in your power deliver me from my tight places in the name of Jesus.
15. Shout fire of deliverance fall on me… 7 times.
16. Evil dreams depart from my life in the name of Jesus.
17. Every power of darkness polluting and attacking my dreams; be arrested by fire in the name of Jesus.
18. By the blood of Jesus, I cancel every effect of evil dreams in my life in the name of Jesus.
19. I cancel every dreams, visions, prophesy and prayers against my life and family in the name of Jesus.
20. Talk to God about your heart desires and your situation.
21. Thank God for answered prayers.

Confession:

"The Lord hath taken away thy judgments, he hath cast out thine enemy: the king of Israel, even the Lord, is in the midst of thee: thou shall not see evil any more" Zephaniah 3:15.

Wisdom for Today:

Training yourself to live in the present—without regretting the past or fearing the future—is a recipe for a happy life"

Read the Bible Today: Jeremiah 41–42

Prayer Points:

1. All good things that household witchcraft has confiscated, I receive them back, in the name of Jesus.
2. All my benefits stolen by the dead, I receive them back sevenfold, in the name of Jesus.
3. Let the clock and timetable of the enemy for my life, marriage, and family, be destroyed, in the name of Jesus.
4. Almighty God let all the efforts of my enemies be reduced to useless exercise in the name of Jesus.
5. I receive favor above my colleagues today, in the name of Jesus.
6. Every messenger of death in this church; depart and enter no more in the name of Jesus.
7. Every evil power that is holding me down, die in the name of Jesus.
8. I move from nothing to something good in the name of Jesus.
9. In this country I shall not be disgraced in the name of Jesus.
10. Every attack in my dream that is now affecting my life; be reversed in the name of Jesus.
11. Evil arrows from my dream come out and go back to sender in the name of Jesus.
12. Powers from my father's house and my mother's house begin to attack yourself in Jesus name.
13. Almighty God I need a break in this country in the name of Jesus.

14. Almighty God, heal me from every area that I have been wounded in the name of Jesus.
15. I cancel every dreams, visions, prophesy and prayers against my life and family in the name of Jesus.
16. Talk to God about your heart desires and your situation.
17. Thank God for answered prayers.

Confession:

"Yea, though I walk through the valley of the shadow of death, I will fear no evil throughout this year: For God is with me; His rod and His staff comfort me" Psalms 23:4.

Wisdom for Today:

"When you feel worried and depressed, consciously form a smile on your face and act upbeat until the happy feeling becomes genuine".

Read the Bible Today: Jeremiah 43–44

Prayer Points:

1. Let every good thing that is dead in my life; begin to receive life now, in the name of Jesus.
2. I command every evil device against me to be disappointed, in the name of Jesus.
3. Let the healing power of God overshadow me now, in Jesus name.
4. I bind every spirit working against answers to my prayers, in the name of Jesus.
5. I disarm any power that has made a covenant with the ground, water, and wind against me, in the name of Jesus.
6. Every power bent on seeing my destiny destroyed, Holy Ghost fire locate and destroy them in the name of Jesus.
7. My ears shall hear good news, my eyes shall see good things, and my hands shall possess good things in the name of Jesus.
8. Almighty God, arise quickly and deliver me from shame in the name of Jesus.
9. Evil arrows my body is not for you in the name of Jesus.
10. Every owner of evil load in my life, carry your load in the name of Jesus.
11. I shall not be wasted; I shall not be useless in the name of Jesus.
12. Every power affecting my joy, lose your power and die in the name of Jesus.
13. I declare I shall not bury my children in the name of Jesus.
14. Every dry bone in my life, receive the touch of resurrection and live in the name of Jesus.
15. Every good door that has been closed against me, lift up your heads and let the King of glory come in in Jesus name.

Apostle A.O. Solomon

16. Almighty God, arise in your mercy and close the old chapter in my life in the name of Jesus.
17. Every word of the enemy waiting for manifestation in my life, die in the name of Jesus.
18. Every maturity date of evil words and prophesies in my life, be nullified in the name of Jesus.
19. I fire back, every arrow of evil prophecy that is pursuing my life; I fire you back in Jesus name.
20. Every satanic assignment, I reject you in my life in the name of Jesus.
21. Every power demanding tears from my eyes before receiving my blessings, die in the name of Jesus.
22. I cancel every dreams, visions, prophesy and prayers against my life and family in the name of Jesus.
23. Talk to God about your heart desires and your situation.
24. Thank God for answered prayers.

Confession:

"Behold, at that time, I will undo all that afflict thee: and I will save her that halteth, and gather her that was driven out: and I will get them praise and fame in every land where they have been put to shame" Zephaniah 3:19.

Wisdom for Today:

"Happiness is when what you think, what you say, and what you do are in harmony. Happiness is not something readymade. It comes from your own actions".

Read the Bible Today: Jeremiah 45–46

Prayer Points:

1. Almighty God, make my life invincible to demonic observers, in the name of Jesus.
2. I bind all remote control spirits fashioned against me, in the name of Jesus.
3. I withdraw all the bullets and ammunition made available to the enemy against my life, in the name of Jesus.
4. Almighty God let the table turn against my enemy today, in the name of Jesus.
5. Let people gather to favor me today, in the name of Jesus.
6. Every power sponsoring weeping in my family; carry your load and die in the name of Jesus.
7. Every witchcraft cage caging my destiny, break by fire in the name of Jesus.
8. Almighty God, deliver me from the strife of tongue in the name of Jesus.
9. Evil arrows go back to your sender in the name of Jesus.
10. Every attack of eaters of flesh and drinkers of blood, back fire in the name of Jesus.
11. I withdraw my blood from witchcraft altar in the name of Jesus.
12. Anything representing me in any kingdom of darkness, I withdraw you by fire in the name of Jesus.
13. I walk out of the prison of evil dreams in the name of Jesus.
14. Every dream of backwardness in my life, die in the name of Jesus.

15. Any power using anything in my past to torment me die in the name of Jesus.
16. By the blood of Jesus, I register my name for solution today in the name of Jesus.
17. I shall not serve my enemies and I shall not serve my friend in the name of Jesus.
18. I disagree with every satanic decision over my life in the name of Jesus.
19. I cancel every former and present agreement with the spirit of Egypt in the name of Jesus.
20. I cancel every dreams, visions, prophesy and prayers against my life and family in the name of Jesus.
21. Talk to God about your heart desires and your situation.
22. Thank God for answered prayers.

Confession:

"Thou art my king, O God; command deliverance for Jacob" Psalms 44:4.

Wisdom for Today:

Nothing is impossible to a willing heart. Isaiah 1:19

Read the Bible Today: Jeremiah 47–48

Prayer Points:

1. I revoke any conscious and unconscious covenant with the spirit of death in my life, in the name of Jesus.
2. Almighty God I submit my tongue to you; take absolute control of it, in the name of Jesus.
3. Let the heavenly surgeon come down and perform surgical operations where necessary in my life, in the name of Jesus.
4. I receive deliverance from all physical, spiritual, and financial bondage, in the name of Jesus.
5. I refuse to wage war against myself, in the name of Jesus.
6. Almighty God command deliverance upon my life, in the name of Jesus.
7. Every agreement with the power of the air, I command you to break in the name of Jesus.
8. I recover every blessing I have lost to spirit of Egypt in the name of Jesus.
9. Almighty God, deliver me from every problem I have brought upon myself in the name of Jesus.
10. I reject every invitation to bondage in the name of Jesus.
11. Almighty God, give me power to overcome pressures in life in the name of Jesus.
12. Almighty God, give me a sign for good and use me for your glory in the name of Jesus.
13. By the anointing of the Holy Ghost, I leap over every negative situation surrounding me in the name of Jesus.
14. My soul hopes and wait on the Lord, for you God is gracious in the name of Jesus.
15. I shall not fail God in the name of Jesus.

16. Almighty God I commit my life to you; organize my scattered life in the name of Jesus.
17. Almighty God, change my story as you did Jabez in the name of Jesus.
18. I cancel every dreams, visions, prophesy and prayers against my life and family in the name of Jesus.
19. Talk to God about your heart desires and your situation.
20. Thank God for answered prayers.

Confession:

"And ye shall tread down the wicked; for they shall be ashes under the sole of your feet in the day that I shall do this, saith the Lord of hosts" Malachi 4:3.

Wisdom for Today:

"Accomplishment of purpose is better than making a profit".

Read the Bible Today: Jeremiah 49–50

Prayer Points:

1. Almighty God, wake me up from any spiritual slumber, in the name of Jesus.
2. Every seed planted by fear in my life, be uprooted by fire now, in the name of Jesus.
3. Almighty God let your kingdom be established in every area of my life, in Jesus name.
4. I cancel all former negotiations with the devil and his agents, in the name of Jesus.
5. Let the presence of God go before and after me today, in the name of Jesus.
6. I receive grace and power to enjoy the blessings of God in the land of the living, in the name of Jesus.
7. I reject automatic failure in my life in the name of Jesus.
8. Every enemy of divine presence in my life, I command you to die in the name of Jesus.
9. Anointing to excel above all my family members fall upon me now in the name of Jesus.
10. I shall experience divine favor throughout the days of my life in Jesus name.
11. Holy Spirit; coordinate me in the name of Jesus.
12. Arrows of the enemy you shall not locate me, go back to your sender in the name of Jesus.
13. Power to sin no more, fall upon me now in the name of Jesus.
14. I put the yoke of Jesus Christ upon myself in the name of Jesus.

15. God shall help me and fight for me in the name of Jesus.
16. I shall not lose my job in the name of Jesus.
17. I cancel every dreams, visions, prophesy and prayers against my life and family in the name of Jesus.
18. Talk to God about your heart desires and your situation.
19. Thank God for answered prayers.

Confession:

"He hath shewed strength with his arm; he hath scattered the proud in the imagination of their hearts. He hath put down the mighty from their seats, and exalted them of low degree" Luke 1:51–52.

Wisdom for Today:

The question should be, "Is it worth trying to do?" not, "Can it be done?" You must motivate yourself every day.

Read the Bible Today: Jeremiah 51–52

Prayer Points:

1. I renounce any ceremony linking me to any evil power, in the name of Jesus.
2. I renounce any signature of my name in satanic possession, in the name of Jesus.
3. I break any bondage of inherited sickness in my life, in the name of Jesus.
4. Spirit of infirmity in my life, come out and enter no more, in the name of Jesus.
5. By the power of God that enabled me to see this day, I will overcome every obstacle and evil on my way today, in Jesus name.
6. My source of money shall not be blocked in this month in the name of Jesus.
7. Throughout this month I shall be blessed and highly favored in the name of Jesus.
8. Where there is no way for others, there shall be way for me this month in the name of Jesus.
9. I reject death in my family and church in the name of Jesus.
10. Almighty God let your hand be upon me for good throughout this month in the name of Jesus.
11. Almighty God, do not give me up to the desires of my enemies in the name of Jesus.
12. Evil shall not prevail against me and my family in the name of Jesus.
13. Sin shall not rule over me in the name of Jesus.
14. Every good thing my hands have started, my hands shall complete and I shall enjoy them in the name of Jesus.

15. My head hear the word of the Lord; you shall not be bewitched in the name of Jesus.
16. I cancel every dreams, visions, prophesy and prayers against my life and family in the name of Jesus.
17. Talk to God about your heart desires and your situation.
18. Thank God for answered prayers.

Confession:

"But thus saith the Lord, even the captives of the mighty shall be taken away, and the prey of the terrible shall be delivered: for I will contend with him that contendeth with thee, and I will save thy children. And I will feed them that oppress thee with their own flesh; and they shall be drunken with their own blood, as with sweet wine: and all flesh shall know that I the Lord am thy Savior and thy redeemer, the mighty one of Jacob" Isaiah 49:25–26.

Wisdom for Today:

"The best motivation always comes from within".

Read the Bible Today: Revelation 3–4

Prayer Points:

1. Almighty God, soak me and my family in the blood of Jesus.
2. I declare that death and sickness have no hold on me and my family in the name of Jesus.
3. Almighty God, help me to fulfill the program of my life, in the name of Jesus.
4. Let all devourers devour themselves today for my sake, in the name of Jesus.
5. Let all evil covenant attached to this day against me and my family be broken now, in the name of Jesus.
6. Almighty God, convert my body to the fire of the Holy Ghost, in the name of Jesus.
7. I shall not become what the enemies want me to be in the name of Jesus.
8. O God of Abraham, Isaac, and Jacob, rearrange this country to favor me in the name of Jesus.
9. Every completed work of my enemies over my life; be destroyed with all your effects in the name of Jesus.
10. I break and lose myself from the stronghold of darkness in the name of Jesus.
11. Any power that wants to replace my peace with war, die suddenly in the name of Jesus.
12. By the blood of Jesus Christ, I rise above limitation in life in the name of Jesus.

Apostle A.O. Solomon

13. Almighty God reign supreme in my life in the name of Jesus.
14. Almighty God set me free from poverty in the name of Jesus.
15. By the power in the word of God, I command every darkness in my life to vanish in the name of Jesus.
16. Every step by step work of the enemy in my life; be destroyed in the name of Jesus.
17. Every perfected works of the enemy in my life; be over turned by the blood of Jesus in the name of Jesus.
18. Every evil altar in my family working against my glory; be consumed by fire in the name of Jesus.
19. I cancel every dreams, visions, prophesy and prayers against my life and family in the name of Jesus.
20. Talk to God about your heart desires and your situation.
21. Thank God for answered prayers.

Confession:

"That I should be saved from my enemies, and from the hand of all that hate me" Luke 1:7.

Wisdom for Today:

"The only difference between saints and sinners is that every saint has a past while every sinner has a future".

Read the Bible Today: 1 Peter 1–2

Prayer Points:

1. Almighty God, ignite the fire of revival in my soul, in the name of Jesus.
2. Let all eaters of flesh and drinkers of blood assigned against me stumble and fall whenever they want to carry out their operations, in Jesus name.
3. Let all my blessings that my enemies have swallowed be vomited now, in Jesus name.
4. All good things that are at the point of death in my life, receive life now, in the name of Jesus.
5. No evil shall prosper over my life and family today, in the name of Jesus.
6. Almighty God, where everyone is stocking up on your bounty, make way for me, in the name of Jesus.
7. Any satanic power assigned to waste my destiny, be wasted, in the name of Jesus.
8. This year I shall not weep before I receive my blessing; I shall be blessed and highly favored, in the name of Jesus.
9. This year I forbid my blessing to be stolen, in the name of Jesus.
10. My blessing, glory, and honor shall not be transferred to another person, in the name of Jesus.
11. All the helpers attached to my greatness in life, be released from your captivity, in the name of Jesus.
12. I cancel every dreams, visions, prophesy and prayers against my life and family in the name of Jesus.
13. Talk to God about your heart desires and your situation.
14. Thank God for answered prayers.

Confession:

"Therefore shall his calamity come suddenly; suddenly shall he be broken without remedy" Proverbs 6:15.

Wisdom for Today:

"At the end of every hard day, find a reason to believe that all shall be well".

Read the Bible Today: Exodus 1–2

Prayer Points:

1. All the wicked intentions of the devil upon my life; be destroyed by fire, in the name of Jesus.
2. I command the hands that cover my blessings to wither and be lifted away now, in the name of Jesus.
3. I command the eggs laid by the enemy against my life to break before hatching, in the name of Jesus.
4. Let the enemy fall into the pit they dug for me today, in Jesus name.
5. Almighty God, clothe me with your fire, in Jesus name.
6. Every good thing the enemy scattered in my life, come together in the name of Jesus.
7. Every power and spirit that has set my life for affliction, I bind you in the name of Jesus.
8. My life shall not follow satanic agenda in the name of Jesus.
9. Almighty God it is time give me rest and comfort me, prospers me in the name of Jesus.
10. By the blood of Jesus, I register my name for solution today in the name of Jesus.
11. I connect myself with the power of God in the name of Jesus.
12. Every pillar of witchcraft in my family, what are you waiting for? I pull you down in the name of Jesus.
13. Witchcraft powers why are you pursuing my life? die in the name of Jesus.
14. It is written suffer not a witch to live, therefore any witchcraft pursuing my life, I command you to die in the name of Jesus.
15. I disagree with failure in the name of Jesus.
16. I cancel every dreams, visions, prophesy and prayers against my life and family in the name of Jesus.
17. Talk to God about your heart desires and your situation.
18. Thank God for answered prayers.

Confession:

"That at the name of Jesus, every knee should bow, of things in heaven and things in earth, and things under the earth. And that every tongue should confess that Jesus Christ is Lord, to the glory of God the Father" Philippians 2:10–11.

Wisdom for Today:

"Faith consists in believing when it is beyond the power of reason to believe. It is enough that a thing be possible for it to be believed".

Read the Bible Today: *Exodus 3–4*

Prayer Points:

1. All anti-progressive forces, I summon you together, and I issue the judgment of the fire of God upon you, in the name of Jesus.
2. Lord Jesus, I invite you to be Lord over every department of my life in the name of Jesus.
3. Father Lord, I confess my sins and ask that you forgive and cleanse me today, in Jesus name.
4. I forgive all those who have hurt or offended me, in the name of Jesus.
5. O Lord, take me from where I am to where you want me to be, in Jesus name.
6. Failure at the edge of good things, depart from my life by the blood of Jesus in the name of Jesus.
7. Witchcraft battle at the edge of my success return to your sender in the name of Jesus.
8. Every evil seed planted by the enemy in my life, be uprooted by fire in the name of Jesus.
9. Every plantation of darkness in my life, come out with all your roots in the name of Jesus.
10. Every evil seed planted into my life through dreams, be uprooted by fire in the name of Jesus.
11. I challenge my system with the fire of God, in the name of Jesus.
12. Every instrument of satanic control in my life, wherever you are be destroyed by fire in the name of Jesus.

Apostle A.O. Solomon

13. Arrows of darkness in my life come out of your hiding places and go back to your sender in the name of Jesus.

14. As from today, life shall be easy for me in the name of Jesus.

15. By the blood of Jesus, I stand in gap for every member of my family in the name of Jesus.

16. Every of my family that is appointed for death, be redeemed by the blood of Jesus in the name of Jesus.

17. Any power that wants to attack me, Holy Ghost fire attack and destroy them in the name of Jesus.

18. Arrows of madness fired against me and any member of my family, gather yourself together and go back to your sender in the name of Jesus.

19. All those in the system of this country that will not favor me, O Lord replace them with people that will favor me in the name of Jesus.

20. I cancel every dreams, visions, prophesy and prayers against my life and family in the name of Jesus.

21. Talk to God about your heart desires and your situation.

22. Thank God for answered prayers.

Confession:

"Heal me, O Lord, and I shall be healed; save me, and I shall be saved: for thou art my praise" Jeremiah 17:14.

Wisdom for Today:

"We must accept finite disappointment, but we must never lose infinite hope".

Read the Bible Today: *Exodus 5–6*

Prayer Points:

1. I claim my freedom from the consequences of all curses, in the name of Jesus.
2. Every demonic reinforcement against my life; be broken unto desolation, in the name of Jesus.
3. Let the power of God be released into my body now, in the name of Jesus.
4. Let every affliction be consumed by fire, in the name of Jesus.
5. Evil strangers, come out of your hiding place in any area of my life, in the name of Jesus.
6. All those who are boasting to fire me in my place of work, let the Holy Ghost fire, fire them in the name of Jesus.
7. I put the yoke of Jesus Christ upon myself in the name of Jesus.
8. Almighty God, help me, and fight for me in the name of Jesus.
9. I shall not lose my job in the name of Jesus.
10. My source of money shall not be blocked this month in the name of Jesus.
11. Throughout this month I shall be blessed and highly favored in the name of Jesus.
12. Where there is no way for others, there shall be way for me this month in the name of Jesus.
13. I cancel every dreams, visions, prophesy and prayers against my life and family in the name of Jesus.
14. Talk to God about your heart desires and your situation.
15. Thank God for answered prayers.

Confession:

"For I will restore health unto thee, and I will heal your wounds, saith the Lord" Jeremiah 30:17.

Wisdom for Today:

"Though you may be under a dark tree, always look for the light shining through the branches".

Read the Bible Today: Exodus 7–8

Prayer Points:

1. I cast out the spirit of evil inheritance, in the name of Jesus.
2. I stand against every addictive evil desire in my life, in the name of Jesus.
3. Let the healing power of God flow into every damaged part of my body, in the name of Jesus.
4. Almighty God, begin to restore me to full abundant life, in the name of Jesus.
5. Almighty God, empower my life with your authority over every demonic force that sets itself against my life, in the name of Jesus.
6. All those who are boasting to fire me in my place of work, let the Holy Ghost fire, fire them in the name of Jesus.
7. Every evil register containing my name, Holy Ghost fire consume them in the name of Jesus.
8. Every broom of darkness sweeping good things away from my life, catch fire in the name of Jesus.
9. Angel of the living God; begin to sweep back all my blessings in the name of Jesus.
10. Every spirit of laboring without achievement; be destroyed in the name of Jesus.
11. I hold the hammer of the word of God and command every padlock ministering evil against my life, break in the name of Jesus.
12. With the garment of fire and power of Jesus, I enter the strong room of the enemy and collect all my blessing in the name of Jesus.
13. I go with the Lord Jesus and the Holy Ghost fire into every witchcraft coven and collect my blessings in the name of Jesus.
14. Any man or woman, attending witchcraft meeting because of me, you shall not return in the name of Jesus.

15. Anyone calling my name for evil in the night, angel of God; slap them in the name of Jesus.
16. Every night captivity in my life, break in the name of Jesus.
17. Anything done against me in the night; be destroyed by fire in the name of Jesus.
18. Every satanic power appearing in my dream, the Lord rebuke you perish in the name of Jesus.
19. I cancel every dreams, visions, prophesy and prayers against my life and family in the name of Jesus.
20. Talk to God about your heart desires and your situation.
21. Thank God for answered prayers.

Confession:

"Every plant, which my heavenly Father hat not planted, shall be uprooted" Matthew 15:13.

Wisdom for Today:

Remember sadness is always temporary. Look at your present situation and say: "This, too, shall pass".

Read the Bible Today: Exodus 9–10

Prayer Points:

1. Almighty God, grant me the power to be fulfilled, successful, and prosperous in life, in the name of Jesus.
2. Every seed of the enemy in my life; be uprooted now by fire, in the name of Jesus.
3. Almighty God, make a way for me where there is no way, in Jesus name.
4. Almighty God, make me break past every obstacle on my way to progress in life, in the name of Jesus.
5. Almighty God, promote me and preserve me, in the name of Jesus.
6. Almighty God let every power behind problems and affliction in my life be consumed by the fire of God, in the name of Jesus.
7. Any fire that the enemy has lighted against me and my family; be quenched by the blood of Jesus in the name of Jesus.
8. Every evil pot caging anything good in my life, break by thunder in the name of Jesus.
9. In the name of Jesus, by fire, by force, I come against every evil force assigned against my life the name of Jesus.
10. Almighty God put upon me now your garment of mercy and favor in the name of Jesus.
11. My spirit man, my body, my soul hear the word of the Lord you shall not answer the call of the enemy day or night in the name of Jesus.
12. Let the voice of God thunder against my enemies and divide them in the name of Jesus.
13. Let the voice of God, divide the fire of my enemy and destroy them in the name of Jesus.

14. Let the voice of God; shake down the camp of my enemies in the name of Jesus.
15. Almighty God, clothe me with mercy and compassion in the name of Jesus.
16. I cancel every dreams, visions, prophesy and prayers against my life and family in the name of Jesus.
17. Talk to God about your heart desires and your situation.
18. Thank God for answered prayers.

Confession:

"Let the weak say, I am strong" Joel 3:10.

Wisdom for Today:

"Trials give you strength, sorrows give understanding and wisdom".

Read the Bible Today: Exodus 11–12

Prayer Points:

1. The joy of the Lord is my strength today; there is no sickness in my body, in the name of Jesus.
2. Almighty God add flavor to my life, in the name of Jesus.
3. Almighty God, add increase to my work and income, in the name of Jesus.
4. Almighty God, add profitability to my work, in the name of Jesus.
5. I reject the plans and agenda of the enemies against my life, in the name of Jesus.
6. I connect myself to God's fullness of joy, in the name of Jesus.
7. Almighty God, empower my hands to profit in the name of Jesus.
8. Every attack against my labor, break and release me in the name of Jesus.
9. Every curse of the enemy against the works of my hands, break by the blood of Jesus.
10. Every physical and spiritual chain upon my hands, break in the name of Jesus.
11. Thou son of David use your key, and set me free from hand cuffs and chains in the name of Jesus.
12. Jesus set me free; I am free indeed in the name of Jesus.
13. I drink the blood of Jesus, and I cover myself with the blood of Jesus.
14. Any power that wants to destroy the works of God in my life, Holy Ghost fire; destroy them in the name of Jesus.
15. Every satanic bondage from evil dreams programmed into my life; break and release me in the name of Jesus.
16. Every sickness introduced into my life as a result of evil dreams die now in the name of Jesus.

17. Every dream of failure in my past; be reversed in the name of Jesus.

18. Every witchcraft power pursuing me in the dream; fall down and die in the name of Jesus.

19. Almighty God, make me holy by your power in the name of Jesus.

20. Every satanic dream attached to my progress, die in the name of Jesus.

21. I come out of every dream prison by the power of the Holy Ghost in the name of Jesus.

22. I cancel every dreams, visions, prophesy and prayers against my life and family in the name of Jesus.

23. Talk to God about your heart desires and your situation.

24. Thank God for answered prayers.

Confession:

"Jesus saith unto him, I am the way, the truth and the life" John 14:6.

Wisdom for Today:

"Concern should drive you into action, not depression".

Read the Bible Today: Exodus 13–14

Prayer Points:

1. Because I am serving the way, there shall be way for me today, in the name of Jesus.
2. Every barrier on my way of progress, clear away by fire, in the name of Jesus.
3. I command every wall of Jericho standing between me and my blessings to fall now, in the name of Jesus.
4. Every demonic transference into the affairs of my life; be broken, in the name of Jesus.
5. Let no evil power trouble me anymore, because I have the marks of Jesus Christ in my body in the name of Jesus.
6. I fire back every witchcraft arrow fired into my dream in the name of Jesus.
7. Every evil dream of the past affecting my life now, die in the name of Jesus.
8. Every witchcraft serpent attacking me in the dream, return to your sender and destroy them in the name of Jesus.
9. Every dream affecting my life, marriage, and career lose your power and die in the name of Jesus.
10. Every good thing I have lost in the dream I repossess you back in Jesus name.
11. Every agent of darkness in my dream life, I command you to die in the name of Jesus.
12. Every evil pronouncement against me in the dream shall not stand, and shall not come to pass in the name of Jesus.
13. My resting time shall not be a trouble time in the name of Jesus.
14. Any power, spirit, personality that wants to trouble me, my God shall trouble you in the name of Jesus.

15. Life shall not be difficult for me in the name of Jesus.
16. I cancel every dreams, visions, prophesy and prayers against my life and family in the name of Jesus.
17. Talk to God about your heart desires and your situation.
18. Thank God for answered prayers.

Confession:

"But unto you that fear my name shall the sun of righteousness arise with healing in his wings; and ye shall go forth, and grow up as the calves of the stall" Malachi 4:2.

Wisdom for Today:

"To accomplish great things, we must not only act, but also dream; not only plan, but also believe".

Read the Bible Today: Exodus 15–16

Prayer Points:

1. Almighty God, establish me in truth, Godliness and faithfulness, in the name of Jesus.
2. I shall not dishonor my God, in the name of Jesus.
3. Let God be first in my life and every other thing behind, in the name of Jesus.
4. Let every weapon and evil design against me fail totally, in the name of Jesus.
5. I reject premature death, in the name of Jesus.
6. I shall be blessed and highly favored today, in the name of Jesus.
7. I reject every form of nakedness physically and spiritually in the name of Jesus.
8. I reject every form of disorder in the name of Jesus.
9. Me and my family shall be for good signs and wonders in the name of Jesus.
10. As the Lord God lives, people will see the good work of God in my life in Jesus name.
11. Almighty God bless all those that will bless me, and let all those that curse me, be cursed in Jesus name.
12. Every completed work of the enemy over my life; be destroyed with all your power in the name of Jesus.
13. I plead the blood of Jesus against every voice speaking against my destiny in the name of Jesus.
14. Every owner of evil load in my life, wherever you are appear and carry your load in Jesus name.
15. I plead the blood of Jesus over everything the devil is holding against me in the name of Jesus.

16. Jesus I belong to you, I disconnect from the iniquity of my ancestors in the name of Jesus.
17. Every ancestral oat that is affecting my life break now by the blood of Jesus in the name of Jesus.
18. Every evil word that is pursuing my destiny, the Lord rebuke you; turn back in the name of Jesus.
19. I cancel every dreams, visions, prophesy and prayers against my life and family in the name of Jesus.
20. Talk to God about your heart desires and your situation.
21. Thank God for answered prayers.

Confession:

"The Lord is my rock and my fortress, and my deliverer; my God, my strength in whom I will trust; my buckler, and the horn of my salvation, and my high tower. I will call upon the Lord, who is worthy to be praised: so shall I be saved from mine enemies" Psalms 18:2–3.

Wisdom for Today:

"Failure is only the opportunity to begin again, this time more wisely".

Read the Bible Today: Exodus 17–18

Prayer Points:

1. I reject nightmares and sudden destruction, in the name of Jesus.
2. I reject dryness in my walk with God and in my daily endeavors, in the name of Jesus.
3. I reject financial debt, in the name of Jesus.
4. I reject lack and famine in my life, in the name of Jesus.
5. I reject physical and spiritual accident in my going in and coming out, in the name of Jesus.
6. Every prophecy demoting my life; lose your hold and die in the name of Jesus.
7. Evil family pattern, break and release me by fire in the name of Jesus.
8. Every evil water flowing in my family, dry up by fire in the name of Jesus.
9. Family bondage affecting my life, break in the name of Jesus.
10. Ancestral evil covenant, I separate myself from you now in the name of Jesus.
11. Every evil register containing my name, be roasted by fire in the name of Jesus.
12. Jesus Christ of Nazareth I confess you as Lord over my life, my spirit, soul and body, my prayers and every situation of my life in Jesus name.
13. Almighty God in your presence there is fullness of Joy bless me with your presence, bless my home, marriage, family, job, finances and everything that concerns me in the name of Jesus.

14. Almighty God open your hands to me, my family, my marriage, my job, my ministry, my children and spouse and fill us with your goodness and our lives shall not remain the same in the name of Jesus.

15. Almighty God, fill our lives with your healing, blessing, goodness, breakthrough, with your abundance, success and your miracle in Jesus name.

16. Almighty God, uphold me and raise me up in the name of Jesus Christ.

17. Almighty God, open your hands and release your miracle upon me in the name of Jesus.

18. Almighty God; open your hands and satisfy the desires of my heart in the name of Jesus.

19. Almighty God; be gracious unto me, open your hands and fill my life with your goodness in the name of Jesus.

20. I command every arrow of the enemy and every negative situation in my life to go down in the name of Jesus.

21. I cancel every dreams, visions, prophesy and prayers against my life and family in the name of Jesus.

22. Talk to God about your heart desires and your situation.

23. Thank God for answered prayers.

Confession:

"For God hath not given us the spirit of fear, but of power, of love, and of a sound mind" 2 Timothy 1:7.

Wisdom for Today:

"Great changes may not happen right away, but with effort even the difficult may become easy".

Read the Bible Today: Exodus 19–20

Prayer Points:

1. I reject sickness in my spirit, soul, and body, in the name of Jesus.
2. I overcome fear in my life by faith in the powerful word of God, in Jesus name.
3. Let the love of Christ envelope my heart, in the name of Jesus.
4. I stand against every evil work in my life, in the name of Jesus.
5. I overcome powerlessness, confusion, and every attack of the enemy, in the name of Jesus.
6. I confess you as Lord over my life, my spirit, soul and body, my prayers and every situation of my life in Jesus name.
7. Almighty God open your hands to me, my family, my marriage, my job, my ministry, my children and spouse and fill us with your goodness and our lives shall not remain the same in the name of Jesus.
8. Almighty God, fill our lives with your healing, blessing, goodness, breakthrough, with your abundance, success and your miracle in Jesus name.
9. Almighty God, uphold and raise me up in the name of Jesus Christ.
10. Almighty God, open your hands and release your miracle upon me in the name of Jesus.
11. Almighty God; open your hands and satisfy the desires of my heart in the name of Jesus.
12. Almighty God; be gracious unto me, open your hands and fill my life with your goodness in the name of Jesus.
13. I command every arrow of the enemy and every negative situation in my life to go down in the name of Jesus.

14. I cancel every dreams, visions, prophesy and prayers against my life and family in the name of Jesus.
15. Talk to God about your heart desires and your situation.
16. Thank God for answered prayers.

Confession:

"For our God is a consuming fire" Hebrews 12:29.

Wisdom for Today:

"Patience and perseverance have a great effect before which difficulties disappear and obstacles vanish." —John Quincy Adams

"A little knowledge that acts is worth infinitely more than much knowledge that is idle." — Kahlil Gibran

Read the Bible Today: Exodus 21–22

Prayer Points:

1. Almighty God, thank you for the gift of life, for the life of my family for the life of my children my job and all that concerns me in the name of Jesus.
2. Almighty God you are the most high, the awesome God, the unquestionable God in the name of Jesus.
3. I declare Jesus Christ is Lord over my life, situation, family, marriage, job and everything I do in Jesus name.
4. Almighty God take all the glory in my life, in my family, in my marriage, and home in the name of Jesus.
5. Almighty God bless me and multiply me greatly, financially, physically, spiritually, maritally in the name of Jesus.
6. Almighty God let me, my children, and my family increase in every area of our lives don't let us decrease in the mighty name of Jesus.
7. You are the God of all flesh there is nothing you cannot do, therefore Lord speak to every area of our lives in the name of Jesus.
8. Almighty God be gracious unto me, bless me and let me multiply greatly, bless my family, my children, spouse, job , finances, ministry contrary to the wish and plans of the enemies and let us multiply greatly in the name of Jesus.
9. Almighty God bless me with joy, healing, all round rest, peace of mind, breakthrough and all the good things of life in the mighty name of Jesus Christ.

10. Almighty God because of your grace, mercy and compassion don't let me suffer any loss of life and property, don't let me lose my children, my spouse, any members of my family, my chances, my seasons and time in life, don't let me lose my destiny in the name of Jesus.
11. Almighty God I commit my all to you let there be testimonies in my life in the name of Jesus.
12. I decree and declare that I shall not lose, I shall not decrease, and I decree it shall be well with me and my household in Jesus name.
13. I decree satan hear the word of God there is no parking for you in my life, my family and job, I decree our lives a danger zone for the devil and enemies in the name of Jesus.
14. I decree satan hear the world of the Lord, whatever you could not find in Jesus you will not find in me, my home, my family, my job, marriage, my children and spouse in Jesus name.
15. Almighty God let me see your work and wonders in all areas of our lives in the name of Jesus.
16. Let the fire of God destroy everything that is causing hostility in my marriage, in the name of Jesus.
17. I command spiritual divorce between me and every power of darkness, in the name of Jesus.
18. Let the fire of God destroy every covenant I have with a spirit wife or husband, in the name of Jesus.
19. Let every poisoned arrow of the enemy in my body be neutralized by the fire of God, in the name of Jesus.
20. I revoke every satanic decree upon my life, in the name of Jesus.
21. I cancel every dreams, visions, prophesy and prayers against my life and family in the name of Jesus.
22. Talk to God about your heart desires and your situation.
23. Thank God for answered prayers.

Apostle A.O. Solomon

Confession:

"For the eyes of the Lord are over the righteous and his ears are open unto their prayers: but the face of the Lord is against them that do evil" 1 Peter 3:12.

Wisdom for Today:

"The only job where you start at the top is digging a hole."

Read the Bible Today: Exodus 23–24

Prayer Points:

1. Almighty God, break all harmful genetic ties in my life, in Jesus name.
2. Almighty God set me free from any negative thing that came against me before I was born, in Jesus name.
3. Almighty God, use your blood to clean my spiritual wounds in the name of Jesus.
4. From now on, I bulldoze my way into supernatural breakthroughs in every area of my life, in the name of Jesus.
5. I render all evil attacks against my potential and destiny impotent, in the name of Jesus.
6. Lord lead us according to your will, help us to pray according to your will, come and guide us and have your way in our lives in Jesus name.
7. Almighty God Lead us and coordinate us in every area of our lives in the name of Jesus.
8. Almighty God raise help for me, my spouse, and my children financially, maritally, spiritually, physically and in every area of our lives from expected and unexpected quarters in the mighty name of Jesus.
9. Almighty God as you promoted Joseph in prison, promote me and my family in the name of Jesus.
10. Unexpected and expected financial income and breakthrough locate me, my family; locate my spouse and children in the name of Jesus.
11. I shall not be stranded financially, my God will surprise me in my finances, marriage, and my job and in every area of my life in Jesus name.

12. As the Lord lives, I shall not be put to shame; my family shall not be put to shame in the mighty name of Jesus.

13. By the blood of Jesus Christ I receive divine solution to my situations in the name of Jesus.

14. Almighty God, be gracious unto me don't let my testimony become history in the name of Jesus.

15. Almighty God; make me financially blessed in the name of Jesus.

16. I decree as from today, money shall not disappoint me in the name of Jesus.

17. I decree as from today, anytime I need money, it shall be available for me in the name of Jesus.

18. Almighty God; direct money to my life and dwelling place in the name of Jesus.

19. Every sorrow in my life, disappear in the name of Jesus.

20. As the Lord lives, I shall see the goodness of the Lord in the Land of the living in the name of Jesus.

21. Almighty God, connect me to your prosperity, attach me to your wealth in the name of Jesus.

22. Almighty God let your kingdom come into my life and let the kingdom of poverty collapse in the name of Jesus.

23. I decree I shall live in prosperity all the days of my life in the name of Jesus.

24. Almighty God; transform my life by your signs and wonders in the name of Jesus.

25. Almighty God, turn my situation to testimony in the name of Jesus.

26. I cancel every dreams, visions, prophesy and prayers against my life and family in the name of Jesus.

27. Talk to God about your heart desires and your situation.

28. Thank God for answered prayers.

Confession:

"And they overcome him by the blood of the lamb, and by the word of their testimony; and they loved not their lives unto the death" *Revelation 12:11.*

Wisdom for Today:

"Defeat is not defeat unless accepted as a reality—in your own mind." —Bruce Lee

Read the Bible Today: Exodus 25–26

Prayer Points:

1. Holy Spirit, anoint me so that I might pray prophetically, in the name of Jesus.
2. Inherited poisons come out of my life by the blood of Jesus, in Jesus name.
3. Almighty God, convert my problems to miracles, in the name of Jesus.
4. I paralyze every progress arrester today, in the name of Jesus.
5. I speak destruction to the roadblocks of the enemy in my way today, in the name of Jesus.
6. Thank you O Lord for another day in your presence, I worship you and thank you for your love; glory be to your name, you are the Most High God; I declare you as Lord.
7. Every knee shall bow and every tongue must confess that you are Lord in the name of Jesus.
8. Almighty God; open new doors for me, my spouse, children, and business, new doors of success, breakthrough, abundance, victory, and upliftment in Jesus name.
9. Almighty God make way for me, my family, my children, and my spouse, in our finances, job, business and every area of our lives in Jesus name.
10. Almighty God, deliver me from the hands of testimony destroyer in the name of Jesus.
11. Every testimony destroyer working against my life, my testimony, my children and spouse testimonies; be destroyed in the name of Jesus.

12. Almighty God; deliver me from the hands of glory destroyer; deliver my spouse, children, business, destiny, in the name of Jesus.

13. Almighty God I am what I am by your grace, I am born to reign and I will never fail in the name of Jesus.

14. Thank you Lord because heaven has declared me a winner, I am a winner because I am born of God and am His property; I am healed in Jesus name.

15. I declare Jesus Christ as the Lord over my life, my family, my business and every area of my life in Jesus name.

16. This is the day the Lord has made for me therefore all my battles, my spouse and children's battle be scattered in the name of Jesus Christ.

17. Today I reject any encounter with sorrow pains, sickness and death in the name of Jesus.

18. This is the day the Lord has made for me; therefore I shall not encounter sorrow, shame, evil arrow, weeping, accident and tragedy in the name of Jesus Christ.

19. I cancel every dreams, visions, prophesy and prayers against my life and family in the name of Jesus.

20. Talk to God about your heart desires and your situation.

21. Thank God for answered prayers.

Confession:

"For whatsoever is born of God overcometh the world: and this is the victory that overcometh the world, even our faith" 1 John 5:4.

Wisdom for Today:

"Most things in life require effort even if, years later, they seem easy".

Read the Bible Today: Exodus 27–28

Prayer Points:

1. I confess every sexual sin that may keep me in bondage, and I ask for forgiveness, in the name of Jesus.
2. As I go into this prayer session, I surround myself with the fire of God, and cover myself with the blood of Jesus, in Jesus name.
3. Every foundational covenant with spirit husband or spirit wife; be destroyed by the blood of Jesus in the name of Jesus.
4. Every parental evil dedication to any water and powers therein; be canceled by the blood of Jesus in the name of Jesus.
5. It is written blessed be the Lord who daily loadeth us with benefits therefore I withdraw my blessings, possessions from the hold of the enemies in the name of Jesus.
6. Almighty God, load me with your benefits in the name of Jesus.
7. In the name of Jesus I declare I am a blessed child of God whether the enemies and the devil like it or not, my children are blessed children of God, my spouse is a blessed child of God in the name of Jesus.
8. Lord I dedicate this day to you as I seek let me find, as I go into this day preserve me, divert sorrow away from me in the name of Jesus.
9. Anyone that has been assigned to disturb my peace of mind, make me lose my job and bring me sorrow will not come my way in the name of Jesus.
10. Any area of my life that is experiencing stagnancy receive the touch of God and be revived in the name of Jesus.
11. Almighty God, open new channel of financial flow for me, new channel of income in the name of Jesus.
12. I shall get to my promise land and prosper in my promised land, surely as the Lord liveth in the name of Jesus.

13. I shall get to my promise land, my spouse and children shall get to their promise land no matter how the storms may be we shall all get to our promised land in Jesus name.
14. Lord Jesus Christ of Nazareth say yes to my healing, blessing, comfort, joy, happiness, freedom, liberty, peace of mind, success, finances, job, marriage, deliverance, and my requests in Jesus mighty name.
15. I decree no oppressor shall oppress me, my spouse, and my children in every area of our life in the name of Jesus.
16. Every evil pattern in my family that is following me about physically, maritally, spiritually and manifesting in any area of my life your time is up break and rise no more in the name of Jesus.
17. Every problem of my parents manifesting on every area of my life, your time is up I command you to die and rise no more in the name of Jesus.
18. Problem in my father's life, my mother's life I silence you and I command you to die in the name of Jesus Christ.
19. Any problem in my life from any member of my family, almighty God remove them, I refuse to go about with such problem in the mighty name of Jesus.
20. I cancel every dreams, visions, prophesy and prayers against my life and family in the name of Jesus.
21. Talk to God about your heart desires and your situation.
22. Thank God for answered prayers.

Confession:

Sickness is not my portion; disease is rejected in my life in the name of Jesus. Every hold of the enemy is broken. Evil pronouncements made into my life are cancelled in the name of Jesus. I thank the Lord in advance for turning every curse into a blessing and every challenge into His favor in Jesus name.

I am what God says I am; I am a Winner; and not a looser.

Wisdom for Today:

"To reach a port we must sail, sometimes with the wind and sometimes against it. But we must not drift or lie at anchor".

Read the Bible Today: 29–30

Prayer Points:

1. I drink the blood of Jesus for healing, and for purging, in Jesus name.
2. Every arrow of darkness fired into my life, relinquish your hold and come out of your hiding place, in the name of Jesus.
3. Every arrow of infirmity in any area of my body, relinquish your hold and come out by fire, in the name of Jesus.
4. Every stronghold of sickness in my life; be pulled down now, in the name of Jesus.
5. Every sickness introduced into my life through dreams, die, in the name of Jesus.
6. Every satanic strongman attached to my health, I bind and paralyze you, in the name of Jesus.
7. I arrest the foundation of any sickness in my life by fire, in the name of Jesus.
8. Every problem in my life from my ex-husband, my ex-wife, ex-boyfriend or girlfriend, be terminated in the name of Jesus.
9. Almighty God let the rain of your blessings fall upon my life and yield results in the name of Jesus.
10. Almighty God Let your rain fall upon my home, spouse, children and all that I do, let your rain of goodness, abundance, success, breakthrough, upliftment, mercy, favor and grace fall upon us today in the name of Jesus Christ.

11. Lord as I call my friends and loved ones and refer them to you, God let it work for me, give me double in the land let me receive your blessings and favor in the name of Jesus.

12. I run into the name of the Lord for safety, healing, deliverance, blessing, it is written the name of the Lord is a strong tower the righteous run into it and is safe therefore I run into the name of the Lord and me and my family are safe in the name of Jesus.

13. Almighty God I am your property, my family is your property; divert evil, tragedy, accident and death away from our lives to the camp of our enemies, let our enemies die for our sake, in the name of Jesus Christ.

14. I declare unto my destiny, my spouse and children's destiny move forward in the name of Jesus.

15. I speak unto my star, the star of my wife and children keep shinning in the name of Jesus Christ.

16. Almighty God, remove the standing place, the foundation of any problem in my life, financially, maritally and in every area of my life in the mighty name of Jesus.

17. Jesus Christ is Lord therefore I shall move from glory to glory in the land of the living, my spouse and children shall move from glory to glory in the land of the living in the name of Jesus.

18. Jesus Christ is Lord therefore, my job, my finances and everything shall move from glory to glory in the name of Jesus.

19. By the blood of Jesus Christ I knock on the door of this day (date) Of the month of (month) in the (year) And I command the door of this day to open for me now, doors of favor, victory, wealth, doors of good news, success, blessings open in the name of Jesus.

20. You doors of (date) open for me today, it is written knock and it shall be opened therefore I knock on the door of this day to open for me, my spouse and children in the name of Jesus.

21. I reject every evil in this day, bad news, stress, sorrow and pain in Jesus name.

22. I cancel every dreams, visions, prophesy and prayers against my life and family in the name of Jesus.

23. Talk to God about your heart desires and your situation.

24. Thank God for answered prayers.

Confession:

"He that leads into captivity shall go into captivity: he that kills with sword must be killed with the sword. Here is the patience and faith of the saints" Revelation 13:10.

Wisdom for Today:

"The heights by great men reached and kept were not obtained by sudden flight. But they, while their companions slept, were toiling upward in the night".

Read the Bible Today: Exodus 31–32

Prayer Points:

1. I command all the enemies of success and prosperity in my business to turn back now, in the name of Jesus.
2. As you are turning back, let the doors of breakthroughs open for me now, in the name of Jesus.
3. Let the angels of God connect me with all those who will move my business forward, in the name of Jesus.
4. Let the name of my business attract favor anywhere it appears, in the name of Jesus.
5. Almighty God, release your favor and prosperity upon my life and business today, in the name of Jesus.
6. I break any curse operating in my life and business, in the name of Jesus.
7. Declare Jesus Christ is Lord.
8. Almighty God; comfort me on every side in the name of Jesus Christ.
9. Every gate and everlasting door preventing me from fulfilling my destiny; be lifted up in the name of Jesus.
10. Every gate and everlasting door disturbing me; be lifted and let the prince of peace reign in my life in the name of Jesus.
11. Every gate and everlasting door preventing me from my testimony; lift up your head and let my testimony come in the name of Jesus.
12. Every gate and everlasting door challenging my joy; be lifted up in the name of Jesus.
13. Every gate and everlasting door that is challenging my glory, be lifted up and let my glory manifest in the name of Jesus.

14. I need a miracle in my marriage, ministry, finances, job, and studies in the name of Jesus.
15. Glory of God manifest in my life in the name of Jesus.
16. Power of the Living God come down on my behalf, and solve my problems with signs and wonders in the name of Jesus.
17. Every power of confusion; present in my life; I bind and cast you out in the name of Jesus.
18. By the blood of Jesus Christ I enter into the covenant of peace with God and my helpers in the name of Jesus.
19. By the blood of Jesus Christ I enter into the covenant of favor in the name of Jesus.
20. By the blood of Jesus Christ I enter into the covenant of prosperity in the name of Jesus.
21. Let the power in the blood of Jesus arise and sustain me in the name of Jesus.
22. Every power attacking me to frustrate the will and purpose of God in my life, I command you to go down into the pit in the name of Jesus.
23. Let the power in the blood of Jesus Christ arise and establish me in every good work in the name of Jesus.
24. I cancel every dreams, visions, prophesy and prayers against my life and family in the name of Jesus.
25. Talk to God about your heart desires and your situation.
26. Thank God for answered prayers.

Confession:

"For thus saith the Lord of hosts. After the glory hath he sent me unto the nation which spoiled you: for he that toucheth you toucheth the apple of his eye" Zechariah 2:3.

Wisdom for Today:

"The toughest part of getting to the top of the ladder is getting through the crowd at the bottom".

Read the Bible Today: Exodus 33–34

Prayer Points:

1. I thank God for making my body a dwelling place of the Holy Spirit in the name of Jesus.
2. I thank God for sending another comforter to live with me in the name of Jesus.
3. Let the rain of God's power fall upon my life now, in the name of Jesus.
4. Almighty God, open the heavens above my head as of the day of Pentecost and release your power and fire upon me, in the name of Jesus.
5. Let the power of the carnal mind die, and let the spirit of God take control, in the name of Jesus.
6. Every anti–Holy Ghost revival in my life, die now, In the name of Jesus.
7. Anything standing between me and the power of God die now, in the name of Jesus.
8. I refuse to carry any evil into the second half of this year, in the name of Jesus.
9. Thank you for another day in your presence, thank you for your love, grace, and mercy, I declare you are Lord over my life, marriage, work, business, spouse, children, spirit soul and body in Jesus name.
10. Almighty God connect me to my vision and destiny fulfillers connect my business, job, my spouse, children, finances and all that concerns me with divine destiny and vision fulfillers in the mighty name of Jesus.

11. Almighty God, deliver me from vision killers and destiny destroyers wherever they may be and whoever they may be in the name of Jesus.

12. Almighty God honor your word and deliver me, my spouse, children, job, finances, business in every area of our lives from vision killers and destiny destroyers in the name of Jesus.

13. Every affliction targeted against my divine vision and destiny die and rise no more in the name of Jesus.

14. Every affliction targeted against my spouse and children's vision, our finances, business, career, and work I come against you and I command you to and rise no more in the name of Jesus.

15. Almighty God divinely connect me, and my family to our burden bearers, connect my spouse, children, business, work, finances and all that concerns us with our burden bearers, those who will help us and make life easier for us in Jesus name.

16. My vision, my destiny receive the power of God for manifestation in the name of Jesus.

17. My visions receive divine provision and divine visitation from above in the mighty name of Jesus.

18. My expectation receive the touch of Jesus for manifestation concerning my life, spouse, children, business, finances and all that concerns me in the name of Jesus Christ.

19. Almighty God, arise and liberate me from vision killers in the name of Jesus.

20. Almighty God, separate me, my spouse, children and finances from vision killers in the mighty name of Jesus.

21. Any vision killer, any destiny destroyer that is already close to me; depart by fire, wherever and whoever they may be I decree divine separation by fire between us in the name of Jesus.

22. I cancel every dreams, visions, prophesy and prayers against my life and family in the name of Jesus.

23. Talk to God about your heart desires and your situation.

24. Thank God for answered prayers.

Confession:

I believe and confess that the Lord is faithful at all times. I praise him for causing me to be favored of him and man. I boldly confess that my eyes are anointed to discover and enjoy the favor of the Lord today, in Jesus name.

Wisdom for Today:

"Nothing could be worse than the fear that one had given up too soon, and left one unexpended effort that might have saved the world." — Jane Addams

Read the Bible Today: Exodus 35–36

Prayer Points:

1. I thank God for what this prayer will do in my life and business in the name of Jesus.
2. I command all the enemies of success and prosperity in my business to turn back now, for God is for me, in the name of Jesus.
3. As you are turning back, let the doors of breakthroughs open for me now, in the name of Jesus.
4. I claim perfection of good things this month, in the name of Jesus.
5. Let the angels of God connect me with all those who will move my business forward, in the name of Jesus.
6. Let the name of my business attract favor anywhere it appears, in the name of Jesus.
7. I commit the second half of the year into God's able hands in the name of Jesus.
8. I soak the second half of this year in the blood of Jesus in the name of Jesus.
9. I shall finish the second half of this year a better person than I was in the first, in the name of Jesus.
10. Every Ahithophel, evil friend and counselor attached to any area of my life, my family, finances, spouse and children be exposed and be disgraced in the name of Jesus.
11. Untimely death hear the word of God depart from my life; depart from my helpers life in the name of Jesus.
12. Almighty God, arise and deliver my helpers from every problem, captivity, and crises, in the name of Jesus.

13. Almighty God I commit all my helpers and vision fulfillers in to your hands; give them peace and rest of mind, and comfort them in the name of Jesus.

14. Every power, spirit, persons in the heart of my vision fulfillers against me you shall not prevail; die in the mighty name of Jesus.

15. Almighty God Arise and Connect me to my vision fulfillers, connect my spouse, children, business, home, finances, job and all that concerns me in the mighty name of Jesus.

16. Almighty God arise in your power bring my burden bearer to me from the north, south, east, west, and wherever they may be bring them to me in the name of Jesus.

17. Almighty God, bring those who will help me with my burden and problem and destroy anything that might be standing against us in the mighty name of Jesus.

18. Almighty God, bring those who will help my spouse and children with their burden and problems in the mighty name of Jesus.

19. I cancel every dreams, visions, prophesy and prayers against my life and family in the name of Jesus.

20. Talk to God about your heart desires and your situation.

21. Thank God for answered prayers.

Confession:

Supernatural breakthrough follows me. I am experiencing God's abundant increase. I am anointed to experience multiple increases. Barrenness is over in my life and business, in Jesus name. I shall increase in spiritual understanding.

Wisdom for Today:

"Our greatest glory is not in ever failing, but in rising up every time we fail".

Read the Bible Today: Exodus 37–38

Prayer Points:

1. I reject failure in my business, in the name of Jesus.
2. Almighty God, give me ideas that will move my business forward, in the name of Jesus.
3. I ask God for divine wisdom that shall proper my business in the name of Jesus.
4. Almighty God, give me the power to attain wealth in the name of Jesus.
5. Almighty God, teach my hands to profit, in the name of Jesus.
6. Almighty God, order my step into prosperity, in the name of Jesus.
7. Almighty God, in this second half of this year, break the yokes I bear and give me total deliverance, in the name of Jesus.
8. I declare Jesus Christ is Lord over my life, home, marriage, work, spouse, children and every situation of my life; He is the immortal and the invisible God, the one who never dies in the name of Jesus.
9. I decree that I shall not run dry, Jesus is my source; I am connected to the source so I shall not run dry financially, spiritually, maritally and in all areas of my life in the name of Jesus.
10. Surely as the Lord liveth my spouse and children shall not run dry physically, financially and in all areas of life in the name of Jesus Christ.
11. Almighty God open the flood gate of heaven upon every dry land in my life, home, work, career, finances, in the life of my spouse and children in the name of Jesus.

12. Almighty God let every evil expectation for my life, my home, work, finances, business and every area of my life be disappointed in the name of Jesus.
13. Evil expectation for my life, home, marriage, career, ministry, my spouse, children and every area of my life break ,and be disappointed in the name of Jesus.
14. Let the power in the blood of Jesus flow into every dead area of my life, into every department of my life, my spouse, children, and let every dry bone in our lives; live in the name of Jesus.
15. I apply the blood of Jesus against every problem in every area of my life in the name of Jesus.
16. My prayers over my life, spouse, children, finances, and work shall not be in vain in the name of Jesus.
17. Lord Jesus, use your mighty power to deliver, heal and bless me, my spouse and children tonight in every area of our lives in the name Jesus name.
18. Almighty God have mercy on me and bring me, my spouse and children out of every mess, shame, fruitless prayer life, sorrow, pains, sickness, bondage and repair our lives in Jesus name.
19. Let the blood of Jesus arise in my life and repair my life in the name of Jesus.
20. I cancel every dreams, visions, prophesy and prayers against my life and family in the name of Jesus.
21. Talk to God about your heart desires and your situation.
22. Thank God for answered prayers.

Confession:

There shall be great increase in blessing, and favor. The days of my small beginnings will turn around to the time of great abundance, in the name of Jesus.

I am what God says I am; I am a Winner; am not a looser.

Wisdom for Today:

"Problems are only opportunities in work clothes".

Read the Bible Today: Exodus 39–40

Prayer Points:

1. Evil plantings in my life; be uprooted by fire, in the name of Jesus.
2. I destroy the power and influence of bewitchment upon my life, in the name of Jesus.
3. I release myself from every evil domination and control, in the name of Jesus.
4. Almighty God walk back to every second of my life and deliver me where I need delivering, heal me where I need healing, and transform me where I need transforming in the name of Jesus.
5. Holy Ghost, purge every impurity from my heart with your fire, in the name of Jesus.
6. Almighty God, create in me a clean heart, in the name of Jesus.
7. Almighty God let me experience the fullness of joy in this second half of the year, in the name of Jesus.
8. Almighty God I ask for your divine intervention concerning every situation in my life, you say we should call upon you in the days of trouble and you will answer us therefore, I call upon you concerning every situation in my life, career, finances, work, business, spouse and children in the name of Jesus.
9. Almighty God let your glory manifest in a new way for me, my household and in every area of our lives in the name of Jesus.
10. Anointing from above, fall upon my head and the head of my spouse and children's head in the name of Jesus.
11. Every evil yoke affecting my life let the anointing break them all today in my life, in the life of my spouse and children in the name of Jesus.

12. I destroy every evil yoke in my life, finances, work, and business, marriage, in the life of my spouse, children and every area of our lives in the name of Jesus.

13. I declare Jesus is Lord over my spirit, soul and body, over my family, work, finances and every area of my life and I decree He is Lord forever in Jesus name.

14. I declare the blessings of God upon my life, job, career, finances, spouse, children and every area of my life in the name of Jesus.

15. It is the blessing of God that makes one rich without adding sorrow, so I decree the blessings of God upon, every area of my life in Jesus name.

16. Almighty God open the heavens of prosperity for me, bless me with business ideas and as you bless me with the ideas, bless me with divine provision in the name of Jesus.

17. Almighty God bless me with revelation and divine vision of business ideas, open my eyes to what I ought to do in Jesus name, God manifest yourself in the mighty name of Jesus.

18. Almighty God open the heavens above my life, finances, my work, business, career, my spouse, my children and all that we do in the mighty name of Jesus Christ.

19. Almighty God give me power to get wealth and establish your covenant of prosperity, long life, joy, comfort, glory, and peace with me, my spouse, my children and in all that we do in the name of Jesus.

20. Almighty God have mercy upon me deliver me from unprofitable hard labor and hard work in Jesus name, I receive deliverance by the power in the blood of Jesus in the name of Jesus.

21. Almighty God arise and destroy the yoke of stagnancy upon my life, the life of my spouse, my children, business, marriage and every area of my life in the name of Jesus.

22. You spirit of stagnancy, lose your hold upon my life, my spouse, children, career, work, business and every area of our life in Jesus name.

23. I cancel every dreams, visions, prophesy and prayers against my life and family in the name of Jesus.

24. Talk to God about your heart desires and your situation.

25. Thank God for answered prayers.

Confession:

"So shall they fear the name of the Lord from the west and his glory from the rising of the sun. When the enemy shall come in as a flood, the spirit of the Lord shall lift up a standard against them" Isaiah 59:19.

Wisdom for Today:

"It is not because things are difficult that we do not dare, it is because we do not dare that they are difficult".

Read the Bible Today: Deuteronomy 1–2

Prayer Points:

1. Almighty God anytime I want to do the wrong thing, frustrate my effort, in the name of Jesus.
2. Any comfort that will send me to hellfire, Lord remove the comfort, in the name of Jesus.
3. Almighty God if I am my own enemy; deliver me now, in the name of Jesus.
4. Any power struggling to bury my destiny, fall down and die, in the name of Jesus.
5. I command deliverance upon my destiny from the hands of darkness, in the name of Jesus.
6. Every barrier to my greatness, comfort, career, success, breakthrough, destiny, fulfillment of dreams, glory, marriage, greatness my spouse and children, be consumed by the fire of God in the name of Jesus.
7. By the blood of Jesus Christ I scatter every power holding evil meeting for my sake physically and spiritually; I command them to scatter in the name of Jesus.
8. Almighty God open your hands to me Lord and, bless my life, family, career, spouse, children, work my labor abundantly and supply all my needs, bless me with your blessing and release good things into my life in Jesus name.
9. Almighty God secure my job for me, anything or anybody that is tormenting me, my work, marriage, finances, breakthrough and success uproot them in the name of Jesus.

10. Any one fighting against me without any cause let God arise and uproot them in the name of Jesus.

11. I decree the spirit of wisdom knowledge and understanding in all I do, for my spouse and children in the name of Jesus.

12. Almighty God have mercy upon me, make this week beginning from now my week of unbeatable, and uncommon results, I will have that breakthrough this week in the name of Jesus.

13. Let the heavens begin to announce me as the heaven announced Jesus and favor me in Jesus name.

14. By the blood of Jesus I command every long standing problem in my life be removed; let fire fall from heaven and consumed them in Jesus name.

15. Almighty God I pray for divine support and provision in the name of Jesus.

16. Thank you Lord because there is no other God besides thee, you are the covenant keeping God, glory be to your holy name, I declare you as Lord and king over my life, home, marriage every area of my life, spirit, soul and body in the name of Jesus.

17. Almighty God I thank you for this day and I dedicate this day into your hands, lead me in the way I should go in the name of Jesus.

18. 18.   , Almighty God have your way this day, this is the day you have made take absolute control of every situation in my life; strengthen my weaknesses because without you I can do nothing in the name of Jesus.

19. Almighty God I commit my prayers into your hands, lead me to pray according to your will, take over my mouth, Holy ghost take over in the name of Jesus.

20. Almighty God give your charge over my life, home, work, spouse, children and every area of my life in Jesus name.

21. Angels of the living God go to the east, west, north and south and begin to bring good things, people and all those that will help me fulfill my destiny in the name of Jesus.

22. I cancel every dreams, visions, prophesy and prayers against my life and family in the name of Jesus.

23. Talk to God about your heart desires and your situation.

24. Thank God for answered prayers.

Confession:

"The blood of Jesus shall be for me a token upon the house where I live and evil shall see the blood, and evil shall pass over me, and the plague shall not be upon me to destroy me" Exodus 12:13.

Wisdom for Today:

"Nothing is as strong as gentleness, and nothing is as gentle as true strength".

Read the Bible Today: Deuteronomy 3–4

Prayer Points:

1. I will see the goodness of the Lord in the land of the living, in the name of Jesus.
2. Let evil pass over me and my family today, in the name of Jesus.
3. Let the blood of Jesus defend me today from evil agenda, in the name of Jesus.
4. Let the blood of Jesus speak favor and deliverance on my behalf today, in the name of Jesus.
5. Angels of the living God surround me and drive affliction far away from my live, home, work, business, spouse children and every area of my life in Jesus name.
6. Every enemy of good things attached to any area of my life whoever they may be, wherever they are be uprooted, in the name of Jesus.
7. Almighty God arise and scatter every envious people that surrounds my life, home, work, finances, spouse and children in the name of Jesus.
8. Every attack against my life, home, marriage, work, spouse, children emanating from my past relationships back fire and be destroyed; it is written by the way it came in by that way it shall return therefore, every attack against my joy to destroy and frustrate me let their power become null and void in the name of Jesus.
9. Whatever the enemies have done against me that is affecting every area of my life; I call on the blood of Jesus to cancel them in the name of Jesus.
10. Whatever the enemy meant for my destruction shall turn on them in the name of Jesus Christ.
11. Every Enchantment against me, my family, my work, and business be destroyed by the blood of Jesus in the name of Jesus.

12. Thank you God for preserving me, for the gift of life, your faithfulness and grace, I declare you as Lord over my life, home, work, marriage, spouse, children in Jesus name.

13. Almighty God have mercy on me every good thing I have lost consciously or unconsciously in my life, work, finances, marriage, locate all those good things and bring them back to me in the name of Jesus.

14. I stretch forth my hands by faith that by the power of the Holy Ghost I possess every good thing in the name of Jesus.

15. It is written upon mount Zion there shall be deliverance and the house of Jacob shall possess their possession therefore, I possess my possession financially, maritally, physically and spiritually, I possess my breakthrough, that big contract , that business idea, that opportunity in the mighty name of Jesus Christ.

16. By the blood of Jesus Christ and the power of the Holy Ghost I recover all my lost ground, wasted years physically, maritally, spiritually , academically, career wise in my life, in the life of my spouse, children and every area of my life in the mighty name of Jesus Christ.

17. Almighty God, make help available for me, my children, spouse, work, business, ministry, finances and in all areas of life in the name of Jesus.

18. I claim my freedom from every curse and its consequences in the name of Jesus.

19. Almighty God, free me, my spouse, children, career, finances, business, work, marriage from every family and ancestral curse in the name of Jesus Christ.

20. By the blood of Jesus I claim my freedom from every consequence of evil pronunciation in all areas of life, in Jesus name.

21. I claim my freedom from evil dream, dream attack, spirit wife, husband, children, and evil covenant in the dream in the name of Jesus Christ.

22. Today I claim my blessings, breakthrough, success, the blessings of God, peace of mind, favor, grace, promotion in the name of Jesus.

23. The good things that are at the point of death in my life, academics, finances, marriage, business, home, in the life of my spouse, children, I command you by the power of resurrection to receive life in Jesus name.

Apostle A.O. Solomon

24. Any part of me that is not functioning well; receive the touch of God and come alive now in Jesus name.
25. I cancel every dreams, visions, prophesy and prayers against my life and family in the name of Jesus.
26. Talk to God about your heart desires and your situation.
27. Thank God for answered prayers.

Confession:

"God is my refuge and strength, a very present help in trouble. Therefore; I will not fear though the earth be removed, though the mountains be carried unto the midst of the sea, though the water thereof roar and be troubled, though the mountains shake with the swelling" Psalms 46:1–3.

Wisdom for Today:

"Never, never, never give up." —Winston Churchill

Read the Bible Today: Deuteronomy 5–6

Prayer Points:

1. It does not matter whether I deserve it or not; I receive unquantifiable favor from the Lord, in the name of Jesus.
2. Almighty God as Abraham received favor, let me receive your favor so that I can excel in every area of my life, in Jesus name.
3. Everything done against me to spoil my joy, receive destruction, in the name of Jesus.
4. My blessings will not be transferred to my neighbor this day, in the name of Jesus.
5. My body, soul, and spirit reject every evil, in the name of Jesus.
6. Almighty God, bless me, surprise me and let me be a blessing in the mighty name of Jesus.
7. Almighty God, help me to fulfill your divine program for my life in the name of Jesus.
8. I shall not die without fulfilling my divine destiny in the name of Jesus.
9. Almighty God I need your help, my spouse and children need your help to fulfill destiny in life in Jesus name.
10. We shall not die in vain; we shall live and declare you as Lord over our lives family, work, ministry business, and every situation of life in the name of Jesus.
11. Almighty God you are the master over our lives and all that concerns us in the name of Jesus.
12. Lord I thank you because you will answer my prayers, glory be to your name in Jesus name.

Apostle A.O. Solomon

13. Almighty God lay your hands upon me today; and make me whole in the name of Jesus.
14. Joy and peace in the Holy Ghost overwhelm my life, my spouse and children's lives and all that concerns us in the name of Jesus.
15. Almighty God, arise and deliver me from every evil of the night and every trouble of the night in the name of Jesus.
16. I decree in the name of Jesus the moon and stars shall not smite me, my spouse and children in the name of Jesus.
17. I decree let every old wicked thing in my life pass away in my life now in the name of Jesus.
18. I am now a new creature every old and wicked things in my life I command you to pass away in Jesus name.
19. Failure of old, bareness, sorrow, shame, disappointment in every area of my life pass away in the name of Jesus.
20. Almighty God today reverse every evil dream in my life in Jesus name.
21. Almighty God open new doors for me, my spouse, and children in Jesus name.
22. Let the power of transfiguration overshadow my life, my spouse and children in the name of Jesus.
23. Almighty God arise in your power and deliver me from every hereditary problem, sickness, poverty, marital problem, that is disturbing my life, my children and spouse, I claim deliverance from every hereditary problems in the name of Jesus.
24. Evil repetitions in my life and in my family, your time is up die in Jesus name.
25. Every evil power of marital failure, sickness, infirmity, yokes, poverty, shame, lack and ill luck pursuing my mother and father and my family at large you shall not pursue me, die in the name of Jesus.
26. I refuse to replay the failure, sickness, marital failure of my parents in my life physically, maritally, and in every area of my life in the name of Jesus.
27. I refuse to inherit any evil of my parents in the mighty name of Jesus.
28. Every blessing of my family gather yourself together and locate me in the name of Jesus.
29. I decree I am a blessed child of God, I am blessed and highly favored; I am blessed of the Lord in the name of Jesus.

30. Almighty God restore me to the perfect way you created me, whatever that has been altered in my life let there be restoration in the name of Jesus.

31. My spirit, soul and body hear the word of the Lord, I say unto you reject bewitchment in the name of Jesus.

32. I command every work of bewitchment; be destroyed in any area of my life in the name of Jesus Christ.

33. Almighty God please put an end to all my troubles financially, maritally, academically, and whatever situation might be bringing sorrow to my life, spouse and children in Jesus name.

34. Almighty God please meet my financial need in the mighty name of Jesus, prosper me, make me live in plenty and abundance, you are a covenant keeping God your word says you will supply all my needs according to your riches in glory therefore, Lord meet me at the point of my need in Jesus name.

35. I cancel every dreams, visions, prophesy and prayers against my life and family in the name of Jesus.

36. Talk to God about your heart desires and your situation.

37. Thank God for answered prayers.

Confession:

God, I remind you that I am a blood covenant child of yours. I am entitled to all your heavenly resources. I am under the blood of your Son Jesus Christ. God is my deliverer; I am dwelling in the secret place of the Most High.

Wisdom for Today:

"You gain strength, courage, and confidence by every experience in which you really stop to look fear in the face. You must do the thing which you think you cannot do."

Read the Bible Today: Deuteronomy 7–8

Prayer Points:

1. I break every covenant with poverty, in the name of Jesus.
2. By the blood of Jesus, I enter into a covenant of perfect health with God, in the name of Jesus.
3. By the blood of Jesus, I enter into a covenant of long life with God, in the name of Jesus.
4. By the blood of Jesus, I enter into a covenant of peace with God, in the name of Jesus.
5. By the blood of Jesus, I enter into a covenant of fruitfulness with God, in the name of Jesus.
6. I declare Jesus as Lord over my life and every situation, I know my redeemer lives, and Jesus Christ is Lord in Jesus name.
7. Holy Spirit of the God I declare that you take over today's prayer and have your way in the name of Jesus.
8. Almighty God this is the day you have made I will rejoice and be glad in it in the name of Jesus.
9. Almighty God, make me to prosper, increase me, and make me to succeed in Jesus name.
10. Every trouble of yesterdays and every trouble in my life, family, destiny, work I forbid you in the name of Jesus Christ.
11. I forbid every evil of my past in the mighty name of Jesus.
12. I take over this day from the hands of failure in the name of Jesus Christ.
13. Let everything that God made to favor me in the name of Jesus.

14. Almighty God, baptize me and my work with uncommon favor in the name of Jesus.
15. Whatever the enemy has prepared against me, my family and work; back fire in the name of Jesus.
16. Anyone attached to my life by the devil to destroy good things in my life, I separate from you by fire in the name of Jesus.
17. Anyone who is close to me and my family but harboring bewitchment, Father Lord; deliver me from them in the name of Jesus.
18. Almighty God; deliver me from anyone pulling my life down; connect me with those that will move my life forward in the name of Jesus.
19. Almighty God; separate our children from evil companion in the name of Jesus Christ.
20. Almighty God; deliver the destiny of my children from the hand of the wicked in the name of Jesus.
21. Every satanic manipulation in the lives of my children; be uprooted by fire in the name of Jesus.
22. Every evil seed planted into the heart of people against my life; die in the name of Jesus.
23. Every good door shut by those who hate me, angels of the living God; open them by fire in the name of Jesus.
24. I cancel every dreams, visions, prophesy and prayers against my life and family in the name of Jesus.
25. Talk to God about your heart desires and your situation.
26. Thank God for answered prayers.

Confession:

I will not be afraid. A thousand shall fall at my side and ten thousand at my right hand, but it shall not come near me. No evil shall befall me. No plague shall come near my dwelling place. God will give his angels charge over me to keep me in all my ways. They shall bear me up in their hands, lest I dash my feet against a stone. I will tread on the lion and serpent: the young lion and dragon will I trample under my feet. Psalm 91

Wisdom for Today:

"With courage you will dare to take risks, have the strength to be compassionate, and the wisdom to be humble. Courage is the foundation of integrity".

Read the Bible Today: Deuteronomy 9–10

Prayer Points:

1. Almighty God, disgrace every power that is out to thwart your program for my life, in the name of Jesus.
2. Every step I take shall lead to outstanding success, in the name of Jesus.
3. I shall prevail with man and with God in every area of my life, in the name of Jesus.
4. Evil foundation in my life, I pull you down today, in the name of Jesus.
5. Let God be glorified in every area of my life, in the name of Jesus.
6. Declare Jesus Christ is Lord.
7. Almighty God; load my life today with divine benefits in the name of Jesus.
8. By the blood of Jesus, I escape from death in the name of Jesus.
9. By the power of the almighty God, I escape from every tragedy and calamity in the name of Jesus Christ.
10. By the power of the Almighty God, I escape out of poverty, shame, disgrace, lack, snare of the devil in the name of Jesus.
11. I escape out of every shame, bondage, failure, witchcraft attack and prison in the name of Jesus.
12. Almighty God; have mercy on me; include me among those you promise to have mercy on in the name of Jesus.

13. Wherever I shall encounter any difficult situation; Almighty God, let mercy appear and turn it around in the name of Jesus.
14. Every problem I encounter let the mercy of God turn it around in the name of Jesus.
15. O God of mercy, have mercy on me and move me from glory to glory in the name of Jesus.
16. Almighty God; by your mercy enlarge my coast in the name of Jesus Christ.
17. O God of mercy, have mercy upon me and let me see your goodness in the land of the living in the name of Jesus.
18. By the blood of Jesus Christ I shall see the mercy of God in the name of Jesus.
19. Almighty God; have mercy on me; by your mercy deliver me from every trouble, in the name of Jesus Christ.
20. I cancel every dreams, visions, prophesy and prayers against my life and family in the name of Jesus.
21. Talk to God about your heart desires and your situation.
22. Thank God for answered prayers.

Confession:

I am protected by God and his holy warring angels. In God have I put my trust; I will not be afraid of what man can do to me. The blood of Jesus is sufficient for my protection. I therefore now resist all satanic attacks, in the mighty name of Jesus.

Wisdom for Today:

"Courage is not the absence of fear, but rather the judgment that something else is more important than fear."

Read the Bible Today: Deuteronomy 11–12

Prayer Points:

1. Evil waters in my body, dry up by fire, in the name of Jesus.
2. I cancel the effect of every evil dedication in my life, in the name of Jesus.
3. Fire of the Holy Ghost; immunize my blood against satanic poison, in the name of Jesus.
4. Almighty God put self-control in my mouth, in the name of Jesus.
5. I refuse to get used to ill health, in the name of Jesus.
6. Declare Jesus Christ is Lord.
7. I escape from death today in the name of Jesus.
8. I escape from depression, poverty, and lack in the name of Jesus.
9. By the power of the Almighty God, I escape from every evil trap set for me in the name of Jesus.
10. Almighty God, connect me today with your mercy in the name of Jesus Christ.
11. Almighty God; let your mercy connect me with great people in the name of Jesus.
12. Almighty God; let your mercy connect me with my Good Samaritan in the name of Jesus.
13. Almighty God; let your mercy take care of my needs in the name of Jesus.
14. Let the wisdom of God rest upon me in the name of Jesus.
15. Every good thing taken away from me, I claim them back in the name of Jesus.

16. Almighty God, have mercy upon me and move my life forward in the name of Jesus Christ.
17. I cancel every dreams, visions, prophesy and prayers against my life and family in the name of Jesus.
18. Talk to God about your heart desires and your situation.
19. Thank God for answered prayers.

Confession:

"I believe and confess that the Lord is good, for I am delivered from the trap of the enemy. The Son of God sets me free and I am free indeed. No evil befalls me. No weapon formed against me shall prosper" Isaiah 54:17.

Wisdom for Today:

"Your current safe boundaries were once unknown frontiers".

Read the Bible Today: Deuteronomy 13–14

Prayer Points:

1. Every door open to infirmity in my life, be permanently closed today, in the name of Jesus.
2. Every power contending with God in my life; be roasted by fire, in the name of Jesus.
3. Every power preventing God's glory from manifesting in my life, be paralyzed, in the name of Jesus.
4. I release myself from the spirit of desolation, in the name of Jesus.
5. Declare Jesus Christ is Lord.
6. Almighty God, send your angels to me in the name of Jesus Christ.
7. Angels of the living God, arise in your strength, minister to my needs in the name of Jesus.
8. Almighty God; I humble myself under your mighty power in the name of Jesus.
9. Almighty God; bless me with divine abilities in the name of Jesus Christ.
10. Every evil hand that is harassing my life, I command you to wither in the name of Jesus.
11. Whatever is killing others shall not come near me in the name of Jesus.
12. Almighty God, bless me with peace; deliver me from restlessness in the name of Jesus.
13. Almighty God; in every situation of my life, let your light shine in my situation in the name of Jesus.
14. Almighty God let your presence be with me in the name of Jesus.

15. Angels of the living God touch me with your miracle hands and let all satanic chain on me break off in the name of Jesus.
16. Every good door closed against me, open in the name of Jesus.
17. Almighty God; deliver me by your signs and wonders in the name of Jesus.
18. Every gate that leads to my breakthrough, open in your accord in the name of Jesus Christ.
19. Almighty God, deliver me from the spirit of Ichabod in the name of Jesus Christ.
20. Almighty God, deliver me from evil expectation and the wish of the enemy in the name of Jesus.
21. Almighty God; bless me financially in the name of Jesus.
22. Let God be God in my home, in the name of Jesus.
23. I cancel every dreams, visions, prophesy and prayers against my life and family in the name of Jesus.
24. Talk to God bout your heart desires and your situation.
25. Thank God for answered prayers.

JULY 11

Christ has redeemed me from the curse of the law. I am free from the power of the evil ones. My freedom is guaranteed in Jesus. I am covered by his precious blood.

Wisdom for Today:

"One isn't necessarily born with courage, but one is born with potential. Without courage, we cannot practice any other virtue with consistency. We can't be kind, true, merciful, generous, or honest".

Read the Bible Today: Deuteronomy 15–16

Prayer Points:

1. Let God be God in my career, in the name of Jesus.
2. Let God be God in my health, in the name of Jesus.
3. Let God be God in my economy, in the name of Jesus.
4. Glory of God; envelop every department of my life, in the name of Jesus.
5. Let the God who answers by fire appear in my situation today, in the name of Jesus.
6. Almighty God, this month give me grace for great accomplishment in the name of Jesus Christ.
7. Almighty God, work for me in the name of Jesus.
8. Declare Jesus Christ is Lord.
9. Almighty God, open the heavens for us in the name of Jesus.
10. Power of God, Mercy of God, and Grace of God come upon us and sustain us in the name of Jesus.
11. Almighty God, perfect all that concerns me in the name of Jesus.
12. Almighty God, by your never failing power, make this month a month of great accomplishment for me in the name of Jesus.
13. Almighty God, make this month, a month of great achievement for me in the name of Jesus.
14. Almighty God, make this month a month of possibilities for me in the name of Jesus.
15. Whatsoever I have been unable to do in the past, I receive divine power to do them in the name of Jesus.
16. Almighty God, connect me this month to my vision fulfillers in the name of Jesus.
17. Almighty God, arrange a divine meeting between me and my vision and destiny fulfillers in the name of Jesus.

18. Almighty God make this month, a month of divine change for me in the name of Jesus.
19. Positive changes come into my life in the name of Jesus.
20. Almighty God, change my times and season for good in the name of Jesus.
21. Almighty God, have mercy on me, don't allow me to suffer any loss in the name of Jesus.
22. Arrows of death, I am not your candidate; my family are not your candidate, go back to your sender in the name of Jesus.
23. I cancel every dreams, visions, prophesy and prayers against my life and family in the name of Jesus.
24. Talk to God about your heart desires and your situation.
25. Thank God for answered prayers.

Confession:

As a child of covenant, I believe and confess that the God is good; for He causes me to have victory through the Lord Jesus Christ. I thank the Lord for defeating Satan on my behalf in the name of Jesus. By faith, I confess that the victory of the Lord will prevail over the challenges that I am facing.

Wisdom for Today:

"I cannot give you the formula for success, but I can give you the formula for failure—which is: Try to please everybody".

Read the Bible Today: Deuteronomy 17–18

Prayer Points:

1. All my enemies shall scatter to rise no more, in the name of Jesus.
2. Blood of Jesus, cry against all gatherings for my sake, in the name of Jesus.
3. Almighty God, convert all my past failures to unlimited victories, in the name of Jesus.
4. Lord Jesus, create room for my advancement in every area of life in the name of Jesus.
5. Almighty God, turn all evil thoughts against me, to breakthroughs for me, in Jesus name
6. Every evil dream, programmed to manifest in my life, I cancel you in the name of Jesus.
7. Almighty God, I have started this month with you, uphold me in the name of Jesus.
8. Almighty God, don't let me end this month with sorrow in the name of Jesus.
9. Every evil conspiracy against my work, back fire in the name of Jesus.
10. Declare Jesus Christ is Lord.
11. I reject oppression and affliction in all areas of my life in the name of Jesus.
12. Every satanic agenda for my life, work and family this month, vanish in the name of Jesus.
13. Every evil association consciously or unconsciously; release me in the name of Jesus.

14. Almighty God, restore back to me all the opportunities I have lost in the name of Jesus.
15. Almighty God, give me a new name in the name of Jesus.
16. Almighty God, connect me with my destiny in the name of Jesus.
17. Almighty God, deliver me from the bondage of impossibility in the name of Jesus.
18. Almighty God, this month of July let my life experience divine acceleration in the name of Jesus.
19. I cancel every dreams, visions, prophesy and prayers against my life and family in the name of Jesus.
20. Talk to God about your heart desires and your situation.
21. Thank God for answered prayers.

Confession:

I confess that the hand of the enemy will not prevail against me. Rather, for every weariness, tiredness and attack of the enemy; I gain victory over them in the name of Jesus.

Wisdom for Today:

"Success does not consist in never making blunders, but in never making the same one a second time."

Read the Bible Today: Deuteronomy 19–20

Prayer Points:

1. Almighty God, release the evil decisions that have been made against me by evil men, in the name of Jesus.
2. Let the showers of astonishing prosperity fall on every department of my life, in the name of Jesus.
3. I claim all my prosperity, in the name of Jesus.
4. Every door of my prosperity that has been shut; be opened now, in the name of Jesus.
5. Almighty God let all grace abound in my life in the name of Jesus.
6. By the power of the Holy Ghost and by the grace of Jesus I receive the wealth of the wicked in the name of Jesus.
7. My body; reject sickness in the name of Jesus.
8. Almighty God let your angels minister to me in my dreams in the name of Jesus.
9. Declare Jesus Christ is Lord.
10. Dedicate the day to the Lord.
11. Almighty God, be magnified in every area of my life in the name of Jesus.
12. Almighty God let me not be ashamed, let not my enemies triumph over me in the name of Jesus.
13. Almighty God, meet me at the point of my financial need in the name of Jesus.
14. Almighty God, don't let money hinder my breakthrough in the name of Jesus.
15. Almighty God, remove my name from the list of evil register in the name of Jesus.

16. Almighty God, deliver me from past ugly experiences in the name of Jesus.
17. Almighty God, have mercy upon me, turn everything making me to weep into joy in the name of Jesus.
18. Almighty God, you are a covenant keeping God, I pray for restoration in the name of Jesus.
19. I cancel every dreams, visions, prophesy and prayers against my life and family in the name of Jesus.
20. Talk to God about your heart desires and your situation.
21. Thank God for answered prayers.

"By faith, I confess that I will succeed in spite of failures, for the Lord will make my life peculiar to Him out of many people. God will cause me to have victory over sin and dominion over situations" Isaiah 43:4.

Wisdom for Today:

"The secret of success in life is for a man to be ready for his opportunity when it comes".

Read the Bible Today: *Deuteronomy 21–22*

Prayer Points:

1. Almighty God convert my poverty to prosperity, in the name of Jesus.
2. Almighty God convert my mistakes to perfection, in the name of Jesus.
3. Almighty God convert my frustration to fulfillment, in the name of Jesus.
4. Almighty God, bring honey out of the rock for me, in the name of Jesus.
5. I stand against every evil covenant of sudden death, in the name of Jesus.
6. Almighty God show me your glory, goodness, and mercy as from today in the name of Jesus.
7. Almighty God, I declare your glory in my life, your wonders in my situation in the name of Jesus.
8. Almighty God, make my life beautiful in the name of Jesus.
9. Almighty God, this month give me grace for great accomplishment in the name of Jesus Christ.
10. Almighty God, work for me in the name of Jesus.
11. Almighty God let it please you to bless me in the name in the name of Jesus.
12. I receive grace to accomplish that which the Lord has ordained for my life in the name of Jesus.
13. As the redeemed of the Lord whatever I say is so in the name of Jesus; therefore I say to myself, it is well with me in the name of Jesus.
14. Almighty God let it be unto me according to your word and declaration in the name of Jesus.

15. Almighty God, preserve my Job in the name of Jesus.
16. Almighty God, bless all that I do and give me profit in all that I do in the name of Jesus.
17. Sudden destruction will not be my lot in the name of Jesus.
18. Almighty God, reverse every curse in my life in the name of Jesus.
19. Every evil covenant that is disturbing any area of my life break in the name of Jesus.
20. You gates of death reject me and my family in the name of Jesus.
21. Every appointment with death, break in the name of Jesus.
22. I cancel every dreams, visions, prophesy and prayers against my life and family in the name of Jesus.
23. Talk to God about your heart desires and your situation.
24. Thank God for answered prayers.

Confession:

By faith, I confess that I will eat the good of the land. I give God praise for turning around famine years and making them harvest times. I bless the name of the Lord because He will bring a harvest as I sow the seed I have.

Wisdom for Today:

"Impatience never commanded success".

Read the Bible Today: Deuteronomy 23–24

Prayer Points:

1. You, stones of death, depart from my ways, in the name of Jesus.
2. Almighty God, make me a voice of deliverance and blessings, in the name of Jesus.
3. I tread upon the high places of the enemies, in the name of Jesus.
4. Every seed I shall sow shall bring me a hundredfold harvest, in the name of Jesus.
5. You, evil current of death, release your grip over my life, in the name of Jesus.
6. Almighty God, this month give me grace for great accomplishment in the name of Jesus Christ.
7. Almighty God, work for me in the name of Jesus.
8. Almighty God I thank you because with you on my side I will not fail in the name of Jesus.
9. Almighty God, cause my heart to be at rest all the time in the name of Jesus.
10. Almighty God, keep me from leaning and relying on my own understanding and intelligence in the name of Jesus.
11. Almighty God, help me to focus on you alone in the name of Jesus.
12. I claim the victory of the cross of Jesus Christ for my life in the name of Jesus.
13. Almighty God, enable me to become the person you created me to be in the name of Jesus.
14. By the blood of Jesus Christ, I receive open heaven for my life in the name of Jesus.
15. I refuse to be the meat of witchcraft in the name of Jesus Christ.

16. I retrieve my destiny out of the hands of the enemy in the name of Jesus.
17. Almighty God, anoint me with the oil of gladness above my fellows in the name of Jesus.
18. My live, family, and members of my church are secured in the name of Jesus.
19. Almighty God, I pray for financial supply in the name of Jesus.
20. Almighty God, register my name among the rich, I refuse to be poor in the name of Jesus.
21. I cancel every dreams, visions, prophesy and prayers against my life and family in the name of Jesus.
22. Talk to God about your heart desires and your situation.
23. Thank God for answered prayers.

Confession:

I praise the name of the Lord because he will destroy every attack of the evil ones against my life. I do not lean on my own understanding, but I totally depend on the grace of God. Every project I lay my hands on will succeed, in Jesus name.

Wisdom for Today:

"Success is the sum of small efforts, repeated day in and day out."

Read the Bible Today: Deuteronomy 25–26

Prayer Points:

1. Fire of protection; cover me and my family in the name of Jesus.
2. Almighty God, make my way perfect, in the name of Jesus.
3. Throughout the days of my life, I shall not be put to shame, in the name of Jesus.
4. I reject every garment of shame, in the name of Jesus.
5. I reject every shoe of shame, in the name of Jesus.
6. Shamefulness shall not be my lot, in the name of Jesus.
7. I hear the sound of abundance; nothing shall hinder the manifestation of bounty in my life, in the name of Jesus.
8. Appreciate the Lord for all He has done.
9. Declare Jesus Christ is Lord.
10. Dedicate the day to God
11. Almighty God, open the heaven for my prayers in the name of Jesus Christ.
12. Almighty God, give me rest from all my troubles and fear in the name of Jesus.
13. Almighty God, lay waste every mountain and hill in the name of Jesus.
14. Almighty God, I lift up my hands to you, hold my hands in the name of Jesus.
15. Almighty God, without you there cannot be me, hold my hands and keep me in the name of Jesus.
16. Almighty God, terminate any problem sharing glory in my life in the name of Jesus.
17. Almighty God, open before me the double doors in the name of Jesus Christ.

18. Almighty God, go before me and make all the crooked places straight in the name of Jesus.
19. O God of Israel arise give me the hidden riches and treasures of hidden places in the name of Jesus.
20. In the name of Jesus, you heavens begin to rain upon my life in the name of Jesus.
21. I cancel every dreams, visions, prophesy and prayers against my life and family in the name of Jesus.
22. Talk to God about your heart desires and your situation.
23. Thank God for answered prayers.

Confession:

The Lord will cause every demonic network to be defeated for my sake. The devil will not prevail over my life and all that belongs to me. The word of God is the basis for my success, and he will link me with those who will bless me.

Wisdom for Today:

"If your actions inspire others to dream more, learn more, do more and become more, you are a leader."

Read the Bible Today: Haggai 1–2

Prayer Points:

1. Every demonic limitation on my progress as a result of shame be removed, in the name of Jesus.
2. Every network of shame around me; be paralyzed, in the name of Jesus.
3. As far as shame is concerned, I shall not record any points for satan, in the name of Jesus.
4. In the name of Jesus, I shall not eat the bread of sorrow, I shall not eat the bread of shame, and I shall not eat the bread of defeat, in the name of Jesus.
5. Almighty God, bring your blessings to my life in Jesus name.
6. Almighty God, give me the power to prevail in life in the name of Jesus.
7. Almighty God, heal me with your power in the name of Jesus.
8. No evil will touch me throughout my life, in the name of Jesus.
9. Almighty God; give me power of problem solving ideas in the name of Jesus.
10. Any family or ancestral curse operating in any area of my life break and release me by the blood of Jesus in the name of Jesus.
11. Let the curses of those I have offended and is now affecting my life be removed in the name of Jesus.
12. Any word spoken by my parents, and any woman in anger, and is now affecting my life, blood of Jesus Christ reverse them in the name of Jesus.

13. Anywhere my parents or anyone has visited on my behalf for solution in the past, almighty God deliver me from them in the name of Jesus.
14. Almighty God, surprise me with pleasant surprises in the name of Jesus.
15. Almighty God, deliver me from the hands of those who are stronger than me in the name of Jesus.
16. O God of all grace, put an end to my suffering, extend all grace to all the areas of my life in the name of Jesus.
17. Perfect me, establish me, settle me O Lord in the name of Jesus.
18. My father in heaven, bless me in the name of Jesus.
19. Almighty God, don't let poverty and lack kill my vision in the name of Jesus.
20. O God of more than enough manifest yourself in my life in the name of Jesus.
21. Almighty God, make room for me in the name of Jesus.
22. I cancel every dreams, visions, prophesy and prayers against my life and family in the name of Jesus.
23. Talk to God about your heart desires and your situation.
24. Thank God for answered prayers.

JULY 18

Confession:

"Thou will show me the path of life: in thy presence is fullness of joy; at thy right hand there are pleasures for evermore" Psalms 16:11.

Wisdom for Today:

"He who has learned how to obey will know how to command."

Read the Bible Today: Habakkuk 1–2

Prayer Points:

1. I shall reach my goal, in the name of Jesus.
2. In every area of my life, my enemies will not catch me, in the name of Jesus.
3. In every area of my life, I shall run and not grow weary; I shall walk and shall not faint, in the name of Jesus.
4. Almighty God let not my life disgrace you, in every area of life in the mighty name of Jesus.
5. I will not be a victim of failure, and I shall not bite my finger for any reason, in the name of Jesus.
6. Almighty God, help me to meet your standard for my life, in the name of Jesus.
7. Give God thanks for His favor.
8. Declare God favors me.
9. Jesus Christ is Lord over my situation in the name of Jesus.
10. Declare Jesus Christ is Lord.
11. Lord I thank you for my family in the name of Jesus.
12. Almighty God, forgive my ancestors in the name of Jesus.
13. Blood of Jesus Christ flow into my life and disconnect me from every evil family blood flow in the name of Jesus.
14. I refuse to suffer for the sins of my parents in the name of Jesus.
15. The glory of my family that is in captivity be released in the name of Jesus.
16. The blessings of my family that is in captivity be released in the name of Jesus.
17. The prosperity of my family that has been buried come out and locate me in the name of Jesus.
18. Almighty God, arise and separate me from every family limitation in the name of Jesus.

19. Almighty God, you are my deliverer, deliver me from every common evil in my life in the name of Jesus.

20. Almighty God, by the greatness of your power; begin something new, something glorious in my life in the name of Jesus.

21. Anything in my father's house, my mother's house caging my destiny, O God arise and consume them by fire in the name of Jesus.

22. Almighty God, pass through my father's family, my mother's family, and uproot any evil tree harboring my blessings in the name of Jesus.

23. Almighty God, have mercy upon me and my family and restore the glory of my family in the name of Jesus.

24. I cancel every dreams, visions, prophesy and prayers against my life and family in the name of Jesus.

25. Talk to God about your heart desires and your situation.

26. Thank God for answered prayers.

Confession:

I have victory over problems and situations. My hands are strengthened by the Lord, and the voice of victory shall not stop in my household. The favor and the blessings of the Lord rest upon my home, for the hand of opposition shall always fail against me.

Wisdom for Today:

"Reputation is what men and women think of us; character is what God and angels know of us." — Thomas Paine

Read the Bible Today: Habakkuk 3

Prayer Points:

1. I refuse to be a candidate for spiritual amputations, in the name of Jesus.
2. I shall move to higher ground with each day of my life, in the name of Jesus.
3. Every spirit of shame set in motion against my life; I bind and paralyze you, in the name of Jesus.
4. Every spirit working against my breakthroughs ; be chained permanently with fetters that cannot be broken, in the name of Jesus.
5. I bind every spirit of slavery, in the name of Jesus.
6. In every day of my life, I disgrace all my evil pursuers, in the name of Jesus.
7. Declare Jesus Christ is Lord.
8. I shall be free indeed in the name of Jesus.
9. I Plead the blood of Jesus over my life in the name of Jesus.
10. I lose myself from every evil from both sides of my family in the name of Jesus.
11. By the power in the blood of Jesus, I break and lose myself from every family struggle in the name of Jesus.
12. Blood of Jesus Christ, ransom me and my family wherever we have been sold off in the name of Jesus.
13. Almighty God, locate and destroy anything that is not making marriage to work in my family, in the name of Jesus.
14. Almighty God, deliver me and my family from every limitation in the name of Jesus.

15. Holy Ghost arise, and pull me out of every evil family coven in the name of Jesus.
16. I claim deliverance from every evil pattern in the name of Jesus.
17. Every sickness running in my family, I attack you by the blood of Jesus die in the name of Jesus.
18. I will reach my goal; nothing will hinder me in the name of Jesus.
19. Every evil covenant and curse upon my life break in the name of Jesus.
20. I cancel every dreams, visions, prophesy and prayers against my life and family in the name of Jesus.
21. Talk to God about your heart desires and your situation.
22. Thank God for answered prayers.

Confession:

The Lord will raise me and make me a testimony of his wealth and riches to the glory of his name, in the precious name of Jesus.

Wisdom for Today:

"Nothing of character is really permanent but virtue and personal worth".

Read the Bible Today: Nahum 1–2

Prayer Points:

1. I thank God for today.
2. I bind every spirit that destroys things at infancy in my life, in the name of Jesus.
3. I speak destruction unto every roadblock erected against my progress in life in the name of Jesus.
4. Almighty God let my breakthroughs baffle my enemies, in the name of Jesus.
5. Declare Jesus Christ is Lord.
6. I plead the blood of Jesus Christ over me and my family in Jesus name.
7. Every curse against my family, blood of Jesus Christ break and turn them to blessings in the name of Jesus.
8. Blood of Jesus minster deliverance to my family in the name of Jesus.
9. Every curse of infirmity issued upon my family break by the blood of Jesus in the name of Jesus.
10. Blood of Jesus turn into a mighty flood and wash away every evil, curse from my family in the name of Jesus.
11. Almighty God; arise and be at the center of my family in the name of Jesus.
12. All my enemies submit yourself to me in the name of Jesus.
13. Almighty God; thoroughly plead my case and give me rest in the name of Jesus.
14. Every witchcraft agent in my life, be arrested and confess in the name of Jesus.
15. Almighty God, destroy every work of internal enemy in my life in the name of Jesus.

16. Almighty God repair everything destroyed in my life and family, in the name of Jesus.
17. Almighty God, according to your word let weeping come to an end in my life in the name of Jesus.
18. I cancel every dreams, visions, prophesy and prayers against my life and family in the name of Jesus.
19. Talk to God about your heart desires and your situation.
20. Thank God for answered prayers.

Apostle A.O. Solomon

Confession:

I give thanks, praise and honor to the Almighty God for the opportunity to be alive and healthy today. I thank the Lord for access to His throne through the precious Lord Jesus Christ. I bless the name of the Lord for proving Himself mighty and strong on my behalf. By the spirit of prophesy and by faith, I confess that the Lord give to me opportunities to touch humanity with my talent. I am a blessing to the human race.

Wisdom for Today:

"A good name will shine forever. " —Proverbs 9:43

Read the Bible Today: Nahum 3

Prayer Points:

1. I paralyze all problem expanders, in the name of Jesus.
2. Almighty God, make me a channel of your blessing, in the name of Jesus.
3. Let my hand be stronger than all opposing hands, in the name of Jesus.
4. I decree that people will always love to bless me, favor me, and be good to me, in the name of Jesus.
5. I choose blessing and life today; I reject curses and death, in the name of Jesus.
6. All shall be well with me today, in the name of Jesus.
7. Declare Jesus Christ is Lord.
8. I plead the blood of Jesus Christ over my family line in the name of Jesus.
9. Almighty God, deliver me and my family from anything that will bring mass destruction in the name of Jesus.
10. Every evil covenant in my family, I come against you by the blood of Jesus Christ break in the name of Jesus.
11. Every evil covenant entered by any member of family, break in the name of Jesus.
12. Almighty God, have mercy upon me and my family deliver us from affliction in the name of Jesus.
13. Almighty God, magnify yourself in my life and the life of my family in the name of Jesus Christ.

14. I bring my family under the covenant of the blood of Jesus in the name of Jesus.

15. I renounce every evil family oat and covenant by the blood of Jesus Christ in the name of Jesus.

16. Almighty God; show my family your mercy in the name of Jesus.

17. I break and lose myself from every evil family covenant in the name of Jesus.

18. I refuse to suffer for the sins of my parents in the name of Jesus Christ.

19. I command peace upon my life in the name of Jesus.

20. Fire of deliverance possess my life and set me free in the name of Jesus Christ.

21. Through Jesus Christ my Lord and savior my family and I are blessed in Jesus name.

22. Untimely death, my life is not your candidate in the name of Jesus.

23. Barrenness my life is not your candidate in the name of Jesus.

24. Poverty, hear the word of the Lord, depart from my life in the name of Jesus.

25. I cancel every dreams, visions, prophesy and prayers against my life and family in the name of Jesus.

26. Talk to God about your heart desires and your situation.

27. Thank God for answered prayers.

Confession:

I take authority over the spirit of disunity, disfavor, and betrayal from finding a way into work, in the name of Jesus. No evil shall befall me, and no danger shall come near my working or dwelling place. God will cause me to shine as light in this crooked world.

Wisdom for Today:

Sow an act, and you reap a habit; sow a habit, and you reap a character; sow a character, and you reap a destiny. – Emerson Ralph Waldo

Read the Bible Today: *Micah 1–2*

Prayer Points:

1. I reject evil invitation to backwardness, in the name of Jesus.
2. Every spirit of Pharaoh; be disgraced in my life, in the name of Jesus.
3. Every Red Sea before me; be parted, in the name of Jesus.
4. All my failures this year; be converted to miracles, in the name of Jesus.
5. I command every stone of hindrance in my life to be rolled away, in the name of Jesus.
6. I claim dominion over prosperity and breakthrough today, in the name of Jesus.
7. Worship the King of Kings.
8. Declare Jesus Christ is Lord.
9. Almighty God, choose me for miracles in the name of Jesus.
10. Almighty God let me experience your visitation today in the name of Jesus.
11. Lord I humble myself under your mighty power in the name of Jesus.
12. Almighty God, restore back the chances I have missed in the name of Jesus.
13. Almighty God, baptize me with the spirit of faith in the name of Jesus Christ.
14. Almighty God, remove failure in my life; baptize me with the spirit of wisdom, knowledge and understanding in the name of Jesus.
15. I plead the blood of Jesus over my life in the name of Jesus.

16. Almighty God; have mercy upon my parents and ancestors that has brought curses upon us; forgive us in the name of Jesus Christ.

17. By the blood of Jesus Christ I separate myself from every evil running in my family in the name of Jesus.

18. By the blood of Jesus Christ I refuse to suffer for the sins of my parents in the name of Jesus Christ.

19. Every affliction in my life, as a result of parental and ancestral sins I plead the blood of Jesus Christ in the name of Jesus.

20. Almighty God, give me a new beginning in the name of Jesus.

21. I cancel every dreams, visions, prophesy and prayers against my life and family in the name of Jesus.

22. Talk to God about your heart desires and your situation.

23. Thank God for answered prayers.

Confession:

I give thanks to the Lord in advance, for my labor will not be in vain. God, himself, will shower his blessing and favor upon me and command fruitfulness on every venture I carry out. I take authority over sickness that tries to hinder me from achieving my vision. I subdue hindrances to my business or work and cancel all such hindrance in the name of Jesus. I receive breakthrough in the area of my finance in the name of Jesus.

Wisdom for Today:

Talents are best nurtured in solitude. Character is best formed in the stormy billows of the world.

Read the Bible Today: Micah 3–4

Prayer Points:

1. Almighty God, roll away every stone of hardship and slavery from my life, in the name of Jesus.
2. Almighty God, roll away every stone of stagnancy stationed at the border of my life and blessings, in the name of Jesus.
3. Let the power from above come upon me now, in the name of Jesus.
4. Declare Jesus Christ is Lord.
5. Lord Jesus; give me the power over all demons and to cure diseases in the name of Jesus.
6. Every work of the enemy in my life, I bind and cast you out in the name of Jesus Christ.
7. Every spirit of fear, poverty and lack, failure at the edge of miracle I bind and cast you out in the name of Jesus.
8. I lose the blessing of God upon my life in the name of Jesus.
9. Anything that satan is using to hinder me let the fire of God consume them in Jesus name.
10. By the blood of Jesus Christ, satan get thee behind me in the name of Jesus.
11. Ask God for a great visitation.
12. Give thanks to the Lord Almighty.
13. Declare Jesus Christ is Lord.

14. Lord Jesus Christ show up in my situation and let every negative thing in my life give up in the name of Jesus.
15. Declare Jesus Christ is Lord.
16. Lord Jesus; give me the power over all demons and to cure diseases in the name of Jesus.
17. Every work of the enemy in my life, I bind and cast you out in the name of Jesus Christ.
18. Every spirit of fear, poverty and lack, failure at the edge of miracle I bind and cast you out in the name of Jesus.
19. I lose the blessing of God upon my life in the name of Jesus.
20. I cancel every dreams, visions, prophesy and prayers against my life and family in the name of Jesus.
21. Talk to God about your heart desires and your situation.
22. Thank God for answered prayers.

Confession:

I bless the name of the Lord because he causes me to increase and gives me profit. All that I have is covered with the blood of Jesus. I give God praise for his faithfulness in Jesus name. I step out into this day with confidence in God, with the blood of Jesus and the Holy Ghost power and fire.

Wisdom for Today:

Our character is but the stamp on our souls of the free choices of good and evil we have made through life.

Read the Bible Today: Micah 5–6

Prayer Points:

1. Almighty God, manifest your power in every area of my life, in the name of Jesus.
2. Almighty God, make me a power generator throughout the days of my life, in the name of Jesus.
3. Let the power to live a holy life throughout the days of my life fall upon me, in the name of Jesus.
4. Let the Spirit of God rest upon the life of my children in the name of Jesus.
5. Almighty God, arise and deliver my children from affliction in the name of Jesus.
6. Almighty God; give me and my family a new beginning in the name of Jesus.
7. By the blood of Jesus Christ we cancel every appointment with death in the name of Jesus.
8. Almighty God, enlarge my coast and bless me indeed in the name of Jesus.
9. Almighty God, command deliverance and blessing upon my life in the name of Jesus.
10. Almighty God visit my life, let my failure, pain, and shortcoming disappear in the name of Jesus.
11. Almighty God, arise and rebuild the damage walls of my life in the mighty name of Jesus.
12. Every satanic whisperer; be silenced in the name of Jesus.

13. Every bewitchment upon my life; be destroyed in the name of Jesus.
14. Almighty God, deliver me from failure at the edge of success in the name of Jesus.
15. Every power, every spirit, any agent arranging battle for me at the edge of my breakthrough in all areas of my life, let fire go before God and consume them in the name of Jesus Christ.
16. Almighty God wherever I have failed, God give me a miracle in the name of Jesus.
17. I cancel every dreams, visions, prophesy and prayers against my life and family in the name of Jesus.
18. Talk to God about your heart desires and your situation.
19. Thank God for answered prayers.

Confession:

By the spirit of prophesy, I believe and confess that God's abundance flows into my life. The Lord will do exceedingly great and mighty things in my life, for the breakthroughs of abundance beyond my imagination rests upon my life. I shall experience blessing in every area of my business and home.

Wisdom for Today:

Reputation is for time; character is for eternity.

Read the Bible Today: Micah 7

Prayer Points:

1. Let the power to prosper throughout the days of my life fall upon me, in the name of Jesus.
2. Let the power to be in good health throughout the days of my life fall upon me, in the name of Jesus.
3. Let the power to disgrace the enemies throughout the days of my life fall upon me, in the name of Jesus.
4. Let the power of Christ rest upon me now, in the name of Jesus.
5. I claim all-round peace and comfort, in the name of Jesus.
6. This second half of the year shall bless me more than the first, in the name of Jesus.
7. Begin to thank the Lord.
8. Almighty God, lay your hand upon me and make me whole in the name of Jesus.
9. Almighty God, lose me from every bond of satan in the name of Jesus.
10. Get thee behind me satan; I overcome you by the blood of the lamb and the words of my testimony in Jesus mighty name.
11. I Command every satanic item in my life to fall in the name of Jesus Christ.
12. Blood of Jesus Christ stand between me and failure in every aspect of my life in Jesus name.
13. Blood of Jesus Christ stand between me and poverty, lack and depression in the name of Jesus.
14. Blood of Jesus Christ stand between me and every problem in my life in the name of Jesus.

15. I reject bad luck in all areas of my life in the name of Jesus Christ.
16. I carry God's divine favor in the mighty name of Jesus.
17. By the blood of Jesus I reject tragedy and misfortune in the mighty name of Jesus.
18. Every power of satan hindering any area of my life, the Lord rebuke you in the name of Jesus.
19. Almighty God separate me from every satanic agent assigned to hinder me in the name of Jesus.
20. I cancel every dreams, visions, prophesy and prayers against my life and family in the name of Jesus.
21. Talk to God about your heart desires and your situation.
22. Thank God for answered prayers.

Apostle A.O. Solomon

Confession:

The grace of God abounds unto me; the Lord opens unto me his abundant treasure. The Lord causes long-suffering and goodness that is abundant toward me to increase. I boldly command every hidden treasure of abundance to be exposed to me that the riches of the ungodly will enter into my hand for favor and blessing, and I shall know the grace of God without trouble.

Wisdom for Today:

Character is a diamond that scratches every other stone.

Read the Bible Today: Jonah 1–2

Prayer Points:

1. Let the power to bind and release fall upon me now, in the name of Jesus.
2. Almighty God let your key of revival unlock every department of my life for your revival fire, in the name of Jesus.
3. Every good area of my life that is at the point of death, receive the touch of resurrection now, in the name of Jesus.
4. Let the word of God prosper in my life without measure, in the name of Jesus.
5. I release the power in the blood of Jesus to my situation in the name of Jesus.
6. Dry bones in my life, receive the blood of Jesus and come alive in the name of Jesus.
7. Every dry bone in my life, receive the blood of Jesus and live in the name of Jesus.
8. I cover my door post with the blood of Jesus in the name of Jesus.
9. Blood of Jesus arise in your power and fight for me in Jesus name.
10. I am made perfect through the blood of the everlasting covenant in Jesus name.
11. I have redemption through the blood of Jesus in the name of Jesus.
12. Every spirit of fear operating in my life, I rebuke you in the name of Jesus.
13. I receive healing through the blood of Jesus in the name of Jesus.

14. I receive deliverance through the blood of Jesus in the name of Jesus.
15. Every evil yoke upon my life break in the name of Jesus.
16. I cancel every dreams, visions, prophesy and prayers against my life and family in the name of Jesus.
17. Talk to God about your heart desires and your situation.
18. Thank God for answered prayers.

Confession:

I believe and confess that the Lord anoints my eyes to see the hidden riches of this world. He causes creativity to flow in my life and business; my ears are anointed to hear what God is saying; my eyes are anointed to see what God has in store; my hands are anointed to touch the blessings set aside for me, in Jesus name.

Wisdom for Today:

In the stormy current of life characters are weights or floats which at one time make us glide along the bottom and at another maintain us on the surface.

Read the Bible Today: Jonah 3–4

Prayer Points:

1. Let the fire of God fall and consume all hindrances to my advancement, in the name of Jesus.
2. You, stubborn problems in my life, receive the fire of the Holy Ghost and disappear, in the name of Jesus.
3. My blessing will not miss me, and I shall not miss my blessings, in the name of Jesus.
4. Let my angels of blessings locate me now, in the name of Jesus.
5. Every history of failure in my family; be changed to success, in the name of Jesus.
6. Every history of marital problems and crisis in my family be changed to peace, in the name of Jesus.
7. Almighty God I come into your presence by the blood of Jesus Christ in the name of Jesus.
8. Almighty God, shine your light to every department of our lives in the name of Jesus.
9. Jesus Christ is Lord over my life therefore; I refuse to live in darkness in the name of Jesus.
10. Blood of Jesus open up all the doors and gates short against me in the name of Jesus.
11. Every evil dream in my life; be cancelled in the name of Jesus.
12. Every good dream and vision in my life; receive the power of God and manifest in the name of Jesus.

13. Any evil dream programmed for manifestation in my life this week, month, this year I cancel you by the blood of Jesus in the name of Jesus.
14. I plead the blood of Jesus over every dream in my life in the name of Jesus.
15. Holy Ghost; baptize our children in the name of Jesus.
16. I cancel every dreams, visions, prophesy and prayers against my life and family in the name of Jesus.
17. Talk to God about your heart desires and your situation.
18. Thank God for answered prayers.

Confession:

There shall be an outbreak of the rain of God's favor in my life. For the Lord will cause my life to be exceedingly blessed. The Lord will cause me to enter his great favor.

Wisdom for Today:

Every human being is intended to have a character of his own; to be what no others are, and to do what no other can do.

Read the Bible Today: Obadiah 1

Prayer Points:

1. Every satanic program of impossibility, I cancel you now by the blood of Jesus, in Jesus name.
2. Every household wickedness and its program of impossibility be paralyzed, in the name of Jesus.
3. No curse will land on my head throughout the days of my life, in the name of Jesus.
4. Throughout the days of my life, I will not waste money on my health; the Lord shall be my healer, in the name of Jesus.
5. Throughout the days of my life, I will not depart from the presence of God, in Jesus name.
6. Every history of sickness and poverty in my family; be reversed, in the name of Jesus.
7. I claim uncommon favor and blessing today, in the name of Jesus.
8. Almighty God I come into your presence by the Blood of Jesus Christ in the name of Jesus.
9. Almighty God, shine your light to every department of our lives in the name of Jesus.
10. Jesus Christ is Lord over my life therefore; I refuse to live in darkness in the name of Jesus.
11. Blood of Jesus open up all the doors and gates short against me in the name of Jesus.
12. Every evil dream in my life be cancelled in the name of Jesus.
13. Every good dream and vision in my life; receive the power of God and manifest in the name of Jesus.

14. Any evil dream programmed for manifestation in my life this week, month, this year I cancel you by the blood of Jesus in the name of Jesus.
15. I plead the blood of Jesus over every dream in my life in the name of Jesus.
16. Let the Spirit of God rest upon the life of my children in the name of Jesus.
17. Almighty God, arise and deliver my children from affliction in the name of Jesus.
18. Almighty God; give me and my family a new beginning in the name of Jesus.
19. By the blood of Jesus Christ we cancel every appointment with death in the name of Jesus.
20. Almighty God, enlarge my coast and bless me indeed in the name of Jesus.
21. Almighty God, command deliverance and blessing upon my life in the name of Jesus.
22. Almighty God visit my life, let my failure, pain, and shortcoming disappear in the name of Jesus.
23. Almighty God, arise and rebuild the damage walls of my life in the name of Jesus.
24. Every satanic whisperer be silenced in the name of Jesus.
25. Every bewitchment upon my life be destroyed in the name of Jesus.
26. Almighty God, deliver me from failure at the edge of success in the name of Jesus.
27. Every power, every spirit, any agent arranging battle for me at the edge of my breakthrough in all areas of my life, let fire go before God and consume them in the name of Jesus Christ.
28. Almighty God wherever I have failed, God give me a miracle in the name of Jesus.
29. I cancel every dreams, visions, prophesy and prayers against my life and family in the name of Jesus.
30. Talk to God about your heart desires and your situation.
31. Thank God for answered prayers.

Confession:

I boldly confess that God makes my spiritual life good and fruitful. He causes prosperity on my business and ventures. I receive by faith, wisdom, knowledge, and divine creativity to excel in life. I boldly declare that I become a point of reference to the glory of God for the Lord causes me to increase even in the midst of my tribulation, and my tribulation will produce an eternal way to glory.

Wisdom for Today:

Every great dream begins with a dreamer. Always remember, you have within you the strength, the patience, and the passion to reach for the stars to change the world.

Read the Bible Today: Amos 1–2

Prayer Points:

1. Throughout the days of my life, I will be in the right place at the right time, in the name of Jesus.
2. Throughout the days of my life, I will not depart from the fire of God's protection, in the name of Jesus.
3. Throughout the days of my life, I will not be a candidate for incurable disease, in the name of Jesus.
4. Every weapon of captivity fashioned against me, be disgraced, in the name of Jesus.
5. I cancel every form of sorrow, bad news, loss, and premature death, in this second half of the year, in the name of Jesus.
6. I plead the blood of Jesus Christ over my prayers in the name of Jesus.
7. Declare Jesus Christ is Lord.
8. Declare, I know that my redeemer liveth in the name of Jesus.
9. Almighty God, manifest your presence in my life in the name of Jesus.
10. Almighty God, show me your kindness in the name of Jesus Christ.
11. Any power that wants to attack me in my dream, perish in the name of Jesus.
12. By the ordinances that establish day and night, I reject every evil dream and attacks in the name of Jesus.

13. By the ordinances that establish day and night, let all those seeking my life, die in the name of Jesus.
14. Almighty God, shift every battle in my life to the camp of my enemies in the name of Jesus.
15. Almighty God, deliver me from harvest eaters and destroyers in the name of Jesus.
16. Every power pushing me away from the road of success and progress be consumed by the anger of God in the name of Jesus.
17. Almighty God if I have been forced away from the road of success and progress, take me back, and establish me in the name of Jesus.
18. Any power, any spirit that want to force me into hiding, die in the name of Jesus.
19. I cancel every dreams, visions, prophesy and prayers against my life and family in the name of Jesus.
20. Talk to God about your heart desires and your situation.
21. Thank God for answered prayers.

Confession:

I boldly declare that the Lord will command every drought and famine area in my life to be transformed to abundance. He will cause his contentment to be upon me. The blessings of Zion flow into my life. The grace of sufficiency abounds unto me, in the precious name of Jesus. I am what God says I am; I am a winner and not a loser.

Wisdom for Today:

Delight yourself in the dreams of the future rather than the history of the past.

Read the Bible Today: Amos 3–4

Prayer Points:

1. Almighty God I need an outstanding miracle and blessing today, in the name of Jesus.
2. Let every attack planned against the progress of my life be frustrated, in the name of Jesus.
3. I command the spirit of harassment and torment to leave me, in the name of Jesus.
4. Almighty God, examine my life today and reveal my weaknesses in prayer to me, in the name of Jesus.
5. Let divine strength come into my life, in the name of Jesus.
6. Declare Jesus Christ is Lord.
7. I reject frustration today in the name of Jesus.
8. By the blood of Jesus Christ, I take over this day in the name of Jesus.
9. Almighty God, give me wisdom, knowledge and understanding to excel in all areas of life in the name of Jesus Christ.
10. I bring myself and my family under the coverage of the blood of Jesus Christ in the name of Jesus.
11. By the blood of Jesus Christ, I reject every evil in this day in the name of Jesus.
12. I withdraw the secret of my life from the hands of the enemy in the name of Jesus Christ.
13. Almighty God, show me your kindness in the name of Jesus.
14. Almighty God, forgive my iniquity and remember my sin no more in the name of Jesus.

15. Almighty God; make a new covenant with me in the name of Jesus.
16. Almighty God, perform the good things which you have promised me in the name of Jesus.
17. By the ordinances that establish the day and night, I command every good door closed against me to open in the name of Jesus.
18. By the ordinances that establish the day and night, I command the pipeline of prosperity to open into my life in the name of Jesus.
19. By the ordinances that establish the day and night, I command every evil dream to die in the name of Jesus.
20. By the ordinances that establish the day and night, I command every power blocking my way in this country, perish in the name of Jesus.
21. I cancel every dreams, visions, prophesy and prayers against my life and family in the name of Jesus.
22. Talk to God about your heart desires and your situation.
23. Thank God for answered prayers.

Confession:

I boldly confess and possess all-round blessings, in Jesus name. I receive God's divine endorsement and proclaim God's divine endorsement now, in all that I do. For the Lord will favor me with his divine direction. The Lord is exposing all my hidden blessings.

Wisdom for Today:

Commitment leads to action. Action brings your dream closer.

Read the Bible Today: Amos 5–6

Prayer Points:

1. Almighty God revive my prayer life by your fire, in the name of Jesus.
2. I receive God's endorsement for my blessings today, in the name of Jesus.
3. Let every evil behind my problems be destroyed in the name of Jesus.
4. Every satanic attempt to downgrade my potential be frustrated now, in the name of Jesus.
5. Let my life begin to show forth the glory of God in all areas, in the name of Jesus.
6. Declare Jesus Christ is Lord.
7. Blood of Jesus Christ begin to flow in my system in the name of Jesus.
8. Almighty God, show me great mercy in the name of Jesus.
9. Let impossibility become possible in my life in the name of Jesus.
10. Almighty God; show me your great mercy and make way for me where there seems to be no way in the name of Jesus.
11. Almighty God; show me the kind of mercy that you showed to David in the name of Jesus.
12. Almighty God; show me the kind of mercy that you showed to Elizabeth in the name of Jesus.
13. Almighty God Let your great mercy begin to defend my life in the name of Jesus.
14. Almighty God I trust in your mercy let my heart rejoice in your salvation in the name of Jesus.

15. Every power and spirit rebelling against my light; be consumed by the fire of God in the name of Jesus.
16. The season is changing in my favor, in the name of Jesus.
17. I cancel every dreams, visions, prophesy and prayers against my life and family in the name of Jesus.
18. Talk to God about your heart desires and your situation.
19. Thank God for answered prayers.

Confession:

"O death, where is thy sting? O grave, where is thy victory?" 1 Corinthians 15:55.

Wisdom for Today:

Our greatest glory consists not in our falling, but in rising every time we fall.

Read the Bible Today: Amos 7–8

Prayer Points:

1. Christ Jesus has redeemed me from the spirit and power of sin and death by his precious blood in the name of Jesus.
2. I cancel every dream of death today by the blood of Jesus, in Jesus name.
3. I cancel every utterance and prophesy of death against me and my family by the blood of Jesus, in Jesus name.
4. I am a living proof of God's abounding power, favor, and mercy, in Jesus name.
5. I will experience only sweetness throughout the days of my life, in Jesus name.
6. I shall not die, but live to declare the works of God in Jesus name.
7. Declare Jesus Christ is Lord.
8. I declare it is my turn in the name of Jesus.
9. Almighty God, deliver me from the spirit of slumber in the name of Jesus.
10. Every power working against my prayers; be destroyed by fire in the name of Jesus.
11. Every delay strategy of the enemy in order to frustrate my life; be destroyed in the name of Jesus Christ.
12. Almighty God; have mercy upon me; restore all the years delay has taken from me; in the name of Jesus.
13. Every yoke of delay upon any area of my life; be destroyed in the name of Jesus.
14. Every yoke of stagnancy upon my life; be destroyed in the name of Jesus.
15. Power of God, break me free and move my life forward in the name of Jesus.

16. Everything holding me down and preventing me from moving forward, be destroyed in the name of Jesus.
17. Every problem sponsored by the enemy to keep me at the same spot; backfire in the name of Jesus.
18. Everything standing as red sea in my life, give way in the name of Jesus.
19. Every power pushing me away from the road of success and progress; be destroyed by the fire of God in the name of Jesus.
20. Almighty God if I have been pushed away take me back and keep me going in the name of Jesus.
21. Any power that wants to force me into hiding, you shall not prevail, you shall not prosper; die in Jesus name.
22. I cancel every dreams, visions, prophesy and prayers against my life and family in the name of Jesus.
23. Talk to God about your heart desires and your situation.
24. Thank God for answered prayers.

Apostle A.O. Solomon

AUGUST 2

Confession:

"Glory in the Lord; O worshipers of God, rejoice. Search for him and for his strength, and keep on searching" Psalms 105:3, 4.

Wisdom for Today:

Press on! A better fate awaits you.

Read the Bible Today: Amos 9 and John 21

Prayer Points:

1. I unplug myself from every evil family socket, in the name of Jesus.
2. I disconnect myself from every family idol, in the name of Jesus.
3. Foundational pollution in my life, vanish by the blood of Jesus in the name of Jesus.
4. Every problem in my life from the womb, die, in the name of Jesus.
5. Anything in my foundation that the enemy is using against me be destroyed by fire, in the name of Jesus.
6. Arrows of deliverance go to my foundation now and deliver me, in the name of Jesus.
7. I declare boldly that the joy of the Lord is my strength today, and I shall not be defeated in the name of Jesus.
8. Almighty God, I stand still before your presence, fight my battles for me in the name of Jesus.
9. Almighty God sanctify and empower my leg, let me be at right place, at the right time in the name of Jesus.
10. Almighty God don't let me be useless in the name of Jesus.
11. Almighty God give me power to fulfill my destiny in the name of Jesus.
12. Bless me Lord and make me a blessing in the name of Jesus.
13. Almighty God, do what no man can do in my life in the name of Jesus.
14. Almighty God let me and my family dwell in safety in the name of Jesus.
15. Almighty God by the greatness of your power let my enemies submit to me in the name of Jesus.
16. Almighty God; don't let me labor in vain in the name of Jesus.

17. You spirit of failure at the edge of success, the Lord rebuke you in my life in the name of Jesus.
18. You spirit of almost there in my life, I command you to depart from my life in the name of Jesus.
19. I decree I shall get to my promised land; and I will reach my goal in the name of Jesus.
20. Almighty God; by your great mercy open the flood gates of heaven in the name of Jesus.
21. Any power making me to move in circles let fire fall and consume them in the name of Jesus.
22. Almighty God, show me great mercy that will cause my neighbor to rejoice with me in the name of Jesus.
23. Almighty God; let your great mercy open doors for me in the name of Jesus.
24. Almighty God Let your great mercy answer for me in every physical and spiritual court in the name of Jesus.
25. Almighty God; show me great mercy, heal and deliver me in the name of Jesus.
26. I cancel every dreams, visions, prophesy and prayers against my life and family in the name of Jesus.
27. Talk to God about your heart desires and your situation.
28. Thank God for answered prayers.

Confession:

"Affliction shall not rise up the second time" Nahum 1:9.

Wisdom for Today:

The important thing in life is to have great aim and to possess the aptitude and the perseverance to attain it.

Read the Bible Today: Joel 1–2

Prayer Points:

1. I destroy every power binding me to poverty by the blood of Jesus, in the name of Jesus name.
2. I destroy every power binding me to failure, in the name of Jesus.
3. I destroy every power of affliction operating in my life, in the name of Jesus.
4. I destroy by the blood of Jesus every power binding me to disappointment, in the name of Jesus.
5. I put off every garment of affliction, and I put on the garment of favor, glory, and comfort, in Jesus name.
6. I am blessed and highly favored, in the name of Jesus.
7. Almighty God, do what only you can do in my life, in the name of Jesus.
8. I give thanks to God.
9. Almighty God, help me to worship you in spirit and in truth in the name of Jesus.
10. Almighty God I present my body on your altar as a living sacrifice in the name of Jesus Christ.
11. Almighty God, help me to do what is right in your sight in the name of Jesus.
12. Almighty God anything that will not allow me to get to my promised, remove them in the name of Jesus.
13. Almighty God, do what no man or woman can do for me before the end of this month in the name of Jesus.
14. Almighty God let my battles expire with this month in the name of Jesus.
15. Almighty God; deliver me from every satanic retaliation in the name of Jesus.

16. Let the blood of Jesus Christ arise and defend me against any satanic retaliation in the name of Jesus.

17. Any man or woman wanting to retaliate against me be silenced in the name of Jesus.

18. Almighty God don't allow affliction to rise again in my life in the name of Jesus.

19. I cancel every dreams, visions, prophesy and prayers against my life and family in the name of Jesus.

20. Talk to God about your heart desires and your situation.

21. Thank God for answered prayers.

Confession:

"Bless my family and me forever" 2 Samuel 7:29.

Wisdom for Today:

Persistent people begin their success where others end in failure.

Read the Bible Today: *Joel 3*

Prayer Points:

1. Almighty God, give me the power to prosper in all areas of life in the name of Jesus.
2. The blessings of God shall never depart from my family, in the name of Jesus.
3. My portion shall not be given to others, in the name of Jesus.
4. Almighty God, fight for me and my family in the name of Jesus.
5. Almighty God disgrace household witchcraft in my family, in the name of Jesus.
6. Declare Jesus Christ is Lord.
7. Every attack against my children; go back to your sender in the name of Jesus.
8. I refuse my children to be used for sacrifice in the name of Jesus.
9. Anointing of success fall upon my children in the name of Jesus.
10. Almighty God; deliver my children from sickness in the name of Jesus.
11. Almighty God; give my children grace and power to excel in the name of Jesus.
12. I prophesy my children shall not cause me sorrow in the name of Jesus.
13. Almighty God; as you blessed Joseph in Egypt; bless me in this land in the name of Jesus.
14. Almighty God; don't allow those who hate me to decide my promotion in the name of Jesus.
15. Almighty God; I know my case cannot be too hard for you; settle me in the name of Jesus.
16. I cancel every dreams, visions, prophesy and prayers against my life and family in the name of Jesus.
17. Talk to God about your heart desires and your situation.
18. Thank God for answered prayers.

Confession:

"If the son therefore shall make you free, ye shall be free indeed"
John 8:36.

Wisdom for Today:

Discipline is the bridge between goals and accomplishment.

Read the Bible Today: Judges 1–2

Prayer Points:

1. Evil family altars catch fire and be destroyed, in the name of Jesus.
2. Every family idol, release my life by fire, in the name of Jesus.
3. Every conscious and unconscious covenant with death, break by the blood of Jesus.
4. Almighty God, transport me to the right place of my destiny, in the name of Jesus.
5. Anything in me strengthening bondage, die now, in the name of Jesus.
6. Evil anointing upon my life, dry up by fire, in the name of Jesus.
7. I disconnect myself from every blood covenant working against my life, in the name of Jesus.
8. You, bondage of past sexual sin, break now, in Jesus name.
9. Declare Jesus Christ is Lord.
10. Almighty God, lead me in the way I should go in the name of Jesus.
11. Almighty God; I commit the labor of my hands to you in the name of Jesus.
12. Almighty God, shift away every battle in my life in the name of Jesus.
13. Almighty God; I commit my family to your hands; keep them in the name of Jesus.
14. Almighty God, consume everything that the devil is using to keep me in the same spot with your fire in the name of Jesus.
15. Fire of God pass through my family and set me free in the name of Jesus.
16. Whatever is killing people in my family, you shall not prevail over my life in the name of Jesus.

Apostle A.O. Solomon

17. Whatever is limiting people in my family, you shall not prevail over my life in the name of Jesus.
18. Almighty God, separate me from friends that are pulling me back in the name of Jesus.
19. Every abandoned good project in my life, almighty God take over and finish them in the name of Jesus.
20. Almighty God, bless me and give me grace and power to enjoy it in the name of Jesus.
21. I cancel every dreams, visions, prophesy and prayers against my life and family in the name of Jesus.
22. Talk to God about your heart desires and your situation.
23. Thank God for answered prayers.

Confession:

"For by grace are ye saved" Ephesians 2:8.

Wisdom for Today:

Don't follow any advice, no matter how good, until you feel as deeply in your spirit as you think in your mind that the counsel is wise.

Read the Bible Today: Judges 3–4

Prayer Points:

1. That which is killing people in my family, relinquish your hold and power over my life, in the mighty name of Jesus.
2. I eat the flesh of Jesus for perfect health, and I drink the blood of Jesus for life, in the name of Jesus.
3. I refuse the enemy to waste my life, in the name of Jesus.
4. I plead and cover myself with the blood of Jesus in the name of Jesus.
5. Almighty God, surround me with your hedge of fire, in the name of Jesus.
6. Every problem defiling my prayers, the Lord rebuke you in the name of Jesus.
7. King of glory; manifest your glory in my life in the name of Jesus.
8. Thou prince of peace, manifest your peace in every area of my life in the name of Jesus.
9. Almighty God set me free from every limitation in the name of Jesus.
10. I drink the blood of Jesus Christ and I obtain healing and deliverance in the name of Jesus.
11. Almighty God, I commit my work to your hands in the name of Jesus.
12. Power of God, possess my hand for healing and deliverance in the name of Jesus Christ.
13. I reject every attack in my dream in the name of Jesus.
14. Almighty God; let the heaven open for me and let me see the visions of God in the name of Jesus.
15. I cancel every dreams, visions, prophesy and prayers against my life and family in the name of Jesus.
16. Talk to God about your heart desires and your situation.
17. Thank God for answered prayers.

Confession:

"The Lord is my rock, and my fortress, and my deliverer; my God, my strength, in whom I will trust" Psalms 18:2.

Wisdom for Today:

From the errors of others, a wise man corrects his own. – Syrus, Publilius

Read the Bible Today: Judges 5–6

Prayer Points:

1. Every habitation of wickedness firing arrows at my destiny, receive the fire of God and be roasted, in the name of Jesus.
2. Almighty God, appear now in the camp of my enemies and scatter them, in the name of Jesus.
3. O God of Elijah let me experience your signs and wonders, in the name of Jesus.
4. Let the fire of God burn away every existence of darkness in my life, in the name of Jesus.
5. Everyone who carries an evil burden into my life, carry that burden away now, in the name of Jesus.
6. Every internal enemy against my destiny and progress; be frustrated in the name of Jesus Christ.
7. Almighty God, show me your great mercy in the name of Jesus.
8. Every satanic strategy to make me lose my blessings, fail woefully in the name of Jesus.
9. Every effort of my enemy to keep me at the same spot, fail woefully in the name of Jesus.
10. Every power impersonating me, die in the name of Jesus.
11. Almighty God, don't let me go empty handed in the name of Jesus.
12. Every problem in my life making people to mock my God, die in the name of Jesus.
13. Every power challenging God in my life, almighty God scatter them in the name of Jesus.
14. Every Goliath boasting against my life, you will not survive in the name of Jesus.
15. Almighty God, defend my personality and defend my interest in the name of Jesus.

16. Almighty God, give me grace to move forward in the name of Jesus.
17. Almighty God wherever I have been trapped, deliver me in the name of Jesus.
18. Almighty God, help me to control my spirit in the name of Jesus.
19. I cancel every dreams, visions, prophesy and prayers against my life and family in the name of Jesus.
20. Talk to God about your heart desires and your situation.
21. Thank God for answered prayers.

Confession:

"Behold, the Lord God will help me; who is he that shall condemn me? Lo, they all shall wax old as a garment; the moth shall eat them up" Isaiah 50:9.

Wisdom for Today:

If you're trying to achieve, there will be roadblocks. I've had them; everybody has had them. But obstacles don't have to stop you. If you run into a wall, don't turn around and give up. Figure out how to climb it, go through it, or work around it.

Read the Bible Today: Judges 7–8

Prayer Points:

1. Almighty God, comfort me on every side in the mighty name of Jesus.
2. Every curse that I have issued consciously or unconsciously against myself, break by the blood of Jesus in the name of Jesus.
3. Every power promoting tears in my life, and the life of my family members die, in the name of Jesus.
4. Almighty God, deliver my eyes from evil tears, in the name of Jesus.
5. I shall weep no more, in the name of Jesus.
6. Jesus Christ is Lord.
7. Every evil stronghold erected against me in this country, I pull you down in the name of Jesus.
8. By the power of the Holy Ghost, I come out of every slavery life in the name of Jesus.
9. Almighty God, deliver me from every limitation in the name of Jesus.
10. By the power of the Holy Ghost, I remove every garment of darkness in the name of Jesus.
11. Almighty God, solve my financial need in the name of Jesus.
12. Almighty God, give me financial miracle and deliverance in the name of Jesus Christ.
13. My hands are blessed in the name of Jesus.
14. Almighty God; heal my heart and spirit in the name of Jesus Christ.

15. Almighty God; open my eyes to the mystery of the kingdom of heaven in the name of Jesus.
16. Almighty God, bless me with your knowledge, wisdom and understanding in the name of Jesus Christ.
17. Almighty God; reveal to me the secret of giving and sowing in the name of Jesus.
18. Almighty God; give me the result of my seed in the name of Jesus Christ.
19. Every power destroying my harvest be destroyed in the name of Jesus.
20. Every power swallowing my money die in the name of Jesus.
21. Every Power assigned to put me on the sick bed; you shall not prosper in the name of Jesus.
22. I cancel every dreams, visions, prophesy and prayers against my life and family in the name of Jesus.
23. Talk to God about your heart desires and your situation.
24. Thank God for answered prayers.

Confession:

"Keep thyself pure" 1 Timothy 5:22.

Wisdom for Today:

In seeking wisdom thou art wise; in imagining that thou hast attained it—thou art a fool.

Read the Bible Today: Judges 9–10

Prayer Points:

1. Almighty God, sanctify my spirit, soul, and body, in the name of Jesus.
2. Every object of bewitchment in my possession, be exposed and be destroyed, in the name of Jesus.
3. I have accepted Jesus Christ as my Lord and Savior; I therefore break every covenant with the kingdom of satan, in Jesus name.
4. I cut myself off from inherited poverty and affliction, in the name of Jesus.
5. As Goliath bowed to David, so shall all my enemies bow and submit themselves unto me, in the name of Jesus.
6. Begin to give thanks unto the Lord.
7. Declare Jesus Christ is Lord.
8. Every satanic strategy to block my blessings fail woefully in the name of Jesus Christ.
9. Almighty God; arise for my sake and fight for me in the name of Jesus.
10. I plead the blood of Jesus Christ over my spirit, soul and body in the name of Jesus.
11. Almighty God; send your angels to help me today in the name of Jesus Christ.
12. Almighty God; send your angels to the north, south, east, and west to bring my blessings in the name of Jesus.
13. Anywhere my blessings has been hiding, I command the angels of God to release them in the name of Jesus.
14. Let my helpers be released from captivity in the name of Jesus.
15. Every attack against my helpers, backfire in the name of Jesus.
16. I speak unto this day, favor me and work against my enemies in the name of Jesus Christ.

17. I refuse my destiny and blessings to be sabotaged in the name of Jesus.
18. Every power sabotaging any area of my life; be destroyed in the name of Jesus.
19. Almighty God; it is written: ask and it shall be given to you, therefore by faith in Jesus Christ I ask for my blessings in the name of Jesus.
20. Almighty God; as you deliver the Israelites out of their tight corner; deliver me in the name of Jesus.
21. Almighty God; make a way for me where there seems to be no way in the name of Jesus.
22. Almighty God; show me your great mercy, deliver me from sadness and sorrow in the name of Jesus.
23. Almighty God; I commit my children to your hand in the name of Jesus.
24. Blood of Jesus Christ come on our lives; mark us for safety and favor in the name of Jesus.
25. I cancel every dreams, visions, prophesy and prayers against my life and family in the name of Jesus.
26. Talk to God about your heart desires and your situation.
27. Thank God for answered prayers.

Confession:

"I am with you, that is all you need. My power shows up best in weak people"

2 Corinthians 12:9.

Wisdom for Today:

It is a characteristic of wisdom not to do desperate things.

Read the Bible Today: Judges 11–13

Prayer Points:

1. Every power that is planting sorrow into my life, family, and business, carry your seeds away and die, in the name of Jesus.
2. I shall laugh last over my enemies, in the name of Jesus.
3. Arrows of sorrow, go back to your sender, in the name of Jesus.
4. I withdraw every support that I have given to the enemies over my life through crying, complaining, sinning, and unforgivingness, in the name of Jesus.
5. I remove myself from the control of every evil authority, in the name of Jesus.
6. Declare Jesus Christ is Lord.
7. Almighty God; have mercy upon me and remember me in the name of Jesus.
8. You spirit of fear and doubt keeping me in the wilderness of life, I bind and cast you out in the name of Jesus.
9. Every confusion holding me captive, break away in the name of Jesus.
10. Every past sin and error that is keeping me down physically, spiritually, financially be removed by the blood of Jesus Christ in the name of Jesus.
11. Almighty God; deliver me from the captivity of wrong counsel in the name of Jesus Christ.
12. Almighty God; deliver me from any human being blocking my success in the name of Jesus.
13. Let the way make way for me in all areas of life in the name of Jesus.
14. Thank the Lord for blessing the works of your hands.
15. Declare Jesus Christ is Lord.

16. Almighty God I give you all the glory in the name of Jesus.
17. Almighty God; I commit my job, school, ministry, business into your hands in the name of Jesus.
18. Almighty God, connect me to that one man that will make the difference in my life in the name of Jesus.
19. Almighty God, connect me with my burden bearer in the name of Jesus.
20. Almighty God, show me your great mercy, breath on me in the name of Jesus.
21. Every witchcraft power attacking the works of my hands, die in the name of Jesus.
22. Almighty God, deliver me from every witchcraft coven in the name of Jesus.
23. Almighty God, show me your great mercy and don't allow the wicked to determine my progress in the name of Jesus.
24. I reject unprofitable hard labor in the name of Jesus.
25. Every witchcraft power urinating on my life, business, work and destiny die in the name of Jesus.
26. You my labor receive deliverance in the name of Jesus Christ.
27. I cancel every dreams, visions, prophesy and prayers against my life and family in the name of Jesus.
28. Talk to God about your heart desires and your situation.
29. Thank God for answered prayers.

Confession:

"The Blood of Jesus shall be for me a token upon the house where I live and evil shall see the blood, and evil shall pass over me, and the plague shall not be upon me to destroy me" Exodus 12:13.

Wisdom for Today:

"It requires wisdom to understand wisdom: the music is nothing if the audience is deaf." —Walter Lippman.

"Knowledge comes, but wisdom lingers." —Alfred Lord Tennyson

"Memory is the mother of all wisdom." —Aeschylus

Read the Bible Today: Judges 14–15

Prayer Points:

1. Almighty God, pump your blood into my blood, in Jesus name.
2. Let impossibilities in my life become possible, in Jesus name.
3. I break every family curse upon my life, in Jesus name.
4. Power to prevail in prayer; fall upon me now, in Jesus name.
5. Almighty God, replace everything needing replacement in my life, in Jesus name.
6. Let the blood of Jesus cleanse me of every evil mark from head to toe, in Jesus name.
7. Declare Jesus Christ is Lord.
8. God of new beginnings visit my life In the name of Jesus Christ.
9. Almighty God; you are my God; I put my trust in you, manifest in the name of Jesus.
10. Almighty God; let heaven release blessing for me in the name of Jesus.
11. Anything in my environment that is limiting my life, I command you to break away in the name of Jesus.
12. Almighty God; I commit my environment into your hands; revive it in the name of Jesus.
13. Everything I need in life let heaven begin to supply in the name of Jesus.
14. Almighty God, open to me your good treasure in the name of Jesus.
15. Almighty God let the heavens give rain to my land in its season in the name of Jesus.

16. Almighty God; Show me your great mercy, let me lend; to many nations in the name of Jesus.

17. I reject demotion in every area of life; I claim promotion in the name of Jesus.

18. Almighty God; arise and take me to my promised land in the name of Jesus.

19. Almighty God; let the victory of the cross of Jesus Christ manifest in all areas of my life in the name of Jesus.

20. I cancel every dreams, visions, prophesy and prayers against my life and family in the name of Jesus.

21. Talk to God about your heart desires and your situation.

22. Thank God for answered prayers.

AUGUST *12*

Confession:

"God is my refuge and strength, a very present help in trouble. Therefore; I will not fear though the earth be removed, though the mountains be carried unto the midst of the sea, though the water thereof roar and be troubled, though the mountains shake with the swelling" Psalms 46:1–3.

Wisdom for Today:

Obstacles are those frightful things you see when you take your eyes off your goal.

Read the Bible Today: Judges 16–17

Prayer Points:

1. I refuse to be shaken by the enemy, in Jesus name.
2. I regain my balance today in all areas of life, in the name of Jesus.
3. I claim abundance in every area of my life, in Jesus name.
4. I reverse all damages done to my life from the womb, in Jesus name.
5. Almighty God, give me power to overcome all the challenges of the enemy, in Jesus name.
6. Give God all the praise.
7. Declare Jesus Christ is Lord.
8. I plead the blood of Jesus against every negative and evil dream in my life and I command them, to be cancelled in the name of Jesus.
9. Almighty God, empower your dreams and visions for my life to come to pass in the name of Jesus Christ.
10. Almighty God, deliver me from every affliction following me about as a result of negative thinking in the name of Jesus.
11. I reject every satanic inspiration in the name of Jesus.
12. Almighty God, open every good door that I have shut against myself, in the name of Jesus.
13. By the blood of Jesus Christ, you failure in my life fall, and I command success to arise in the name of Jesus.
14. Every kingdom of failure, barrenness, I command you to fall and rise no more in the name of Jesus.
15. Almighty God, supply all that I need in the name of Jesus.

16. You spirit of pride, get thee behind me in Jesus name.
17. Almighty God, I humble myself under your mighty power, exalt me in due season in the name of Jesus.
18. I cancel every dreams, visions, prophesy and prayers against my life and family in the name of Jesus.
19. Talk to God about your heart desires and your situation.
20. Thank God for answered prayers.

Apostle A.O. Solomon

Confession:

I am a blood covenant child of God. I am entitled to all heavenly resources; I am under the blood of Jesus Christ. God is my deliverer. I am dwelling in the secret place of the Most High.

Wisdom for Today:

Patience is the companion of wisdom.

Read the Bible Today: Judges 18–19

Prayer Points:

1. Let the blood of Jesus remove every curse placed upon my family, in Jesus name.
2. Let my breakthroughs begin to locate me and gravitate toward me, in Jesus name.
3. Every agent of shame be paralyzed, in Jesus name.
4. Every demonic resistance to my prayers be broken by fire, in Jesus name.
5. Almighty God let all those who do not want to see me around go for me, in the name of Jesus.
6. Declare Jesus Christ is Lord.
7. Almighty God, manifest your great power in the name of Jesus.
8. Almighty God; by your power subdue my enemies, and problems in the name of Jesus.
9. Almighty God; let your great power change my story tonight in the name of Jesus.
10. Great power of the living God, subdue every opposition to my glory in the name of Jesus.
11. Great power of the living God, make new ways for me in the name of Jesus.
12. By the power of the living God, I decree no opposition shall prevail over my life and destiny in the name of Jesus.
13. Almighty God, help me to identify and operate in my territory in the name of Jesus.
14. I prevail over every opposition in the name of Jesus.
15. Every stranger occupying my God given territory I cast you out in the name of Jesus Christ.
16. Almighty God, show me your great mercy in the name of Jesus.

17. By the stripes of Jesus I am healed in the name of Jesus.
18. I am complete in Christ Jesus in the name of Jesus.
19. I cancel every dreams, visions, prophesy and prayers against my life and family in the name of Jesus.
20. Talk to God about your heart desires and your situation.
21. Thank God for answered prayers.

Confession:

"I will not be afraid. A thousand shall fall at my side and ten thousand at my right hand, but it shall not come near me" Psalms 91:7.

Wisdom for Today:

"To be satisfied with a little is the greatest wisdom; and he that increaseth his riches increaseth his cares; but a contented mind is a hidden treasure, and trouble findeth it not." —Akhenaton

Read the Bible Today: Judges 20–21

Prayer Points:

1. I claim my freedom from the consequences of attitude problems, in Jesus name.
2. I claim my freedom from the consequences of idolatry, in Jesus name.
3. I claim my freedom from the consequences of sins by the blood of Jesus, in Jesus name.
4. Let the healing power of God flow into every damaged part of my body, in Jesus name.
5. I release the creative miracle of God into every department of my life and marriage, in Jesus name.
6. Declare Jesus Christ is Lord.
7. Almighty God, help me not to fight useless battles in the name of Jesus.
8. Help me Lord, to fight the good fight of faith in the name of Jesus.
9. Almighty God; give me a heart that perceive, an eye that sees and ear that hears in the name of Jesus.
10. Almighty God, help me to recognize your voice in the name of Jesus.
11. I shall not die in the battle field in the name of Jesus.
12. You spirit of stubbornness, I bind and cast you out of my life in the name of Jesus.
13. Almighty God; hide me in your secret place, from the plots of men in the name of Jesus.
14. Almighty God; arise destroy and divide the tongues of my enemies in the name of Jesus.

15. Almighty God; lift me up before those who are pulling me down in the name of Jesus.
16. Almighty God, lead me to prosperity and success in the name of Jesus Christ.
17. I prevail over my enemies in all areas of life in the name of Jesus.
18. I triumph over sickness, failure, poverty, dream attack, family crisis, in the name of Jesus.
19. Every waster in my life, depart in the name of Jesus.
20. Every destroyer in my life, I cast you out in the name of Jesus.
21. Every emptier, in my life, I cast you out depart in the name of Jesus.
22. I refuse to labor for my enemies in the name of Jesus.
23. I reject wasted efforts in the name of Jesus.
24. Every power attacking my labor and my profit; you shall not prevail in the name of Jesus.
25. Almighty God; show me your great power and promote me by signs and wonders in the name of Jesus.
26. Angels of the living God; guide me to my promised land in the name of Jesus.
27. Every good door I closed against myself, I open you now by fire, by force in the name of Jesus.
28. Holy Spirit, arise and control the affairs of my life in the name of Jesus.
29. I cancel every dreams, visions, prophesy and prayers against my life and family in the name of Jesus.
30. Talk to God about your heart desires and your situation.
31. Thank God for answered prayers.

Confession:

"No evil shall befall me. No plague shall come near my dwelling place" Psalms 91:10.

Wisdom for Today:

To conquer fear is the beginning of wisdom. Turn your wounds into wisdom.

Read the Bible Today: Proverbs 1–2

Prayer Points:

1. Almighty God, restore me fully, in Jesus name.
2. Almighty God, empower my life with your authority over every demonic force that sets itself against my life, in Jesus name.
3. Almighty God, take me from where I am to where you want me to be, in Jesus name.
4. I refuse to be in any tight corner in life, in the name of Jesus.
5. Almighty God, break me and remold me, in Jesus name.
6. Holy Spirit of God, breathe upon my dry bones and make me fruitful in the name of Jesus.
7. Holy Spirit of God spread your wings over my life and cover me with your shadow in the name of Jesus.
8. I shall not pray in vain, I shall see the result of prayer in the name of Jesus.
9. I shall not pray when it is too late in the name of Jesus
10. Almighty God, encourage me to pray in the name of Jesus.
11. Holy Spirit of God, possess me now and let me mount with wings as eagles in the name of Jesus.
12. My prayer life receive deliverance in the name of Jesus.
13. My prayer life receive revival in the name of Jesus.
14. Result of my prayers wherever you are manifest in the name of Jesus.
15. Frustration at hour of prayer my life is not your candidate, die and rise no more in the name of Jesus.
16. Distraction and confusion at the hour of prayer, my life is not your candidate, die and rise no more in the name of Jesus.
17. I cancel every dreams, visions, prophesy and prayers against my life and family in the name of Jesus.
18. Talk to God about your heart desires and your situation.
19. Thank God for answered prayers.

Confession:

"God will give his angels charge over me to keep me in all my ways. They shall bear me up in their hands, lest I dash my feet against a stone" Psalms 91:11–12.

Wisdom for Today:

We are made wise not by the recollection of our past, but by the responsibility for our future.

Read the Bible Today: Proverbs 3–4

Prayer Points:

1. Almighty God, make me break through into astonishing miracles in all areas of my life, in Jesus name.
2. By your power, O Lord, I break out of every obstacle on my way to progress, in Jesus name.
3. Almighty God add flavor to my life, work, and marriage, in Jesus name.
4. Every witchcraft battle at the edge of my breakthroughs be defeated by the blood of Jesus in the name of Jesus.
5. Almighty God, turn my weaknesses into strengths, in the name of Jesus.
6. Declare Jesus Christ is Lord.
7. Lord Jesus let your blood bring positive change and good result to my prayers in the name of Jesus.
8. Every enemy of my prayer be consumed by the fire of God in the name of Jesus.
9. I claim my divine benefits today in the name of Jesus.
10. Almighty God; have mercy upon me; show me your great mercy and uncommon favor in the name of Jesus.
11. I break and lose myself from every satanic control and domination in the name of Jesus.
12. I cancel every evil dream in the name of Jesus.
13. I shall not be afraid for the Lord God is with me in the name of Jesus.
14. I refuse to limit God in my life in the name of Jesus Christ.
15. Almighty God undertake for me in the name of Jesus.

16. I refuse to fight another man's battle in the mighty name of Jesus Christ.
17. I refuse to carry another man's load and problem in the name of Jesus.
18. You powers hijacking blessings, you shall not hijack my blessings in the name of Jesus.
19. Almighty God; help me to keep your covenant in the name of Jesus.
20. Anyone that is saying that certain things cannot be possible in my life, you are not God, be disappointed in the name of Jesus.
21. Whatever has been declared impossible in my life, become possible in the name of Jesus.
22. I shall not die but live and declare the works of God in the name of Jesus.
23. Almighty God; redeem my spirit, soul and body from death in the name of Jesus.
24. I cancel every dreams, visions, prophesy and prayers against my life and family in the name of Jesus.
25. Talk to God about your heart desires and your situation.
26. Thank God for answered prayers.

Confession:

"I will tread on the lion and serpent: the young lion and dragon will I trample under my feet" Psalms 91:13.

Wisdom for Today:

Truth has no special time of its own. Its hour is now—always.

Read the Bible Today: *Proverbs 5–6*

Prayer Points:

1. O God, confront all those who confront me with evil and disgrace them, in the name of Jesus.
2. Almighty God, make me an instrument of blessings, in Jesus name.
3. I refuse to labor under any curse, in the name of Jesus.
4. I revoke every curse under which I labor, in Jesus name.
5. Every power causing warfare at the edge of my breakthroughs be defeated permanently by fire, in Jesus name.
6. Holy Ghost, connect me to my breakthroughs, in Jesus name.
7. Declare Jesus Christ is Lord.
8. I claim the life in the blood of Jesus in the name of Jesus.
9. I claim the victory of the blood of Jesus over death in my life and family in the name of Jesus.
10. I overcome the spirit of death operating in any area of my life in the name of Jesus.
11. Let the power that raise Jesus from the dead rest upon me and my family in the name of Jesus.
12. Every dead marriage; come alive in the name of Jesus.
13. Every spirit and power killing people before their time in my family and around me, die in the name of Jesus Christ.
14. Every attack of death upon me and my family back fire in the name of Jesus. Declare Jesus Christ is Lord.
15. Blood of Jesus Christ flow like a destroying flood and sweep the enemies of my life in the name of Jesus.
16. Almighty God you are the great deliverer come down and deliver me from death in the name of Jesus.

Apostle A.O. Solomon

17. Almighty God; let the deliverance that cannot be forgotten com upon me tonight in the name of Jesus.
18. The anointing that rejects insult; come upon my life in the name of Jesus.
19. Every evil yoke affecting my life, break by the anointing in the name of Jesus.
20. I cancel every dreams, visions, prophesy and prayers against my life and family in the name of Jesus.
21. Talk to God about your heart desires and your situation.
22. Thank God for answered prayers.

Confession:

I am protected by God and his holy warring angels. In God have I put my trust; I will not be afraid of what man can do to me.

Wisdom for Today:

Wisdom is the sharing of wise experiences and knowledge, but a lot of it is common sense. The difference is how we apply this common sense—we all have the ability to keep going even when we face challenges in our lives—basically it comes down to your attitude—is it positive or negative?

Read the Bible Today: Psalm 91

Prayer Points:

1. Thou sword of deliverance, cut down the tree of family affliction, in the name of Jesus.
2. Every robber of favor, die, in the name of Jesus.
3. Every affliction targeted at the edge of breakthroughs in my life, die, in the name of Jesus.
4. Every dream of affliction, die, in the name of Jesus.
5. Let the road of affliction close, in the name of Jesus.
6. Every satanic register containing my life span and the life span of my family catch fire in the name of Jesus.
7. Whatever is killing people in my family, I am not your candidate; die in the name of Jesus.
8. Every mark of death upon me and my family; be cancelled by the blood of Jesus in the name of Jesus.
9. Almighty God; in the battle of my destiny, I need total deliverance in the name of Jesus.
10. The spirit of the Lord God is in charge of my life; therefore satan; get thee behind me in the name of Jesus.
11. You evil powers controlling people in my family; release me in the name of Jesus.
12. The deliverance that will change failure to success, sorrow to joy and poverty to prosperity let it fall upon me in the name of Jesus.
13. The deliverance that will restore my lost glory, possess my life in the name of Jesus.
14. Thank God for rescuing you.

15. Lord I thank you for not allowing trouble to swallow me up in the name of Jesus.
16. Almighty God I thank you for you derive pleasure in my wellbeing in the name of Jesus.
17. Thank you Lord for preserving and keeping my soul from evil in the name of Jesus.
18. Lord I thank you for subduing my enemies in the name of Jesus.
19. Declare Jesus Christ is Lord.
20. I refuse to be a living dead in the name of Jesus.
21. Almighty God, help me to always be at the right place at the right time in the name of Jesus.
22. Almighty God; bless the works of my hands, and deliver my labor from debt in the name of Jesus.
23. Almighty God, help me to always appreciate you and to give you all the glory due unto you for the rest of my life in the name of Jesus.
24. Every arrow of death fired against me and my family, you shall not prosper in the name of Jesus.
25. Almighty God, send your angels to deliver my children from death and calamity in the name of Jesus.
26. I cancel every dreams, visions, prophesy and prayers against my life and family in the name of Jesus.
27. Talk to God about your heart desires and your situation.
28. Thank God for answered prayers.

Confession:

The blood of Jesus is sufficient for my protection. I therefore now resist all satanic attacks, in the mighty name of Jesus.

Wisdom for Today:

All you need is a word from God and your life will never remain the same.

Read the Bible Today: Proverb 3

Prayer Points:

1. Thou covenant of hardship, break by the blood of Jesus, in the name of Jesus.
2. Thou serpent and scorpion of affliction, die, in the name of Jesus.
3. Every grave clothe binding my hands be burned away, in the name of Jesus.
4. Every evil power binding my life, release me and let me go now, in the name of Jesus.
5. Every evil power binding my life, release me and let me go now, in the name of Jesus.
6. I reject untimely death In the name of Jesus.
7. Every good thing that is dead or at the point of death, in my life come alive by the blood of Jesus Christ in the name of Jesus.
8. Every power suffocating and killing good things in my life, the Lord rebuke you, be destroyed in the name of Jesus.
9. I come out of the grave by the power of the Holy Ghost in the name of Jesus.
10. Every death on my way, clear away in the name of Jesus.
11. Every sentence of death over my life and family, I reverse you in the name of Jesus.
12. I cancel every evil decision against my life in the name of Jesus.
13. Every stubborn power pursing my life; turn back and perish in the name of Jesus.
14. Every untimely death hovering over my life and family, catch fire in the name of Jesus.
15. Almighty God according to the greatness of your power, preserve all those who are appointed to die in the name of Jesus.
16. This year I reject the loss of life and property in the name of Jesus.

17. I shall not die but live, the number of my days shall be fulfilled in the name of Jesus.
18. Almighty God, answer me speedily show me your great mercy in the name of Jesus Christ.
19. Cause me O Lord to know your loving kindness in the name of Jesus.
20. I cancel every dreams, visions, prophesy and prayers against my life and family in the name of Jesus.
21. Talk to God about your heart desires and your situation.
22. Thank God for answered prayers.

Confession:

I can do all things through Christ which strengthens me.

Wisdom for Today:

Christ has redeemed me from the curse of the law. I am free from the power of the evil ones. My freedom is guaranteed in Jesus. I am covered by his precious blood.

Read the Bible Today: Psalm 7

Prayer Points:

1. You, dream of diverse vanities, vanish, in the name of Jesus.
2. Every power turning the clock of my life, die, in the name of Jesus.
3. Any power hiding my key of promotion, release it unto me now and die, in the name of Jesus.
4. I remove my name from every satanic family record, in the name of Jesus.
5. Satanic blood link between me and my family break, in the name of Jesus.
6. Arise O Lord and fight for me with jealousy in the name of Jesus.
7. Almighty God I thank you because I will not see trouble throughout this month in the name of Jesus.
8. Every storm prepared for me and my family; be diverted away in the name of Jesus.
9. Thank the Lord for the month that the Lord has made.
10. Every mark of bewitchment upon my life; lose your power and be erased in the name of Jesus.
11. Every evil hand writing upon my life; be erased in the name of Jesus.
12. Every witchcraft operation in my life, family, and church; die in the name of Jesus.
13. Every power attacking me from the land of the dead; die the second time in the name of Jesus.
14. Almighty God, use my life to confuse the enemy in the name of Jesus.
15. Every appointment with death in this month; I reject you in the name of Jesus.

Apostle A.O. Solomon

16. Every pillar of sorrow in my life; I pull you down in the name of Jesus.
17. Anything standing as a pillar of sorrow in this country in my life; I pull you down in the name of Jesus.
18. O thou that troubled my Israel be pulled down now in the name of Jesus.
19. I reject tragedy and calamity throughout this month in the name of Jesus.
20. Sorrow shall not branch in my dwelling place throughout this month in the name of Jesus.
21. I shall not carry any evil load throughout this month in the name of Jesus.
22. Every maturity day of affliction; be nullified by the blood of Jesus in the name of Jesus.
23. Every incantation against me; be cancelled, the Lord rebuke you in the name of Jesus.
24. I cancel every dreams, visions, prophesy and prayers against my life and family in the name of Jesus.
25. Talk to God about your heart desires and your situation.
26. Thank God for answered prayers.

Confession:

"By faith, I confess that the victory of the Lord will prevail over the challenges that I am facing" Hebrews 11:6.

Wisdom for Today:

In all things shewing thyself a pattern of good works: in doctrine shewing incorruptness, gravity, sincerity. Titus 2:7

Read the Bible Today: Psalm 86

Prayer Points:

1. I break the power of territorial curses over my life, in the name of Jesus.
2. Every demonic information center, scatter, in the name of Jesus.
3. Every power pursuing me with death, die, in the name of Jesus.
4. Every power that has singled me out for affliction, die, in the name of Jesus.
5. Ancestral witchcraft embargo, break now, in the name of Jesus.
6. Thou power of unprofitable struggling, die, in the name of Jesus.
7. Every owner of evil load in my life, appear and carry your load in the name of Jesus.
8. Every perfected work of the enemy over my life; die in the name of Jesus.
9. By the Blood of Jesus, I receive freedom from every financial bondage in the name of Jesus.
10. You spirit of frustration I reject you in my life in the name of Jesus.
11. I refuse to be wasted, any power that wants to waste my life be wasted in the name of Jesus.
12. Every waster of my prosperity wherever you are; be arrested in the name of Jesus.
13. Every aggression of the enemy against my prosperity; be paralyzed in the name of Jesus.
14. Shout 21 Halleluiah.
15. My blessings you shall not be stagnant, move, and locate me in the name of Jesus.
16. Every clever and hidden devourer, working in my life collapse and die in the name of Jesus.

17. Every handshake of poverty, come out with all your roots in the name of Jesus.
18. Every witchcraft problem in my life come out and go back to your sender and destroy them in the name of Jesus.
19. Every defeat that I have ever suffered in the dream be converted to victory in the name of Jesus.
20. Fresh power of God, over shadow my life in the name of Jesus.
21. Almighty God open my spiritual ears and let me hear what you want me to hear in the name of Jesus.
22. I cancel every dreams, visions, prophesy and prayers against my life and family in the name of Jesus.
23. Talk to God about your heart desires and your situation.
24. Thank God for answered prayers.

Confession:

I give thanks, praise and honor to the Almighty God for the opportunity to be alive and healthy today. I thank the Lord for access to his throne through the precious Lord Jesus Christ.

Wisdom for Today:

Obey God at all cost, never be rebellious, destiny is on the other side of obedience.

Read the Bible Today: Hebrew 10

Prayer Points:

1. Magnets that attract failure to my life die, in the name of Jesus.
2. Almighty God, prove your name in my situations, in the name of Jesus.
3. Anyone collecting satanic power because of me die with your power, in the name of Jesus.
4. Thunder of the Holy Ghost; pursue my pursuers, in the name of Jesus.
5. Strangers of darkness in my life, come out by fire and die, in the name of Jesus.
6. Every internal failure in my life come out in the name of Jesus.
7. Every seed of sorrow in my life come out in the name of Jesus.
8. Anything standing as problem in my life; fall down and die in the name of Jesus.
9. I bind and render to knot every evil counsel and imagination against my life, marriage and family in the name of Jesus.
10. Let the entrance door of poverty into my life be closed now in the name of Jesus.
11. Every power adding problem to my problem, what are you waiting for? die in the name of Jesus.
12. You doors of my prosperity, open now in the name of Jesus.
13. Let my enemies bow before me and congratulate me in the name of Jesus.
14. Almighty God, remove from my life every garment of suffering like you did for Joseph in the name of Jesus.
15. Any power that wants me to die, die for my sake in the name of Jesus.

Apostle A.O. Solomon

16. Every owner of evil load; in my life, I command you to carry your load in the name of Jesus.
17. I will prosper and be in good health in this country in the name of Jesus.
18. This country is not complete without me; I shall possess my possession in the name of Jesus.
19. I will not cry in this country again in Jesus name.
20. Every power that does not want me to see the days of joy die in the name of Jesus.
21. I cancel every dreams, visions, prophesy and prayers against my life and family in the name of Jesus.
22. Talk to God about your heart desires and your situation.
23. Thank God for answered prayers.

Confession:

And the God of peace shall bruise Satan under my feet shortly. The grace of our Lord Jesus Christ is with me. Amen. Romans 16:20

Wisdom for Today:

Adjust your attitude if you are going to step into God's blessings and best.

Read the Bible Today: Psalm 16

Prayer Points:

1. Wicked arrows of the night, come out and die, in the name of Jesus.
2. Every wickedness planted in my body, be uprooted, in the name of Jesus.
3. Everyone who carries any evil burden into my life, carry that burden away now, in the name of Jesus.
4. Internal battles against my breakthroughs, die, in the name of Jesus.
5. Every unconscious darkness planted within me, come out and die, in the name of Jesus.
6. I refuse to lose in the name of Jesus.
7. Witchcraft covenant upon my life, I command you to break in the name of Jesus.
8. Every general curse working against my life; break and release me in the name of Jesus.
9. Family evil strongman or woman; release my life by fire in the name of Jesus.
10. Water spirit release me by fire, I belong to Jesus in the name of Jesus.
11. Any covenant binding me with marine spirit, break by the blood of Jesus in the name of Jesus.
12. Every curse upon my life as a result of the wickedness of my ancestors break and release me in Jesus name.
13. Every curse standing in the way of my children's blessing, break in the name of Jesus.
14. I forbid every storm in my life this year in the name of Jesus.

Apostle A.O. Solomon

15. Every power destroying good things in my life; be destroyed by fire in the name of Jesus.
16. Every covenant of late blessing, break and release my life in the name of Jesus.
17. I cancel every dreams, visions, prophesy and prayers against my life and family in the name of Jesus.
18. Talk to God about your heart desires and your situation.
19. Thank God for answered prayers.

Confession:

"Yea, the Lord shall give that which is good; and our land shall yield her increase" Psalms 85:12.

Wisdom for Today:

Never settle for less but God's best.

Read the Bible Today: Isaiah 58

Prayer Points:

1. Every program of death prepared for me, be turned to life, in the name of Jesus.
2. Thou power and spirit of death pursuing me and my family be paralyzed by the blood of Jesus.
3. Every ordination of death prepared for my business, be turned to breakthrough, in the name of Jesus.
4. Every program of death prepared for my career, be turned to promotion, in the name of Jesus.
5. Every personality of death in my life, get out by fire, in the name of Jesus.
6. I am that I am, arise and manifest your power in my life in the name of Jesus.
7. I am that I am, arise and destroy my poverty in the name of Jesus.
8. I am that I am, arise and destroy the bondage in my family in the name of Jesus.
9. Blood of Jesus Christ speak better things to my life in the name of Jesus.
10. Anything that will take me away from divine protection, come out of my life and enter no more in the name of Jesus.
11. Almighty God, hold me up for I put my hope in you in the name of Jesus.
12. Almighty God, empower me for victory today in the name of Jesus.
13. Every operation of the enemies in my dreams; fail woefully in the name of Jesus.
14. Any manifestation of the enemy in my dream, I command you to be consumed by the fire in the name of Jesus.

15. Every appointment with weeping, I reject you in the name of Jesus.
16. I refuse to weep for the enemies to rejoice in the name of Jesus.
17. Any area of secret tears in my life, receive the touch of God's miracle in the name of Jesus.
18. Almighty God go back to every second of my past and remove anything that is causing problem in my life in the name of Jesus.
19. Almighty God arise and nullify every word of human being that is manifesting in my life in the name of Jesus.
20. I cancel every dreams, visions, prophesy and prayers against my life and family in the name of Jesus.
21. Talk to God about your heart desires and your situation.
22. Thank God for answered prayers.

✂ *Confession:*

"Thou will show me the path of life: in thy presence is fullness of joy; at thy right hand there are pleasures for evermore" Psalms 16:11.

Wisdom for Today:

Get up now if you are going to rise above the crisis, success is not based upon expectation, but upon preparation.

Read the Bible Today: Judges 6

Prayer Points:

1. I refuse to pray when it is too late, in the name of Jesus.
2. My prayers shall not become abomination to God, in the name of Jesus.
3. Power of sin in my life, die, in the name of Jesus.
4. Almighty God, deliver me from carnality, in the name of Jesus.
5. Holy Spirit of God, give me your understanding, in the name of Jesus.
6. Every evil programmed into the day against me and my household be destroyed by fire, in the name of Jesus.
7. Almighty God enough of reproach in my life, family, and ministry in the name of Jesus.
8. I cancel every evil dream with the blood of Jesus in the name of Jesus.
9. All my good dreams; be empowered for speedy manifestation in the name of Jesus.
10. Every power fuelling problems in my life your time is up; die in the name of Jesus.
11. I release myself from every curse working in my family in the name of Jesus.
12. Every spiritual dedication against me and my family; receive the stones of fire and die in the name of Jesus.
13. You messenger of death assigned against me and my family, go back to your sender in the name of Jesus.
14. Evil Seed planted in my life be uprooted by fire in the name of Jesus.
15. Every evil wisdom working against my breakthroughs; be disgraced in the name of Jesus.

Apostle A.O. Solomon

16. I put every evil under my feet in the name of Jesus.
17. Thou power of sin and iniquity in my life, the Lord rebuke you, die in the name of Jesus.
18. Every evil desire in my life; the Lord rebuke you in the name of Jesus.
19. I cancel every dreams, visions, prophesy and prayers against my life and family in the name of Jesus.
20. Talk to God about your heart desires and your situation.
21. Thank God for answered prayers.

Confession:

"Being justified by faith, we have peace with god through our Lord Jesus Christ" Romans 5:1.

Wisdom for Today:

Stretch your faith, if it's going to be it's up to you. If it does not work change it.

Read the Bible Today: *Isaiah 60*

Prayer Points:

1. Almighty God, search the land of the living and that of the dead and recover my stolen blessings for me, in Jesus name.
2. Almighty God let my life become too hot for the enemy to handle, in the name of Jesus.
3. Every power that says I will not have breakthroughs in this land, die, in the name of Jesus.
4. I refuse to allow my angels of blessings to depart, in the name of Jesus.
5. I am seated with Christ in the heavenly places, far above principalities and powers in the name of Jesus.
6. Anointing of deliverance fall upon me now in the name of Jesus.
7. Every power that pursued my parents and now pursuing me, what are you waiting for, die in the name of Jesus.
8. Every problem in the life of my parents that is now appearing in my life; vanish in the name of Jesus.
9. Every pillar of disgrace in my life, I pull you down in the name of Jesus.
10. Every evil preparation to disgrace me; be destroyed by fire in the name of Jesus.
11. Every power that has singled me out for affliction, Holy Ghost fire, locate and destroy them in the name of Jesus.
12. Every evil mark upon my body, wherever you are vanish in the name of Jesus.
13. Almighty God restore all my wasted years in the name of Jesus Christ.
14. Every power covering my glory, fall down and die in the name of Jesus.
15. You my glory arise and shine in the name of Jesus.

16. Every seed of the enemy in my life come out by fire in the name of Jesus.
17. Every seed of poverty in my life come out by fire in the name of Jesus.
18. Every dream of poverty, I cancel you by the blood of Jesus in the name of Jesus.
19. Every evil burial for my sake, be destroyed by fire in the mighty name of Jesus.
20. I break the power of death over my life in the name of Jesus.
21. Every hold of the enemy over my blood break by fire in the name of Jesus.
22. Every messenger of death on assignment against me and my family, die in the name of Jesus.
23. I cancel every dreams, visions, prophesy and prayers against my life and family in the name of Jesus.
24. Talk to God about your heart desires and your situation.
25. Thank God for answered prayers.

Confession:

"What a wonderful God we have.... Who so wonderfully comforts and strengthens us" 2 Corinthians 1:3–4.

Wisdom for Today:

Failure to plan is a plan to fail.

Read the Bible Today: Deuteronomy 1

Prayer Points:

1. Almighty God, bless my going out and my coming in today, in the name of Jesus.
2. I paralyze all satanic antagonism from the womb, in the name of Jesus.
3. Almighty God, bring honey out of the rock for me, in the name of Jesus.
4. Almighty God, open up all the good doors of my life that household wickedness has shut, in the name of Jesus.
5. Let all anti-breakthrough designs against my life be shattered to pieces and burnt to ashes, in the name of Jesus.
6. Good dreams in my life, hear the word of God, come alive and manifest in the name of Jesus.
7. Every weapon of demotion fashioned against my life, scatter in the name of Jesus.
8. I send back every evil arrow fired against my life, go back to sender in the name of Jesus.
9. Anything packaged to destroy my joy in this country be destroyed by fire in the name of Jesus.
10. Foundation of sorrow in my life; be broken to pieces in the name of Jesus.
11. I proclaim that your joy shall last forever in the name of Jesus.
12. Evil deposit in my life, in my body, your time is up, come out in the name of Jesus.
13. Every attempt to cover my glory; be frustrated in the name of Jesus.
14. Every evil power monitoring the gates of my prosperity why are you still alive, I command you to die in Jesus name.

15. Every evil arrow fired to useless my life, come out and go back to your sender in the name of Jesus.
16. Spirit of poverty come out of my life and enter no more in the name of Jesus.
17. Any power that is making my family to suffer your time is up, die in the name of Jesus.
18. I shall not answer the call of any evil spirit in the name of Jesus Christ.
19. Every power hired to curse me, curse my destiny, what are you waiting for, die in the name of Jesus.
20. Any power or covenant of my father's house that wants to waste my life and calling, die in the name of Jesus.
21. I cancel every dreams, visions, prophesy and prayers against my life and family in the name of Jesus.
22. Talk to God about your heart desires and your situation.
23. Thank God for answered prayers.

Confession:

"I will dwell in the house of the Lord forever" Psalms 23:6.

Wisdom for Today:

The challenge that you face is never bigger than God.

Read the Bible Today: Colossians 2

Prayer Points:

1. I break every evil unity organized against me, in the name of Jesus.
2. Almighty God, fill me with the desire of heavenly things, in the name of Jesus.
3. The presence and glory of God shall never depart from me, in Jesus name.
4. I will prosper in all good areas today, in the name of Jesus.
5. Stubborn pursuers of my life, die in the name of Jesus.
6. Every evil stamp of the enemy; be removed in the name of Jesus.
7. Almighty God; turn my failures to success in the name of Jesus.
8. Every gate in this nation shot against me, open now in the name of Jesus.
9. Every curse that is delaying good things in my life; break and release me in the name of Jesus.
10. Every spirit of this world attached to my mind, I cut you off in the name of Jesus.
11. Spirit of God, reign in my life in the name of Jesus.
12. Almighty God, teach my hand to war tonight in the name of Jesus.
13. Arise O God and prevail over my enemies in Jesus name.
14. Let the wicked and their wickedness be consumed by fire in the name of Jesus.
15. Let every stubborn enemy that has risen against me; be defeated now in the name of Jesus.
16. By the power of the Holy Ghost, I destroy the enemies and their work in my life in the name of Jesus.
17. Let the dwelling place of my enemies come to nothing, and let those who hate me be put to shame in the name of Jesus.

Apostle A.O. Solomon

18. Let every weapon of my enemies back fire and destroy them in the name of Jesus.
19. I cancel every dreams, visions, prophesy and prayers against my life and family in the name of Jesus.
20. Talk to God about your heart desires and your situation.
21. Thank God for answered prayers.

Confession:

"Therefore I shall see no more vanity, nor divine divination: for God will deliver his people out of the hand of the wicked: and ye shall know that I am the Lord" Ezekiel 13:23.

Wisdom for Today:

Chart your course to victory, God is still in control.

Read the Bible Today: 2 Corinthians 2

Prayer Points:

1. Every evil bird of the night flying for my sake, fall down and die, in the name of Jesus.
2. Satanic calendar against me and my family I destroy you today, in Jesus name.
3. I command this month to vomit my portion now, in the name Jesus.
4. This day hear the Word of God take hold of the ends of the earth and shake away every wickedness against my life, in the name of Jesus.
5. There shall be help for me today, in Jesus name.
6. Almighty God, reveal to me the secret of becoming a winner in life in the name of Jesus.
7. Blood of Jesus, make way for me tonight in the name of Jesus.
8. Let the power of God clear way for my prayers tonight in the name of Jesus.
9. Let the angels of God come to my aid, support me tonight in the name of Jesus.
10. Holy Ghost, arise in your power deliver me from my tight places in the name of Jesus.
11. Shout fire of deliverance fall on me... 7 times.
12. Evil dreams depart from my life in the name of Jesus.
13. Every power of darkness polluting and attacking my dreams; be arrested by fire in the name of Jesus.
14. By the blood of Jesus, I cancel every effect of evil dreams in my life in the name of Jesus.
15. Every messenger of death in my church depart and enter no more in the name of Jesus.

16. Every evil power that is holding me down, die in the name of Jesus.
17. I move from nothing to something good in the name of Jesus.
18. In this country I shall not be disgraced in the name of Jesus.
19. Every attack in my dream that is now affecting my life be reversed in the name of Jesus.
20. I cancel every dreams, visions, prophesy and prayers against my life and family in the name of Jesus.
21. Talk to God about your heart desires and your situation.
22. Thank God for answered prayers.

Confession:

Whosoever blesses me shall be blessed; anyone who curses me shall bear the curses, because I am anointed of the Lord.

Wisdom for Today:

After you have done the will of God, you need to endure even when you are going through storms. Hold on to your confidence in God.

Read the Bible Today: Hebrews 10

Prayer Points:

1. Let all evil counselors against me be destroyed in the name of Jesus.
2. Almighty God, enlarge my horizons beyond my wildest dream, in the name of Jesus.
3. My eyes shall see good things today, my ears shall hear good news, and my hands shall possess good things, in the name of Jesus.
4. Holy Ghost, seal all the holes in my pockets, in Jesus name.
5. I will rise and shine above all my colleagues today, in the name of Jesus.
6. Evil arrows from my dream come out and go back to sender in the name of Jesus.
7. Powers from my father and mother's house begin to attack yourself in Jesus name.
8. Almighty God I need a break in this country in the name of Jesus.
9. Lord, heal me from every area that I have been wounded in the name of Jesus.
10. Every power bent on seeing my destiny destroyed, Holy Ghost fire locate and destroy them in the name of Jesus.
11. My ears shall hear good news, my eyes shall see good things, and my hands shall possess good things in the name of Jesus.
12. Almighty God, arise quickly and deliver me from shame in the name of Jesus.
13. Evil arrows my body is not for you in the name of Jesus.
14. Every owner of evil load in my life, carry your load in the name of Jesus.
15. I shall not be wasted; I shall not be useless in the name of Jesus.

16. Every power affecting my joy, lose your power and die in the name of Jesus.
17. I shall not bury my children in the name of Jesus.
18. Every dry bone in my life, receive the touch of resurrection and life in the name of Jesus.
19. Every good door that has been closed against my life, lift up your heads and let the King of glory come in the name of Jesus.
20. Almighty God, arise in your mercy and close the old chapter in my life in the name of Jesus.
21. Evil prophecy waiting for manifestation in my life, die in the name of Jesus.
22. Every maturity date of evil words and prophesies in my life; be nullified in the name of Jesus.
23. I cancel every dreams, visions, prophesy and prayers against my life and family in the name of Jesus.
24. Talk to God about your heart desires and your situation.
25. Thank God for answered prayers.

Confession:

"Every good gift and perfect gift is from above" James 1:17.

Wisdom for Today:

Your position and location is very important in fulfilling your destiny.

Read the Bible Today: Romans 9:17

Prayer Points:

1. No dark meeting held against me shall prosper, in the name of Jesus.
2. I claim back my goods, which presently reside in wrong hands, in the name of Jesus.
3. Let all financial failure in my life receive termination, in the name of Jesus.
4. I refuse to reap any satanic harvest in any area of my life, in the name of Jesus.
5. I command everything that is hindering me from greatness to begin to give way now, in the name of Jesus.
6. I fire back, every arrow of evil prophecy that is pursuing my life in Jesus name.
7. Every satanic assignment, I reject you in my life in the name of Jesus.
8. Every power demanding tears from my eyes before receiving my blessings, die in the name of Jesus.
9. Every power sponsoring weeping in my family; carry your load and die in the name of Jesus.
10. Every witchcraft cage, caging my destiny, break by the fire of God in the name of Jesus.
11. Almighty God, deliver me from the strife of tongue in the name of Jesus.
12. Evil arrows go back to your sender in the name of Jesus.
13. Every attack of eaters of flesh and drinkers of blood, back fire in the name of Jesus.
14. I withdraw my blood from witchcraft altar in the name of Jesus.
15. Anything representing me in any kingdom of darkness, I withdraw you by fire in the name of Jesus.
16. I walk out of the prison of evil dreams in the name of Jesus.

17. Every dream of backwardness in my life die in the name of Jesus.
18. Any power using anything in my past to torment me, die in the name of Jesus.
19. By the blood of Jesus, I register my name for solution today in the name of Jesus.
20. I cancel every dreams, visions, prophesy and prayers against my life and family in the name of Jesus.
21. Talk to God about your heart desires and your situation.
22. Thank God for answered prayers.

Confession:

"For in him we live and move and are!" (Acts 17:28, TLB)

Wisdom for Today:

Understanding the level of your commitment will let you live and enjoy what God promised.

Read the Bible Today: John 1

Prayer Points:

1. Almighty God guide and direct me as I rectify any problem I have with my business, work, and studies, in Jesus name.
2. Lord, forgive me for any wrong decision, action, or thought I have engaged in, in Jesus name.
3. Almighty God, help me to see my mistakes and faults, give me power to correct and overcome them in Jesus name.
4. Almighty God, show me what to do so that business and work crises will not arise in my life again, in the name of Jesus.
5. Lord, give unto me the eagle eye and the eyes of Elisha to foresee breakthroughs in all areas, in Jesus name.
6. I shall not serve my enemies and I shall not serve my friend in the name of Jesus.
7. I disagree with every satanic decision over my life in the name of Jesus.
8. I cancel every former and present agreement with the spirit of Egypt in the name of Jesus.
9. Every agreement with the power of the air, I command you to break in the name of Jesus.
10. I recover every blessing I have lost to spirit of Egypt in the name of Jesus.
11. Almighty God, deliver me from every problem I have brought upon myself in the name of Jesus.
12. I reject every invitation to bondage in the name of Jesus.
13. Almighty God, give me power to overcome pressures in life in the name of Jesus.
14. Almighty God, make me a good sign and use me for your glory in the name of Jesus.

15. By the anointing of the Holy Ghost, I leap over every negative situation surrounding me in the name of Jesus.
16. I cancel every dreams, visions, prophesy and prayers against my life and family in the name of Jesus.
17. Talk to God about your heart desires and your situation.
18. Thank God for answered prayers.

September 2

Confession:

"Being justified freely by his grace through the redemption that is in Christ Jesus" Romans 3:24.

Wisdom for Today:

Keep your head up and encourage yourself at all times.

Read the Bible Today: Psalm 107

1. Almighty God, give me wisdom to walk out of any unfavorable situations, in Jesus name.
2. Almighty God, help me to formulate a plan of recovery to keep me at the top always, in the name of Jesus.
3. Almighty God, send me divine counselors who can help me with my business, in the name of Jesus.
4. Almighty God, always help me to identify evil business traps, and deliver me from falling into them, in the name of Jesus.
5. Almighty God, help me to erect safeguards to prevent marital, career, and business failures, in the name of Jesus.
6. Almighty God I put my trust in you let me not be ashamed, let not my enemy triumph over me in the name of Jesus.
7. In the name Of Jesus I shall not fail God in the name of Jesus.
8. Almighty God, I commit my life to you; organize my scattered life in the name of Jesus.
9. Almighty God, change my story as you did Jabez in the name of Jesus.
10. I reject automatic failure in my life in the name of Jesus.
11. Every enemy of divine presence in my life, I command you to die in the name of Jesus.
12. Anointing to excel above all my family members fall upon me now in the name of Jesus.
13. I shall experience divine favor throughout the days of my life in Jesus name.
14. Holy Spirit; coordinate me in the name of Jesus.
15. Arrows of the enemy you shall not locate me, go back to your sender in the name of Jesus.
16. Power to sin no more, fall upon me now in the name of Jesus.
17. I cancel every dreams, visions, prophesy and prayers against my life and family in the name of Jesus.
18. Talk to God about your heart desires and your situation.
19. Thank God for answered prayers.

Confession:

"Heaven and earth shall pass away, but my words shall not pass away" Matthew 24:35.

Wisdom for Today:

Hold steady right now, no matter what comes, no matter what moves.

Read the Bible Today: Ephesians 4

Prayer Points:

1. Lord, help me to submit to your will every day of my life, in the name of Jesus.
2. Almighty God cause me to be spiritually and mentally alert in my place of work, in Jesus name.
3. Let all my plans and purposes for my business bring honor and glory to God in Jesus name.
4. Almighty God let your angels lift up my business in their hands so that it does not strike its foot against a stone, in the name of Jesus.
5. Let all decisions made for my business be originated by the Holy Ghost, in the name of Jesus.
6. I reject death in my family and church in the name of Jesus.
7. Almighty God let your hand be upon me for good throughout this month in the name of Jesus.
8. Almighty God do not give me up to the desires of my enemies in the name of Jesus.
9. Evil shall not prevail against me and my family in the name of Jesus.
10. Sin shall not rule over me in the name of Jesus.
11. Every good thing my hands have started, my hands shall complete, and I shall enjoy them in the name of Jesus.
12. My head hear the word of the Lord; you shall not be bewitched in the name of Jesus.
13. I shall not become what the enemies want me to be in the name of Jesus.
14. O God of Abraham, Isaac, and Jacob rearrange this country to favor me in the name of Jesus.

15. Every completed work of my enemies over my life; be destroyed with all your effects in the name of Jesus.

16. I break and lose myself from the stronghold of darkness in the name of Jesus.

17. Any power that wants to replace my peace with war, die suddenly in the name of Jesus.

18. By the blood of Jesus Christ, I rise above limitation in life in the name of Jesus.

19. I cancel every dreams, visions, prophesy and prayers against my life and family in the name of Jesus.

20. Talk to God about your heart desires and your situation.

21. Thank God for answered prayers.

Confession:

"The kingdoms of this world are become the kingdom of our Lord, and of his Christ; and he shall reign forever and ever" Revelation 11:15.

Wisdom for Today:

Expecting is the key to receiving from God, what you believe is what you receive – Daniel N. Brown

Read the Bible Today: Mark 11

Prayer Points:

1. O Lord, let the influence of the Holy Ghost be upon me and every member of my family, in the name of Jesus.
2. Let increased productivity and profit be the lot of my business, in the name of Jesus.
3. Let my business continue to grow and expand in all areas, in the name of Jesus.
4. Almighty God give me direction and guidance at all times, in the name of Jesus.
5. Almighty God let my business prosper and have good success, in the name of Jesus.
6. Almighty God let my path grow brighter and brighter until it reaches the full light of the day, in the name of Jesus.
7. Almighty God reign supreme in my life in the name of Jesus.
8. Almighty God set me free from poverty in the name of Jesus.
9. I command every darkness in my life to vanish in the name of Jesus.
10. Every step by step work of the enemy in my life be destroyed in the name of Jesus.
11. Every perfected works of the enemy in my life be over turned by the blood of Jesus in the name of Jesus.
12. Every evil altar in my family working against my glory, be consumed by fire in the name of Jesus.
13. Every good thing the enemy scattered in my life, come together in the name of Jesus.
14. Every power and spirit that has set my life for affliction, I bind you in the name of Jesus.

15. In the name of Jesus, my life shall not follow satanic agenda in the name of Jesus.
16. Almighty God it is time give me rest and comfort me, prosper me in the name of Jesus.
17. By the blood of Jesus, I register my name for solution today in the name of Jesus.
18. I cancel every dreams, visions, prophesy and prayers against my life and family in the name of Jesus.
19. Talk to God about your heart desires and your situation.
20. Thank God for answered prayers.

Apostle A.O. Solomon

Confession:

"If the Son therefore shall make you free, ye shall be free indeed"
John 8:36.

Wisdom for Today:

Forgiveness is of God, the more you know the more you forgive.

Read the Bible Today: Romans 8

Prayer Points:

1. I cancel my name and the names of my family members from the register of death by the blood of Jesus, in the name of Jesus.
2. Every weapon of destruction fashioned against me, be destroyed by the fire of God, in the name of Jesus.
3. Fire of God, fight for me in every area of my life, in Jesus name.
4. Every hindrance to my promotion be melted by the fire of God, in the name of Jesus.
5. Every evil gathering against me, be scattered by the thunder and fire of God, in the name of Jesus.
6. I connect myself with the power of God in the name of Jesus.
7. I pulled down every pillar of witchcraft in my family in the name of Jesus.
8. Witchcraft powers why are you pursuing my life? die in the name of Jesus.
9. It is suffer not a witch to live, therefore any witchcraft pursuing my life, I command you to die in the name of Jesus.
10. I disagree with failure in the name of Jesus.
11. Failure at the edge of good things, depart from my life by the blood of Jesus in the name of Jesus.
12. Witchcraft battle at the edge of my success, return to your sender in the name of Jesus.
13. Every evil seed planted by the enemy in my life, be uprooted by fire in the name of Jesus.
14. Every plantation of darkness in my life, come out with all your roots in the name of Jesus.
15. Every evil seed planted into my life through dreams, be uprooted by fire in the name of Jesus.
16. I challenge my system with the fire of God, in the name of Jesus.

17. Every instrument of satanic control in my life, wherever you are be destroyed by fire in the name of Jesus.
18. I cancel every dreams, visions, prophesy and prayers against my life and family in the name of Jesus.
19. Talk to God about your heart desires and your situation.
20. Thank God for answered prayers.

Confession:

"The God of my mercy shall prevent me: God shall let me see my desire upon mine enemies" Psalms 59:10.

Wisdom for Today:

"Hope is like the sun, which, as we journey toward it, casts the shadow of our burden behind us". – Samuel Smiles

Read the Bible Today: 2 Thessalonians 1

Prayer Points:

1. Almighty God let your fire destroy every evil list containing my name, in Jesus name.
2. All failures of the past in my life be converted to successes, in Jesus name.
3. Almighty God let your blessing pour down on me now like rain, in the name of Jesus.
4. Almighty God let the failure mechanism of the enemy designed against my success be frustrated, in the name of Jesus.
5. I receive power from on high, to paralyze all the powers of darkness that are diverting my blessings, in the name of Jesus.
6. Arrows of darkness in my life come out of your hiding places and go back to your sender in the name of Jesus.
7. As from today, life shall be easy for me in the name of Jesus.
8. By the blood of Jesus, I stand in gap for every member of my family in the name of Jesus.
9. Every of my family that is appointed for death, be redeemed by the blood of Jesus in the name of Jesus.
10. Any power that wants to attack me, Holy Ghost fire attack and destroy them in the name of Jesus.
11. Arrows of madness fired against me and any member of my family, gather yourself together and go back to your sender in the name of Jesus.
12. Almighty God, replace all those in the system of this country that will not favor me, with the people that will favor me in the name of Jesus.
13. All those who are boasting to fire me in my place of work, let the Holy Ghost fire, fire them in the name of Jesus.

14. Every evil register containing my name, Holy Ghost fire consume them in the name of Jesus.
15. Every broom of darkness sweeping good things away from my life, catch fire in the name of Jesus.
16. I cancel every dreams, visions, prophesy and prayers against my life and family in the name of Jesus.
17. Talk to God about your heart desires and your situation.
18. Thank God for answered prayers.

Confession:

"Yea, though I walk through the valley of the shadow of death, I will fear no evil: For thou art with me; thy rod and thy staff they comfort me" Psalms 23:4.

Wisdom for Today:

The darkest of the night is before the dawn, weeping may endure for a night but joy comes in the morning.

Read the Bible Today: Psalm 71

Prayer Points:

1. From this day forward, I employ the services of the angels of God to open unto me every door of opportunity, in the name of Jesus.
2. I will not go around in circles again; I will make progress, in the name of Jesus.
3. I shall not build for another to inhabit, and I shall not plant for another to eat, in the name of Jesus.
4. I paralyze the powers of the emptier concerning my handwork, in the name of Jesus.
5. Let the angel of the living God; begin to sweep back all my blessings in the name of Jesus.
6. Every spirit of laboring without achievement; be destroyed in the name of Jesus.
7. I hold the hammer of the word of God and command every padlock ministering evil against my life, break in the name of Jesus.
8. I enter the strong room of the enemy and collect all my blessing in the name of Jesus.
9. Any man or woman, attending witchcraft meeting because of me, you shall not return in the name of Jesus.
10. Anyone calling my name for evil in the night, angel of God; slap them in the name of Jesus.
11. Every night captivity in my life, break in the name of Jesus.
12. Anything done against me in the night; be destroyed by fire in the name of Jesus.
13. Every satanic power appearing in my dream, the Lord rebuke you perish in the name of Jesus.

14. Any fire that the enemy has lighted against me and my family be quenched by the blood of Jesus in the name of Jesus.
15. Every evil pot caging anything good in my life, break by the thunder of God in the name of Jesus.
16. Almighty God put upon me your garment of mercy and favor in the name of Jesus.
17. My spirit man, my body, and my soul hear the word of the Lord you shall not answer the call of the enemy day or night in the name of Jesus.
18. I cancel every dreams, visions, prophesy and prayers against my life and family in the name of Jesus.
19. Talk to God about your heart desires and your situation.
20. Thank God for answered prayers.

Confession:

"Because greater is he that is in me, than he that is in the world"
1 John 4:4.

Wisdom for Today:

"The best way to cheer yourself up is to cheer someone else up". Mark Twain

Read the Bible Today: Philippians 4

Prayer Points:

1. The enemy shall not spoil my testimonies in life, in the name of Jesus.
2. I reject every backward journey, and I move forward by God's unfailing power, in the name of Jesus.
3. I paralyze every evil strongman attached to any area of my life, in the name of Jesus.
4. Let every agent of shame fashioned to work against my life be paralyzed, in the name of Jesus.
5. I paralyze the activities of household wickedness over my life, in the name of Jesus.
6. Let the voice of God thunder against my enemies and divide them in the name of Jesus.
7. Let the voice of God, divide the fire of my enemy and destroy them in the name of Jesus.
8. Let the voice of God, shake down the camp of my enemies in the name of Jesus
9. Almighty God, clothe me with mercy and compassion in the name of Jesus.
10. Almighty God, empower my hands for profit in the name of Jesus.
11. Every attack against my labor, break and release me in the name of Jesus.
12. Every curse of the enemy against the works of my hands, break by the blood of Jesus in the name of Jesus.
13. Every physical and spiritual chain upon my hands, break in the name of Jesus.
14. Thou son of David use your key, and set me free from hand cuffs and chains in the name of Jesus.

15. Jesus set me free; I am free indeed in the name of Jesus.
16. I cancel every dreams, visions, prophesy and prayers against my life and family in the name of Jesus.
17. Talk to God about your heart desires and your situation.
18. Thank God for answered prayers.

Confession:

"And there shall be no more curse" Revelation 22:3.

Wisdom for Today:

Do not despair no matter what you are going through.

Read the Bible Today: Isaiah 61:1

Prayer Points:

1. I quench every strange fire emanating from evil tongues against me, in the name of Jesus.
2. Almighty God, give me power for maximum achievement in the name of Jesus.
3. Almighty God, give me comforting authority to achieve my goal in the name of Jesus.
4. Almighty God, fortify me with your power, in the name of Jesus.
5. I decree any curse of profitless hard work upon my life break now, in the name of Jesus.
6. I drink the blood of Jesus, and cover myself with the blood of Jesus in the name of Jesus.
7. Any power that wants to destroy the works of God in my life, Holy Ghost fire; destroy them in the name of Jesus.
8. Every satanic bondage from evil dreams programmed into my life; break and release me in the name of Jesus.
9. Every sickness introduced into my life as a result of evil dreams die now in the name of Jesus.
10. Every dream of failure in my past be reversed in the name of Jesus.
11. Every witchcraft power pursuing me in the dream fall down and die in the name of Jesus.
12. Almighty God, make me holy by your power in the name of Jesus.
13. Every satanic dream attached to my progress, die in the name of Jesus.
14. I come out of every dream prison by the power of the Holy Ghost in the name of Jesus.
15. I fire back every witchcraft arrow fired into my dream in the name of Jesus.

16. Every evil dream of the past affecting my life now, die in the name of Jesus.
17. I cancel every dreams, visions, prophesy and prayers against my life and family in the name of Jesus.
18. Talk to God about your heart desires and your situation.
19. Thank God for answered prayers.

Confession:

"And there shall be no night there; and they need no candle, neither light of the sun; for the Lord God giveth them light: and they shall reign forever and ever". Revelation 22:5

Wisdom for Today:

It takes vision to set out on a mission. Before you embark on any mission, be sure of a revelation from heaven. When the unexpected happens on your way to your mission, it is what God has told or showed you that will keep you on the move.

Read the Bible Today: Proverb 3: 5-6

Prayer Points:

1. I decree that every curse that has prevented me from achieving my goal break in the name of Jesus.
2. Every curse of backwardness, break, in the name of Jesus.
3. I paralyze every spirit of disobedience in my life, in Jesus name.
4. I refuse to disobey the voice of God, in the name of Jesus.
5. Every root of rebellion in my life be uprooted, in Jesus name.
6. Every witchcraft serpent attacking me in the dream, return to your sender and destroy them in the name of Jesus.
7. Every dream affecting my life, marriage, and career lose your power and die in the name of Jesus.
8. Every good thing I have lost in the dream I repossess you back in Jesus name.
9. Every agent of darkness in my dream life, I command you to die in the name of Jesus.
10. Every evil pronouncement against me in the dream you shall not stand, you shall not come to pass in the name of Jesus.
11. My resting time shall not be a trouble time in the name of Jesus.
12. Almighty God trouble any power, spirit, and personality troubling me in the name of Jesus.
13. Life shall not be difficult for me in the name of Jesus.
14. I reject spiritual and physical nakedness in the name of Jesus.
15. I reject every form of disorder in the name of Jesus.
16. Me and my family shall be for good signs and wonders in the name of Jesus.

17. As the Lord God lives, people will see the good work of God in my life in Jesus name.
18. Almighty God, bless all those that bless me, and curse all those that curses me, in Jesus name.
19. I cancel every dreams, visions, prophesy and prayers against my life and family in the name of Jesus.
20. Talk to God about your heart desires and your situation.
21. Thank God for answered prayers.

Confession:

"And I brake the jaws of the wicked, and plucked the spoil out of his teeth" Job 29:17.

Wisdom for Today:

The question should be, "Is it worth trying to do?" not, "Can it be done?" You must motivate yourself every day.

Read the Bible Today: Ephesians 6:10, 11, and 16

Prayer Points:

1. Fountain of rebellion in my life, dry up, in the name of Jesus.
2. Contrary powers that fuel rebellion in my life die now, in Jesus name.
3. Every inspiration of witchcraft in my family be destroyed, in the name of Jesus.
4. Blood of Jesus, blot out every evil mark of witchcraft in my life, in the name of Jesus.
5. Every garment put upon me by witchcraft, be torn to pieces, in the name of Jesus.
6. I plead the blood of Jesus against every voice speaking against my destiny in the name of Jesus.
7. Every owner of evil load in my life, wherever you are appear and carry your load in Jesus name.
8. I plead the blood of Jesus over everything the devil is holding against me in the name of Jesus.
9. Jesus I belong to you, I disconnect from the iniquity of my ancestors in the name of Jesus.
10. Every ancestral oat that is affecting my life now break by the blood of Jesus in the name of Jesus.
11. Every evil word that is pursuing my destiny, the Lord rebuke you; turn back in the name of Jesus.
12. Every prophecy demoting my life lose your hold and die in the name of Jesus.
13. Evil family pattern, break and release me by fire in the name of Jesus.
14. Every evil water flowing in my family, dry up by fire in the name of Jesus.

15. Family bondage affecting my life, break in the name of Jesus.
16. Ancestral evil covenant, I separate myself from you now in the name of Jesus.
17. Every evil register containing my name, be roasted by fire in the name of Jesus.
18. I cancel every dreams, visions, prophesy and prayers against my life and family in the name of Jesus.
19. Talk to God about your heart desires and your situation.
20. Thank God for answered prayers.

Confession:

"He will keep in perfect peace all those who trust in him, whose thoughts turn often to the Lord" Isaiah 26:3, TLB.

Wisdom for Today

"Just don't give up trying to do what you really want to do. Where there is love and inspiration I don't think you can go wrong". - Ella Fitzerald

Read the Bible Today: Isaiah 40:31

Prayer Points:

1. Angels of God pursue my household enemies and let their ways be dark and slippery, in the name of Jesus.
2. Almighty God, confuse my household enemies and turn them against themselves, in Jesus name.
3. I break every evil unconscious agreement with household enemies that gets in the way of my miracles, in the name of Jesus.
4. Household witchcraft, fall down and die, in the name of Jesus.
5. Almighty God, drag all the household wickedness to the Dead Sea and drown them in the name of Jesus.
6. Give thanks unto the Lord.
7. Thank God for turn of events.
8. Declare Jesus Christ is Lord.
9. Almighty God; open the book of remembrance for me in the name of Jesus.
10. Almighty God; make this day fulfilling of turn of events in the name of Jesus.
11. Every dream of nakedness; I revise you by the power of the almighty God in the name of Jesus.
12. Almighty God, reverse every dream tragedy in the name of Jesus.
13. Every dream of failure and limitation I reverse you in the name of Jesus.
14. Every dream of seeing dead friends, dead relative, coffin and casket; be reversed in the name of Jesus.
15. Almighty God; divert death away from my life to every evil gathering in the name of Jesus.
16. It is written I am God's property therefore, you devil take off your hands from the affairs of my life in the name of Jesus.

17. Almighty God; bestow your honor and your glory upon me in the name of Jesus Christ.
18. I am complete in Christ Jesus in the name of Jesus.
19. Almighty God; perfect all that concerns my life in the name of Jesus.
20. I cancel every appointment with death in the name of Jesus.
21. Almighty God; redeem my soul from the power of the grave in the name of Jesus.
22. I cancel every dreams, visions, prophesy and prayers against my life and family in the name of Jesus.
23. Talk to God about your heart desires and your situation.
24. Thank God for answered prayers.

Confession:

"Be sober, be vigilant; because your adversary the devil as a roaring lion walketh about, seeking whom he may devour" 1 Peter 5:8.

Wisdom for Today:

"Wisdom is knowing what to do next; virtue is doing it". - David Starr Jordan

Read the Bible Today: Romans 8

Prayer Points:

1. Almighty God I refuse to follow the evil pattern of my household enemies, in the name of Jesus.
2. My life, jump out from the cage of household wickedness, in the name of Jesus.
3. I command that all my blessings and potentials buried by wicked household enemies be exhumed, in the name of Jesus.
4. I will see the goodness of the Lord in the land of the living, in the name of Jesus.
5. Everything done against me to spoil my joy, receive destruction, in the name of Jesus.
6. Any power, any spirit, any one that wants me to fight battle until I die, fire of God consume them in the name of Jesus.
7. I decree that my battles shall expire today in the name of Jesus.
8. Almighty God, today I command my tears and weeping to cease in the name of Jesus.
9. Any Power, any spirit, anyone that wants me to weep or cry before I receive my blessing; die in the name of Jesus.
10. Any idol demanding worship, sacrifice or ritual from me before I receive my blessing and miracle; let fire go before God and consume them in the name of Jesus.
11. Give thanks unto the Lord.
12. I plead the blood of Jesus Christ over my spirit, soul, and body in the name of Jesus.
13. Almighty God; Visit me specially today in the name of Jesus.
14. Almighty God anoint me with your fresh oil in the name Jesus.
15. Almighty God; answer me speedily in the name of Jesus.
16. Almighty God; it is your blessing that makes one rich; bless the works of my hands in the name of Jesus.

17. I cancel every dreams, visions, prophesy and prayers against my life and family in the name of Jesus.
18. Talk to God about your heart desires and your situation.
19. Thank God for answered prayers.

Confession:

By the spirit of prophesy, I believe and confess that God's abundance flows into my life. The Lord will do exceedingly great and mighty things in my life, for the breakthroughs of abundance beyond my imagination rest upon my life.

Wisdom for Today:

"Life is a sum of all your choices. Our joy comes from living our own lives simply and gratefully—never from making any demands whatsoever upon others".

Read the Bible Today: Psalm 27

Prayer Points:

1. Almighty God as Abraham found favor with you, let me find favor with you so that I can excel in every area of my life, in Jesus name.
2. It does not matter whether I deserve it or not, I receive immeasurable favor from the Lord, in the name of Jesus.
3. Every blessing God has attributed to me today will not pass me by, in the name of Jesus.
4. My blessing will not be transferred to my neighbor, in the name of Jesus.
5. Every spirit that abandons good things, come out of my life and enter no more in the name of Jesus.
6. Jesus Christ is Lord over my spirit, soul, and body therefore every evil load in my life be consumed by fire in Jesus mighty name.
7. Almighty God have mercy upon me remove my shoulder from every satanic burden in the name of Jesus.
8. Almighty God; have mercy upon me deliver me from the spirit of slavery and servitude in the name of Jesus.
9. Almighty God increase my greatness and comfort me on every side in the name of Jesus.
10. Almighty God; as from this moment let me go from strength to strength in the name of Jesus.
11. Almighty God answer my prayers speedily in the name of Jesus.
12. Almighty God make your face to shine upon me in the mighty name of Jesus.

13. Almighty God; you are my song and my shield, give me grace and glory in the name of Jesus.
14. Almighty God; as from today, help me to work up rightly in the name of Jesus.
15. Almighty God; as from today never allow me to lack any good thing in the name of Jesus.
16. Almighty God; show me your mercy and grant me your salvation in the name of Jesus.
17. Almighty God; let your salvation never depart from my life and let your glory dwell in my life, in my family and church in the name of Jesus.
18. I cancel every dreams, visions, prophesy and prayers against my life and family in the name of Jesus.
19. Talk to God about your heart desires and your situation.
20. Thank God for answered prayers.

SEPTEMBER 15

Confession:

I shall experience blessing in every area of my business and home. The grace of God abounds unto me; the Lord opens unto me his abundant treasure.

Wisdom for Today:

"Be of good courage, and he shall strengthen your heart, all ye that hope in the Lord" Psalm 31: 24

Read the Bible Today: Isaiah 51:11

Prayer Points:

1. Almighty God disgrace every power that is out to thwart your program for my life, in the name of Jesus.
2. Every step I take shall lead to outstanding success, in Jesus name.
3. I shall prevail with man and with God in every area of my life, in the name of Jesus.
4. Every habitation of infirmity in my life, break to pieces, in the name of Jesus.
5. My body, soul, and spirit shall reject every evil oppression in Jesus name.
6. Almighty God; let the truth spring out of my life in the name of Jesus.
7. Almighty God; come down from heaven and bless my life in the name of Jesus.
8. Almighty God; in this land wherever I go from today, give me what is good in the name of Jesus.
9. Almighty God; make your footsteps my path way in Jesus name.
10. Almighty God; have mercy upon me and bless me more and more in the name of Jesus.
11. Almighty God; give me rest of mind in the name of Jesus.
12. Almighty God; remember me for good today and manifest yourself in my life in the name of Jesus.
13. O heavens open for my prayers in the name of Jesus.
14. Almighty God; manifest yourself and take away yoke of problem from my neck in the name of Jesus.
15. Almighty God; take away every evil family burden from my shoulder in the name of Jesus.

16. Every wind behind any storm in my life; I command you now be still in the name of Jesus.
17. Almighty God calm every storm in my life in the mighty name of Jesus.
18. Almighty God; arise and deliver me from every curse that is in my life in the name of Jesus.
19. It is written my husband is my maker therefore every spirit wife, spirit husband, remove your hands from the affairs of my life in the name of Jesus.
20. You spirit wife, and husband release all my blessing in your custody in the name of Jesus.
21. Every covenant in my life supporting any problem; break in the name of Jesus.
22. Anything that is keeping problem in place in my life; be destroyed by the fire of God in the name of Jesus.
23. I cancel every dreams, visions, prophesy and prayers against my life and family in the name of Jesus.
24. Talk to God about your heart desires and your situation.
25. Thank God for answered prayers.

Confession:

The Lord causes increasing abundance and goodness to come to me.

Wisdom for Today:

"Be careful for nothing; but in everything by prayer and supplication with thanksgiving let your request be made known unto God". Philippians 4: 6-7

Read the Bible Today: James 5

Prayer Points:

1. Give thanks to the Lord.
2. Evil foundation in my life, I pull you down today, in the mighty name of Jesus.
3. Every inherited sickness in my life, depart from me now, in the name of Jesus. Evil waters in my body dry up by fire, in the name of Jesus.
4. I cancel the effect of every evil dedication in my life, in the name of Jesus.
5. Fire of the Holy Ghost; immunize my blood against satanic poisons, in the name of Jesus.
6. Almighty God; stretch forth your mighty hand a second time against my enemy for my recovery in the name of Jesus.
7. In the name of Jesus I recover all my lost grounds in the name of Jesus.
8. Almighty God; remember me for good and let me have a turn of event in my life in the name of Jesus.
9. Almighty God; bless my life with peace; deliver me from confusion in the name of Jesus.
10. Rock of ages; arise and collide with my mountain of problem, grind them to powder, and let the east wind blow them away in the name of Jesus.
11. Declare Jesus Christ is Lord.
12. Declare it is well with you.
13. Almighty God; have your way in my life in the name of Jesus.
14. Almighty God; I have no power of my own, arise and deliver me from unprofitable hard labor in the name of Jesus.

15. Almighty God; revive my spiritual life and set me on fire for you in the name of Jesus.
16. Almighty God; make me untouchable for any evil spirit in the name of Jesus.
17. I cancel every dreams, visions, prophesy and prayers against my life and family in the name of Jesus.
18. Talk to God about your heart desires and your situation.
19. Thank God for answered prayers.

Apostle A.O. Solomon

Confession:

I boldly command every hidden treasure of abundance to be exposed to me that the riches of the ungodly will enter into my hand for favor and blessing, and I shall know the grace of God without trouble.

Wisdom for Today:

"He that keepeth his mouth keepeth his life: but he that openeth wide his lips shall have destruction". Proverbs 13:2, 3

Read the Bible Today: Genesis 26

Prayer Points:

1. Almighty God put self-control into my mouth, in the name of Jesus.
2. I refuse to get used to ill health, in the name of Jesus.
3. Every door open to infirmity in my life, be permanently closed today, in the name of Jesus.
4. Every power contending with God in my life be roasted by fire, in the name of Jesus.
5. Every power preventing God's glory from manifesting in my life, be paralyzed, in the name of Jesus.
6. Almighty God; keep me fresh; give me oil in my lamp in the name of Jesus.
7. My spirit man; receive the fire of revival and reject oppression in the name of Jesus.
8. Almighty God; give me rest in the name of Jesus.
9. Almighty God let me have rest from my trouble, problem, fear, hard bondage, in the name of Jesus.
10. Almighty God; remove my name from the register of beggars in the name of Jesus.
11. Almighty God; deliver me; don't let me use debt to settle debt again in the name of Jesus.
12. Almighty God; bless me in such a way that even the blessed will call me blessed in the name of Jesus.
13. Begin to give thanks to the King of kings and Lord of lords.
14. Thank God for one more day.
15. Declare Jesus Christ is Lord.

16. Almighty God; let your grace be sufficient for me in the name of Jesus.
17. Have your way Lord in my life and situation in the name of Jesus.
18. Almighty God; I pray for a divine visitation in the name of Jesus.
19. Almighty God let your fire consume everything that is limiting my life in the name of Jesus.
20. Everything that is stagnating my life; Almighty God arise and consume them by your fire in the name of Jesus.
21. I cancel every dreams, visions, prophesy and prayers against my life and family in the name of Jesus.
22. Talk to God about your heart desires and your situation.
23. Thank God for answered prayers.

Confession:

I believe and confess that the Lord anoints my eyes to see the hidden riches of this world. He causes creativity to flow in my life and business. My ears are anointed to hear what God is saying, my eyes are anointed to see what God has in store, my hands are anointed to touch the blessings set aside for me.

Wisdom for Today:

"The Lord is not slack concerning his promise, as some men count slackness; but is longsuffering to us-ward, not willing that any should perish, but that all should come to repentance". II Peter 3:9

Read the Bible Today: Phillippians 1:

Prayer Points:

1. I release myself from the spirit of desolation and confusion, in the name of Jesus.
2. Let God be God in my home, in the name of Jesus.
3. Let God be God in my health, in the name of Jesus.
4. Let God be God in my career, in the name of Jesus.
5. Let God be God in my finances, in the name of Jesus.
6. Everything eating up my joy, almighty God; consume them by your fire in the name of Jesus.
7. Whatever is eating up my peace, almighty God; consume them by fire in the name of Jesus.
8. Almighty God; according to your word settle me today in the name of Jesus.
9. Any power, any spirit, anyone saying no to my testimony, almighty God; remove them from my way in the name of Jesus.
10. Almighty God; deliver me from my strong enemies in the name of Jesus.
11. Every power, every spirit of impossibility on my way be removed in the name of Jesus.
12. Whatever the enemies declared impossible in my life, O God arise and make them possible in the name of Jesus.
13. Almighty God; let there be a turn of event in my life in the name of Jesus.

14. Almighty God; take me to that position where my enemies can never pull me down in the name of Jesus.
15. Almighty God; bless me in such a way that even the blessed will call me blessed in the name of Jesus.
16. Any power, any spirit, anyone boasting against my joy, peace, you shall not survive today in the name of Jesus.
17. Almighty God; I need a major breakthrough in the name of Jesus.
18. I cancel every dreams, visions, prophesy and prayers against my life and family in the name of Jesus.
19. Talk to God about your heart desires and your situation.
20. Thank God for answered prayers.

Confession:

There shall be an outbreak of the rain of God's favor in my life. For the Lord will cause my life to be exceedingly blessed. The Lord will cause me to enter his great favor.

Wisdom for Today:

"Take therefore no thought for tomorrow: for the morrow shall take thought for the things of itself. Sufficient unto the day is the evil thereof". Mathew 6:34

Read the Bible Today: Psalm 38

Prayer Points:

1. Almighty God enlarge my horizons beyond my wildest dreams, in the name of Jesus.
2. Almighty God let every evil trend directing my affairs be reversed, in the name of Jesus.
3. Lord Jesus, uproot every evil thing from my life in the name of Jesus.
4. Almighty God plant good things in my life, in the name of Jesus.
5. Almighty God let every financial failure in my life be turned to financial breakthrough in the name of Jesus.
6. Declare Jesus Christ is Lord.
7. Almighty God have your way in my life in the name of Jesus.
8. Almighty God; keep me out of every trouble in the name of Jesus.
9. Almighty God; stretch forth your hand against the anger of my enemy in the name of Jesus.
10. Almighty God; do not forsake the works of your hand, perfect that which concerns me in the name of Jesus.
11. Almighty God; surprise me with pleasant surprise in the name of Jesus.
12. Almighty God; don't allow my fear to come to pass in the name of Jesus.
13. Almighty God; in you I take refuge do not leave my soul destitute in the name of Jesus.
14. Almighty God; keep me and my family away from the trap of the workers of iniquity in the name of Jesus.

15. Almighty God; let my enemy fall into their own net, while I escape safely in the name of Jesus.
16. I cancel every dreams, visions, prophesy and prayers against my life and family in the name of Jesus.
17. Talk to God about your heart desires and your situation.
18. Thank God for answered prayers.

Confession:

I boldly confess that God makes my spiritual life good and fruitful.

Wisdom for Today:

"Casting all your care upon him; for he careth for you"

Read the Bible Today: Psalm 91

Prayer Points:

1. Any negative transactions currently affecting my life physically and spiritually be canceled by the fire of God, in Jesus name.
2. I release myself from any dark spirit, in the name of Jesus.
3. Let all incantations and enchantments against me be canceled by the blood of Jesus, in Jesus name.
4. Almighty God let all my oppressors retreat and flee in defeat this moment, in the name of Jesus.
5. I bind and paralyze every strongman who has my goods in his possessions, in the name of Jesus.
6. Almighty God; have mercy upon me let there be turn of event in my life to the glory and praise of your name in the name of Jesus.
7. Almighty God let anyone going through struggle; receive deliverance in the name of Jesus.
8. Evil yokes in my life; be destroyed in the name of Jesus.
9. Through the poverty of Jesus Christ, I receive my prosperity in the name of Jesus.
10. Almighty God; frustrate every evil desire against me in the name of Jesus.
11. Lift up your voice and thank the Lord.
12. Declare Jesus Christ is Lord.
13. Almighty God let today's prayer take me to another level of glory, favor, and mercy in the name of Jesus.
14. Almighty God I commit my prayers to your hand have your way in the name of Jesus.
15. I drink the blood of Jesus and I eat the flesh of Jesus in the name of Jesus.
16. Every spirit of infirmity in my life I bind and I cast you out in the name of Jesus Christ.

17. Any power using sickness or any infirmity to delay my life; be consumed by fire in the name of Jesus.
18. Every instrument of delay operating in any area of my life come out by fire and enter no more in the name of Jesus.
19. Almighty God; have mercy upon me; take me to another level of your glory, favor, power, and anointing in the name of Jesus.
20. Almighty God take me away from the captivity of the mighty in the name of Jesus.
21. I cancel every dreams, visions, prophesy and prayers against my life and family in the name of Jesus.
22. Talk to God about your heart desires and your situation.
23. Thank God for answered prayers.

Confession:

God causes prosperity on my business and ventures. I receive by faith, wisdom, knowledge, and divine creativity to excel in life.

Wisdom for Today:

"Fear thou not: for I am with thee: be not dismayed; yea, I will help thee; yea, I will uphold thee with the right hand of my righteousness". Isaiah 41:10

Read the Bible Today: Isaiah 49

Prayer Points:

1. Glory of God; envelop every department of my life, in the name of Jesus.
2. The Lord who answers by fire is my God, in the name of Jesus.
3. Today, all my enemies shall scatter and rise no more, in the name of Jesus.
4. Blood of Jesus, cry against all evil gatherings arranged for my sake, in the name of Jesus.
5. Father Lord, convert all my past failures to unlimited victories and successes, in the name of Jesus.
6. Lord Jesus, create room for my advancement in every area of my life in the name of Jesus.
7. Father make today my miracle day in the name of Jesus.
8. Almighty God save us and our children from the attack of the enemy in the name of Jesus.
9. Almighty God, deliver me and my family from death in the name of Jesus.
10. I cancel every dream of death by the blood of Jesus in the name of Jesus.
11. Almighty God bless me more and more O Lord in the name of Jesus.
12. Almighty God; give me seed to sow always and give me harvest in the name of Jesus.
13. I reject every evil in this day in the name of Jesus.
14. I refuse to enter into any coffin this year in the name of Jesus.
15. I cancel every dreams, visions, prophesy and prayers against my life and family in the name of Jesus.
16. Talk to God about your heart desires and your situation.
17. Thank God for answered prayers.

Confession:

I boldly declare that I become a point of reference to the glory of God, for the Lord causes me to increase even in the midst of my tribulation, and my tribulation will produce an eternal way to glory.

Wisdom for Today:

"It is good that a man should both hope and quietly wait for the salvation of the Lord". Lamentations 3:26

Read the Bible Today: Psalm 27

Prayer Points:

1. Almighty God turn all evil thoughts against me to goodness, in the name of Jesus.
2. Almighty God reverse any evil decisions that have been made against me, in the name of Jesus.
3. Almighty God give me amazing prosperity in my life, in the name of Jesus.
4. Let the showers of amazing prosperity fall upon every department of my life, in the name of Jesus.
5. I claim all my prosperity this day, in the name of Jesus.
6. Every door of my prosperity that has been shut be opened now, in the name of Jesus.
7. Go ahead and worship and appreciate God.
8. Almighty God manifest yourself in my life as the Lord of lords in the name of Jesus.
9. Every satanic knee in my life, I command you to bow in the name of Jesus.
10. I command every knee contesting my glory to bow in the name of Jesus.
11. Any power chasing good things from me, exchanging it with evil let fire fall and consume them in the name of a Jesus.
12. Almighty God; enough is enough; take me to another level of glory in the name of Jesus.
13. I cancel every dreams, visions, prophesy and prayers against my life and family in the name of Jesus.
14. Talk to God about your heart desires and your situation.
15. Thank God for answered prayers.

Confession:

I boldly declare that the Lord will command every drought and famine area in my life to be transformed to abundance. He will cause his contentment to be upon me, and the blessings of Zion to flow into my life.

Wisdom for Today:

"Cast not away therefore your confidence, which hath great recompence of reward. For ye have need of patience, that, after ye have done the will of God, ye might receive the promise". Hebrews 10:35-37

Read the Bible Today: Hebrew 12

Prayer Points:

1. Almighty God convert my poverty to prosperity, in the name of Jesus.
2. Almighty God convert my mistakes to perfection, in the name of Jesus.
3. Almighty God convert my frustrations to fulfillment, in the name of Jesus.
4. Almighty God bring honey out of the rock for me, in the name of Jesus.
5. I stand against every evil covenant of sudden death, in the name of Jesus.
6. Almighty God take me to my next level; give me rest in the name of Jesus.
7. Almighty God; let me prosper and continue prospering in the name of Jesus.
8. Almighty God show me your way that I may know you more and more in the name of Jesus.
9. Almighty God; let your presence go with me and give me rest in the name of Jesus.
10. Almighty God stretch forth your mighty hand and bring back to me, my family and children all the blessings that we have lost in the name of Jesus.
11. I declare today as my day of uncommon blessing in the name of Jesus.

12. The gates of hell shall not prevail against the church in the name of Jesus.
13. Declare Jesus Christ is Lord.
14. Plead the blood of Jesus Christ.
15. I approach the throne of mercy with the blood of Jesus Christ in the name of Jesus.
16. Let the spirit and anointing of Zion rest upon me in the name of Jesus.
17. Almighty God; I commit this day into your hands in the name of Jesus.
18. I cancel every dreams, visions, prophesy and prayers against my life and family in the name of Jesus.
19. Talk to God about your heart desires and your situation.
20. Thank God for answered prayers.

Confession:

The grace of sufficiency abounds unto me, in the precious name of Jesus.

Wisdom for Today:

"Cease from anger, and forsake wrath: fret not thyself in any wise to do evil. For evildoers shall be cut off: but those that wait upon the Lord, they shall inherit the earth". Psalm 37;8, 9

Read the Bible Today: Psalm 40

Prayer Points:

1. I break every conscious and unconscious evil covenant of untimely death, in the name of Jesus.
2. You, spirit of death and hell, you have no right to be in my life, in the name of Jesus.
3. You, stones of death, depart from my paths, in the name of Jesus.
4. Almighty God make me a voice of deliverance and blessing, in the name of Jesus.
5. I tread upon the high places of the enemies, in the name of Jesus.
6. Let there be turn of event in my life in the name.
7. Almighty God; fulfill your promises in my life in the name of Jesus.
8. Every evil dream, I bury you in the blood of Jesus, and I command you to die in the name of Jesus.
9. Every evil desire fashioned against me and my family back fire in the name of Jesus.
10. Anything standing as a reproach in my life, almighty God; remove them in the name of Jesus.
11. Every evil kingdom, contesting against the Kingdom of God in my life, almighty God; destroy them in the mighty name of Jesus.
12. Every power, every spirit diverting the blessing of God away from my life, my family Holy Ghost fire consume them in the name of Jesus.
13. All my diverted blessing; hear the word of the living God; gather yourself together and come back to me in the name of Jesus.

14. Every problem I am having in my academics, my work my business and family, almighty God; reduce them to nothing in the name of Jesus.
15. I cancel every dreams, visions, prophesy and prayers against my life and family in the name of Jesus.
16. Talk to God about your heart desires and your situation.
17. Thank God for answered prayers.

Confession:

God always causes me to have victory through the Lord Jesus, as I rely on his word. The Lord will favor me with an all-round blessing that cannot be overlooked.

Wisdom for Today:

"For whatsoever things were written aforetime were written for our learning, that we through patience and comfort of the scriptures might have hope. Now the God of patience and consolation grant you to be likeminded one toward another according to Christ Jesus". Romans 15: 4-5

Read the Bible Today: Deuteronomy 33

Prayer Points:

1. You, evil current of death, relinquish your grip over my life and burn to ashes, in the name of Jesus.
2. I frustrate evil decisions over me and my family in the name of Jesus.
3. Fire of protection; cover me and my family in the name of Jesus.
4. Almighty God make my way perfect, in the name of Jesus.
5. Throughout the days of my life, I shall not be put to shame, in the name of Jesus.
6. Success that cannot vanish, that the enemy cannot overcome, come upon my life and overtake my failure in the name of Jesus.
7. Almighty God; have mercy upon me in the name of Jesus.
8. Almighty God I need your mercy in the name of Jesus.
9. Almighty God; let your mercy heal me and deliver in the name of Jesus.
10. Almighty God by your mercy answer my prayers in the name of Jesus.
11. God of Abraham, Isaac, and Jacob manifest yourself in my life; let me experience a turn of event in the name of Jesus.
12. Give thanks unto the Lord.
13. Almighty God; deliver me from the hands of my oppressors in the name of Jesus.
14. Almighty God; deliver all our children from the hands of wasters in the name of Jesus.

15. Almighty God; anoint me and all my children to succeed in the name of Jesus.
16. Any power that wants to use my children to make me cry; die in the name of Jesus.
17. Any power attacking my children because of me; die in the name of Jesus.
18. Almighty God give me rest of mind in the name of Jesus.
19. 19. Intercede for any one that you know is looking for the fruit of the womb, let almighty God make them fruitful and multiply in the name of Jesus.
20. Also pray for those that are looking for job, let there be miracles in the name of Jesus.
21. I cancel every dreams, visions, prophesy and prayers against my life and family in the name of Jesus.
22. Talk to God about your heart desires and your situation.
23. Thank God for answered prayers.

Confession:

Whosoever blesses me shall be blessed; whosoever curses me shall bear the curses, because I am anointed of the Lord.

Wisdom for Today:

"The steps of a good man are ordered by the Lord: and he delighted in his way". Psalm 37:23

Read the Bible Today: Psalm 32

Prayer Points:

1. I reject every garment of shame, in the name of Jesus.
2. I reject every shoe of shame, in the name of Jesus.
3. I reject every headgear and cap of shame, in the name of Jesus.
4. Shamefulness shall not be my lot, in the name of Jesus.
5. Every limitation on my progress due to reproach in my life, be removed, in the name of Jesus.
6. Almighty God deliver me from every evil spiritual court in the name of Jesus.
7. Pray for the country where you are that the kingdom of God will come into the land in the name of Jesus.
8. Every enemy of this country be exposed and be disgraced in the name of Jesus.
9. I plead the blood of Jesus against natural disaster in the name of Jesus.
10. Almighty God I lift you up in my life, draw blessings, prosperity and goodness to my life in the name of Jesus.
11. Declare Jesus Christ is Lord.
12. Plead the blood of Jesus Christ.
13. I approach the throne of mercy by the blood of Jesus Christ in the name of Jesus.
14. Let the spirit and anointing of Zion rest upon me in the name of Jesus.
15. Almighty God; I commit this day into your hands in the name of Jesus.
16. Let there be turn of event in my life in the name of Jesus.
17. Almighty God; fulfill your promises in my life in the name of Jesus.

18. Every evil dream in my life, I bury you by the blood of Jesus, and I command you to die in the name of Jesus.
19. I cancel every dreams, visions, prophesy and prayers against my life and family in the name of Jesus.
20. Talk to God about your heart desires and your situation.
21. Thank God for answered prayers.

Confession:

I am what God says I am—I am a winner and not a looser.

Wisdom for Today:

Being confident of this very thing, that he which hath begun a good word in you will perform it until the day of Jesus Christ: Philippians 1:6

Read the Bible Today: Luke 10

Prayer Points:

1. Every network of shame around me be paralyzed, in the name of Jesus.
2. I decree all those who are seeking for my shame shall die in shame, in the name of Jesus.
3. I decree as far as shame is concerned, I shall not record any point for satan, in the name of Jesus.
4. I shall not eat the bread of sorrow, I shall not eat the bread of shame, and I shall not eat the bread of defeat, in the name of Jesus.
5. No evil will touch me throughout my life, in the name of Jesus.
6. Every evil desire fashioned against me and my family back fire in the name of Jesus.
7. Anything standing as a reproach in my life, almighty God; uproot and remove them in the name of Jesus.
8. Every evil kingdom, contesting against the kingdom of God in my life, almighty God; destroy them in the mighty name of Jesus.
9. Every power, spirits diverting the blessing of God away from my life, my family, Holy Ghost fire consume them in the name of Jesus.
10. All my diverted blessing; hear the word of the living God; gather yourself together and come back to me in the name of Jesus.
11. Every problem I am having in my academics, work, business and family, almighty God; reduce them to nothing in the name of Jesus.
12. Almighty God; have mercy upon me in the name of Jesus.
13. Almighty God I need your mercy in the name of Jesus.
14. Almighty God; let your mercy heal me and deliver in the name of Jesus.
15. Almighty God by your mercy answer my prayers in the name of Jesus.

16. I cancel every dreams, visions, prophesy and prayers against my life and family in the name of Jesus.
17. Talk to God about your heart desires and your situation.
18. Thank God for answered prayers.

Confession:

I believe and confess that the Lord is good for he has redeemed me from the curse of the law. By faith I confess that the curse of disobedience to parents over my life is broken in the name of Jesus.

Wisdom for Today:

"Obey them that have rule over you, and submit yourselves: for they watch for your souls, as they that must give account, that they may do it with joy, and not with grief: for that is unprofitable for you". Hebrews 13:17

Read the Bible Today: Psalm 1:1-3

Prayer Points:

1. I shall reach my goal no matter how severe the storms against me may be, in the name of Jesus.
2. In every area of my life, my enemies will not catch me, in the name of Jesus.
3. In every area of my life, I shall run and not grow weary; I shall walk and shall not faint, for the joy of the Lord is my strength, in Jesus name.
4. Almighty God please don't let my life disgrace you in any way in the name of Jesus.
5. I will not be a victim of failure for any reason, and I will not bite my finger in regret in the name of Jesus.
6. Give thanks unto the Lord.
7. Almighty God; deliver me from the hands of my oppressors in the name of Jesus.
8. Almighty God; deliver all our children from the hands of wasters in the name of Jesus.
9. Almighty God; anoint all our children to succeed in the name of Jesus.
10. Any power that wants to use my children to make me cry; die in the name of Jesus.
11. Any power attacking my children because of me; die in the name of Jesus.
12. Almighty God; give me rest of mind in the name of Jesus.

13. I plead the blood of Jesus against natural disaster in the name of Jesus.
14. I cancel every dreams, visions, prophesy and prayers against my life and family in the name of Jesus.
15. Talk to God about your heart desires and your situation.
16. Thank God for answered prayers.

Confession:

I believe and confess that I am free from the yoke of bondage. I believe and confess that I am free from the curse that makes a family downtrodden. Slavery is not my portion.

Wisdom for Today:

Know therefore that the Lord thy God, he is God, the faithful of God, which keepeth convenant and mercy with them that love him and keep his commandments to a thousand generations; Deuteronomy 7:8-9

Read the Bible Today: Joshua 23

Prayer Points:

1. Almighty God help me to meet up with your standard for my life, in Jesus name.
2. I refuse to be a candidate of every physical and spiritual amputator in the name of Jesus.
3. With each day of my life, I shall move to higher ground, in the name of Jesus.
4. Every spirit of shame set in motion against my life; I bind you, in the name of Jesus.
5. Every spirit competing against my breakthroughs, be arrested and be destroyed in the name of Jesus.
6. I bind and cast out every spirit of slavery, in the name of Jesus.
7. Begin to worship God.
8. Declare Jesus Christ is Lord.
9. Give thanks unto the Lord.
10. Almighty God I thank you for there shall be a turn of events in my life in the name of Jesus.
11. Almighty God; open the heavens for our prayer in the name of Jesus.
12. Almighty God; let your hand be upon me for good in the name of Jesus.
13. Almighty God lead us in the way we should go in the name of Jesus.
14. As the Lord liveth, I shall triumph over my enemies in the name of Jesus.

15. Almighty God please remember me for good in the name of Jesus.
16. I cancel every dreams, visions, prophesy and prayers against my life and family in the name of Jesus.
17. Talk to God about your heart desires and your situation.
18. Thank God for answered prayers.

Confession:

I thank the Lord in advance for turning every curse into a blessing and every challenge into his favor in Jesus name. I am what God says I am; I am a winner and not a looser.

Wisdom for Today:

"Faithful is he that calleth you, who also will do it". I Thessalonians 5:24

Read the Bible Today: Joshua 23:14

Prayer Points:

1. I disgrace all my stubborn pursuers, in the name of Jesus.
2. I bind every spirit of Herod, in the name of Jesus.
3. Every spirit challenging my God be disgraced, in Jesus name.
4. Every Red Sea before me be parted, in the name of Jesus.
5. I command every spirit of bad endings to be bound in every area of my life, in the name of Jesus.
6. Holy Spirit of God; bless my life in the name of Jesus.
7. Almighty God let your blessing be upon my life in the name of Jesus.
8. Almighty God; deliver me from my stubborn enemy in the name of Jesus.
9. Almighty God; heal every area of my life in the name of Jesus.
10. Almighty God; take over my labor and bless me in the name of Jesus.
11. Almighty God; remember my life, and my family in the name of Jesus.
12. Almighty God; turn my life around in the name of Jesus.
13. I unseat any power sitting upon my blessing in the name of Jesus.
14. Almighty God; you have done it before do it again in the name of Jesus.
15. Almighty God; I commit this land into your hand; bless it with your peace in the name of Jesus.
16. I cancel every dreams, visions, prophesy and prayers against my life and family in the name of Jesus.
17. Talk to God about your heart desires and your situation.
18. Thank God for answered prayers.

Confession:

I believe and confess that God's plan is to prosper me and not to harm me. God's plan is to elevate me and not to demote me because, eye hath not seen, ear hath not heard nor hath it come into our understanding what God still hath in store for me.

Wisdom for Today:

"He will not suffer thy foot to be moved: he that keepeth thee will not slumber. Behold, he that keepeth thee Israel shall neither slumber nor sleep".

Read the Bible Today: Psalm 1

Prayer Points:

1. Every spirit of Saul be disgraced in my life, in the name of Jesus.
2. Every spirit of Pharaoh be disgraced in my life, in Jesus name.
3. I reject every evil invitation to backwardness, in Jesus name.
4. I command every stone of hindrance in my life to be rolled away, in the name of Jesus.
5. Almighty God roll away every stone of poverty from my life, in the name Jesus.
6. Every wicked intention against my life be frustrated in the name of Jesus.
7. Almighty God; bless our going out and coming in, in the mighty name of Jesus.
8. Almighty God; deliver me from trouble in this land in the name of Jesus.
9. Go ahead and thank God for the season of turn of events in Jesus name.
10. Blood of Jesus Christ wash me from every known and unknown sin in the name of Jesus.
11. Almighty God; have your way in my life in the name of Jesus.
12. Declare Jesus Christ is Lord.
13. Jesus Christ is Lord 3x Hallelujah.
14. Almighty God; open the book of remembrance for me in the name of Jesus.
15. Almighty God; have mercy upon me, bring back my good season in the name of Jesus.

Apostle A.O. Solomon

16. Almighty God; I believe that I will have a turn of event in the name of Jesus.
17. I am serving the bright and morning star, I command every area of my life to shine forth in Jesus name.
18. I cancel every dreams, visions, prophesy and prayers against my life and family in the name of Jesus.
19. Talk to God about your heart desires and your situation.
20. Thank God for answered prayers.

Confession:

"Christ died and rose again ....so that he can be our lord both while we live and when we die". Romans 14:9, TLB.

Wisdom for Today:

"Let the word of Christ dwell in you richly in all wisdom; teaching and admonishing one another in psalms and hymns and spiritual songs, singing with grace in your hearts to the Lord". Colossians 1:9-11

Read the Bible Today: John 14

Prayer Points:

1. Let every stone of infertility in my life, business, marriage, and children be rolled away, in the name of Jesus.
2. Let every stone of nonachievement in my life be rolled away, in the name of Jesus.
3. Almighty God roll away every stone of hardship and slavery from my life, in the name of Jesus.
4. Almighty God roll away every stone of failure in my life, my home, and my business, in the name of Jesus.
5. You, stones of hindrance, planted at the edge of my breakthroughs, be rolled away, in the name of Jesus.
6. Lord Jesus Christ, you are my bright and morning star, shine on my path way in the name of Jesus.
7. I reject self-pity, depression, sorrow, and sickness in the name of Jesus.
8. Almighty God; have mercy upon me change my destiny for good in the name of Jesus.
9. Where the world and enemies has said it is finished for me, almighty God; arise and show yourself in the name of Jesus.
10. All the benefits that the Lord has blessed me with; manifest in the name of Jesus.
11. All that the enemy has swallowed in my life, I command them to be vomited in the name of Jesus.
12. Every bad dream in my life, I cancel you in the name of Jesus.
13. Almighty God; by your power cause all my good dreams to manifest speedily in the name of Jesus.

14. Almighty God; by your mercy and power cause the good dreams of our children to manifest in the name of Jesus.
15. Almighty God, do something new that will make the world to congratulate me in the name of Jesus.
16. Almighty God; manifest yourself in my life and take me to my next level in the name of Jesus.
17. I cancel every dreams, visions, prophesy and prayers against my life and family in the name of Jesus.
18. Talk to God about your heart desires and your situation.
19. Thank God for answered prayers.

Confession:

The Lord is giving me joy in all things, causing favor and blessing to flow toward me. The favor of the Lord goes with me everywhere, and the Lord's blessing is manifest even in adverse situations.

Wisdom for Today:

Wherefore, my beloved brethren, let every man be swift to hear, slow to speak, slow to wrath: 2For the wrath of man worketh not the righteousness of God. James 1: 19-20.

Read the Bible Today: *Colossians 3*

Prayer Points:

1. You, stones of stagnancy stationed at the border of my life, be rolled away, in the name of Jesus.
2. My God, let every stone of the destroyers planted at the beginning of my life, at the middle of my life, and at the end of my life, be rolled away, in the name of Jesus.
3. Almighty God I thank you for all the stones you have rolled away, I forbid their return, in the name of Jesus.
4. Let the power from above come upon me, in the name of Jesus.
5. Almighty God manifest your power in every area of my life, in the name of Jesus.
6. I thank God for the season of turn of events in the name of Jesus.
7. Blood of Jesus Christ wash me from every known and unknown sin in the name of Jesus.
8. Almighty God; have your way in my life in the name of Jesus.
9. Declare Jesus Christ is Lord.
10. Jesus Christ is Lord 3x Hallelujah.
11. Almighty God; open the book of remembrance for me in the name of Jesus.
12. Almighty God; have mercy upon me, bring back my good season in the name of Jesus.
13. Almighty God let there be a turn of event in my life in the name of Jesus.
14. Lord Jesus Christ, you are my bright and morning star, let your light shine on my path way in the name if Jesus.

15. I reject self-pity, depression, sorrow, and sickness in the name of Jesus.
16. I cancel every dreams, visions, prophesy and prayers against my life and family in the name of Jesus.
17. Talk to God about your heart desires and your situation.
18. Thank God for answered prayers.

Confession:

God's favor to collect the goods from the wicked ones rests upon me. God's divine elevation in the sight of the enemy rests upon my life.

Wisdom for Today:

"Ye shall walk in all the ways which the Lord your God hath commandeth you that ye may live, and that it may be well with you, and that ye may prolong your days in the land which ye shall possess".

Read the Bible Today: *Jeremiah 7:23*

Prayer Points:

1. Almighty God make me a power generator throughout the days of my life, in the name of Jesus.
2. Let the power to live a holy life throughout the days of my life fall upon me, in the name of Jesus.
3. Let the power to live a victorious life throughout the days of my life fall upon me, in the name of Jesus.
4. Let the power to prosper throughout the days of my life fall upon me, in the name of Jesus.
5. Let the power to be in good health throughout the days of my life fall upon me, in the name of Jesus.
6. Let the power to disgrace my enemies throughout the days of my life fall upon me, in the name of Jesus.
7. Almighty God; have mercy upon me change my destiny for good in the name of Jesus.
8. Where the world and my enemies has said it is finished for me, almighty God; arise and show yourself in the name of Jesus.
9. I command all the benefits that the Lord has blessed me with to manifest in the name of Jesus.
10. I command all the enemy has swallowed in my life be vomited in the name of Jesus.
11. Every bad dream in my life, I cancel you in the name of Jesus.
12. Almighty God; by your power cause all my good dreams to manifest speedily in the name of Jesus.
13. Almighty God; by your mercy and power cause the good dreams of my children to manifest in the name of Jesus.

14. Almighty God; do something new in my life that will make the world to congratulate me in the name of Jesus.
15. I cancel every dreams, visions, prophesy and prayers against my life and family in the name of Jesus.
16. Talk to God about your heart desires and your situation.
17. Thank God for answered prayers.

Confession:

The eyes of the Lord go with me and cause me to stand before kings and to have favor with all men.

Wisdom for Today:

"Is any sick among you? Let him call for the elders of the church; and let them pray over him, anointing him with oil in the name of the Lord: And the prayer of faith shall save the sick, and the Lord shall raise him up; and if he have committed sins, they shall be forgiven him". James 5: 14-15

Read the Bible Today: Exodus 15

Prayer Points:

1. Let the healing power of Jesus Christ rest upon me now, in the name of Jesus.
2. Let the power to bind and release come upon me now, in the name of Jesus.
3. Almighty God let your key of revival unlock every department of my life for your revival fire, in the name of Jesus.
4. Every area of my life that is at the point of death, receive the touch of revival, in the name of Jesus.
5. Almighty God send down your fire and anoint my life, in the name of Jesus.
6. Every area of my life that is not crucified, receive the touch of fire and be crucified, in the name of Jesus.
7. Almighty God; manifest yourself in my life and take me to my next level in the name of Jesus.
8. Go ahead and worship the Lord.
9. Lord I thank you for open door in Jesus name.
10. Almighty God; accept my praise, worship and thanksgiving today in the name of Jesus.
11. Almighty God; empower and strengthen me to pray and to prevail in prayers in Jesus mighty Name.
12. I declare Jesus Christ is Lord over my spirit, soul and body in the name of Jesus.
13. Almighty God; I commit my prayers to you; have your way in the name of Jesus.

14. Almighty God, give me good health to serve you in the name of Jesus.
15. Any strategy of the devil, to use infirmity and sickness to drain my finances; be frustrated in the name of Jesus.
16. Almighty God; have mercy upon me; remove sickness far away from my family in the name of Jess.
17. I cancel every dreams, visions, prophesy and prayers against my life and family in the name of Jesus.
18. Talk to God about your heart desires and your situation.
19. Thank God for answered prayers.

Confession:

The favor of the Lord helps me recognize those who will bless and promote me. God's destined program will bring favor to my life at all time.

Wisdom for Today:

"Mark the perfect man, and behold the upright: for the end of that man is life and peace". Psalm 37:37

Read the Bible Today: Psalm 119

Prayer Points:

1. Let the fire of God fall and consume all hindrances to my advancement, in the name of Jesus.
2. You, stubborn problems in my life, be demolished by the power of the Holy Ghost, in the name of Jesus.
3. You the result, the testimony and the blessing of my past prayer and fasting receive the touch of God and manifest in the name of Jesus.
4. Holy Ghost fire; baptize me with prayer miracle, in Jesus name.
5. Every area of my life that needs deliverance, receive the touch of fire and be delivered, in the name of Jesus.
6. Almighty God replace any part of my body that is not functioning well, in Jesus name.
7. You spirit of depression and heaviness, my life is not your candidate, pack your load and depart from my life in the name of Jesus.
8. Almighty God; give me a miracle over my fear in the name of Jesus.
9. Almighty God make today the best day of my life in the name of Jesus.
10. Almighty God; it is a new day; give me a new song, a new blessing in the name of Jesus.
11. Almighty God; it is written you will have mercy on whom you will have mercy; show me the uncommon mercy of David in the name of Jesus.
12. Almighty God; I call on you today; show me great and mighty things in the name of Jesus.

13. Any power changing position to attack me; die in the name of Jesus.
14. Any power that wants to use my children to make me cry, Holy Ghost fire, consume them in the name of Jesus.
15. I decree as from today, my children shall bring joy and not sorrow in the name of Jesus.
16. Almighty God; let your blessing be upon me and all that I do in the name of Jesus.
17. Almighty God; deliver me from unprofitable hard labor in the name of Jesus.
18. Almighty God; let your blessing and your favor be upon me in the name of Jesus.
19. Almighty God; bless me with ideas that will prosper, promote and supply all my needs in the name of Jesus.
20. Almighty God; don't let me labor in vain, reward my labor in the name of Jesus.
21. Almighty God; let there be something for me to rejoice over in the name of Jesus.
22. I cancel every dreams, visions, prophesy and prayers against my life and family in the name of Jesus.
23. Talk to God about your heart desires and your situation.
24. Thank God for answered prayers.

Confession:

I believe and confess that the favor and honor, which will frustrate the enemy, has rested upon my life. The favor of the Lord God Jehovah that brings good understanding is coming my way.

Wisdom for Today:

"But the meek shall inherit the earth; and shall delight themselves in the abundance of peace".

Read the Bible Today: Romans15

Prayer Points:

1. Let my angels of blessing locate me today, in the name of Jesus.
2. Every satanic program of impossibility, I cancel you now, in the name of Jesus.
3. I command household wickedness and its program of impossibility to be paralyzed now, in the name of Jesus.
4. No curse will land on my head, marriage, children, and family, in the name of Jesus.
5. Throughout the days of my life, I will not waste money on my health; the Lord shall be my healer, in the name of Jesus.
6. Declare Jesus Christ is Lord.
7. Every power forcing me into strange journey be consumed by the fire of God in the name of Jesus.
8. My head reject evil load, my body reject evil manipulation in the name of Jesus.
9. Almighty God use the hours of the night to settle my calling, career, ministry, marriage, academics in the name of Jesus.
10. Any mistake that I made today, almighty God cancel such mistakes by the blood of Jesus Christ in the name of Jesus.
11. Any power, witches and wizard that want to attend any evil meeting tonight because of me and my family, you shall not return in the name of Jesus.
12. Any agent of darkness that transforms into any animal to attack me; Holy Ghost fire consume them in the name of Jesus.
13. Almighty God; surround where I sleep with your fire in Jesus name.

14. Almighty God; if you are God; do something great to deliver me, heal me, bless me in the name of Jesus.
15. Almighty God; visit my life today let every unshakeable mountains shake, and unmovable mountains move in the name of Jesus.
16. Almighty God; let the ordinances of the day and night fight for me in the name of Jesus.
17. I command the moon and the stars to arise tonight and begin to fight against anyone planning my down fall in Jesus mighty name.
18. Tonight I command the midnight hour to arise and set me free, and condemn my enemies in the name of Jesus.
19. Almighty God; concerning the issues in my life intervene in the name of Jesus.
20. I cancel every dreams, visions, prophesy and prayers against my life and family in the name of Jesus.
21. Talk to God about your heart desires and your situation.
22. Thank God for answered prayers.

Confession:

I believe and confess that I will be patient until the day of my promotion. I confess boldly that the kindness of the Lord upon my life extends to the heavens.

Wisdom for Today:

"Only take heed to thyself, and keep thy soul diligently, lest thou forget the things which thine eyes have seen, and lest they depart from thy heart all the days of thy life: but teach them thy sons, and thy son' sons;

Read the Bible Today: Habakkuk 2

Prayer Points:

1. Throughout the days of my life, I will be in the right place at the right time, in the name of Jesus.
2. Throughout the days of my life, I will not depart from the fire of God's protection, in the name of Jesus.
3. Throughout the days of my life, I will not be a candidate for incurable disease, in the name of Jesus.
4. Every weapon of captivity in my life be disgraced, in the name of Jesus.
5. Almighty God before the end of this month, I need an outstanding miracle in every area of my life, in the name of Jesus.
6. Any power that wants to buy and sell in my spirit, soul and body; Holy Ghost fire consume them in the name of Jesus.
7. Almighty God; I present my body to you as a living sacrifice in the name of Jesus.
8. Begin to appreciate God.
9. Declare Jesus Christ is Lord.
10. Shout hallelujah. 7 times.
11. Every curse upon my life move away in the name of Jesus.
12. Almighty God; remove every problem, tragedy, calamity and sorrow from my way in the name of Jesus.
13. Almighty God; have mercy upon me and make way for me in the name of Jesus.
14. Almighty God help me to serve you with diligence in the name of Jesus.

15. Almighty God Fill my life with your glory in a new way in the name of Jesus.
16. I cancel every dreams, visions, prophesy and prayers against my life and family in the name of Jesus.
17. Talk to God about your heart desires and your situation.
18. Thank God for answered prayers.

Confession:

"God satisfies my mouth with good things". Psalm 103:5 "He took my mourning and gave me laughter. Weeping may have been for a night but my joy has come forth". Psalm 30:5

Wisdom for Today:

"Let us hold fast the profession of our faith without wavering; for he is faithful that promised;

Read the Bible Today: I Peter 4

Prayer Points:

1. I shall not weep over what is giving me joy, in the name of Jesus.
2. Let every attack planned against the progress of my life be frustrated, in the name of Jesus.
3. I command the spirits of harassment and torment to leave me, in the name of Jesus.
4. Almighty God speak soundness into my mind and being, in the name of Jesus.
5. I reverse every witchcraft curse issued against my progress, in the name of Jesus.
6. Anything in my place of birth that the enemy is using against me, fire of God; locate and destroy them in the name of Jesus.
7. Failure and frustration minus me in the name of Jesus Christ.
8. I recover all in Jesus mighty name.
9. Worship the King of Kings, the Lord of lord.
10. Declare Jesus Christ is Lord.
11. Almighty God; we give thanks to you in the name of Jesus.
12. Almighty God; take away from me all sickness, according to your word in the name of Jesus.
13. Almighty God; do not lay me and my family with any terrible disease of Egypt but lay them on those who hate us in the name of Jesus.
14. Almighty God; wash my head with the blood of Jesus Christ and don't let my head reject your blessing in the name of Jesus.
15. Let the everlasting covenant of the blood of Jesus, arise and begin to speak for me in the name of Jesus.

Apostle A.O. Solomon

16. Let the blood of Jesus Christ, arise and deliver me from every evil covenant in the name of Jesus.
17. I cancel every dreams, visions, prophesy and prayers against my life and family in the name of Jesus.
18. Talk to God about your heart desires and your situation.
19. Thank God for answered prayers.

Confession:

The favor of God's anointing and strength is upon my life; it flows in me and causes me to rise above all situations.

Wisdom for Today:

"A good man leaveth an inheritance to his children's children: and the wealth of the sinner is laid up for the just".

Read the Bible Today: John 11

Prayer Points:

1. If others are making it in this country, I will make it, in the name of Jesus.
2. If others are prospering in this country, I will prosper and be in good health, in the name of Jesus.
3. Where there is no way for others, there shall be way for me, in the name of Jesus.
4. Where others are failing, I [say your name] will succeed and excel, in Jesus name.
5. I will rise and shine above all my colleagues and the unbelievers around me, in the name of Jesus.
6. Almighty God; arise and remove whatever is delaying my testimony in the name of Jesus.
7. Whatever is sleeping in my life, awake in the name of Jesus.
8. Lord Jesus Christ of Nazareth; help me ask God for my breakthrough in the name of Jesus.
9. Almighty God; as I go out today let me encounter your favor in the name of Jesus.
10. As I leave my home Lord, keep me from all evil in the name of Jesus.
11. Almighty God; let your covenant with this day fight for me in the name of Jesus.
12. Go ahead and magnify the Lord.
13. Almighty God I thank you for deliverance from the spirit of death and healing in the name of Jesus.
14. Declare Jesus Christ is Lord.
15. I know my redeemer lives in the name of Jesus.

16. Lord Jesus Christ of Nazareth; deliver me and my family from death in the name of Jesus.
17. Every mark of death; be wiped off by the blood of Jesus.
18. Any power that has marked me for death; almighty God arise and destroy them in the name of Jesus.
19. I cancel every dreams, visions, prophesy and prayers against my life and family in the name of Jesus.
20. Talk to God about your heart desires and your situation.
21. Thank God for answered prayers.

Confession:

The favor, which follows a wise servant, is upon my life. I am blessed and highly favored, in the name of Jesus.

Wisdom for Today:

"Therefore take no thought, saying, what shall we drink? For after all these things do the Gentiles seek :) for your heavenly Father knoweth that ye have need of all these things. But seek ye first the kingdom of God, and his righteousness; and all these things shall be added unto you" Mathew 6:31-33

Read the Bible Today: Isaiah 43

Prayer Points:

1. I condemn all the spirits that condemn me, in the name of Jesus.
2. Let divine accuracy come into my life and my operations, in the name of Jesus.
3. No evil directive will manifest in my life, in the name of Jesus.
4. Let the plans and purposes of heaven be fulfilled in my life, in the name of Jesus.
5. Almighty God bring to me friends that will reverence your name, and keep all others away, in the name of Jesus.
6. Lord Jesus Christ; redeem my spirit, soul, and body from death in the name of Jesus.
7. I cancel every dream and vision of death by the blood of Jesus in the name of Jesus.
8. I shall not die but live and declare the works of God in the mighty name of Jesus Christ.
9. Almighty God; satisfy me and my family with long life and show us your salvation in the name of Jesus.
10. Almighty God deliver me and my family from the eaters of flesh and drinkers of blood in the name of Jesus.
11. I shall not enter any coffin this year in the name of Jesus.
12. Almighty God; according to your word, let my enemy die for me in the name of Jesus.
13. I cover my spirit, soul and body with the blood of Jesus Christ in the name of Jesus.
14. Almighty God; let all those who hate me, end in everlasting confusion in the name of Jesus.

15. Almighty God; let all those who use their mouth to run me down, serve me in the name of Jesus.
16. Lord Jesus draw men unto yourself in the name of Jesus.
17. I cancel every dreams, visions, prophesy and prayers against my life and family in the name of Jesus.
18. Talk to God about your heart desires and your situation.
19. Thank God for answered prayers.

Confession:

I believe and confess that the Lord is good. He is faithful at all times, and keeps his word. God will not withhold good things from those who love him. I give praise to the Lord for his work of healing in my life.

Wisdom for Today:

"Upon the first day of the week let every one of you lay by him in store, as God hath prospered him, that there be no gatherings when I come". I Corintians 16:2

Read the Bible Today: *Isaiah 30*

Prayer Points:

1. Let divine strength come into my life, in the name of Jesus.
2. Almighty God cause yourself to be real in my life, in the name of Jesus.
3. Almighty God show yourself in my life today, in the name of Jesus.
4. Let every stronghold working against my peace be destroyed, in the name of Jesus.
5. Let the power to destroy every decree of darkness operating in my life fall upon me now, in the name of Jesus.
6. Thank God for a new day.
7. Begin to call on the blood of Jesus.
8. I plead the blood of Jesus over my going out and coming in the name of Jesus.
9. Declare Jesus Christ is Lord.
10. I take over this day by the blood of Jesus Christ.
11. By the blood of Jesus Christ, I overcome every terror of the night in the name of Jesus.
12. By the covenant of God with the day, arrows that fly shall not locate me in the name of Jesus.
13. By the covenant of God with day, I declare today my day of recovery in the name of Jesus.
14. I reject every evil in this day in the name of Jesus.
15. Lord Jesus Christ of Nazareth have mercy upon me; cleanse me with your precious blood in the name of Jesus.

Apostle A.O. Solomon

16. I cancel every dreams, visions, prophesy and prayers against my life and family in the name of Jesus.
17. Talk to God about your heart desires and your situation.
18. Thank God for answered prayers.

Confession:

The Lord God is my Jehovah Rapha. He remembers my tears of affliction and takes away tears from members of my household. I believe and confess that I have inner healing for ailments I cannot see, in Jesus name.

Wisdom for Today:

Ye are the light of the world. A city that is set on an hill cannot be hid. Both do men light a candle, and put it under a bushel, but on a candle stick; and it giveth light unto all that are in the house. Mathew 5:13-16

Read the Bible Today: Proverb 12

Prayer Points:

1. Almighty God deliver my tongue from evil silence, in the name of Jesus.
2. Lord, let my tongue tell others of your goodness in my life, in Jesus name.
3. Lord, loosen my tongue and use it for your glory, in Jesus name.
4. Lord, let my tongue bring straying sheep back to the fold, in Jesus name.
5. Lord, let my tongue strengthen those who are discouraged, in Jesus name.
6. Lord, let my tongue guide the sad and the lonely, in Jesus name.
7. Almighty God baptize my tongue with your fire, in the name of Jesus.
8. Everything my enemies have programmed into this day, I command them to back fire in the name of Jesus.
9. Almighty God; today in the presence of my enemies, catapult me into my success in the name of Jesus.
10. Almighty God prepare a table for me in the presence of my enemies in the name of Jesus.
11. Almighty God; as from today anyone that runs me down with their mouth, make them bow before me in the name of Jesus.
12. Almighty God; lift me up above the imagination and expectation of my enemies in the name of Jesus.
13. Almighty God; anyone that I have associated with that is using my glory to shine, separate me from them in the name of Jesus.

14. In this new and blessed day I (your name) reject worry, depression, fear, sickness in my life, in the life of my spouse and children in the name of Jesus.
15. Anything that my enemies plan to cage me with, almighty God turn it to their sorrow and destruction in the name of Jesus.
16. I claim all the goodness of God in this day in the name of Jesus.
17. I cancel every dreams, visions, prophesy and prayers against my life and family in the name of Jesus.
18. Talk to God about your heart desires and your situation.
19. Thank God for answered prayers.

OCTOBER 14

Confession:

Affliction is not my portion. I reject every problem of blood disease and receive healing for every area of my life.

Wisdom for Today:

"Cast thy burden upon the Lord, and he shall sustain thee: he shall never suffer the righteous to be moved". Psalm 55:22

Read the Bible Today: Jeremiah 32

Prayer Points:

1. Let every unrepentant and stubborn pursuer be disgraced in my life, in the name of Jesus.
2. Let every iron-like curse working against my life be broken by the blood of Jesus, in the name of Jesus.
3. Let every problem designed to disgrace me receive open shame, in the name of Jesus.
4. Let every problem anchor in my life be heaved up, in Jesus name.
5. Multiple evil covenants, be broken by the blood of Jesus, in the name of Jesus.
6. By the covenant of the almighty God with the day and night no evil shall come to pass in my life in the name of Jesus.
7. I reject any destruction at noon day in the name of Jesus.
8. Lord Jesus Christ put your mark upon my life in the name of Jesus.
9. Almighty God remember my kindness in the name of Jesus.
10. This is my year of compensation; I receive my rewards in the name of Jesus.
11. Declare Jesus Christ is Lord.
12. Almighty God; make me rich; bless me exceedingly in the name of Jesus.
13. Almighty God; answer me suddenly before the end of this month in the name of Jesus.
14. Almighty God before the end of this month; decorate and beautify my life in the name of Jesus.
15. Almighty God; before the end of this month, give me a new song in all areas of my life in the name of Jesus.

16. Almighty God; you are the God that changes times and season, arise and move my destiny from the valley to the mountain top in the name of Jesus.

17. I shall be surrounded with goodness and mercy in the name of Jesus.

18. I cancel every dreams, visions, prophesy and prayers against my life and family in the name of Jesus.

19. Talk to God about your heart desires and your situation.

20. Thank God for answered prayers.

Confession:

"Understand therefore this day, that the Lord thy God is he which goeth over before thee; as a consuming fire he shall destroy them, and he shall bring them down before thy face: so shalt thou drive them out, and destroy them quickly, as the Lord hath said unto thee" Deuteronomy 9:3.

Wisdom for Today:

"For we are made partakers of Christ, if we hold the beginning of our confidence steadfast unto the end". Hebrews 3:14

Read the Bible Today: Isaiah 25

Prayer Points:

1. Multiple curses, be broken by the blood of Jesus, in the name of Jesus.
2. Every good thing locked away from me with evil padlocks, be opened up to me by the blood of Jesus, in the name of Jesus.
3. Everything done against me at any crossroads be nullified by the blood of Jesus, in the name of Jesus.
4. Let every stubborn and prayer-resisting demon receive stones of fire and thunder, in the name of Jesus.
5. Every stubborn and prayer-resisting sickness, relinquish your evil hold upon my life, in the name of Jesus.
6. Every problem associated with the dead, be smashed by the blood of Jesus, in the name of Jesus.
7. I recover my stolen property sevenfold, in the name of Jesus.
8. Power of resurrection arise and give life to my dry bones in the name of Jesus.
9. Almighty God; arise in the name of Jesus and nourish my life in the name of Jesus.
10. Sorrow from the consequences of my past mistakes; vanish in the name of Jesus.
11. I cancel every dreams, visions, prophesy and prayers against my life and family in the name of Jesus.
12. Talk to God about your heart desires and your situation.
13. Thank God for answered prayers.

Confession:

I boldly confess that I am anointed to bring healing to people. The Lord shall deliver those in bondage through me. The ministry of healing shall flow forth through me, in the name of Jesus.

Wisdom for Today:

"Herein is love, not that we loved God, but that he loved us, and sent his Son to be the propitiation for our sins. Beloved, if God so loved us, we ought also to love one another".

Read the Bible Today: John 14:18-21

Prayer Points:

1. Let every evil memory about me be erased by the blood of Jesus, in Jesus name.
2. I disallow my breakthroughs from being caged, in Jesus name.
3. Let the sun of my prosperity arise and scatter every cloud of poverty, in Jesus name.
4. I decree unstoppable advancement upon my life, in Jesus name.
5. I soak every day of my life in the blood of Jesus and in signs and wonders, in the name of Jesus.
6. Anywhere I appear, sickness, failure, and poverty shall disappear, in the name of Jesus.
7. I appreciate God for keeping me alive in the name of Jesus.
8. Call the blood of Jesus.
9. Almighty God lead us to pray by your holy spirit in the name of Jesus.
10. Almighty God have your way in my prayers in the name of Jesus.
11. Almighty God; order my steps, and my doings in the name of Jesus.
12. Almighty God; anything that I will do that will bring your anger upon me, I plead the blood of Jesus in the name of Jesus.
13. Almighty God in your house; have mercy upon me deliver me from error in the name of Jesus Christ.
14. Almighty God; help me not to involve myself in the matters that will put me in trouble, in the name of Jesus.
15. Almighty God deliver us from the spirit of error in the name of Jesus.

16. Almighty God I believe you for a miracle in the name of Jesus.
17. I cancel every dreams, visions, prophesy and prayers against my life and family in the name of Jesus.
18. Talk to God about your heart desires and your situation.
19. Thank God for answered prayers.

Confession:

"There shall no man be able to stand before me: for the Lord my God shall lay my fear and dread upon all the land that I shall tread upon, as he hath said unto me" Deuteronomy 11:25.

Wisdom for Today:

Love not the world, neither the things that are in the world, if any man love the world, the love of the Father is not in him. I John 2:15

Read the Bible Today: Revelation 12

Prayer Points:

1. I break every stronghold of oppression in my life, in Jesus name.
2. Let every satanic joy over my life be terminated, in the name of Jesus.
3. I paralyze every household wickedness, in the name of Jesus.
4. Let every river that carries satanic oppression dry up by the fire of God, in the name of Jesus.
5. I bind all ancestral spirits and command them to relinquish their hold over my life, in the name of Jesus.
6. Ancestral spirits pack your possessions and go out of my life, in the name of Jesus.
7. I thank God for preserving my life in the name of Jesus.
8. Give thanks to the Lord, the Almighty God.
9. Declare Jesus Christ is Lord.
10. Almighty God you are my Alpha and Omega, I started this month with you, father let me end it with good news and blessings in the name of Jesus.
11. Every evil, and sorrow programmed into this day against me; be consumed by the fire of God in the name of Jesus.
12. Almighty God visit my life and water it in the name of Jesus.
13. Almighty God; let all those who hate me become desolate in the name of Jesus.
14. Almighty God water the dry area of my life and soften the rigid area of my life that is not yielding to you in the name of Jesus.
15. Almighty God; settle every area of my life in the name of Jesus.
16. Almighty God make life easy for me in the name of Jesus.

17. Almighty God; bless me, and move my life forward in the name of Jesus.
18. Almighty God; crown the rest of the year with your abundance and goodness in the name of Jesus.
19. Almighty God let your blessings, goodness, and mercy drop on the pastures of my life in the name of Jesus.
20. Almighty God from this day let me rejoice on every side in the name of Jesus.
21. I cancel every dreams, visions, prophesy and prayers against my life and family in the name of Jesus.
22. Talk to God about your heart desires and your situation.
23. Thank God for answered prayers.

Confession:

"The Lord shall cause thine enemies that rise up against thee to be smitten before thy face: they shall come against thee one way, and flee before thee seven ways" Deuteronomy 28:7.

Wisdom for Today:

"Beloved, believe not every spirit, but try the spirits whether they are of God: because many false prophets are gone out into the world". I John 4:1

Read the Bible Today: Psalm 65

Prayer Points:

1. Almighty God enter the camp of my enemies and destroy them in the name of Jesus.
2. I command every satanic embargo on my goodness and prosperity to be broken to irreparable pieces, in the name of Jesus.
3. Let every door of attack on my spiritual progress be closed, in Jesus name.
4. Holy Spirit set me on fire for God, in Jesus name.
5. I command all my imprisoned benefits to be released unto me now, in Jesus name.
6. Almighty God; clothe the pastures of my life with your glory, your favor, and abundance, in the name of Jesus.
7. All that I pursued from the month of January that I could not get father Lord manifest your power and deliver them unto me in the name of Jesus.
8. Almighty God your ways are supernatural, make it my super deliverance, healing, and blessing in the name of Jesus.
9. Almighty God; wherever I have been forgotten, let me be remembered in the name of Jesus.
10. Begin to worship the King of kings.
11. Give thanks to the Lord most High.
12. Almighty God envelope my mouth with power, fill my mouth with your great power in the name of Jesus.
13. Declare Jesus Christ is Lord.
14. Almighty God; have mercy upon me and my children; don't let us have trouble and sorrow again in the name of Jesus.

15. I declare my children are blessed and highly favored in Jesus mighty name.
16. Almighty God; all those you are going to use to bless me; don't let me fall out of favor with them in the name of Jesus.
17. Almighty God let your purpose for my life this year come to pass in the name of Jesus.
18. Any human power looking for opportunity to exploit me, you shall not succeed in the name of Jesus.
19. All my God ordained glory in the hands of evil powers; begin to work against them, and come back to me in the name of Jesus.
20. I cancel every dreams, visions, prophesy and prayers against my life and family in the name of Jesus.
21. Talk to God about your heart desires and your situation.
22. Thank God for answered prayers.

Confession:

"For the wicked shall no more pass through thee: he is utterly cut off" Nahum 1:15.

Wisdom for Today:

"Take heed to yourselves: if thy brother trespass against thee, rebuke him; and if he repent, forgive him".

Read the Bible Today: Mathew 6

Prayer Points:

1. Let the thunder of God strike down all demonic strongholds manufactured against me, in the name of Jesus.
2. Almighty God anoint me with the power to pursue, overtake, and recover my stolen properties from the enemy, in the name of Jesus.
3. Almighty God bring to naught every evil counselor and counsel against me, in Jesus name.
4. The enemy shall not have a hiding place in my life, in Jesus name.
5. Let all blocked ways of prosperity be open unto me, in Jesus name.
6. I command the devil to remove his influence from my finances, in the name of Jesus.
7. Any animal spirit that is attacking my life, die in the name of Jesus.
8. Powers polluting my dream, fire of God consume them in the name of Jesus.
9. Doors that have refused to open for me open for me now and give me uncommon blessing in the name of Jesus.
10. Almighty God; let my success, and my glory begin to shine above the expectation of my enemies in the name of Jesus.
11. Almighty God I thank you for preserving my life in the name of Jesus.
12. Give thanks to, the almighty God.
13. Declare Jesus Christ is Lord.
14. Lord Jesus Christ have your way in my life in the name of Jesus.

15. Almighty God you are my Alpha and Omega, I started this month with you, let me end it with good news, blessings and breakthroughs in the name of Jesus.
16. I cancel every dreams, visions, prophesy and prayers against my life and family in the name of Jesus.
17. Talk to God about your heart desires and your situation.
18. Thank God for answered prayers.

Confession:

"Whatsoever things are pure..... Think on these things" Philippians 4:8.

Wisdom for Today:

"Thou wilt keep him in perfect peace, whose mind is stayed on thee: because he trusteth in thee". Isaiah 26:3

Read the Bible Today: *Colossians 3: 2-5*

Prayer Points:

1. Almighty God guide my heart today, and let me think only on things that will glorify you, in the name of Jesus.
2. I break the curse of automatic failure working upon my life, marriage, and career, in the name of Jesus.
3. Fire of the Holy Ghost; purge my heart, in the name of Jesus.
4. Let my steps and thoughts be ordered by God today, in the name of Jesus.
5. Let every step I take today defeat my enemies, in the name of Jesus.
6. Almighty God water the ridges of my life abundantly in the name of Jesus.
7. Almighty God; settle every area and of my life in the name of Jesus.
8. Almighty God; bless me and my family in the name of Jesus.
9. Almighty God let your blessings, goodness, and mercy drop on the pastures of my life in the name of Jesus.
10. Almighty God from this day let there be a turn of events in my life in the name of Jesus.
11. Almighty God; clothe the pastures of my life with your glory, your favor, and abundance in the name of Jesus.
12. Almighty God; wherever I have been forgotten, let me be remembered in the name of Jesus.
13. I cancel every dreams, visions, prophesy and prayers against my life and family in the name of Jesus.
14. Talk to God about your heart desires and your situation.
15. Thank God for answered prayers.

Confession:

"Smite through the loins of them that rise against me and of them that hate me that they rise not again" Deuteronomy 33:11.

Wisdom for Today:

"Let us therefore come boldly unto the throne of grace that we may obtain mercy, and find grace to help in time of need". Hebrews 4:16

Read the Bible Today: Psalm 56

Prayer Points:

1. In the name of Jesus, I refuse to be afraid, for God has not given me the spirit of fear; but of power and of love, and of a sound mind in the name of Jesus.
2. I bind the spirit of fear in my life, in the name of Jesus.
3. I break every evil covenant that has brought fear into my life, in the name of Jesus.
4. I command every terror of the night that has brought fear into my life to stop and move from my environment, in the name of Jesus.
5. You, spirit of fear, relinquish your hold upon my life and my family, in the name of Jesus.
6. Any satanic power assigned to waste my destiny, be wasted, in the name of Jesus.
7. This year I shall not weep before I receive my blessing; I shall be blessed and highly favored, in the name of Jesus.
8. This year I forbid my blessing to be stolen, in the name of Jesus.
9. My blessing, glory, and honor shall not be transferred to another person, in the name of Jesus.
10. All the helpers attached to my greatness in life, be released from your captivity, in the name of Jesus.
11. All the helpers attached to my success and greatness in life, be released from your captivity, in the name of Jesus.
12. Every negative information about my life in the hands of my helpers be consumed by fire, in the name of Jesus.
13. Every evil information about me in the heart of my helpers be erased by the blood of Jesus, in Jesus name.
14. Every strategy to chase my helpers away from me, fail woefully, in the name of Jesus.

Apostle A.O. Solomon

15. Almighty God, whatever you need to do for my helpers to show up, do it now, in the name of Jesus Christ.
16. Every satanic stronghold erected in the heart of my helpers, I pull you down, in the name of Jesus.
17. Any character in me that is chasing my helpers away, fire of God consume them, in the name of Jesus.
18. Almighty God raise expected and unexpected help for me, in the name of Jesus.
19. I cancel every dreams, visions, prophesy and prayers against my life and family in the name of Jesus.
20. Talk to God about your heart desires and your situation.
21. Thank God for answered prayers.

Confession:

"The Lord will be terrible unto them; for he will famish all the gods of the earth; and men shall worship him, everyone from his place, even all the isles of the heathen" Zephaniah 2:11.

Wisdom for Today:

Fear not; for I am with thee: be not dismayed; for I am thy God; I will strengthen thee; yea, I will help thee; yea, I will uphold thee with the right hand of my righteousness". Isaiah 41:10

Read the Bible Today: Isaiah 50 7-10

Prayer Points:

1. All human and satanic agents using the spirit of fear to torment me day and night be consumed by the fire of God in the name of Jesus.
2. The fear and terror of the unbelievers shall not be my lot, in the name of Jesus.
3. My tomorrow is blessed in Christ Jesus; therefore, you, spirit that is responsible for the fear of tomorrow in my life, I bind you, in the name of Jesus.
4. My destiny is attached to God; therefore, I decree that I can never fail, in the name of Jesus.
5. All bondage that I am subjecting myself to because of the spirit of fear, I break you, in the name of Jesus.
6. Lord let me experience a great change in the name of Jesus.
7. Almighty God; fill my mouth with your power and cause my prayer to prevail in the name of Jesus.
8. Every spirit of toiling, I bind and cast you out in the name of Jesus.
9. You spirit of unprofitable hard work, I bind and cast you out in the name of Jesus.
10. Almighty God raise me out of the dust of poverty in the name of Jesus.
11. Almighty God release your blessing that will make me rich in the name of Jesus.

12. Almighty God remember all my tithes and offerings and fulfill your promises in my life, give me a dumbfounding harvest in the name of Jesus.
13. Almighty God let the rain of blessing begin to fall in my life in the name of Jesus.
14. Shout the name of Jesus Christ 7 times.
15. Almighty God let your mighty power move me forward financially in the name of Jesus.
16. Almighty God arise in your power and speaking deliverance to my situation in the name of Jesus.
17. Dry bones in my finances receive the blood of Jesus Christ in the name of Jesus.
18. By the power in the blood of Jesus; I break and lose myself from every yoke and covenant of poverty in the name of Jesus.
19. Anointing of wealth and prosperity possess me in the name of Jesus.
20. My prosperity, my wealth, my riches in the possession of the enemy be released in the name of Jesus.
21. All that the enemy has swallowed in my life; be vomited now in the name of Jesus.
22. Every satanic power that has swallowed my riches, my prosperity, vomit them now in the mighty name of Jesus.
23. The glory of my family that my ancestors have missed; arise and locate me in the name of Jesus.
24. The glory of my family that was traded away; I recover them back by the blood of Jesus in the name of Jesus.
25. If no one has been destined to be rich in my family; today I command the rule to change by the blood of Jesus in the name of Jesus.
26. The glory of my life that the enemies say will never be revealed; receive the touch of Jesus and manifest in the mighty name of Jesus.
27. I cancel every evil dreams, visions, prophesy and prayers against my life and family in the name of Jesus.
28. Talk to God about your heart desires and your situation.
29. Thank God for answered prayers.

Confession:

I believe and confess that the Lord is faithful at all times. I praise him for causing me to be favored by him and man. I boldly confess that my eyes are anointed to discover and enjoy the favor of the Lord.

Wisdom for Today:

"Great peace have they which love the law: and nothing shall offend them". Psalm 119:165

Read the Bible Today: Luke 13

Prayer Points:

1. All negative doors that the spirit of fear has opened in the past in my life be closed now, in the name of Jesus.
2. Every disease, oppression, and depression that came into my life as a result of fear, disappear now, in the name of Jesus.
3. I refuse to be intimidated by any demonic nightmare, in the name of Jesus.
4. Every enchantment of death and fear made against me, I neutralize you, by the blood of Jesus in the name of Jesus.
5. Every confederacy between my enemies in my home and my enemies outside my home shall not stand, in the name of Jesus.
6. Let all elemental forces of this day cooperate with me and favor me, in the name of Jesus.
7. Weeping shall not be my lot as this year comes to an end, in the name of Jesus.
8. Declare Jesus Christ is Lord.
9. Almighty God; don't let my case be too hard for you in the name of Jesus.
10. Almighty God; comfort me in the name of Jesus.
11. Lord Jesus Christ of Nazareth; set me lose from my infirmities in the name of Jesus.
12. Almighty God; help me to serve you with faithfulness in the name of Jesus.
13. Almighty God; let your kingdom come into the nations of the world in the name of Jesus.

Apostle A.O. Solomon

14. Almighty God; let me serve and worship you in spirit and in truth in the name of Jesus.
15. Almighty God; perfect all that concerns me in the name of Jesus.
16. Almighty God; do not allow satan to hinder me in the name of Jesus.
17. Almighty God; don't let me miss your kingdom, whatever will make me miss your kingdom take them away in the name of Jesus.
18. Almighty God; give me peace yourself always in the name of Jesus.
19. Almighty God; reveal to me the mystery of faith; empower me to hold onto it with pure conscience in the name of Jesus.
20. Almighty God; deliver me from the dangers of this end time in the name of Jesus.
21. It is well with my soul in the name of Jesus.
22. I cancel every evil dreams, visions, prophesy and prayers against my life and family in the name of Jesus.
23. Talk to God about your heart desires and your situation.
24. Thank God for answered prayers.

Confession:

I confess the blessings of God on my business and everything I lay my hands on. Supernatural breakthrough follows me. I am experiencing God's abundant increase. I am anointed to experience multiple increases, in Jesus name.

Wisdom for Today:

"Wherefore seeing we also are compassed about with so great a cloud of witnesses, let us lay aside every weight, and the sin which doth so easily beset us, and let us run with patience the race that is set before us". Hebrews 12:1

Read the Bible Today: Hebrews 10

Prayer Points:

1. All arrangements of the devil concerning me and my home shall not stand; neither shall they come to pass, in the name of Jesus.
2. I destroy all efforts of the enemy to frustrate my work, in the name of Jesus.
3. I nullify all writings, agreements, or covenants against my work, in the name of Jesus.
4. Almighty God, increase my greatness and comfort me on every side, in the name of Jesus.
5. Almighty God, as you delight in my prosperity, I pray that you bless me indeed in my work, let no household enemy control my well-being any longer, in the name of Jesus.
6. Go ahead and worship the Lord.
7. Worship the beauty of Holiness.
8. Declare Jesus Christ is Lord.
9. Let the blood of Jesus speak for us in the name of Jesus.
10. Let the angels of the Lord begin to ascend and descend for my sake in the name of Jesus.
11. Almighty God; prosper my job in the name of Jesus.
12. Almighty God; make me a financial pillar in the name of Jesus.
13. Almighty God; bless me and let me be a blessing to my generation in the name of Jesus.
14. Almighty God enlarge my coast in the name of Jesus.
15. Almighty God; give me divine ideas to prosper my life and help me to appropriate them in the name of Jesus.

16. Almighty God; for one door that has been shut against me, open seven doors in the name of Jesus.
17. Every good door that has been shut against me; open in the name of Jesus.
18. Every opportunity and divine chance that I have missed from the beginning of this year, I recover them back in the name of Jesus.
19. I cancel every evil dreams, visions, prophesy and prayers against my life and family in the name of Jesus.
20. Talk to God about your heart desires and your situation.
21. Thank God for answered prayers.

Confession:

Barrenness is over in my life and business, in Jesus name. I shall increase in spiritual understanding. There shall be great increase in blessing and favor. The days of my small beginnings will turn around to a time of great abundance, in the name of Jesus.

Wisdom for Today:

"Better is the end of a thing than the beginning thereof: and the patient in spirit is better than the proud in spirit. Be not hasty in thy spirit to be angry: for anger resteth in the bosom of fools". Ecclesiastes 7:8-9

Read the Bible Today: Psalm 37

Prayer Points:

1. Let all those who are against me without a cause in my place of work turn back and be brought to confusion, in the name of Jesus.
2. I close every door through which my enemies have been working against my work, in the name of Jesus.
3. No weapon of satan and his agents fashioned against me shall prosper, in the name of Jesus.
4. My life is bound with Christ in God; therefore nobody can kill me or harm me, in the name of Jesus.
5. I open wide all doors leading to my blessings, victories, and breakthroughs, which the enemies have closed, in the name of Jesus.
6. Almighty God; I commit the rest of this month into your hand, surprise me in the name of Jesus.
7. Almighty God; increase my income abundantly, in the name of Jesus.
8. I refuse the enemy to have control over my finances in the name of Jesus.
9. I decree the enemy shall not determine my success and progress in the name of Jesus.
10. Almighty God bless me with a humble heart and spirit in the name of Jesus.
11. Almighty God; arise and send my next helper to me in the name of Jesus.

Apostle A.O. Solomon

12. Almighty God; bless my current helpers and sustain them in the name of Jesus.
13. Almighty God; order my steps to outstanding blessing, and breakthrough in the name of Jesus.
14. I cancel every dreams, visions, prophesy and prayers against my life and family in the name of Jesus.
15. Talk to God about your heart desires and your situation.
16. Thank God for answered prayers.

Confession:

I bless the name of the Lord for his daily leading. I thank him for not withholding any good thing from me, because my trust is in him. I boldly confess that all things will work together for my good, because I love the Lord.

Wisdom for Today:

"For to be carnally minded is death: but to be spiritually minded is life and peace". Romans 8:6

Read the Bible Today: Romans 14:17-19

Prayer Points:

1. Let every territorial spirit working against me in my neighborhood be frustrated, bound, and cast out, in the name of Jesus.
2. Let every power contrary to the power of God operating to suppress people in my area be neutralized, in the name of Jesus.
3. I bind every spirit of frustration, defeat, delayed blessing, and fear in my environment, in the name of Jesus.
4. I banish every enemy of progress in my neighborhood, in the name of Jesus.
5. I bind the spirit of death, armed robbery, and assassination in my neighborhood, in the name of Jesus.
6. Almighty God let me experience a great change in the name of Jesus.
7. Almighty God; help me to serve you more, with my whole heart in the name of Jesus.
8. Every satanic compromise I reject you in the name of Jesus.
9. Almighty God; give me peace of mind in the name of Jesus.
10. Almighty God; lay your mighty hand upon my life and revive me in the name of Jesus.
11. I reject every strange voice in the name of Jesus.
12. My spirit man; receive revival fire in the name of Jesus.
13. Almighty God open my eyes that I may see in the name of Jesus.
14. Almighty God; lay your hands upon my eyes a second time and let me see well in the name of Jesus.
15. Almighty God bless me with the spiritual gifts that I need to excel in my life in the name of Jesus.

16. Almighty God; help me out of the problem I brought upon myself in the name of Jesus.
17. Almighty God; have mercy upon me; don't let the devil take money from me by force in the name of Jesus.
18. I cover myself with the blood of Jesus Christ in the name of Jesus.
19. I am a blessed child of God in the name of Jesus.
20. I cancel every evil dreams, visions, prophesy and prayers against my life and family in the name of Jesus.
21. Talk to God about your heart desires and your situation.
22. Thank God for answered prayers.

Confession: *I declare Jesus Christ is Lord over my life, over my spirit, soul and body, I am more than conqueror.*

The future of my marriage is secure in the Lord. The future of my children is secure in the Lord. The future of my work and business is secure in the Lord. My future will portray God's manifest blessing, in Jesus name.

Wisdom for Today:

"If we have forgotten the name of our god, or stretched out our hands to a strange god: Shall not God search this out? For he knoweth he secrets of the heart". Psalm 44:20-21

Read the Bible Today: *Hebrews 3*

Prayer Points:

1. I reject, renounce, and destroy every evil covenant, in the name of Jesus.
2. By the blood of Jesus, I nullify the effects of the operation of evil forces around my house and workplace, in the name of Jesus.
3. Almighty God, occupy all my stubborn pursuers with unprofitable assignments, in the name of Jesus.
4. I fire back every evil arrow, spiritual bullet, and satanic missile fired at me in the name of Jesus.
5. Almighty God, reveal the secrets and expose all my enemies disguising as my friends, in the name of Jesus.
6. Almighty God make it impossible for my enemies to use my footmarks, urine, blood, sweat, hair, clothing, or shoes against me in the name of Jesus.
7. Go ahead and give thanks to the Lord.
8. Almighty God; show me uncommon mercy in the name of Jesus.
9. Almighty God lead me in the way I should go in the name of Jesus.
10. Almighty God order my step in the name of Jesus.
11. Almighty God; give me grace to follow you in the name of Jesus.
12. Almighty God; let every valley of my finances be exalted in the name of Jesus.

13. Every mountain and hill of problem in my life; be brought low in the name of Jesus.
14. I cancel every evil dreams, visions, prophesy and prayers against my life and family in the name of Jesus.
15. Talk to God about your heart desires and your situation.
16. Thank God for answered prayers.

Confession:

I boldly confess that the Lord is my shepherd; therefore, I shall not miss my purpose, for the Lord has built his hedge of fire around me to give me protection and guarantee my future.

Wisdom for Today:

"Looking diligently lest any man fall of the grace of God; lest any root of bitterness springing up trouble you, and thereby many be defiled; Hebrew 12:15

Read the Bible Today: *Isaiah 48*

Prayer Points:

1. I thank God for what he has done for me this year in the name of Jesus.
2. Let frustration and disappointment be the portion of anyone wishing me and my family, evil in the name of Jesus.
3. Every tie to polluted objects and items between my life and family, break, in the name of Jesus.
4. Every unspoken curse against my life, break, in the name of Jesus.
5. Every curse pronounced inwardly against my destiny, break, in the name of Jesus.
6. Almighty God; make every crooked way in my life straight in the name of Jesus.
7. Almighty God smooth every rough place in my life in the name of Jesus. Almighty God let your glory be revealed in every area of my life in the name of Jesus.
8. Almighty God deliver me from confusion in the name of Jesus.
9. Almighty God reveal my blessings to me in the name of Jesus.
10. Holy Spirit; of the living God; lead and guide me for outstanding success and breakthrough in the name of Jesus.
11. Almighty God; give me grace to hear you in the name of Jesus.
12. Almighty God open my ears to hear your voice in the name of Jesus.
13. I cancel every evil dreams, visions, prophesy and prayers against my life and family in the name of Jesus.
14. Talk to God about your heart desires and your situation.
15. Thank God for answered prayers.

Apostle A.O. Solomon

Confession:

Everything I lay my hands on shall be accomplished, for the Lord makes success to attend all that I do. Because Jesus lives I can face tomorrow. I undo every evil projected against my future by the blood of Jesus. I am not afraid of what man can do to me, for God will not give me to the hands and will of my enemy.

Wisdom for Today:

But God commendeth his love toward us, in that, while we were yet sinners, Christ died for us". Roman 5:8

Read the Bible Today: II Peter 3

Prayer Points:

1. You, inward curses militating against my virtues, break, in the name of Jesus.
2. Any power given the mandate to curse and hinder my progress, fall down and die, in the name of Jesus.
3. Let every spirit of Balaam hired to curse my progress fall down and die, in the name of Jesus.
4. Every curse that I have brought into my life through ignorance and disobedience, break by the blood of Jesus, in Jesus name.
5. Every power that is attracting physical and spiritual curses to me, I raise the blood of Jesus against you, and I challenge you by fire, in the name of Jesus.
6. Almighty God turn all my self-imposed curses to blessings, in the name of Jesus.
7. Go ahead and worship the Lord.
8. Declare Jesus Christ is Lord.
9. Almighty God; I need a special visitation in the name of Jesus.
10. Almighty God breathe upon me your breath of life in the name of Jesus.
11. Our Lord Jesus Christ became poor so that I may be rich, in the name of Jesus.
12. Almighty God; arise and lay your hands upon me and take away my sorrow in the name of Jesus.

13. Almighty God; I pray for financial surprise and supply in the name of Jesus.
14. Every problem that money has caused in my life, family, my church, business; almighty God settle them in the name of Jesus.
15. Almighty God; by the greatness of your power, let money begin to answer for me in the name of Jesus.
16. Almighty God; stare up the deep places of the earth to bless and favor me in the name of Jesus.
17. Almighty God; arise and help me in the name of Jesus.
18. Almighty God; stare up your throne and pour out your blessings upon me in the name of Jesus.
19. I Speak to the north, the south, the west and the east, and I command all my helpers to arise and locate me in the name of Jesus.
20. I cancel every evil dreams, visions, prophesy and prayers against my life and family in the name of Jesus.
21. Talk to God about your heart desires and your situation.
22. Thank God for answered prayers.

Confession:

I believe and confess that the Lord is good. Every good word of the Lord in my life shall bring forth fruit. I boldly declare that I have received grace to grow in my relationship with him. The seed of God's word will fall on good soil in my life.

Wisdom for Today:

"Rejoice, and be exceedingly glad: for great is your reward in heaven: for so persecuted they the prophets which were before you". Mathew 5:10-12

Read the Bible Today: I Peter 2

Prayer Points:

1. Every instrument put in place to frustrate me, become impotent, in the name of Jesus.
2. I reject every cycle of frustration, in the name of Jesus.
3. Every agent assigned to frustrate me, perish by fire, in the name of Jesus.
4. Every power tormenting me, die by the sword, in the name of Jesus.
5. I destroy the power of every satanic setback in my life, in the name of Jesus.
6. All satanic agents that are holding me back release me by fire, in the mighty name of of Jesus.
7. Everything that is representing me in the demonic world against my career be destroyed by the fire of God, in the name of Jesus.
8. Declare Jesus Christ is Lord.
9. Lord Jesus Christ of Nazareth, be glorified through everything am going through in the name of Jesus.
10. Lord Jesus Christ of Nazareth; wake up everything that is sleeping in my life in the name of Jesus.
11. Almighty God; meet all my financial need in the name of Jesus.
12. You angels of the living God, I command you to roll away every stone blocking any area of my life in the name of Jesus.
13. My destiny, my Lazarus, come out of the grave in the name of Jesus.
14. Let the power of resurrection over shadow my life in the name of Jesus.

15. Lord Jesus Christ of Nazareth; remove every grave clothe that the enemy used to bind my hands and legs in the name of Jesus.

16. Almighty God; breath on me your breath of life in the name of Jesus.

17. I cancel every evil dreams, visions, prophesy and prayers against my life and family in the name of Jesus.

18. Talk to God about your heart desires and your situation.

19. Thank God for answered prayers.

Confession:

By faith I confess that I have received grace to walk with God and to understand his word. His word bears fruit in my life, for the success of the Lord answers to all I do. I boldly declare that I receive grace to put away immature behaviors and to grow more in the Lord, in Jesus name.

Wisdom for Today:

"God is faithful, by whom ye were called unto the fellowship f his Son Jesus Christ our Lord". I Corinthians 1:9

Read the Bible Today: II Peter 3

Prayer Points:

1. Spirit of the living God, quicken my whole being, in the name of Jesus.
2. Almighty God empower me and renew my strength, in the name of Jesus.
3. Holy Spirit, open my eyes to see beyond the visible and the invisible, in the name of Jesus.
4. Almighty God, ignite my career with your fire, in the name of Jesus.
5. Almighty God, liberate my spirit to follow the the Holy Spirit, in the name of Jesus.
6. Holy Spirit, teach and empower me to pray and receive breakthroughs, in the name of Jesus.
7. Almighty God deliver me from the lies I tell myself, in the name of Jesus.
8. Go ahead and give thanks to the Lord.
9. Declare Jesus Christ is Lord.
10. Almighty God, I am the work of your hands, restore whatever the enemy has taken from my life, and remove whatever the enemy has added to my life, in the name of Jesus.
11. Almighty God; bless my day in the name of Jesus.
12. I cancel every evil dreams, visions, prophesy and prayers against my life and family in the name of Jesus.
13. Talk to God about your heart desires and your situation.
14. Thank God for answered prayers.

Confession:

My eyes are open to the deeper things of God. I am increasing in the knowledge of the Lord. I soar above all situations like an eagle. Death is defeated in my life and on my way by the blood of Jesus.

Wisdom for Today:

When God speaks to you, it will glorify his name, it will cause you to worship him, it will agree with scriptures, and it will impart the knowledge of God. So, think well about the voice you say you are hearing.

Read the Bible Today: *Genesis 12–14*

Prayer Points:

1. Every evil spiritual padlock and evil chain hindering my success be melted in the name of Jesus.
2. I rebuke every spirit of spiritual deafness and blindness in my life, in the name of Jesus.
3. Almighty God empower me to resist satan and cause him to flee, in the name of Jesus.
4. I chose to believe the report of the Lord and no other, in the name of Jesus.
5. Almighty God, anoint my eyes and my ears that they may see and hear wondrous things from heaven in the name of Jesus.
6. Almighty God, anoint me to pray without ceasing, in the name of Jesus.
7. Almighty God; speak healing and blessing to my life in the name of Jesus.
8. Almighty God let your blessing be upon me in this country in the name of Jesus.
9. Stubborn problems in my life I conquer you by the blood of Jesus in the name of Jesus.
10. Almighty God; bless me to be a blessing to others all the days of my life in the name of Jesus.
11. Declare Jesus Christ is Lord.
12. Almighty God; make me a corner stone in the name of Jesus Christ.

13. Almighty God make me the chief corner stone in the name of Jesus.
14. Almighty God; I pray for divine approval in the name of Jesus.
15. Almighty God; don't let me labor in vain, bombard me with uncommon blessing in the name of Jesus.
16. Power of God possesses my hand in the name of Jesus.
17. I cancel every evil dreams, visions, prophesy and prayers against my life and family in the name of Jesus.
18. Talk to God about your heart desires and your situation.
19. Thank God for answered prayers.

Confession:

I am experiencing an all-round growth. I will not decline physically or spiritually, in the most precious name of Jesus. The hand of my God upholds me to keep me from falling. I am a winner and not a looser.

Wisdom for Today:

Mohammed is still in his grave. Buddha is still in his grave. Confucius, Joseph Smith—all are still in their graves. Only in Christianity do we find a resurrected Lord.

Only faith in Christ is valid because only Jesus rose from the dead. No other religious leader defeated death, so no other can make these claims. The resurrected Lord is the central event of our faith. And, because of Easter, we know that God in Christ Jesus is more powerful than anything in life—even death.

The resurrection is not just another Christian belief; it is the very center of our faith. Everything hinges on the resurrection. And we realize this when life smacks us in the face, in our deepest and darkest moments, when we don't think it can ever get better. The resurrection gives us hope that it can. When we are in the midst of day one or day two, the resurrection gives us hope that there is a day three, and victory is coming.

Read the Bible Today: John 20

Prayer Points:

1. In the name of Jesus, I capture every power behind any career failure in my life, in the name of Jesus.
2. Holy Spirit, rain on me now, in the name of Jesus.
3. Holy Spirit, uncover my darkest secrets and deliver me from shame, in the name of Jesus.
4. You, spirit of confusion, release your hold over my life, in the name of Jesus.
5. In the name of Jesus and the power of the Holy Spirit, I defy satan's power upon my life, career, and marriage, in the name of Jesus.
6. Let water of life flush out every unwanted stranger in my life, in the name of Jesus.
7. You, the enemies of my income, career, and marriage, be paralyzed, in the name of Jesus.
8. My spirit, soul, and body; be delivered in the name of Jesus.

9. I command the blessings of God upon my life in the name of Jesus.
10. Power of God over shadow my life in the name of Jesus.
11. I command healing upon my spirit, soul and body in the name of Jesus.
12. Power to get wealth; come upon my life in the name of Jesus.
13. Almighty God comfort me on every side in the name of Jesus Christ.
14. Almighty God; have mercy upon me; don't let me cry before I receive blessing in the name of Jesus.
15. Almighty God; let it please you to bless me in the name of Jesus.
16. Blood of Jesus Christ arise with your power and reconcile me with the blessing of God in the name of Jesus.
17. I cancel every evil dreams, visions, prophesy and prayers against my life and family in the name of Jesus.
18. Talk to God about your heart desires and your situation.
19. Thank God for answered prayers.

Confession:

"Even when we were dead in sins, hath quickened us together with Christ, (by grace ye are saved)" Ephesians 2:5.

Wisdom for Today:

Tell the enemy, "I am saved not because I am perfect or holy, but by God's grace. Jesus is my righteousness in God."

Read the Bible Today: Isaiah 54

Prayer Points:

1. Every destiny destroyed by family conflict, be repaired, in the name of Jesus.
2. Every witchcraft power working against my destiny, fall down and die, in the name of Jesus.
3. Every incantation and ritual working against my destiny be disgraced, in the name of Jesus.
4. Every power of darkness assigned against my destiny, fall down and die, in the name of Jesus.
5. Every evil power trying to reprogram my life, fall down and die, in the name of Jesus.
6. Almighty God; you are a consuming fire; turn me to fire in the name of Jesus.
7. Almighty God; surround my dwelling place with the hedge of fire in the name of Jesus.
8. Almighty God; send your angels to minister to our needs in the name of Jesus.
9. Almighty God, bless me indeed in the name of Jesus.
10. Almighty God cause a deep sleep on all my enemies, don't allow them to carry out their evil assignment in the name of Jesus.
11. Almighty God stretch out your hand and push poverty out of my life in the name of Jesus.
12. Almighty God; solve my financial problem in the name of Jesus.
13. Almighty God destroy every enemy working against my life in the name of Jesus.
14. I cancel every evil dreams, visions, prophesy and prayers against my life and family in the name of Jesus.
15. Talk to God about your heart desires and your situation.
16. Thank God for answered prayers.

Apostle A.O. Solomon

Confession:

"And hath raised us up together, and made us sit together in heavenly places in Christ Jesus" Ephesians 2:6.

Wisdom for Today:

Stop limiting your destiny; know your position in Christ Jesus, and the devil cannot displace you.

Read the Bible Today: *Ephesians 2:1–22*

Prayer Points:

1. I reject every rearrangement of my destiny by the forces of wickedness, in the name of Jesus.
2. Almighty God lead me in the way I should go in the name of Jesus.
3. I refuse to be removed from the divine agenda of God in the name of Jesus.
4. I refuse to be limited by any power of darkness, in the name of Jesus.
5. Every quencher of my destiny, fall down and die, in the name of Jesus.
6. 6. Begin to thank the Lord.
7. 7. Begin to declare Jesus Christ is Lord.
8. 8. I know my redeemer liveth, change is coming my way in the name of Jesus.
9. 9. You stars in heaven arise and fight for me in the name of Jesus.
10. 10. Lion of the tribe of Judah arise and fight for me in the name of Jesus.
11. 11. Any habitations of darkness in my house, let fire go before the Lord and consume them in the name of Jesus.
12. 12. All you my enemies, hear the word of the Lord, your calamity is at hand and
13. your affliction comes quickly in the name of Jesus.
14. 13 I cancel every evil dreams, visions, prophesy and prayers against my life and family in the name of Jesus.
15. Talk to God about your heart desires and your situation.
16. Thank God for answered prayers.

Confession: I can do all things through

"Having abolished in his flesh the enmity, even the law of command-ments contained in ordinances; for to make in himself of twain one new man, so making peace" Ephesians 2:15.

Wisdom for Today:

You are no longer the miserable sinner you used to be; now you are a friend of God through Christ Jesus who took away your sins. Now you can shout, "Praise the Lord, I am saved!"

Read the Bible Today: Philippians 1–2

Prayer Points:

1. Lord, let my divine destiny appear, and let perverted destiny disappear, in Jesus name.
2. I reject every satanic rearrangement of my destiny, in the name of Jesus.
3. I refuse to live below my divine standard, in Jesus name.
4. Every evil power having negative awareness of my destiny be impotent, in the name of Jesus.
5. I paralyze every polluter of my destiny, in the name of Jesus.
6. By the authority in the blood of Jesus Christ, I possess my possession in the name of Jesus.
7. By the authority in the blood of Jesus Christ, I declare a new season in the name of Jesus.
8. By the authority in the blood of Jesus Christ, I decree I will make it in the name of Jesus.
9. By the authority in the blood of Jesus Christ, I receive power from above in the name of Jesus.
10. By the authority in the blood of Jesus Christ, something good will come out of my life in the name of Jesus.
11. Declare Jesus Christ is Lord.
12. Take all the glory Lord in the name of Jesus.
13. Almighty God; empower me to triumph over my enemies in the name of Jesus.
14. Let the anointing of God come afresh upon my life in the name of Jesus.

15. I cancel every evil dreams, visions, prophesy and prayers against my life and family in the name of Jesus.
16. Talk to God about your heart desires and your situation.
17. Thank God for answered prayers.

Confession:

"Having predestinated us unto the adoption of children by Jesus Christ to himself, according to the good pleasure of his will, to the praise of the glory of his grace, wherein he hath made us accepted in the beloved" Ephesians 1:5–6.

Wisdom for Today:

Know your worth in God, because when you don't know your worth, you become worthless.

Read the Bible Today: Isaiah 43 and 62

Prayer Points:

1. I praise and thank God for allowing me to see yet another day by his grace.
2. Every damage done to my destiny be repaired now, in the name of Jesus.
3. The enemy will not convert my body to rags, in the name of Jesus.
4. The enemy will not convert my destiny to rags, in the name of Jesus.
5. Almighty God, restore me to your original design for my life in the name of Jesus.
6. I reject destiny-demoting names, in the name of Jesus.
7. Almighty God; open my eyes to see what you want me to see, my ears to hear what you want me to hear in the name of Jesus.
8. Henceforth let no principality or power trouble me for I bear the mark of our Lord Jesus Christ in the name of Jesus.
9. Almighty God; insert your pillar of fire into my body in the name of Jesus.
10. Blood of Jesus minister success and favor into my life in the name of Jesus.
11. I reject evil dreams and visitation in the name of Jesus.
12. I decree my joy to come in the morning in the name of Jesus Christ.
13. I command every form of weeping to end in my life in the name of Jesus.
14. Almighty God; visit my life, my family, and my church with good news in the name of Jesus.

Apostle A.O. Solomon

15. Almighty God; change the times and events of my life for good in the name of Jesus.
16. Let divine revelation and vision of heaven replace evil dreams in my life in the name of Jesus.
17. I cancel every evil dreams, visions, prophesy and prayers against my life and family in the name of Jesus.
18. Talk to God about your heart desires and your situation.
19. Thank God for answered prayers.

Confession:

"But now in Christ Jesus ye who sometimes were far off are made nigh by the blood of Christ" Ephesians 2:13.

Wisdom for Today:

God is closer to you than you know or think. Keep holding onto him, and don't lose focus, for in his presence is fullness of joy.

Read the Bible Today: Psalms 16

Prayer Points:

1. I praise and thank God for this beautiful day.
2. Almighty God, enlarge my horizons, in the name of Jesus.
3. I refuse to operate below my divine destiny, in the name of Jesus.
4. Almighty God, anoint my eyes, hands, and legs that I may locate my divine purpose in the name of Jesus.
5. Every power contending with my divine destiny, scatter unto desolation, in the name of Jesus.
6. Let the spirit of excellence come upon me, in Jesus name.
7. I plead the blood of Jesus Christ over my spirit, soul, and body in the name of Jesus.
8. Thou consuming fire, pass through my life with your fire in the name of Jesus.
9. Almighty God; let there be solution to the situation of my life in the name of Jesus.
10. Declare Jesus Christ is Lord.
11. I overcome every evil in my life by the blood of Jesus in the name of Jesus.
12. Let the blood of Jesus arise in its power and begin to fight for me in the name of Jesus.
13. Every storm in my life, I challenge you by the blood of Jesus Christ in the name of Jesus.
14. Almighty God; give me rest of mind and bless me with your peace in the name of Jesus.
15. Almighty God; Let me laugh and rejoice over all that have made me cry in the name of Jesus.
16. I cancel every evil dreams, visions, prophesy and prayers against my life and family in the name of Jesus.
17. Talk to God about your heart desires and your situation.
18. Thank God for answered prayers.

Apostle A.O. Solomon

Confession:

"Unto every one of us is given grace according to the measure of the gift of Christ" Ephesians 4:7.

Wisdom for Today:

Most of what we grumble or complain about is a result of our lack of patience or our fear of trying again after a failure. You have what it takes to make the difference. Christ is in you the hope of glory.

Read the Bible Today: Luke 5

Prayer Points:

1. I thank God for sending yet another day of victory, power, blessings, and glory.
2. I resist and rebuke satan's effort to change the good things in my destiny in the name of Jesus.
3. I remove from satan the right to rob me of my divine destiny in the name of Jesus.
4. I command all powers of darkness assigned to my destiny to leave and never return, in the name of Jesus.
5. Let earthquake, seaquake and air quake destroy every power assigned to demote my destiny, in the name of Jesus.
6. I command all the enemies of Jesus Christ that have access to my progress to leave and never return, in the name of Jesus.
7. Almighty God let there be a turn of event in my life before the end of this month in the name of Jesus.
8. Almighty God; give me a new song before the end of this month in the name of Jesus.
9. Almighty God; take over the situation of my life; let me have a victory dance before the end of this month in the name of Jesus.
10. Almighty God before the end of this month solve my financial needs in the name of Jesus.
11. Almighty God, connect me with the right people that will make the difference in my life in the name of Jesus.
12. Almighty God frustrate anything that the devil and my enemies are doing to frustrate my divine helpers in the name of Jesus.

13. Almighty God; don't let my helpers give up on me because you never gave up on me in the name of Jesus.
14. I cancel every evil dreams, visions, prophesy and prayers against my life and family in the name of Jesus.
15. Talk to God about your heart desires and your situation.
16. Thank God for answered prayers.

Confession:

"Just as you used to be slaves to all kinds of sin, so now you must let yourself be slaves to all that is right and holy" Romans 6:19, TLB.

Wisdom for Today:

Instead of filling your mind with resentments, abusing your body by sinful diversion, and damaging your soul by willfulness, humbly give all over to God. Your conflicts will disappear, and your inner tensions will vanish into thin air. Then your life will begin to count for something.

Read the Bible Today: Philippians 4

Prayer Points:

1. I praise and thank God for allowing me to see yet another day by his grace.
2. I paralyze every satanic opportunity that is working against my life, in the name of Jesus.
3. Every incantation, ritual, and witchcraft power against my destiny, fall down and die, in the name of Jesus.
4. I render null and void the influence of destiny swallowers, in the name of Jesus.
5. Every household wickedness struggling to rearrange my destiny, relinquish your hold, in the name of Jesus.
6. The rod of the wicked shall not rest upon my life, in the name of Jesus.
7. Almighty God preserve my job in the name of Jesus.
8. Lord I ask for strength and power to prevail in prayer in the name of Jesus.
9. By the blood of Jesus Christ; let the heaven open to my prayer in the name of Jesus.
10. Almighty God; baptize my name with your favor in the name of Jesus.
11. As from today I claim dominion over every evil dream in the name of Jesus.
12. Henceforth no evil dream shall come to pass in my life in the name Jesus.
13. Every evil dominion dedicated against me be dethroned in the name of Jesus.

14. Every crown of evil power militating against my life be destroyed by fire in the name of Jesus.
15. Holy Spirit of God; provoke better things in my life in the name of Jesus.
16. Almighty God; put my life in the center of signs and wonder in the name of Jesus.
17. Every negative appointment with my destiny, I terminate you in the name of Jesus.
18. I cancel every evil dreams, visions, prophesy and prayers against my life and family in the name of Jesus.
19. Talk to God about your heart desires and your situation.
20. Thank God for answered prayers.

Confession:

"For he that soweth to his flesh shall of the flesh reap corruption; but he that soweth to the Spirit shall of the Spirit reap life everlasting" Galatians 6:8.

Wisdom for Today:

The Christian life is never spoken of in the Bible as a bed of roses. It is uphill because society is headed in one direction and Christians are headed in the opposite direction. So, avoid compromise, and don't always give your flesh what he wants.

Read the Bible Today: Galatians 6

Prayer Points:

1. I praise and thank God for allowing me to see yet another day by his grace.
2. I refuse to be removed from the divine agenda God has planned for my life, in the name of Jesus.
3. Holy Spirit, I invite you into my imagination today, in Jesus name.
4. Almighty God, bring to light every darkness that shields my potential, in the name of Jesus.
5. I break every curse of backwardness, in the name of Jesus.
6. I recover myself from every evil diversion, in Jesus name.
7. Almighty God; give me wisdom that will bless my life in the name of Jesus.
8. Almighty God; give me adequate skills in the name of Jesus.
9. Blood of Jesus Christ minister healing and deliverance to me in the name of Jesus.
10. Almighty God; arise and glorify yourself in my life in the name of Jesus.
11. Any satanic prophecy concerning my life; be nullified by the blood of Jesus in the name of Jesus.
12. I receive power to fulfill positive promises in the name of Jesus.
13. Let the heavens fight for me in the name of Jesus.
14. Almighty God redeem; any member of my family that has been appointed to die in the name of Jesus.

15. You spirit of death assigned to anyone in my family go back to your sender in the name of Jesus.
16. Almighty God; put the mark of the blood of Jesus upon my head in the name of Jesus.
17. I cancel every evil dreams, visions, prophesy and prayers against my life and family in the name of Jesus.
18. Talk to God about your heart desires and your situation.
19. Thank God for answered prayers.

Apostle A.O. Solomon

Confession:

"For if a man think himself to be something, when he is nothing, he deceiveth himself." Galatians 6:3.

Wisdom for Today:

Always remember that God resists the proud and gives grace to the humble. Even John the Baptist said, "I shall decrease and he shall increase." John 3:30

Read the Bible Today: Matthew 3

Prayer Points:

1. I thank God for today.
2. I shall not come to the world in vain, in the name of Jesus.
3. Every demon of the forest and rock assigned against me, fall down and die, in the name of Jesus.
4. Every local charm burnt against me; attack your sender, in the name of Jesus.
5. I release myself from ungodly parental linkage, in the name of Jesus.
6. Lord Jesus, manifest yourself in my life in the name of Jesus.
7. Declare Jesus Christ is Lord.
8. Almighty God; in the move of your power tonight, pay special attention to my needs in the name of Jesus.
9. Almighty God; have your way in my life in the name of Jesus.
10. Almighty God; deliver me from every foundational pharaoh in the name of Jesus.
11. Every water, river, and sea that is harboring bewitchment against my life; dry up by fire in the name of Jesus.
12. All my blessings inside any river arise come out and locate me in the name of Jesus.
13. Every physical or spiritual padlock used to lock my blessings and success break in the name of Jesus.
14. Almighty God; have mercy upon me; raise help for me from unexpected source in the name of Jesus.
15. Almighty God; don't let anything happen to me that will make me cry in the name of Jesus.
16. I thank God for glory and manifestation in the name of Jesus.
17. I reject career failure in the name of Jesus.

18. I cancel every evil dreams, visions, prophesy and prayers against my life and family in the name of Jesus.
19. Talk to God about your heart desires and your situation.
20. Thank God for answered prayers.

Confession:

"It is written; Man shall not live by bread alone, but by every word that proceedeth out of the mouth of God" Matthew 4:4.

Wisdom for Today:

Stop complaining about what you have not received, look back and count your blessings and always give thanks to God. "God makes all things good at its own time". Ecclesiastes 3:11

Read the Bible Today: Matthew 6

Prayer Points:

1. I praise and thank God for allowing me to see yet another day by his grace.
2. Every bird of death assigned against me, fall down and die, in the name of Jesus.
3. I withdraw any food and drink that nourishes my problems, in the name of Jesus.
4. No river of evil shall flow into my life, in Jesus name.
5. I banish every satanic regulation and domination that threatens my progress, in the name of Jesus.
6. Every garment of darkness be roasted by fire, in the name of Jesus.
7. Declare Jesus Christ is Lord.
8. I receive the rain and blessing from heaven upon my life in the name of Jesus.
9. The heavens were created to be a blessing to my life therefore; you heaven arise and bless my life in the name of Jesus.
10. Let the heavens arise and make way for me in all areas of life in the name of Jesus.
11. Let the heavens arise and fight for me in the name of Jesus.
12. Almighty God have mercy upon me; bow down your heaven and come to my help in the name of Jesus.
13. I renounce every covenant with satan consciously or unconsciously in the name of Jesus.
14. Every evil addiction I renounce you in the name of Jesus.
15. I renounce every agreement consciously or unconsciously with spirit wife and spirit husband in the name of Jesus.

16. By the blood of Jesus Christ I renounce every evil dream, prophesy, and vision in the name of Jesus.
17. I renounce every work of satan and his kingdom in the name of Jesus.
18. Every assignment of the enemy on my finances fail woefully in the name of Jesus.
19. Almighty God; you are the Lord God my healer manifest your healing power in my life in the name of Jesus.
20. I cancel every evil dreams, visions, prophesy and prayers against my life and family in the name of Jesus.
21. Talk to God about your heart desires and your situation.
22. Thank God for answered prayers.

Confession:

"Jesus said unto him, It is written, Thou shall not tempt the Lord thy God" Matthew 4:7.

Wisdom for Today:

Are you under any satanic attack? Launch a counterattack against the devil and his agents with the written word of God. Search the scripture and find a passage in the Bible that fits your case. Quote it again and again until you see a change in your situation. Why don't you be like Jesus and begin to say to your challenges, "It is written …

Read the Bible Today: Psalms 119:9–16 and Psalms 129–136

Prayer Points:

1. I thank God for yet another day.
2. I refuse to live a floating life, in the name of Jesus.
3. Every deeply entrenched problem, dry to the roots, in the name of Jesus.
4. I destroy the weapons of satanic night raiders, in the name of Jesus.
5. Every stronghold of failure be broken, in Jesus name.
6. All internal warfare in my life be removed in the name of Jesus.
7. Go ahead and worship the Lord.
8. Almighty God; hear and answer my prayers tonight in the name of Jesus.
9. Anointing to prosper in all areas of life, fall upon me now in the name of Jesus.
10. Almighty God; have mercy on me let me dwell in safety; let your heaven drop dew upon my life in the name of Jesus.
11. Almighty God; Give me the dew of heaven in the name of Jesus.
12. Almighty God; have mercy upon me, bow down your heavens and come to my help in the name of Jesus.
13. Almighty God let every mountain in my life become a plain in the name of Jesus.
14. In the name of Jesus Christ whatever defeated people in my family shall not defeat me in the name of Jesus.
15. All those who are gathered to celebrate my defeat and failure scatter in the name of Jesus.

16. I cancel every evil dreams, visions, prophesy and prayers against my life and family in the name of Jesus.
17. Talk to God about your heart desires and your situation.
18. Thank God for answered prayers.

Apostle A.O. Solomon

Confession:

"Then saith Jesus unto him, Get thee hence, Satan: for it is written, Thou shall worship the Lord thy God, and him only shall thou serve" Matthew 4:10.

Wisdom for Today:

Refuse to bow to any power, spirit, or personality that demands obedience before you receive your blessings. God will not share his glory in your life with anything or anyone.

Read the Bible Today: *Matthew 4:1–11*

Prayer Points:

1. I thank God for today.
2. Every internal thief, be exposed, in the name of Jesus.
3. Anything planted in my life by my enemies, come out with all your roots, in the name of Jesus.
4. Let the handwriting of household wickedness be rubbed off, in the name of Jesus.
5. Almighty God let thieves, who have stolen my divine rights, return them now, in the name of Jesus.
6. I shall have no cause to weep as the year comes to an end, in the name of Jesus.
7. Almighty God; heal every area of my life in the name of Jesus.
8. Almighty God; take away my reproach in the name of Jesus.
9. Almighty God; lay your hands of miracle upon my hands and take away poverty in the name of Jesus.
10. Almighty God; let the dew of heaven fall upon my hand in the name of Jesus.
11. Almighty God; make my hands the instrument of deliverance in the name of Jesus.
12. I command deliverance upon my spirit, soul, and body in the name of Jesus.
13. Every vow of the enemy to afflict my life and family; be frustrated in the name of Jesus.
14. Strength and power to overcome be renewed in my life in the name of Jesus.
15. Heavens of my miracle, open now in the name of Jesus.

16. Blood of Jesus reconcile me with my helpers in the name of Jesus.
17. Holy Spirit quicken my life now to encounter divine presence in the name of Jesus.
18. I escape out of every bondage; witchcraft captivity, by the seal of the almighty God in the name of Jesus.
19. I decree that the zeal of the Lord shall perform glorious sign and wonders in my life in the mighty name of Jesus.
20. In any area of my life where I have been defeated; I claim back my victory in the name of Jesus.
21. I cancel every evil dreams, visions, prophesy and prayers against my life and family in the name of Jesus.
22. Talk to God about your heart desires and your situation.
23. Thank God for answered prayers.

Confession:

"Lay not up for yourselves treasures upon earth, where moth and rust doth corrupt, and where thieves break through and steal" Matthew 6:19.

Wisdom for Today:

Every tithe you give will always remove you from tight corners in life. Pay your tithes so that situations will not be tight for you.

Read the Bible Today: Malachi 3

Prayer Points:

1. I thank God for this day.
2. Almighty God empower me to always focus on heavenly things, in the name of Jesus.
3. I refuse to live a wasted life, in the name of Jesus.
4. Almighty God, baptize me with your special favor today, in the name of Jesus.
5. Every evil power assigned against my blessing, favor, and income today, be destroyed by fire, in the name of Jesus.
6. Almighty God show yourself in all my affairs today, in the name of Jesus.
7. Power and anointing to overcome every opposition come upon me now in the name of Jesus.
8. Almighty God; be the only one in charge of the affairs of my life in the name of Jesus.
9. In the heart of my helpers, let the lines fall in pleasant places in the name of Jesus.
10. Almighty God; satisfy me early in the name of Jesus.
11. Almighty God; we commit the month into your hands; have your way in the name of Jesus.
12. Almighty God; bless my going out and my coming in the name of Jesus.
13. By the blood of Jesus Christ I take over this month in the name of Jesus.
14. Almighty God; all the battles that I have been fighting for so long, bring them to an end in the name of Jesus.

15. Almighty God; let this month be stress free for me in the name of Jesus.
16. Any evil dream programmed to come to pass in this month, die in the name of Jesus.
17. I cancel every evil dreams, visions, prophesy and prayers against my life and family in the name of Jesus.
18. Talk to God about your heart desires and your situation.
19. Thank God for answered prayers.

Confession:

"Should ye not hear the words which the Lord hath cried by the former prophets, when Jerusalem was inhabited and in prosperity, and the cities thereof round about her" Zechariah 7:7.

Wisdom for Today:

God is faithful enough to bring all your good dreams to pass, but you must pray until it happens. Remember Daniel and the evil prince of Persia (Daniel 10). Keep on praying that miracles, blessings, and prosperity belong to you. Do not quit until you get it.

Read the Bible Today: Daniel 10

Prayer Points:

1. Every power making life difficult for me be destroyed by fire, in the name of Jesus.
2. From now on, life shall be easy for me, in the name of Jesus.
3. To acquire money shall not be difficult for me, in the name of Jesus.
4. Almighty God, teach my hand to profit, in Jesus name.
5. Almighty God, give me power to acquire wealth easily, in the name of Jesus.
6. Owners of evil dream, carry your load in the name of Jesus.
7. Almighty God; baptize me with your special favor in the name of Jesus.
8. Almighty God; let things get better for me in the name of Jesus.
9. Almighty God; let total freedom and everlasting joy be my portion in the name of Jesus.
10. Let the liberty of the Holy Spirit flow into every department of my life in the name of Jesus.
11. Every satanic spider and cobwebs assigned to block my way, roast in the name of Jesus.
12. Every cobweb that hindered me in the past you shall not prosper in the name of Jesus.
13. Almighty God; I commit this month into your hands; make this month my miracle month in the name of Jesus.
14. I decree whatever was not able to stop Jesus Christ from resurrecting shall not be able to stop me in the name of Jesus.

15. Let God arise and cancel every evil dream and utterance in the name of Jesus.
16. I fire back every evil arrow fired against my life in the name of Jesus.
17. I cancel every evil dreams, visions, prophesy and prayers against my life and family in the name of Jesus.
18. Talk to God about your heart desires and your situation.
19. Thank God for answered prayers.

Confession:

"The Lord bringeth the counsel of the heathen to nought: he maketh the devices of the people of none effect" Psalms 33:10.

Wisdom for Today:

God looks at a wounded man and says, "You are still my child. You blew it. You messed up and did a whole lot of things you shouldn't have done. You said some things you shouldn't have said and hurt some people you shouldn't have hurt. But you are still mine. I will not give you unto the desire of the enemy."

Read the Bible Today: Isaiah 43

Prayer Points:

1. I thank God for today.
2. Almighty God lay your hands of fire upon me and change my destiny in the name of Jesus.
3. I receive explosive breakthroughs; I reject weak breakthroughs, in the name of Jesus.
4. Almighty God change my destiny for the better, in the name of Jesus.
5. Every evil power struggling to reprogram my life, fall down and die, in the name of Jesus.
6. Almighty God shake me until I come to my senses whenever I make mistakes, in the name of Jesus.
7. I thank the Lord Jesus for scattering the enemies of my divine destiny in the name of Jesus.
8. Every evil dream causing any problem in my life be canceled now in the name of Jesus.
9. Lay your right hand on your fore head and pray; almighty God; remove every label of failure in my life in the name of Jesus.
10. Every evil identification mark upon my life; be removed in the name of Jesus.
11. Almighty God; wash me clean with the blood of Jesus Christ; remove every evil odor in the name of Jesus Christ.
12. Almighty God; let this month open good doors for me in the name of Jesus.
13. Almighty God; make this month my month of advancement in the name of Jesus.

14. Almighty God; justify me this month in the name of Jesus.
15. Almighty God; accept all my offerings this month in the name of Jesus.
16. Every messenger of death, assigned against me and my family die and rise no more in the name of Jesus.
17. Almighty God; deliver me from every tragedy and accident in the name of Jesus.
18. I am not ready to die now, any power that wants me dead, die in the name of Jesus.
19. I cancel every evil dreams, visions, prophesy and prayers against my life and family in the name of Jesus.
20. Talk to God about your heart desires and your situation.
21. Thank God for answered prayers.

Confession:

"I am living a brand-new kind of life ... more and more like Christ Jesus who created this new life within me" Colossians 3:10.

Wisdom for Today:

Underneath all your troubles will be the "still waters" that the Great Shepherd can provide. Many people are trying to steady themselves by taking tranquilizers. Jesus is the greatest tranquilizer of all. He can straighten out your life and put you back on center. Let him take full control. You'll go on your way rejoicing.

Read the Bible Today: John 3

Prayer Points:

1. I thank God for a new day.
2. Every unprofitable love targeted against me, be broken now, in the name of Jesus.
3. Every evil affliction prepared by household wickedness, be smashed unto desolation, in the name of Jesus.
4. Every stubborn curse, be broken by fire, in Jesus name.
5. I dash onto a wall of fire every evil clock that controls my life, in the name of Jesus.
6. Almighty God, arrest and disgrace all those creating problems for me at work, and school, in the name of Jesus.
7. Declare Jesus Christ is Lord.
8. Almighty God; I commit this month into your hand, let your kingdom come and, let your Will be done in the name of Jesus.
9. Almighty God; I commit this month into your hands; let your light shine upon my way in the name of Jesus.
10. Almighty God; make this month the month of special divine favor for me in the name of Jesus.
11. Almighty God; make this month the month of testimonies and promotion for me and my family in the name of Jesus.
12. Every coffin prepared for me and my family; be consumed by fire in the name of Jesus.
13. Every grave dug for me and my family be covered by the blood of Jesus in the name of Jesus.
14. I prophesy victory shall be my portion in the name of Jesus.

15. Throughout this month, all things shall work together for my good in the name of Jesus.
16. I remove my name from every evil register in the name of Jesus.
17. I prophesy throughout this month, I shall not have any break down in the name of Jesus.
18. Almighty God; make way for me where there seems to be no way in the name of Jesus.
19. I reject every evil in this month in the name of Jesus.
20. I claim the goodness of God in the name of Jesus.
21. Almighty God; give your angels charge over me in the name of Jesus.
22. In the name of Jesus, let everything God has made begin to work for my favor in the name of Jesus.
23. I cancel every evil dreams, visions, prophesy and prayers against my life and family in the name of Jesus.
24. Talk to God about your heart desires and your situation.
25. Thank God for answered prayers.

Confession:

"And I will rejoice in Jerusalem, and joy in my people: and the voice of weeping shall be no more heard in her, nor the voice of crying" Isaiah 65:19.

Wisdom for Today:

When the devil, cares of this world, and anxiety come knocking at the door of your life and heart, don't answer it. Send Jesus to the door. They will bow and flee.

Read the Bible Today: Job 14:7–15

Prayer Points:

1. I thank God for today.
2. Almighty God, comfort my heart, in the name of Jesus.
3. Almighty God, establish me in every good work, in the name of Jesus.
4. Almighty God, establish me in every good word, in the name of Jesus.
5. God of peace, establish me in your peace, in the name of Jesus.
6. Almighty God let my spirit, soul and body, be preserved and blameless unto thee, in the name of Jesus.
7. Almighty God; raise helpers for me; let my helpers locate me in the name of Jesus.
8. Every mountain before me; be made plain in the name of Jesus.
9. Begin to declare Jesus Christ is Lord.
10. Ask God to have His way in the name of Jesus.
11. Holy Spirit of God; empower and revive my prayer life in the name of Jesus.
12. Every arrow of spiritual laziness and weaknesses fired into my life come out and; go back to your sender in the name of Jesus.
13. Every spirit and power of backwardness I bind and cast you out in the name of Jesus.
14. Every satanic network fashioned against my progress physically or spiritually; be scattered by fire in the name of Jesus.
15. Every satanic hand pulling me backward; wither in the name of Jesus.

16. Every evil power sitting upon my glory; fall down and die in the name of Jesus.
17. Anything stolen from my destiny in the womb; I recover them back in the name of Jesus.
18. Almighty God; magnify yourself this month in my life in the name of Jesus.
19. Almighty God; release your power of deliverance upon my spirit, soul and body in the name of Jesus.
20. I cancel every evil dreams, visions, prophesy and prayers against my life and family in the name of Jesus.
21. Talk to God about your heart desires and your situation.
22. Thank God for answered prayers.

Confession:

"Though thy beginning was small, yet thy latter end should greatly increase" Job 8:7.

Wisdom for Today:

Don't despise small blessings or miracles. Don't be afraid of starting small. Every great thing starts in a small way. The Bible says, "He that is faithful in that which is least is faithful also in much" Luke 16:10, KJV. Thank God for little things.

Read the Bible Today: Matthew 14 and Job 8

Prayer Points:

1. I thank God for yet another day.
2. Almighty God let me be filled with the knowledge of your will, in Jesus name.
3. Almighty God let me be filled with all wisdom and spiritual understanding, in the name of Jesus.
4. Almighty God help me to walk a path that is worthy of you and pleasing to you, in the name of Jesus.
5. Almighty God let me be fruitful in every good work, in Jesus name.
6. Almighty God, increase me in the knowledge of God in the name of Jesus.
7. I reject career, academic, ministerial, and destiny failure in the name of Jesus.
8. Whatever the enemy is using to hold me down break off in the name of Jesus.
9. Every padlock used to lock any area of my life; break in the name of Jesus.
10. Declare Jesus Christ is Lord.
11. Any power, spirit, any personality waiting for my day of honor, glory, joy; I command you to perish in the name of Jesus.
12. Almighty God; let the years of my life be increased in the name of Jesus.
13. Every power and spirit prolonging captivity and bondage in my life, rock of ages fall upon them in the name of Jesus.
14. By the word of God that can never fail, those who bless me shall be blessed; those who curse me shall be cursed in the name of Jesus.

15. By the blood of Jesus Christ; I forbid death to branch in my house, church, and family in the name of Jesus.
16. I shall not be demoted; I shall go from glory to glory in the name of Jesus.
17. Every spiritual funeral procession organized for my family and ministry, scatter in the name of Jesus.
18. Every spiritual and witchcraft attack coming from both side of my spouse's family backfire in the name of Jesus.
19. Almighty God comfort me in the name of Jesus.
20. I soak yourself in the blood of Jesus in the name of Jesus.
21. I cancel every evil dreams, visions, prophesy and prayers against my life and family in the name of Jesus.
22. Talk to God about your heart desires and your situation.
23. Thank God for answered prayers.

Confession:

"Jesus spake unto them, saying, be of good cheer; it is I; be not afraid" Matthew 14:27.

Wisdom for Today:

A little girl was running toward the cemetery as the darkness of evening began to fall. She passed a friend who asked her if she was not afraid to go through the graveyard at night. "Oh, no," she said, "I'm not afraid. Though I walk through the valley of the shadow of death, God is always by my side." Today faith and confidence in the resurrected Christ can change your fear to hope and your disappointment to joy.

Read the Bible Today: Matthew 14

Prayer Points:

1. I thank God for another beautiful day.
2. Almighty God let me be filled with all the fullness of God in the name of Jesus.
3. Almighty God help me comprehend the breadth, length, depth, and height of the love of Christ, in the name of Jesus.
4. Every coffin physically or spiritually programmed for me, be consumed by fire, in the name of Jesus.
5. I fire back every evil arrow fired against my life, in the name of Jesus.
6. I bind and cast out the spirits of fear and intimidation from my life, in the name of Jesus.
7. I am a crown of glory, in the name of Jesus.
8. Let the word of the Lord have free course through me and be glorified in me, in the name of Jesus.
9. Let the Lord of peace give me peace in all areas of life, in the name of Jesus.
10. Almighty God strengthen me to pray in the name of Jesus.
11. Almighty God; you are the omnipotent God reign in my life in the name of Jesus.
12. Almighty God; reign in my situation in the name of Jesus.
13. I take over this day by the power in the blood of Jesus Christ in the name of Jesus.

14. Every evil programmed into this day I reject you in the name of Jesus.
15. Almighty God; I commit this day into your hand; let your presence bless my life in the name of Jesus.
16. Almighty God; give me peace always in every area of my life in the name of Jesus.
17. You spirit of fear I bind and cast you out of my life in the name of Jesus.
18. Blood of Jesus Christ flush bitterness and anguish out of my life in the name of Jesus.
19. Blood of Jesus Christ heal me from emotional damage in the mighty name of Jesus.
20. Almighty God; don't allow what I fear to come upon me in the name of Jesus.
21. Glory of the living God overwhelm my life in the name of Jesus.
22. Every fiery dart of the enemy fired into my heart come out and go back to your sender in the name of Jesus.
23. You spirit of heaviness I bind and cast you out of my life in the name of Jesus.
24. Every satanic power; buying and selling in my mind scatter unto desolation in the name of Jesus.
25. Lord Jesus Christ reign in my thought and imagination in the name of Jesus.
26. Almighty God; accept my offering and remember me for good in the name of Jesus.
27. Almighty God perfect what is lacking in my faith in the name of Jesus.
28. I cancel every evil dreams, visions, prophesy and prayers against my life and family in the name of Jesus.
29. Talk to God about your heart desires and your situation.
30. Thank God for answered prayers.

Confession:

"What a wonderful God we have ... who so wonderfully comforts and strengthens us" 2 Corinthians 1: 3–4, TLB

Wisdom for Today:

The Bible teaches unmistakably that we can triumph over bereavement. David said, "Weeping may endure for a night, but joy cometh in the morning" Psalms 30:5, AKJV). Self-pity cannot bring any comfort. The fact is, it will only add to your misery.

Read the Bible Today: Psalm 30

Prayer Points:

1. I thank God for today.
2. Lord God, feed me with the foods of the champions, in the name of Jesus.
3. Lord God, boost my energy to run the race set before me, in Jesus name.
4. I receive the comforting anointing and power in the Holy Ghost, in the name of Jesus.
5. Any power that wants me to weep before I receive my blessings, die, in the name of Jesus.
6. Let the arm of the Lord defend me today, in the name of Jesus.
7. I command the evil things in my life to die, in the name of Jesus.
8. I receive the unsearchable wisdom in the Holy Ghost, in the name of Jesus.
9. I take the shield of faith to deflect every fiery dart of the enemy, in the name of Jesus.
10. Declare Jesus Christ is Lord.
11. Almighty God; manifest your power in my life today in the name of Jesus.
12. Almighty God; do something unusual in my life in the name of Jesus.
13. Almighty God; never allow my enemies to prevail against me in the name of Jesus.
14. Almighty God; you are the most high, never allow the enemy to meet me where they left me in the name of Jesus.

15. Almighty God; you are the most high God, never allow the enemy to meet my marriage where they left my marriage in the name of Jesus.
16. Almighty God; every good chance that I have lost, have mercy Lord and restore them back to me in the name of Jesus.
17. You spirit of fear that wants to rob me of my chances in life, I bind and cast you out in the name of Jesus.
18. Any evil habit or character in me hindering good chances in my life; I command you to die in the name of Jesus.
19. I cancel every evil dreams, visions, prophesy and prayers against my life and family in the name of Jesus.
20. Talk to God about your heart desires and your situation.
21. Thank God for answered prayers.

Confession:

"If it be so, our God whom we serve is able to deliver us from the burning fiery furnace, and he will deliver us out of thine hand, O king" Daniel 3:17.

Wisdom for Today:

The best time to know those who serve God and really trust in him is when storms rise against them and Jesus is taking a nap at a corner in the ship. Can God depend upon you in times of problems?

Read the Bible Today: Daniel 3

Prayer Points:

1. I thank God for today.
2. I take cover in the name of the Lord, who is a strong tower, and I am safe, in the name of Jesus.
3. Let the arm of the Lord dash to pieces every pillar that supports problems in my life and marriage, in the name of Jesus.
4. Let every power that supports any evil power against me collapse and die, in the name of Jesus.
5. Let my faith come alive by the power of God, in the name of Jesus.
6. Almighty God always make me drink from your everlasting well of joy, in the name of Jesus.
7. I thank God for the new spiritual height he has lifted me to in the name of Jesus.
8. The rest of the days in this year shall yield favor, blessings, and honor unto me, in the name of Jesus.
9. Declare Jesus Christ is Lord.
10. Almighty God; manifest your power in my life today in the name of Jesus.
11. Almighty God; do something unusual in my life in the name of Jesus.
12. Almighty God; never allow my enemies to prevail against me in the name of Jesus.
13. Almighty God every good chance that I have lost, have mercy Lord and restore them back to me in the name of Jesus.

14. You spirit of fear that wants to rob me of my chances in life, I bind and cast you out in the name of Jesus.
15. I cancel every evil dreams, visions, prophesy and prayers against my life and family in the name of Jesus.
16. Talk to God about your heart desires and your situation.
17. Thank God for answered prayers.

Apostle A.O. Solomon

Confession:

The Lord will raise me and make me a testimony of his wealth and riches to the glory of his name, in the precious name of Jesus.

Wisdom for Today:

The very pain that's been tormenting and traumatizing you could be the very pain that pushes you to touch God. Remember the woman with the issue of blood.

Read the Bible Today: Luke 8

Prayer Points:

1. I thank God for another good day.
2. Almighty God, plant good things in my life, in the name of Jesus.
3. Almighty God uproot evil things from my life, in the name of Jesus.
4. Every witchcraft pronouncement against me be nullified, in the name of Jesus.
5. Let the heavens of favor open for me today, in the name of Jesus.
6. Let the heavens of prosperity open for my work today, in the name of Jesus.
7. I cancel every unconscious negative agreement, in Jesus name.
8. Lord, make me your battle-axe, in the name of Jesus.
9. I recall all the evil dreams in my past that are affecting me, back to the sender, in the name of Jesus.
10. Almighty God let every spiritual weakness in my life receive termination now, in the name of Jesus.
11. Almighty God; take all the glory in my life and situation in the name of Jesus.
12. Begin to declare Jesus Christ is Lord.
13. Almighty God; Have mercy upon me in the name of Jesus.
14. Almighty God; arise and scatter every power blocking my prayer in the name of Jesus.
15. Almighty God; I pray for deliverance, manifest your deliverance power in my life in the name of Jesus.
16. Almighty God; I pray for healing, manifest your healing power in my life today in the name of Jesus.

17. Almighty God; where I have fallen, pick me up in the name of Jesus.
18. I cancel every evil dreams, visions, prophesy and prayers against my life and family in the name of Jesus.
19. Talk to God about your heart desires and your situation.
20. Thank God for answered prayers.

Confession:

"Behold, I will do a new thing; now it shall spring forth; shall ye not know it? I will even make a way in the wilderness and rivers in the desert" Isaiah 43:19.

Wisdom for Today:

In all ages, Christians have found it possible to maintain the spirit of joy in the hour of trial. In circumstances that would have felled most men, they have so completely risen above them that they actually have used the circumstances to serve and glorify Christ. Forget about the pains of yesterday; God will do a new thing today.

Read the Bible Today: Ephesians 1 and 2

Prayer Points:

1. I thank God for today.
2. Let every financial failure in my life receive termination now, in the name of Jesus.
3. Let every sickness in my life receive termination now, in the name of Jesus.
4. Let every architect of problems in my life receive termination now, in the name of Jesus.
5. Any problem sponsored by the devil in my life, I overcome you now, by the blood of the Lamb of God in the name of Jesus.
6. Anything programmed to disgrace my life, marriage, and calling, be disgraced, in the name of Jesus.
7. I receive wisdom to prevail today, in the name of Jesus.
8. I paralyze all spiritual wolves working against my life, in the name of Jesus.
9. Let that which hinders me from greatness begin to give way now, in the mighty name of Jesus.
10. Almighty God baptize me with your favor today, in the name of Jesus.
11. Almighty God; wherever I have been crushed down in all areas, raise me up and fix my life in the name of Jesus.
12. Almighty God; where I have been wounded, heal me today in the name of Jesus.

13. Almighty God; where I have been damaged, repair me in the name of Jesus.
14. Almighty God; I need a miracle in the name of Jesus.
15. Every power destroying good things in my life, arise O Lord and destroy them in the name of Jesus.
16. Almighty God; have mercy upon me, every opportunity that I have missed restore them back to me in the name of Jesus.
17. Any evil habit and character in my life die and rise no more in the name of Jesus.
18. I cancel every evil dreams, visions, prophesy and prayers against my life and family in the name of Jesus.
19. Talk to God about your heart desires and your situation.
20. Thank God for answered prayers.

Confession:

"May the God of peace ... produce in you through the power of Christ all that is pleasing to him" Hebrews 13:20–21, TLB.

Wisdom for Today:

People may not like what say or do, but if your actions are pleasing to God, ride on.

Read the Bible Today: Galatians 3 and 4

Prayer Points:

1. I thank God for today.
2. I command all my imprisoned and buried potentials to come forth now, in the name of Jesus.
3. You, unfriendly helpers, I command you, to depart from me in the name of Jesus.
4. Let every negative transactions currently affecting my life negatively be canceled, in the name of Jesus.
5. I command all the dark works done against my life in secret to be exposed and be nullified, in the name of Jesus.
6. I release myself from any evil spirit, in the name of Jesus.
7. Let the wisdom of God speak and shine forth in my life, in the name of Jesus.
8. Let the favor of God baptize me today, in the name of Jesus.
9. Give thanks to the Lord
10. Declare Jesus Christ is Lord.
11. Any power, any spirit, anyone that will resist my prayers today; let God scatter them in the name of Jesus.
12. Holy Spirit of God; manifest yourself in my life in the name of Jesus.
13. Almighty God; open my eyes to recognize and identify my time of divine visitation in the name of Jesus.
14. Any evil habit and character shutting good things away from me; die in the name of Jesus.
15. Almighty God; arise and separate me from any man or woman that is pulling down my destiny in the name of Jesus.
16. I cancel every evil dreams, visions, prophesy and prayers against my life and family in the name of Jesus.
17. Talk to God about your heart desires and your situation.
18. Thank God for answered prayers.

Confession:

"But my God shall supply all my need according to his riches in glory by Christ Jesus" Philippians 4:19.

Wisdom for Today:

He may not come at your own time or in your own way, but God never comes late. He provided for the Israelites; he will surely meet you at the very point of your needs, not your wants.

Read the Bible Today: Psalm 78

Prayer Points:

1. I praise and thank God for allowing me to see yet another day by his grace.
2. Almighty God if my life is on the wrong course, correct me, in Jesus name.
3. Let every antiprogressive altar fashioned against me be destroyed with the thunder and fire of God, in the name of Jesus.
4. I command my destiny to change for the better, in Jesus name.
5. I command the foundation of bewitchment in my life to be destroyed, in the name of Jesus.
6. I receive the wisdom to prosper in life, in the name of Jesus.
7. Let my hand become a sword of fire to cut down demonic trees, in the name of Jesus.
8. Let the fire of God consume everything that is making me weep, in the name of Jesus.
9. All boasting powers delegated against me, be silenced permanently, in the name of Jesus.
10. Almighty God soak me in your favor today, in the name of Jesus.
11. Every evil dream in my life, I cancel you by the blood of Jesus in the name of Jesus.
12. Almighty God; I commit my children unto your hands, release the grace and power to fulfill destiny upon them in the name of Jesus.
13. Almighty God; lay your mighty Hand upon our children in the name of Jesus.
14. Almighty God; separate my children from satanic friends in the name of Jesus.

15. Almighty God; let the spirit of revival baptize our children in the name of Jesus.
16. Almighty God; fill our children with the love for things of heaven in the name of Jesus.
17. In the name of Jesus Christ; death, sickness, and the devil shall not take away my children from me in the name of Jesus.
18. Any evil agent, power, spirit, man or woman that want to use my children for ritual or sacrifice, die in the name of Jesus.
19. Any evil agent, power, spirit, man or woman; that is blocking the way of my children, angel of the Lord clear them away in the name of Jesus.
20. I cancel every evil dreams, visions, prophesy and prayers against my life and family in the name of Jesus.
21. Talk to God about your heart desires and your situation.
22. Thank God for answered prayers.

Confession:

"And we know that all things work together for good to them that love God, to them who are the called according to his purpose" Romans 8:28.

Wisdom for Today:

When you are assured of your purpose, you are not fearful of men or of external personal conflicts that attempt to hinder you.

Read the Bible Today: Romans 8

Prayer Points:

1. I thank God for today.
2. I withdraw all my benefits from the hands of the oppressors, in the name of Jesus.
3. Let all unprofitable marks in my life be erased, in Jesus name.
4. Let every power chasing away my blessings be paralyzed, in the name of Jesus.
5. Let every good thing in my life eaten up by the enemy be vomited back to me now, in the name of Jesus.
6. Let the anointing for spiritual breakthroughs fall upon me now, in the name of Jesus.
7. Almighty God anoint me for special favor today, in the name of Jesus.
8. I shall not fall out of God's favor and mercy, in the name of Jesus.
9. The enemy shall not take over the gate of my joy and comfort, in the name of Jesus.
10. The enemy shall not take over the gate of my destiny and marriage, in the name of Jesus.
11. My life and destiny shall not experience disorder, in the name of Jesus.
12. Almighty God; don't let me weep over my children in the name of Jesus.
13. Almighty God; have mercy upon me and my children in the name of Jesus.
14. Almighty God; have mercy upon our children and deliver them from negative influence in the name of Jesus.

15. Almighty God; have mercy upon me; don't let me regret over my children in the name of Jesus.
16. Contrary to the wish of the enemy, my children shall be the head and not the tail in the name of Jesus.
17. Almighty God; I offer my children unto you as a living sacrifice holy and acceptable unto you in the name of Jesus.
18. I cancel every appointment with death in the name of Jesus.
19. Any man or woman digging any pit for me; fall into your pit in the name of Jesus.
20. I cancel every evil dreams, visions, prophesy and prayers against my life and family in the name of Jesus.
21. Talk to God about your heart desires and your situation.
22. Thank God for answered prayers.

Confession:

"Thou shall rejoice in every good thing which the Lord thy God hath given unto thee" Deuteronomy 26:11.

Wisdom for Today:

The secret of soul satisfaction is this: Let your soul delight itself in fatness. Remove the obstructions, tear down the barriers, and let your soul find the fulfillment of its deepest longings in fellowship with God. True satisfaction is only in God.

Read the Bible Today: Psalms 119:89–144

Prayer Points:

1. I thank God for today.
2. My nakedness shall not be exposed to the world, in the name of Jesus.
3. Almighty God make me a prayer addict, in the name of Jesus.
4. Almighty God, ignite my prayer life with your fire, in the name of Jesus.
5. Almighty God, empower my prayer altar, in the name of Jesus.
6. I reject every spiritual contamination, in the name of Jesus.
7. Almighty God give me power to overcome all obstacles to my breakthroughs, in the name of Jesus.
8. Almighty God let my life attract special favor today, in the name of Jesus.
9. Declare Jesus Christ is Lord.
10. Almighty God; let the heaven open upon me now in the name of Jesus.
11. Almighty God; arise and be God over every issue in my life in the name of Jesus.
12. I remove my name from the register of untimely death by the blood of Jesus Christ in the name of Jesus.
13. Almighty God; revive my spirit, soul and body in the name of Jesus.
14. Holy Ghost fire possess my spirit, soul and body in the name of Jesus.
15. I refuse to operate under any satanic influence in the name of Jesus.

16. Almighty God dry every troubled water in my family in the name of Jesus.
17. Every power that wants to deny me of my destiny; be destroyed by fire in the name of Jesus.
18. Power of redemption locate me in the name of Jesus.
19. I cancel every evil dreams, visions, prophesy and prayers against my life and family in the name of Jesus.
20. Talk to God about your heart desires and your situation.
21. Thank God for answered prayers.

Confession:

"For we wrestle not against flesh and blood, but against principalities, against powers, against the rulers of the darkness of this world, against spiritual wickedness in high places" Ephesians 6:12.

Wisdom for Today:

God answers prayer; but there are evil forces that hinder prayer. It is refusing to give up in prayer that makes you one who is able to overcome. Pray without ceasing. Pray until the angel bringing your blessings receives assistance and delivers your blessings to you Daniel 10.

Read the Bible Today: Psalm 35 and Revelation 1

Prayer Points:

1. I thank God for today.
2. Almighty God, give me divine prescription to solve my problems, in the name of Jesus.
3. I break all curses that caused my blessings to leak away from me, in the name of Jesus.
4. Let all spiritual holes in my life be closed by the blood of Jesus, in the name of Jesus.
5. Almighty God help me to locate the defect in the clay of my life in Jesus name.
6. Almighty God let me be at the right place at the right time in the name of Jesus.
7. Fire of God's deliverance, burn from the crown of my head to the soles of my feet, in the name of Jesus.
8. Anointing of fire, possess my life, in the name of Jesus.
9. Almighty God anoint me to be more than a conqueror according to the word of God, in the name of Jesus.
10. Almighty God, favor me in all areas of life today, in the name of Jesus.
11. Almighty God; connect me to your glory in the name of Jesus.
12. Almighty God; deliver me and my destiny from suffering in the name of Jesus.
13. Almighty God; have mercy upon me; open a new chapter for me in the name of Jesus.

14. Chapter of failure, disappointment, and evil; be closed in the name of Jesus.
15. Chapter of sorrow, depression, stress be shut in the name of Jesus.
16. Almighty God; have mercy upon me restore unto me the good chances I have missed in the name of Jesus.
17. I cancel every evil dreams, visions, prophesy and prayers against my life and family in the name of Jesus.
18. Talk to God about your heart desires and your situation.
19. Thank God for answered prayers.

Confession:

"Not by might, nor by power, but by my Spirit, says the Lord of Hosts" Zechariah 4:6.

Wisdom for Today:

The Holy Spirit is the custodian of God's power. When the earth was void and shapeless, it was the Spirit that reshaped it. Call for his service today, and you will experience a good and dramatic turn around.

Read the Bible Today: John 16

Prayer Points:

1. I thank God for another new month.
2. I disarm every household enemy today, in the name of Jesus.
3. Let my enemies pitch their battles against one another, in the name of Jesus.
4. I frustrate and disappoint every instrument of the enemy fashioned against me this month, in the name of Jesus.
5. I seal my victory with the blood of Jesus.
6. I take the head position in everything I do today, in the name of Jesus.
7. You, my life and destiny, hear the word of the living God; come out of every cage of darkness, in the name of Jesus.
8. Anyone who is close to me and is, at the same time, working against me, be exposed and be disgraced, in the name of Jesus.
9. Almighty God baptize me with your special favor throughout this month, in the name of Jesus.
10. No evil shall befall me throughout this month, in the name of Jesus.
11. Go ahead and thank the Lord.
12. Declare Jesus Christ is Lord.
13. Blood of Jesus Christ touch and sanctify this day for me in the name of Jesus.
14. I cover my spirit soul and body with the blood of Jesus in the name of Jesus.
15. Anything that will hinder my prayer; father forgive me in the name of Jesus.

Apostle A.O. Solomon

16. I declare my day shall be blessed and prosperous for me in the name of Jesus.
17. Almighty God; transform my life for testimonies and for great achievement in life in the name of Jesus.
18. Almighty God; let your blessing be upon everything I lay hands on to do in the name of Jesus.
19. I cancel every evil dreams, visions, prophesy and prayers against my life and family in the name of Jesus.
20. Talk to God about your heart desires and your situation.
21. Thank God for answered prayers.

Confession:

"Remember ye not the former things of things, neither consider the things of old. Behold, I will do a new thing; now it shall spring forth; shall ye not know it? I will even make a way in the wilderness and rivers in the desert" Isaiah 43:18–19.

Wisdom for Today:

Get rid of your ugly past experiences and look ahead; there is a bright future ahead. Until you decide where you would rather be, you will never leave where you are. You can create any future you want.

Read the Bible Today: John 15

Prayer Points:

1. I thank the Lord for today and bless the Lord who always causes me to triumph in Christ Jesus.
2. Almighty God, answer my prayers today by your fire, in the name of Jesus.
3. Any power in the air, in the seas, in the earth, and under this earth that is ready to resist me and my prayers today, be roasted, in the name of Jesus.
4. Let the angels of God arrest the traffic of demons channeled across my community, in the name of Jesus.
5. I forbid the gathering of witches and wizards in my environment, day or night in the name of Jesus.
6. Let the glory of God overshadow me today, in the name of Jesus.
7. Almighty God baptize me with your special favor, in the name of Jesus.
8. Let everything in my environment that is causing limitations in my life be completely destroyed, in the name of Jesus.
9. I command every net or trap set for me today to backfire, in the name of Jesus.
10. You, my star, become unlimited by the blood of Jesus Christ in the name of Jesus.
11. Every plan to disgrace my life; come to naught in the name of Jesus.
12. Almighty God; have mercy upon me; let your counsel for my life stand forever in the name of Jesus.

13. Almighty God; my times are in your hands let the times and season of life favor me as from today in the name of Jesus.
14. Every evil against my life, marriage, blessing; die in the name of Jesus.
15. Every power attacking me in the night the Lord rebuke you, be consumed by fire in the name of Jesus.
16. Every agreement made by evil power against my life, my family; be cancelled by the blood of Jesus in the name of Jesus.
17. Every agreement made by any member of my family with satan, you shall not stand, I command you to scatter in the name of Jesus.
18. Every agreement made by my ancestors with dark powers be cancelled in the name of Jesus.
19. Every water and animal power working against my life; be destroyed by fire in the name of Jesus.
20. Almighty God; let your blessing be upon the works of my life, and my family in the name of Jesus.
21. Almighty God; remove the names of my family members, from the register of untimely death in the name of Jesus.
22. Almighty God; have mercy upon me and family, don't let me weep over my family, don't let my family weep over me in the name of Jesus.
23. Almighty God; I lift up the names of my family members, let the mark of the blood of Jesus be upon this names in the name of Jesus.
24. Almighty God; I lift up this names unto you, deliver us from the eaters of flesh and drinkers of blood in Jesus name.
25. Almighty God let your favor baptize us in the name of Jesus.
26. Every spiritual marriage with water spirit and familiar spirit break by the blood of Jesus in the name of Jesus.
27. Every evil spoken against me before I was born be cancelled in the name of Jesus.
28. I will not bow to evil authorities; I will only surrender to Jesus Christ my savior in the name of Jesus.
29. My enemies must acknowledge the finger of God in the name of Jesus.
30. Let the finger of God begin to do work of healing and deliverance in my life in the name of Jesus.
31. I cancel every evil dreams, visions, prophesy and prayers against my life and family in the name of Jesus.
32. Talk to God about your heart desires and your situation.
33. Thank God for answered prayers.

Confession:

"Brethren, I count not myself to have apprehended: but this one thing I do, forgetting those things whish are behind, and reaching forth unto those things which are before, I press toward the mark for the prize of the high calling of God in Christ Jesus" Philippians 3:13–14.

Wisdom for Today:

I don't know how many times you have failed from January 1 to today, but I do know that God promises restoration for all his children. Cheer up! There are still twenty-nine more days in the year, counting today. The God that created the earth and all its fullness within six days can also change your fortune within a twinkling of an eye. You are entering into the New Year with blessings and testimonies, in Jesus name.

Read the Bible Today: Genesis 1

Prayer Points:

1. I thank God for today.
2. Any evil power of the night warming up to attack me tonight, begin to attack yourself, in the name of Jesus.
3. Anywhere my name has been mentioned for spiritual wickedness today; fire of God answer them, in the name of Jesus.
4. Every instrument of spiritual wickedness due to be launched out against me day or night, backfire, in the name of Jesus.
5. Any evil tongue already sharpened and employed to chant evil into my life today, be condemned and be roasted, in the name of Jesus.
6. I bring the blood of Jesus against any evil power attacking me from my childhood, in the name of Jesus.
7. Let my oil of favor begin to overflow, in the name of Jesus.
8. Every trouble of the night bow to the name of Jesus Christ.
9. Every spirit of distress, I bind and cast you out of my life in the name of Jesus.
10. Every spirit of tragedy I bind and cast you out of my life in the name of Jesus.
11. Stubborn problems in my life be buried in the name of Jesus.
12. Every power wasting my efforts; be buried in the name of Jesus.

13. I shall not labor in vain, every power of vain I command you to die in the name of Jesus.
14. Every evil dream in my life, I cancel you in my life in the name of Jesus.
15. Every gate of delay; lift up your head in the name of Jesus.
16. Every gate of delay; be broken in the name of Jesus.
17. Every gate of failure and everlasting doors of defeat; be destroyed completely in the name of Jesus.
18. I cancel every evil dreams, visions, prophesy and prayers against my life and family in the name of Jesus.
19. Talk to God about your heart desires and your situation.
20. Thank God for answered prayers.

Confession:

"And the Lord answered me, and said, Write the vision, and make it plain upon tables, that he may run that readeth it" Habakkuk 2:2.

Wisdom for Today:

Document your goals. Take the time to write down carefully what you want to accomplish with your life. When you write down your goals, you become more decisive. Be a good planner. Planners can predict their success.

Read the Bible Today: *Genesis 2 and 3*

Prayer Points:

1. I thank God for today.
2. I bless the Lord for his enduring mercies and faithfulness in the name of Jesus.
3. Almighty God just as you killed the firstborn of the Egyptians in the night, kill any power that will not allow me to serve you with peace of mind, in Jesus name.
4. Almighty God, as you parted the Red Sea for the Israelites, part away every power of the night hindering my greatness, in the name of Jesus.
5. Almighty God, as you withdrew sleep from King Ahasuerus until he had discovered that Mordecai was not yet rewarded for his kind acts, let anybody in the position to advance and promote me and refusing have no rest until he has done so, in the name of Jesus.
6. Father Lord, as you slew Belshazzar who defiled your vessel, so slay any power defiling my body day or night, in the name of Jesus.
7. God's vision for my life and destiny shall not be aborted, in the name of Jesus.
8. I enlist myself in the register of God's favor today, in the name of Jesus.
9. Every power planning my downfall and demotion, be frustrated and be disgraced, in the name of Jesus.
10. The word of God shall have root in my life, in the name of Jesus.
11. My destiny shall not be manipulated or caged, in the name of Jesus.
12. Every gate of impossibility and everlasting door of no way; working against my life be destroyed in the name of Jesus.

13. Every astral projection against my life; I cut you off in the name of Jesus.
14. Thunder of God locate and destroy every spiritual pot assigned against my life in the name of Jesus.
15. Almighty God Let this day; bless me and favor me in the name of Jesus.
16. Angels of the Living God arise and scatter all those plotting against my destiny in the name of Jesus.
17. Every dry bone in my life; come alive in Jesus mighty name.
18. Almighty God; you are the Lord that healeth me; take away my infirmity in the name of Jesus.
19. Almighty God; remove every evil mark from my life in the name of Jesus.
20. Almighty God; lift up my head above my enemies in the name of Jesus.
21. Almighty God; accept my offering in the name of Jesus.
22. I cancel every evil dreams, visions, prophesy and prayers against my life and family in the name of Jesus.
23. Talk to God about your heart desires and your situation.
24. Thank God for answered prayers.

Confession:

"Be still, and know that I am God: I will be exalted among the heathen, I will be exalted in the earth" Psalms 46:10.

Wisdom for Today:

Certainly, the eye of faith sees much evidence of the supernatural display of God's power and glory. God is still in business. When you are tempted by Satan, always remember that God's angels are around you.

Read the Bible Today: Judges 6 and Psalm 34

Prayer Points:

1. I thank God for today.
2. I refuse to allow the enemy to destabilize me, in the name of Jesus.
3. Jehovah God is with me as a mighty and terrible one, I will not be afraid of what man can do to me, in Jesus name.
4. Accident and tragedy shall not be my portion as the year runs to an end, in the name of Jesus.
5. Let the blood of Jesus cancel every evil dream affecting my life, in Jesus name.
6. Let the fire of God stand against every power standing against my blessings and progress, in the name of Jesus.
7. I shall receive all-round favor today, in the name of Jesus.
8. Declare Jesus Christ is Lord.
9. Holy Spirit of God help me today in the name of Jesus.
10. I decree as from today, my background shall no longer be a barrier to my prosperity in life in the name of Jesus.
11. Almighty God; bring health and healing to my life in the name of Jesus.
12. Almighty God; reveal unto me abundance of favor peace, wealth, and every good thing in the name of Jesus.
13. Almighty God; it is written there is nothing too hard for you, arise and solve every problem in my life in the name of Jesus.
14. Almighty God; fill my life with your love in the name of Jesus.
15. Bread of heaven feed me till I want no more in the name of Jesus.
16. Almighty God; let the blessing of this day be my portion in the name of Jesus.

17. I cancel every evil dreams, visions, prophesy and prayers against my life and family in the name of Jesus.
18. Talk to God about your heart desires and your situation.
19. Thank God for answered prayers.

December 6

Confession:

"In hope of eternal life, which God, that cannot lie, promised before the world began" Titus 1:2.

Wisdom for Today:

Life is a glorious opportunity, if it is used to condition us for eternity. If we fail in this, though, we succeed in everything else, and our life will be a failure. There is no escape for the man who squanders his opportunity to prepare to meet God.

Read the Bible Today: Revelation 21

Prayer Points:

1. I thank God for a new day.
2. Let the name of the Lord God of Jacob defend me today, in the name of Jesus.
3. Holy Spirit, lead me in the way that I should go today, in the name of Jesus.
4. I refuse to live a wasted life, in the name of Jesus.
5. Holy Spirit, order my steps today, in the name of Jesus.
6. Let the glory and presence of God overshadow me throughout today, in the name of Jesus.
7. I shall not be a victim of any evil decisions, in the name of Jesus.
8. I command every failure I have experienced so far this year to depart from me now, in the name of Jesus.
9. I receive favor to triumph over hatred and rejection today, in the name of Jesus.
10. I cast down every evil imagination against me today, in the name of Jesus.
11. Almighty God destroy every power of delay in my life in the name of Jesus.
12. I reject every evil dream and their manifestation in the name of Jesus.
13. Any power that will want to attack me in the dream let fire fall and consume them in the name of Jesus.
14. Declare Jesus Christ is Lord.
15. Holy Spirit of God help me tonight in the name of Jesus.
16. I decree as from tonight, my background shall no longer be a barrier to my prosperity in life in the name of Jesus.

United States Postal Service®

Sorry We Missed You! We ReDeliver for You

Today's Date

Sender's Name

For Redelivery
Go to *usps.com/redelivery*
or see reverse

Item is at:
— Post Office™ (See back)

Available for Pick-up After

Date:

Time:

☐ If checked, you or your agent must be present at time of delivery to sign for item.

USPS Tracking # or Article Number(s)

— Letter

For Delivery: (Enter total number of items delivered by service type.)

— Large envelope, magazine, catalog, etc.

For Notice Left: (Check applicable item)
— Priority Mail Express™
— Insured Mail

— Parcel
— Certified Mail™ (Must claim within 15 days or article will be returned)
— Return Receipt for Merchandise

— Perishable Item
— Restricted Delivery
— Adult Signature

— Other:
— Registered Mail™
— Signature Confirmation™

Notice Left Section
Customer Name and Address

Article Requiring Payment
☐ Postage Due ☐ COD ☐ Customs

Amount Due
$

☐ **Final Notice:** Article will be returned to sender on

Delivered By and Date

usps.com

PS Form **3849**, July 2013

Delivery Notice/Reminder/Receipt

We will redeliver OR you or your agent can pick up your mail at the Post Office. *(Bring this form and proper ID.)*
If your agent will pick up, sign below in item 2, and enter agent's name here):

1.
     a. Check all that apply in section 3;

     ▼ b. Sign in section 2 below;

     c. *Leave this notice where the carrier can see it.*

2. Sign Here to authorize redelivery or to authorize an agent to sign for you:

3. ☐ **Redeliver** *(Enter day of week.)*:

     (Allow at least two delivery days for redelivery, or go to usps.com/redelivery or call 800-275-8777 to arrange redelivery.)

☐ **Leave item at my address**
(not available if you or your agent must be present)

     (Specify where to leave. Example: "porch", "side door". This option is not available if box is checked on the front requiring your signature at time of delivery.)

☐ Refused ☐ Forward ☐ Return

PS Form 3849, July 2013 *(Reverse)*

CUMMING MAIN POST OFFICE - USPS
525 TRIBBLE GAP RD. CUMMING, GA 30040
MON-FRI 8:00AM-6:00 PM SAT8:30 AM-2:00PM
PHONE: 770-886-2388
www.usps.com/redelivery or 800-ASK-USPS (275-8777)

	Delivery Section
Signature	X
Printed Name	Charles Anney
Delivery Address	

USPS

5293 0533 9184 2950

17. Almighty God; bring health and healing to my life in the name of Jesus.
18. Almighty God; reveal unto me abundance of favor peace, wealth, and every good thing in the name of Jesus.
19. Almighty God; it is written there is nothing too hard for you, arise and solve every problem in my life in the name of Jesus.
20. Almighty God; fill my life with your love in the name of Jesus.
21. Bread of heaven feed me till I want no more in the name of Jesus.
22. Almighty God; let the blessing of this day be my portion in the name of Jesus.
23. I cancel every evil dreams, visions, prophesy and prayers against my life and family in the name of Jesus.
24. Talk to God about your heart desires and your situation.
25. Thank God for answered prayers.

Confession:

"He is the image of the invisible God" Colossians 1:15.

Wisdom for Today:

Christ came to give us a visible expression of a God who is invisible. Jesus said, "He who has seen me has seen the Father" John 14:9. That is why no one with access to a Bible can claim ignorance of what God is like. As a believer, are you like Jesus in words, deeds, prayer, and in good works?

Read the Bible Today: *Genesis 3 and Colossians 1*

Prayer Points:

1. I thank God for today.
2. Almighty God baptize me with the spirit of Jesus Christ in the name of Jesus.
3. My life shall not be a disgrace to Jesus, in the name of Jesus.
4. I scatter all evil forces shedding blood on my behalf, in the name of Jesus.
5. I plead the blood of Jesus against every evil that remains in this year, in the name of Jesus.
6. I raise the blood of Jesus against any evil voice that may want to speak against me today, in the name of Jesus.
7. Almighty God baptize me with your special favor, in the name of Jesus.
8. Almighty God let my name attract divine favor today, in the name of Jesus.
9. I choose to follow the will and purpose of God for my life, in the name of Jesus.
10. I receive the power to fulfill my purpose in life, in the name of Jesus.
11. Almighty God increase my zeal and commitment to the things of heaven, in Jesus name.
12. I reject every evil dream and their manifestation in the name of Jesus.
13. Give God the praise.
14. I reject every evil dream and their manifestation in the name of Jesus.

15. Every problem mocking God in my life, I command you to die in the name of Jesus.
16. I cancel every evil dreams, visions, prophesy and prayers against my life and family in the name of Jesus.
17. Talk to God about your heart desires and your situation.
18. Thank God for answered prayers.

Confession:

"For by him all things were created: things in heaven and on earth, visible and invisible, whether thrones or powers or rulers or authorities; all things were created by him and for him. He is before all things" Colossians 1:16–17.

Wisdom for Today:

When you know that everything was created by Jesus and for him, you'll live your life by him and for him alone. You will obey his commandments. You'll give when he says give, come when he says come, go and preach the gospel as he commanded us all, and pay your tithes to store up treasures for yourself in heaven.

Read the Bible Today: John 15 and Matthew 28

Prayer Points:

1. I thank God for today.
2. Lord Jesus, help me to always acknowledge that I live through, by, and for you in everything I do in the name of Jesus.
3. My life shall not follow any evil pattern followed by any member of my family, in the name of Jesus.
4. I reject the failures of my father in every area of my life, in the name of Jesus.
5. I reject the failures of my mother in every area of my life, in the name of Jesus.
6. I cancel all evil dreams and their effects upon my life with the blood of Jesus, in Jesus name.
7. Almighty God let me swim in the pool of your favor throughout today, in Jesus name.
8. Every power and spirit mocking God in my life die in the name of Jesus.
9. Every power challenging God in my life let God arise and scatter them in the name of Jesus.
10. Almighty God; anoint my head with your fresh oil in the name of Jesus.
11. Every arrow of death fired against me and my family go back to your sender in the name of Jesus.
12. Every power advertising coffin in my dream, die in the name of Jesus.

Apostle A.O. Solomon

13. Every coffin prepared for me and my family, roast in the name of Jesus.
14. Almighty God; I commit myself and family into your hands lead us away from every evil and trouble in the name of Jesus.
15. My spirit, soul and body reject bewitchment in the name of Jesus.
16. You my destiny receive the power of God and manifest in the name of Jesus.
17. Almighty God; lay your hands upon me and move me from glory to glory in the name of Jesus.
18. Blood of Jesus redeem me and my family from death in the name of Jesus.
19. I drink the blood of Jesus Christ and obtain health in the name of Jesus.
20. Every power and spirit that has marked me for death; die in the name of Jesus.
21. Almighty God; don't let my family weep over me in the name of Jesus.
22. Almighty God; make way for me in the name of Jesus.
23. Every red sea lose your power and give way in the name of Jesus.
24. Every burial ceremony prepared against me and family scatter by fire in the name of Jesus.
25. I cancel every evil dreams, visions, prophesy and prayers against my life and family in the name of Jesus.
26. Talk to God about your heart desires and your situation.
27. Thank God for answered prayers.

Confession:

"In him all things hold together" Colossians 1:17.

Wisdom for Today:

Consider an egg. It is comprised of the shell, the yoke, and the embryo. Jesus held them together. Have you ever seen the pillars that have held the heavens up above us for so long a time? When they were about to fall upon us, Jesus held them together. Are segments of your life fragmented against each other? Jesus can still hold them together. Just tell him to handle it for you.

Read the Bible Today: *Ezekiel 37 and Matthew 11*

Prayer Points:

1. I thank God for today.
2. Almighty God, rearrange my life for testimonies in the name of Jesus.
3. Almighty God, rearrange my life, my marriage, and family to glorify your name in the name of Jesus.
4. Every power attacking the tree of my prosperity and success, fall down and die, in the name of Jesus.
5. Almighty God, by your power, let my Lazarus come back to life, in the name of Jesus.
6. Almighty God from now on, let people see your glory in my life, my marriage, and family, in the name of Jesus.
7. Almighty God lay your hand of favor upon me today, in the name of Jesus.
8. Thank God for the privilege of being alive in the name of Jesus.
1. Hallelujah …
2. Declare Jesus Christ is Lord.
3. Almighty God; Baptize my life with unusual favor in the name of Jesus.
4. Almighty God bless me with your presence in the name of Jesus.
5. Almighty God; as the waters cover the sea; let your glory cover my life in the name of Jesus.
6. Every problem mocking God in my life, your time is up; die in the name of Jesus.
7. Every power and spirit mocking God in my life die in the name of Jesus.

Apostle A.O. Solomon

8. Every power challenging God in my life; almighty God arise and scatter them in the name of Jesus.

9. Almighty God; anoint my head with your fresh oil today in the name of Jesus.

10. Every arrow of death fired against me and my family; Go back to your sender in the name of Jesus.

11. Every power advertising coffin in my dream; die in the name of Jesus.

12. Every coffin prepared for me and my family; roast in the name of Jesus.

13. Almighty God; I commit myself and family in to your hands lead us away from trouble in the name of Jesus.

14. My spirit, soul, and body reject bewitchment in the name of Jesus.

15. You my destiny receive the power of God and manifest in the name of Jesus.

16. Almighty God; lay your hands upon me; take me from where I am to glory in the name of Jesus.

17. Blood of Jesus Christ redeem me and my family from death in the name of Jesus.

18. I drink the blood of Jesus Christ and I obtain victory over sickness, death, and infirmity in the name of Jesus.

19. Every power, spirit, man or woman that has marked me for death; die in the name of Jesus.

20. I cancel every appointment with death by the blood of Jesus in the name of Jesus.

21. Almighty God; don't let me weep over any member of my family; don't let my family weep over me in the name of Jesus.

22. Almighty God; bless me in this land; don't let me suffer in the name of Jesus.

23. Every red sea before me lose your power and give way for me in the name of Jesus.

24. Every burial ceremony organized for me and my family; scatter unto desolation in the name of Jesus.

25. I cover myself and family with the blood of Jesus Christ in the name of Jesus.

26. I cancel every evil dreams, visions, prophesy and prayers against my life and family in the name of Jesus.

27. Talk to God about your heart desires and your situation.

28. Thank God for answered prayers.

Confession:

"For God was pleased...through him to reconcile to himself all things, whether things on earth or things in heaven, making peace through his blood, shed on the cross" Colossians 1:19–20.

Wisdom for Today:

Do you appreciate who Jesus is and what he has done for you? I'm not asking if you have accepted Christ as your Savior. I hope that you have, and that if you haven't, you will. What I'm wondering about is the depth of your affection for Jesus himself, as your Friend, Brother, Savior, God, and Lord. Take some time now to treasure this Jesus.

Read the Bible Today: *Isaiah 53 and John 14*

Prayer Points:

1. I thank God for today.
2. I thank God for reconciling me to himself through the blood Jesus that was shed on the cross.
3. The devil shall not harvest my soul in hell, in the name of Jesus.
4. Every coffin prepared for me and my family be destroyed by fire, in the name of Jesus.
5. I cancel every evil program against me today by the blood of Jesus, in Jesus name.
6. Today I shall be lifted above all my colleagues, in the name of Jesus.
7. Almighty God let your favor answer to me today, in the name of Jesus.
8. Every red sea before me lose your power and give way for me in the name of Jesus.
9. Every burial ceremony organized for me and my family; scatter unto desolation in the name of Jesus.
10. I cover myself and family with the blood of Jesus Christ in the name of Jesus.
11. Declare Jesus Christ is Lord.
12. Every problem that came into my life while I was in my mother's womb; die in the name of Jesus.
13. Every problem that came into my life through any inheritance, your time is up die in the name of Jesus.

14. Every problem that came into my life through the blood of my parents; die in the name of Jesus.
15. Every problem that came into my life through anything I have swallowed physically or spiritually I command you to die in the name of Jesus.
16. Every problem that came into my life through dream; die in the name of Jesus.
17. Every problem that came into my life through any friend; die in the name of Jesus.
18. Every problem that came into my life through the house that am living or that I lived in the past; die in the name of Jesus.
19. Every evil spirit operating in this house, I bind and cast you out in the name of Jesus.
20. The spirit of the former landlord fighting against me; die in the name of Jesus.
21. Every problem that came into my life through ex –husband, ex-wife, boyfriend and girlfriend; die in the name of Jesus.
22. Foundational problems of my wife's family that is affecting my life; die in the name of Jesus.
23. Every problem that came into my life through my actions on others; father comfort them and take the problem away in the name of Jesus.
24. Every problem that came into my life through bad habits; die in the name of Jesus.
25. I cancel every evil dreams, visions, prophesy and prayers against my life and family in the name of Jesus.
26. Talk to God about your heart desires and your situation.
27. Thank God for answered prayers.

Confession:

"Will a man rob God? Yet you have robbed me. But you say, wherein have we robbed you? In tithes and offerings. Bring you all the tithes into the storehouse, that there may be meat in my house, and prove me now herewith, said the Lord of hosts, if I will not open you the windows of heaven, and pour you out a blessing, that there shall not be room enough to receive it" Malachi 3; 8–10, AKJV.

Wisdom for Today:

Although all our money actually belongs to God, the Bible suggests that we tithe as a minimum response in gratitude to God. You cannot get around it; the Bible promises material and spiritual blessing to the person who gives to God. You cannot out give God. I challenge you to try it and see.

Read the Bible Today: Luke 6

Prayer Points:

1. I thank God for today.
2. Almighty God help me to always be faithful to you in tithes and in offerings, in Jesus name.
3. Every devourer of my finances, fall down and die, in the name of Jesus.
4. Almighty God, bless all my efforts today, in the name of Jesus.
5. Almighty God let all those who will move my life forward locate me, in the name of Jesus.
6. Almighty God baptize me with your favor today, in the name of Jesus.
7. Every problem that came into my life through my naming ceremony; die in the name of Jesus.
8. Every problem that came into my life through the first person that carried me when I came into this world; die in the name of Jesus.
9. Every problem that came into my life through any burial ceremony; die in the name of Jesus.
10. Every problem that came into my life through anything I have stepped upon I command you to die in the name of Jesus.
11. Every problem that came into my life through any relationship and marriage; die in the name of Jesus.

12. Every problem that came into my life through known and unknown sources; Father destroy them in the name of Jesus.
13. Almighty God; have mercy upon me; deliver me from problems in the name of Jesus.
14. Every problem that came into my life through dreams, covenants, and curses die in the name of Jesus.
15. Every problem that came into my life through any relationship with any agent of darkness die in the name of Jesus.
16. Blood of Jesus Christ redeem my spirit, soul, and body from satanic control in the name of Jesus.
17. Almighty God; fill me with your fresh anointing in the name of Jesus.
18. I cancel every evil dreams, visions, prophesy and prayers against my life and family in the name of Jesus.
19. Talk to God about your heart desires and your situation.
20. Thank God for answered prayers.

Confession:

"For you did not receive a spirit that makes you a slave again to fear, but you receive the Spirit of sonship. And by him we cry, Abba Father.' The Spirit himself testifies with our spirit that we are God's children" Romans 8:15–16, NIV.

Wisdom for Today:

The Lord is mindful of us. He has promised his presence, provision, and protection for us. Get addicted to his love and all your fears will vanish.

Read the Bible Today: *John 17 and Revelation 2*

Prayer Points:

1. I thank God for today.
2. I command the evil works of the enemies in my life to be completely neutralized through the night by the blood of Jesus Chris in the name of Jesus.

3. I announce that greater is the one that is in me than any devil on the side of my enemies. It is written; "The righteous is as bold as a lion. By my faith in Christ Jesus, I am righteous. I receive my divine boldness. The angels of the Lord encamped round about them that fear Him. The angels of God are with me, I have no basis to fear any man, any evil, and any evil spirit. Because the Lord of hosts *is with me, I take my confidence in Him. It is written; 'If God be for us who can be against us?' God is with me, I have no reason to be afraid, in the name of Jesus. It is written, The Lord is my light and my salvation whom shall I fear? The Lord is the defense of my life of whom shall I be afraid? Though a host of demons encamp against me, my heart will not fear; though war rises against me, even in this I shall be confident. The Lord is with me like a mighty terrible one. I am not afraid. I cannot be threatened. My persecutors shall stumble and fumble. Their everlasting confusion and disgrace shall never be forgotten. God has commanded me to fear not. Of the 366 days in a year, no single day is allowed for me to fear. So, I refuse to be afraid of anything. You spirit of fear, you are not in God's agenda for me. I dismiss you from my life now, in the name of Jesus. Jesus said even the very hairs of my head are not only counted but numbered. Not one single strand can be removed without God's knowledge and permission. Therefore, I put my confidence in the Lord, Who takes so such care of me.*

4. Almighty God anoint me with your special favor, and let my life attract your blessings today, in the name of Jesus.

5. Thank God for good health.

6. Declare Jesus Christ is Lord.

7. Holy Spirit; empower my prayer life in the name of Jesus.

8. The root of every problem in my life, receive the blood of Jesus and die in the name of Jesus.

9. I declare all good things are possible for me by the blood of Jesus in the name of Jesus.

10. I refuse to be a victim of the arrows that flies by noon day in the name of Jesus.

11. Every umbilical cord bondage in my life break in the name of Jesus.

12. Every spiritual umbilical cord, I command you to break and leave me now in the name of Jesus.

13. Almighty God; don't let my good times and season turn to bad in the name of Jesus.

14. Almighty God; turn around my bad times and season in the name of Jesus.

15. I cancel every evil dreams, visions, prophesy and prayers against my life and family in the name of Jesus.
16. Talk to God about your heart desires and your situation.
17. Thank God for answered prayers.

Confession:

"He ... canceled the written code, with its regulation, that was against us and that stood opposed to us; he took it away, nailing it to the cross" Colossians 2:13–14.

Wisdom for Today:

The cross does not mean that Jesus died for us, but that we died with him. It means we died to all that Jesus Christ died for. The cross means you died to all that was necessary for Christ to die for. Why go on in bondage to it? You don't have to be. You're free! No more evil codes, from henceforth let no man trouble me: for I bear in my body the marks of the Lord Jesus. (Galatians 6:17). It is only the cross that liberates.

Read the Bible Today: 1 Peter 2

Prayer Points:

1. I bless the Lord because he has always been with me as a mighty terrible one.
2. Almighty God answer me by your fire today, in the name of Jesus.
3. Almighty God, send your fire of deliverance into my body now, in the name of Jesus.
4. I vomit every deposit of the powers of the night inside me, in the name of Jesus.
5. Every arrow ever fired into my head in the night, come out by fire in the name of Jesus.
6. Every bewitchment fashioned against my head by the powers of the night, release your hold by fire in the name of Jesus.
7. Almighty God anoint me for special favor today, in the name of Jesus.
8. Declare Jesus Christ is Lord.
9. Almighty God; have mercy upon me don't let my good time and season turn to bad in the name of Jesus.
10. As from today let times and season of life favor me in the name of Jesus.
11. Almighty God; I come before you magnify Jesus in my life in the name of Jesus.

12. Almighty God; let it please you to bless my life in the name of Jesus.
13. Every law of death over my life and the lives of my family; break in the name of Jesus.
14. Almighty God; I lift up all the names of my family members remove them from the register of untimely death in the name of Jesus.
15. I soak all these names in the blood of Jesus Christ in the name of Jesus.
16. Every coffin prepared for us; be destroyed in Jesus mighty name.
17. Almighty God; save me and my family from accident and tragedy in the name of Jesus.
18. Almighty God; let your mighty hand be revealed in my life in the name of Jesus.
19. I overcome the devil through the blood of Jesus Christ in the name of Jesus.
20. I overcome death through the blood of Jesus Christ in the name of Jesus.
21. I cancel every evil dreams, visions, prophesy and prayers against my life and family in the name of Jesus.
22. Talk to God about your heart desires and your situation.
23. Thank God for answered prayers.

Confession:

"Blessed is the man whom the Lord chastens. God's blessing is upon me and all that I do, in the name of Jesus" Psalms 94:12.

Wisdom for Today:

God sometimes allows Christians to suffer in order that they might learn the secret of obedience. David said in Psalms 119:67, "Before I was afflicted, I went astray; but now have I kept thy Words." It was after a great sorrow and much affliction that David learned obedience to God. Not all problems are from the enemy or the devil. In your time of troubles, ask God to open your understanding to what he wants you to learn and know. You will never remain the same.

Read the Bible Today: Matthew 24

Prayer Points:

1. I thank God for another day.
2. Any curse ever fired as an arrow into my head by the powers of darkness, come out and go back to your shooters, in the name of Jesus.
3. Every witchcraft bondage programmed into my life while I was asleep, come out by fire, in the name of Jesus.
4. Every evil affliction placed upon me while I was asleep, be removed by fire now, in the name of Jesus.
5. Almighty God open my eyes of understanding today, in the name of Jesus.
6. I cancel every evil dream and its effect by the blood of Jesus in the name of Jesus.
7. Almighty God draw me to your special favor today, in the name of Jesus.
8. I overcome death through the blood of Jesus Christ in the name of Jesus.
9. I overcome sickness in my life through the blood of Jesus Christ in the name of Jesus.
10. I overcome pain and discomfort through the blood of Jesus in the mighty name of Jesus.
11. I overcome failure, bareness, poverty, affliction through the blood of Jesus in the name of Jesus.

12. I put the mark of the blood of Jesus Christ upon the names of my family members in the name of Jesus.

13. I receive the blessings of God by the blood of Jesus Christ in the name of Jesus.

14. I receive deliverance through the blood of Jesus Christ in the name of Jesus.

15. I receive abundance and prosperity through the blood of Jesus Christ in the name of Jesus.

16. I receive the fullness of the Holy Spirit through the blood of Jesus in the name of Jesus.

17. In this land I receive prosperity and fruitfulness by the blood of Jesus in the name of Jesus.

18. Let the way make way for me in the name of Jesus.

19. Every good thing that belongs to me; locate me in the name of Jesus.

20. I cancel every evil dreams, visions, prophesy and prayers against my life and family in the name of Jesus.

21. Talk to God about your heart desires and your situation.

22. Thank God for answered prayers.

Confession:

I am made in the image of Jehovah God, I am curiously made, I am fearfully and wonderfully made, I am the crown of God's creation, I am created a dominion child of God, I am an express image of Elohim, his workmanship in Christ Jesus for good works. Psalm 139:14

Wisdom for Today:

God purpose for Christ's crucifixion was to draw men unto himself. As his workmanship in Christ Jesus was created for good works, will you join him in winning souls today? Try and tell someone about Jesus today, or invite someone to church.

Read the Bible Today: Matthew 28 and Acts 1

Prayer Points:

1. I thank God for today.
2. Let the spirit of evangelism fall upon me, in the name of Jesus.
3. Let the anointing to prosper fall upon me now, in the name of Jesus.
4. Let all antiprogressive altars fashioned against me be destroyed with the fire of God, in the name of Jesus.
5. I use the blood of Jesus to cancel and reverse every evil dream in my life, in the name of Jesus.
6. I command my destiny to change for the better, in the name of Jesus.
7. Almighty God favor me in every area of life today, in the name of Jesus.
8. I destroy the agenda of the wasters over me and my family, in the name of Jesus.
9. Every mountain programmed into any month of the year be removed and be cast into the sea in the name of Jesus.
10. Almighty God; let every second, week, and month of the year bless and favor me in the name of Jesus.
11. You month vomit my blessing in you in the name of Jesus.
12. Almighty God; arise and perfect all that concerns me in the name of Jesus.
13. Give thanks to the Lord.

14. Declare Jesus Christ is Lord.
15. Holy Spirit; empower me today in the name of Jesus.
16. Power to struggle no more; fall upon me in the name of Jesus.
17. Holy Spirit; anoint me with wisdom, knowledge and understanding in the name of Jesus.
18. I release the blood of Jesus into this land, begin to favor me, yield your increase unto me in the name of Jesus.
19. Almighty God stretch forth your right hand and fight for me in the name of Jesus.
20. I cancel every evil dreams, visions, prophesy and prayers against my life and family in the name of Jesus.
21. Talk to God about your heart desires and your situation.

Thank God for answered prayers.

Apostle A.O. Solomon

Confession:

Oh, Lord my God, how excellent is your name in all the earth. When I consider your heavens, the works of your fingers, the moon, the stars, which you have ordained, what is in me that you are mindful of me, then I remember that I am no longer the former miserable sinner, but Christ has come and died for me to restore all things, that once again and forever I should exercise dominion over every work of your hand.

Wisdom for Today:

Remember, you are not better than others; you are only privileged. Never despise a person or look down on anyone lest God sees it and lifts that person above you. Also, refuse to believe the lies the devil is telling you, but rather choose to believe the opposite of what you're afraid of.

Read the Bible Today: *Genesis 12 and 1 John 1*

Prayer Points:

1. I thank God for today.
2. I pray for [say the name of someone you know who is in need].
3. All boasting evil powers delegated against me, be silenced, in the name of Jesus.
4. I withdraw my benefits from the hands of the oppressors today, in the name of Jesus.
5. Almighty God enlarge my horizons and comfort me on every side, in the name of Jesus.
6. I shall not fall into the pits the enemy dug for me, in the name of Jesus.
7. Almighty God favor my going out and coming in today, in the name of Jesus.
8. Almighty God; lay your hand upon me for good in the name of Jesus.
9. Today my enemies shall acknowledge the finger of God in the name of Jesus.
10. The root of problems in my life receive the blood of Jesus and die in the name of Jesus.
11. The root of sickness; receive the blood of Jesus and die in the name of Jesus.

12. Root of affliction in my life; receive the blood of Jesus and die in the name of Jesus.
13. Every power of oppressors in my life; I terminate you by fire in the name of Jesus.
14. Every attack against my children; backfire in the name of Jesus.
15. Almighty God; lead our children in the way that they should go in the name of Jesus.
16. Almighty God; don't let me see trouble in my career, job and life in the name of Jesus.
17. Almighty God; arise where I have received promises let my miracles manifest today in the name of Jesus.
18. Almighty God; where I have been forgotten for good, open the book of remembrance for me in the name of Jesus.
19. I cancel every evil dreams, visions, prophesy and prayers against my life and the life of my family in the name of Jesus.
20. Talk to God about your heart desires and your situation.
21. Thank God for answered prayers.

Confession:

For thus says the Lord who created me and formed me and called me by my name, that I should not fear! Since I am precious in his sight I have been honored, therefore, will he give men for me, and people for my life.

Wisdom for Today:

You are special in the sight of God; you are a child of destiny. You are seated with Christ in the heavenly places. Believe in God and in your ability today; say this to yourself, "I can make it; I will succeed today, in Jesus name." Look at the challenges in front of you with the eyes of faith; look at them as stepping-stones to your promotion and progress.

Read the Bible Today: Numbers 23 and Exodus 14

Prayer Points:

22. I thank God for today.
23. Let all unprofitable marks in my life be erased by the blood of Jesus, in Jesus name.
24. Let every power and personality chasing blessings away from me be paralyzed, in the name of Jesus.
25. Let the enemies vomit every good thing they have eaten up in my life, in the name of Jesus.
26. Almighty God give me power to overcome every obstacle in the way of my breakthroughs, in the name of Jesus.
27. I break all curses that inhibit my blessings, in the name of Jesus.
28. Almighty God convert all my defeats to victories today, in the name of Jesus.
29. Almighty God baptize me with your favor today, in the name of Jesus.
30. By the power of the living God; I pull down every stronghold of untimely death in the name of Jesus.
31. Almighty God; I lift up my family deliver us from tragedy in the name of Jesus.
32. I shall not be wasted; any power that wants to waste my life, be wasted in the name of Jesus.
33. Every chain of family bondage; break asunder in the name of Jesus.

34. Evil family pattern; break asunder in the name of Jesus.
35. Almighty God bless and prosper my family in the name of Jesus.
36. Every reoccurrence of evil in my life be terminated by the blood of Jesus in the name of Jesus.
37. I receive my marital breakthrough in the name of Jesus.
38. Almighty God; remember all my offerings, good works and sacrifices in the name of Jesus.
39. I cancel every evil dreams, visions, prophesy and prayers against my life and family in the name of Jesus.
40. Talk to God about your heart desires and your situation.
41. Thank God for answered prayers.

Confession:

Whosoever shall gather together against me that is not of Lord shall be scattered unto desolation and they that are incensed against me shall fall for my sake. The Lord will fight against them that fight against me, he will curse them that curse me, and those that oppress me will he feed with their own flesh and make them drunken with their own blood as with sweet wine.

Wisdom for Today:

You have an ego—a consciousness of being an individual. Of course, you do. But that doesn't mean that you are to worship yourself, to think constantly of yourself, and to live entirely for yourself. Common sense tells you that your life would be miserable if you followed that course. God is infinitely more concerned about your happiness than you could possibly be, he says, Deny yourself, carry your cross, and follow me.

Read the Bible Today: Esther 4 and 5

Prayer Points:

1. I thank God for yet another day.
2. Let everything organized to hinder or limit my blessings today be dismantled by the fire of God, in the name of Jesus.
3. I bind every strongman who tries to cheat me out of my blessings, in the name of Jesus.
4. I clear my goods from the warehouse of the strongman, in the name of Jesus.
5. Let every satanic kingdom working against me fail woefully, in the name of Jesus.
6. Let all hidden arrows that bring trouble to my life be chased out of their hiding places, in the name of Jesus.
7. I frustrate and disappoint every instrument of the enemy fashioned against me today, in the name of Jesus.
8. Almighty God let your favor answer to me throughout this day, in the name of Jesus.
9. Declare Jesus Christ is Lord.
10. Almighty God; Have your way in my life In the name of Jesus.
11. You spirit of toiling; be cut off from my life in the name of Jesus.
12. Kingdom of flesh in my life; be overthrown in the name of Jesus.

13. I overthrow the kingdom of witchcraft in my life by the power of the Holy Ghost in the name of Jesus.
14. I overthrow the kingdom of failure in my life in the name of Jesus.
15. I overthrow the kingdom of debt in my life in the name of Jesus.
16. I overthrow the kingdom of disobedience and stubbornness by the power of the Holy Ghost in the name of Jesus.
17. I overthrow the kingdom of sickness and infirmity in the name of Jesus.
18. I overthrow every evil kingdom in my life in the name of Jesus.
19. Almighty God; let your kingdom come and be established in my life in the name of Jesus.
20. I cancel every evil dreams, visions, prophesy and prayers against my life and family in the name of Jesus.
21. Talk to God about your heart desires and your situation.
22. Thank God for answered prayers.

Confession:

The desire and purpose of God for me is that the sun shall not smite me by day nor the moon by night; therefore, any power projecting into the sun and moon to program evil against me, I decree double destruction upon you. Any power that has turned my time of rest into a time of restlessness and warfare, receive the undiluted wrath of God.

Wisdom for Today:

There are higher levels of living that we have never attained. There is peace, satisfaction, and joy that we have never experienced. God is trying to break through to us. The heavens are calling. God is speaking! Let man hear.

Read the Bible Today: Hebrews 1 and 12

Prayer Points:

1. I thank God for today.
2. Any power removing my ladder of success, fall down and die, in the name of Jesus.
3. Every personal Jericho hindering my progress in life be pulled down by the power of God today, in the name of Jesus.
4. Anything in me that is making people hate me in my place of work, come out now by fire, in the name of Jesus.
5. Every seed and tree of problems in my family be destroyed to the root by God's fire, in the name of Jesus.
6. Almighty God let life be easy for me from now on, in the name of Jesus.
7. Almighty God lay your healing power upon me today, in the name of Jesus.
8. Almighty God, baptize me with your special favor, in the name of Jesus.
9. Almighty God; don't let my children give me sorrow in the name of Jesus.
10. Every pit prepared for me and my family; I cover you with the blood of Jesus in the name of Jesus.
11. Almighty God; have mercy upon me don't allow the enemy to rule my life in the name of Jesus.

12. Every appointment with the kingdom of darkness; be terminated in the name of Jesus.

13. By the power of the Holy Ghost I take over this day in the name of Jesus.

14. I reject every evil in this day in the name of Jesus.

15. I claim every good thing that belongs to me; locate me in the name of Jesus.

16. Almighty God; remove any man or woman that will not favor me out of my way in the name of Jesus.

17. Every curse of limitation and stagnation in my life, break in the name of Jesus.

18. I cancel every satanic mark upon my life in the name of Jesus.

19. Every power delaying the manifestation of my blessing, testimony, joy, and glory; roast by fire in the name of Jesus.

20. I command deliverance upon my certificate in the name of Jesus.

21. Anointing of prosperity fall upon my hands in the name of Jesus.

22. Almighty God; in this country make room for me in the name of Jesus.

23. Almighty God; in your name and your power I enter into your inheritance and posses my possession in the name of Jesus.

24. By the spirit of prophecy I declare as from today, I will begin to see the goodness of God in the land of the living in the name of Jesus.

25. Every terminal problem that is counting years against my success, health, achievement; be terminated in the name of Jesus.

26. Almighty God; lay your hands upon my life and separate me from every evil in the name of Jesus.

27. Every evil running in my family; run out in the name of Jesus.

28. I cancel every evil dreams, visions, prophesy and prayers against my life and family in the name of Jesus.

29. Talk to God about your heart desires and your situation.

30. Thank God for answered prayers.

Confession:

I bring myself afresh under the covenant and cover of the Passover blood of the Lamb of God today, and I will say of the Lord, he is my refuge and my fortress; surely he will deliver me from the snare of the fowler and from the perilous pestilence. He shall cover me with his feathers, and under his wings I shall take my refuge; I shall not be afraid of the terror by night, nor of the arrow that flies by day nor the pestilence that walks in darkness.

Wisdom for Today:

Respect your dreams and goals. What you respect, you will attract. Respect is needed for excitement. Excitement is needed for energy. Energy is needed for completion of your dreams and goals. You have all it takes to fulfill your destiny through Christ. The Bible says, "I can do all things through Christ who strengthens me."

Read the Bible Today: Philippians 3 and Genesis 12

Prayer Points:

1. I thank God for today.
2. Almighty God let my adversaries make mistake that will advance my cause, in the name of Jesus.
3. Let every evil tongue that utters unprofitable things about my life be completely silenced, in the name of Jesus.
4. I command every evil power and vessel sitting on my rights and goodness to be violently overthrown, in the name of Jesus.
5. I pursue and overtake my enemies and recover my properties from their hands, in the name of Jesus.
6. All pronouncements of destruction against my life be nullified, in the name of Jesus.
7. I list myself in the book of God's favor today, in the name of Jesus.
8. Let the power of God shield me from every evil today, in the name of Jesus.
9. Declare Jesus Christ is Lord.
10. Almighty God; visit me in a new way in the name of Jesus.
11. Holy Spirit of God; empower my prayers to bring results in the name of Jesus.

12. Almighty God; redeem me and ransom me from the hands of those stronger than me in the name of Jesus.
13. Almighty God; turn my mourning into joy, comfort me, make me to rejoice instead of sorrow in the name of Jesus.
14. Almighty God; satiate my life with the abundance of your glory, goodness and blessing in the name of Jesus.
15. Almighty God; let me be satisfied with your goodness in the name of Jesus.
16. Almighty God; this month perform the good things you promised me in the name of Jesus.
17. By the ordinances of the heavens; I command the blessing of God upon all these certificates and letters in the name of Jesus.
18. Almighty God; you are the only one who can pour out the bottles of heaven upon all these documents in the name of Jesus.
19. Almighty God; undertake for me against every oppression in my life the name of Jesus.
20. Almighty God; bless me and make me a blessing in the name of Jesus.
21. I cancel every evil dreams, visions, prophesy and prayers against my life and family in the name of Jesus.
22. Talk to God about your heart desires and your situation.
23. Thank God for answered prayers.

Confession:

Because I have made the Lord my refuge and the Most High my dwelling place, no evil shall befall me; neither shall any plague come near my dwelling. He will give his angels charge over me to keep me in all my ways. Therefore, let the angels of God take their position to keep me from all evil today, in Jesus mighty name.

Wisdom for Today:

God does, indeed, want us to live according to his word and commandments. And he does, indeed, want us to pray to him. However, our attitude about ourselves and how we pray is of utmost importance. If we think more of ourselves than other people, then our prayers are empty ones. And eventually, God will see that we are humbled, one way or another. How much better it is when we have the attitude like the tax collector who realized that he was a sinner and needed God's mercy. God's word tells us that, when we have that sort of attitude, then we will be exalted! So, remember, when you think of yourself and others and when you pray, it's all in the attitude.

Read the Bible Today: Numbers 14

Prayer Points:

1. I thank God for today.
2. I will not allow my tongue to destroy me, in the name of Jesus.
3. Every evil word from my mouth that affects my life, I cancel you today by the blood of Jesus, in the name of Jesus.
4. You, arrow of destruction, you will not locate me, in the name of Jesus.
5. Any evil person who commands the throne in any area of my life, I dethrone you, in the name of Jesus.
6. Every power contrary to the power of the Holy Spirit in my life, I challenge you with the fire of God; come out and die, in the name of Jesus.
7. Power of God; fill every area of my life, miracles of God, fill every area of my life, in the name of Jesus.
8. Declare Jesus Christ is Lord.
9. I take over this day by the blood of Jesus in the name of Jesus.
10. Almighty God; magnify Jesus in my life in the name of Jesus.
11. Almighty God be magnified in the name of Jesus.

12. Almighty God; encourage me and strengthen my heart in the name of Jesus.
13. Almighty God; put wisdom in my mind and give understanding to my heart in the name of Jesus.
14. Almighty God; pour the bottles of heaven over my life in the name of Jesus.
15. By the ordinances of heaven, let my helpers arise and locate me in the name of Jesus.
16. By the ordinances of heaven, I set my dominion over the works of darkness in the name of Jesus Christ.
17. I cancel every evil dreams, visions, prophesy and prayers against my life and family in the name of Jesus.
18. Talk to God about your heart desires and your situation.
19. Thank God for answered prayers.

Confession:

"Only be thou strong and very courageous, that thou mayest observe to do according to all the law, which Moses my servant commanded thee: turn not from it to the right hand or to the left, that thou mayest prosper whithersoever thou goest" Joshua 1:7.

Wisdom for Today:

Focus on one task at a time. Commit yourself totally to each hour. Remember that Satan's greatest goal is broken focus. Focus creates momentum.

Read the Bible Today: *Hebrews 12 and Joshua 1 and 2*

Prayer Points:

1. I thank God for today.
2. I soak the rest of the days in this year into the blood of Jesus, in Jesus name.
3. I claim divine protection and favor throughout the remaining days in this year, in the name of Jesus.
4. I release myself from the influence of any evil power trying to control my life, in the name of Jesus.
5. I cancel all evil vows and promises that are affecting me negatively, in the name of Jesus.
6. Every power of any family idol affecting my life, my home, and my work, be broken, in the name of Jesus.
7. I command every satanic reinforcement against me to scatter into pieces, in the name of Jesus.
8. By the ordinances of heaven, let the doors of favor, and glory open for me in the name of Jesus.
9. By the ordinances of heaven, every good door closed against me open in the name of Jesus.
10. By the ordinances of heaven, every door open for the enemies, be closed in the name of Jesus.
11. By the ordinances of heaven, every waster working against my life; be wasted in the name of Jesus.
12. By the ordinances of heaven every destroyer assigned against my life, family and ministry; be destroyed in the name of Jesus.
13. By the ordinances of heaven, let this land begin to favor me and yield her increase unto me in the name of Jesus.

14. By the ordinances of heaven, I decree I shall prosper and be blessed in the name of Jesus.
15. By the ordinances of heaven, let all my enemies scatter in the name of Jesus.
16. By the ordinances of heaven, I receive healings, deliverance, breakthrough and prosperity in the name of Jesus.
17. I cancel every evil dreams, visions, prophesy and prayers against my life and family in the name of Jesus.
18. Talk to God about your heart desires and your situation.
19. Thank God for answered prayers.

Confession:

"A wise man will hear, and will increase learning; and a man of understanding shall attain unto wise counsels" Proverbs 1:5.

Wisdom for Today:

Your mentor is anyone who consistently teaches you what you want to know. It was a secret of Elijah and Elisha, Moses and Joshua, Paul and Timothy. Mentorship is accepting perfect knowledge from an imperfect man. Pursue and extract the knowledge of the mentors that God has made available to your life. Do not pay attention to the weaknesses in their lives. You will never travel beyond your wisdom.

Read the Bible Today: 1 Kings 19 and Proverbs 1

Prayer Points:

1. I thank God for today.
2. Almighty God fill me with your wisdom today, in the name of Jesus.
3. Almighty God empower me to prosper throughout the days of my life, in the name of Jesus.
4. Almighty God connect me with those who will move my life forward, in the name of Jesus.
5. Almighty God let the remaining days in this year bring laughter to me and my family in the name of Jesus.
6. Almighty God let me be blessed for the remaining days of this year, in the name of Jesus.
7. Almighty God, baptize me with undeniable favor today, in the name of Jesus.
8. Declare Jesus Christ is Lord.
9. I take over this day by the blood of Jesus in the name of Jesus.
10. Almighty God; magnify Jesus in my life in the name of Jesus.
11. Almighty God be magnified in my life in the name of Jesus.
12. I overcome evil in this day by the power in the blood of Jesus Christ in the name of Jesus.
13. Almighty God; encourage me and strengthen my heart in the name of Jesus.
14. Almighty God; put wisdom in my mind and give understanding to my heart in the name of Jesus.

15. Almighty God; pour the bottles of heaven over my life in the name of Jesus.
16. By the ordinances of heaven, let my helpers arise and locate me in the name of Jesus.
17. By the ordinances of heaven, I set my dominion over the works of darkness in the name of Jesus Christ.
18. I cancel every evil dreams, visions, prophesy and prayers against my life and family in the name of Jesus.
19. Talk to God about your heart desires and your situation.
20. Thank God for answered prayers.

Apostle A.O. Solomon

Confession:

"And thou shall love the Lord thy God with all thy heart, and with all thy soul, and with all thy mind" Mark 12:30.

Wisdom for Today:

The Bible teaches us to show proper respect to those in authority and others. Respect means "to feel or show honor for." Respecting others is usually not difficult. But did you know that you are to show respect for those in authority even when they are wrong, don't act properly, or don't de7serve it? Yes, it is true. Why? Because you will set a good example for others. If you didn't show respect, you might cause others to think badly of God because of your behavior. Please understand that showing respect does not mean that you have to blindly follow an order if you know it is the wrong thing to do. Even adults worthy of our respect can be mistaken. However, when you believe someone is wrong, you can still avoid being disrespectful by calmly and politely explaining your belief or side to him or her.

Read the Bible Today: Luke 19

Prayer Points:

1. I thank God for today.
1. Almighty God, empower me to succeed today, in the name of Jesus.
2. Whatever is standing in my way, give way now in the name of Jesus.
3. Whatever will not let me go, whatever will not let my blessings locate me, depart from me today, in the name of Jesus.
4. Whatever must break for me to have breakthroughs, break now by fire, in the name of Jesus.
5. Almighty God, take over my battle today, in the name of Jesus.
6. Almighty God announce my name for blessings, favor, and honor today, in the name of Jesus.
7. By the ordinances of heaven, let the doors of favor, and glory open for me in the name of Jesus.
8. By the ordinances of heaven, every good door closed against me open in the name of Jesus.
9. By the ordinances of heaven, every door open for the enemies, be closed in the name of Jesus.

10. By the ordinances of heaven, every waster working against my life; be wasted in the name of Jesus.
11. By the ordinances of heaven, let this land begin to favor me and yield her increase unto me in the name of Jesus.
12. By the ordinances of heaven, I decree I shall prosper and be blessed in the name of Jesus.
13. By the ordinances of heaven, let all my enemies scatter in the name of Jesus.
14. By the ordinances of heaven, I receive healings, deliverance, breakthrough and prosperity in the name of Jesus.
15. I cancel every evil dreams, visions, prophesy and prayers against my life and family in the name of Jesus.
16. Talk to God about your heart desires and your situation.
17. Thank God for answered prayers.

Confession:

"The Lord is my rock and my fortress, and my deliverer, my God, my strength in whom I will trust; my buckler, and the horn of my salvation, and my high tower. I will call upon the Lord, who is worthy to be praised: so shall I be saved from mine enemies" Psalms 18:2–3.

Wisdom for Today:

Have you ever been in total darkness before? I mean the kind of darkness in which you cannot see anything at all, even when it is right in front of your nose? If you have, then you know how difficult it would be to walk in that darkness without bumping into or falling over something. It would be hard to find anything in that darkness. But if even the smallest bit of light is brought into the darkness, then we aren't "blinded" by that darkness anymore. Instead, we can see something, even if it's just a shadow. And the more light that is added, the more we are able to see—the more we are able to move about safely and the more we can see and do. Walk in the light. There's a verse in the Bible that compares God's word, the Bible, to a lamp and a light: Psalms 119:105

Read the Bible Today: Romans 8

Prayer Points:

1. Almighty God, I thank you for the days that remain in this year, in the name of Jesus.
2. I plead the blood of Jesus against every voice speaking against my destiny, in the name of Jesus.
3. I plead the blood of Jesus against everything the devil is holding against me, in the name of Jesus.
4. I plead the blood of Jesus against every weapon of the enemy fashioned against me and my family in the name of Jesus.
5. Let God arise, and let all my enemies scatter unto desolation, in the name of Jesus.
6. Every arrow of death fired against me and my family return to your sender, in the name of Jesus.
7. Everyone who carries an evil oppression into my life, carry your oppression away now, in the name of Jesus.
8. Anyone fighting against my blessing and promotion, sleep to death, in Jesus name.

9. Every incantation and enchantment against me and my family release your power and die, in the name of Jesus.
10. Let all those planning to drink my blood collapse and die, in the name of Jesus.
11. Let all those making me run up and down; be destroyed by fire, in Jesus name.
12. Every power that says I will not rise be crushed to pieces, in the name of Jesus.
13. Every power that says I will have no peace, die with your word, in the name of Jesus.
14. Almighty God gather my broken life together by your power, in the name of Jesus.
15. Almighty God let my situations be rearranged to favor me, in Jesus name.
16. With the sword of fire, I cut off every hand of darkness from my spirit, soul, and body, in the name of Jesus.
17. I refuse to carry debt into the New Year, in the name of Jesus.
18. I refuse to enter the New Year with sorrow, in Jesus name.
19. I refuse to enter the New Year with sickness and infirmity, in Jesus name.
20. My enemies shall not laugh last over my life, marriage, and family, in Jesus name.
21. By the blood of Jesus and the power of Jehovah God, I rise above limitations and I begin to shine, in the name of Jesus.
22. I cancel every evil dreams, visions, prophesy and prayers against my life and family in the name of Jesus.
23. Talk to God about your heart desires and your situation.
24. Thank God for answered prayers.

Apostle A.O. Solomon

Confession:

"Let them be confounded and put to shame that seek after my soul: let them be turned back and brought to confusion that device my hurt. Let them be as chaff before the wind: and let the angel of Lord chase them. Let their way be dark and slippery: and let the angel of the Lord persecute them" Psalms 35:4–6.

Wisdom for Today:

Have you ever been afraid? Maybe late at night you find yourself lying in bed and you hear a noise. You start thinking of what it could be. Is it a "monster" coming up the stairs? Is there something under your bed? When we are alone, or when it is dark, it is easy to think of bad things and become frightened. But there is always someone we can call on for help. The Lord is always there. We sometimes forget this in times of fright, but he is always there. The next time you feel the urge to be afraid, remember the Lord is there and call on him. Put your trust in him.

Read the Bible Today: 2 Chronicles 20

Prayer Points:

1. I thank God for today.
2. Lord Jesus, stand for me today, go ahead of me and level every mountain of blockages and opposition, and bring me to my possession, in the name of Jesus.
3. Almighty God let your word settle my case today, in the name of Jesus.
4. Let the enemies enter into the grave they dug for me and my family by fire and by force, in the name of Jesus.
5. I cancel every dream of death against me and my family by the blood of Jesus in the name of Jesus.
6. I break the power of death over my life and family, by the blood of Jesus in the name of Jesus.
7. Let all those planning my shame be put to eternal shame, in the name of Jesus.
8. Let the blood of Jesus begin to speak on my behalf, in the name of Jesus.
9. Almighty God sanctify me unto yourself, in the name of Jesus.

10. Almighty God heal every wounded area of my life, destiny, and marriage, in Jesuss name.
11. I take authority over every spirit and power of affliction targeted against me and my family in the name of Jesus.
12. I refuse to be divided against myself, in the name of Jesus.
13. Every power of satanic limitation upon my life, die now, in the name of Jesus.
14. Almighty God encircle me and my family with your wall of fire, in Jesus name.
15. Almighty God encircle me and my family with the wall of your blood, in Jesus name.
16. Almighty God encircle me and my family with the wall of your angels, in Jesus name.
17. Almighty God bless me indeed, in the name of Jesus.
18. Almighty God promote me from minimum to maximum, in the name of Jesus.
19. Almighty God you are the God of perfection, perfect everything that concerns me and my family, in the name of Jesus.
20. Almighty God arise and blow away every wicked power working against me and my family in the name of Jesus.
21. Let the traps of my enemies catch my enemies, in Jesus name.
22. All eaters of flesh and drinkers of blood fashioned against my family eat your own flesh and drink your own blood, in Jesus name.
23. I disagree with every evil decision over my life, marriage, and family, in Jesus name.
24. By the blood of Jesus, I rise above every limitation and shine, in Jesus name.
25. I cancel every evil dreams, visions, prophesy and prayers against my life and family in the name of Jesus.
26. Talk to God about your heart desires and your situation.
27. Thank God for answered prayers.

Confession:

"For thou hast delivered my soul from death, mine eyes from tears, and my feet from falling. I will walk before the Lord in the land of the living" Psalms 116:8–9.

Wisdom for Today:

Have you ever done something you've seen someone else do? This is what it means to imitate. The Bible tells us to be careful about what we imitate, though: We must think carefully before we imitate the actions of others. Is what they are doing good or evil? Let's look at some examples. Is one of your friends getting good grades by cheating? Good grades are good, but cheating is evil. Don't imitate the cheating. Does someone you know get a bigger allowance than you do, even though he bosses his parents around? The allowance might be good, but the disrespect for parents is evil. Don't imitate and be disrespectful toward your parents. Do you know someone who is really smart who always criticizes others? Intelligence is usually good, but being nasty to others is evil. Don't imitate and treat others badly. Those are just a few examples of how we must be careful not to imitate evil actions, even though they might accompany good things.

Read the Bible Today: *Proverbs 3 and 16*

Prayer Points:

1. I thank God for today.
2. Every evil agreement against me and my family, scatter unto desolation, in Jesus name.
3. Any tree harboring anything against me, dry to the root, in the name of Jesus.
4. Every witchcraft collaboration against me and my family be uprooted by fire, in the name of Jesus.
5. I break every witchcraft pot with the cross of Jesus Christ, in Jesus name.
6. Let the fire of God expose and disgrace every witch in my family, in the name of Jesus.
7. Anyone who entered into witchcraft because of me and my family die with your power, in the name of Jesus.
8. I command a change for better in my life by the blood of Jesus, in Jesus name.

9. Every power working against my better living, die, in the name of Jesus.
10. Any power that wants me to die in bad condition, die now, in the name of Jesus.
11. Let all those who entered into any evil covenant in order to kill or destroy me, die with their evil covenant, in the name of Jesus.
12. I shall not eat the bread of sorrow, in the name of Jesus.
13. I shall not drink the water of affliction, in the name of Jesus.
14. Any power that will not let me go when God says go, die, in the name of Jesus.
15. Every power working against my prayer in my life, come out and die, in the name of Jesus.
16. Let my prayer life receive deliverance by fire, in the name of Jesus.
17. I refuse to die physically and spiritually, in the name of Jesus.
18. Let the angels of God chase away every evil power that pursues me from my father's house, in the name of Jesus.
19. Let the angels of God chase away every evil power that pursues me from my mother's house, in the name of Jesus.
20. The voice of the enemy shall not prevail over my life and marriage, in Jesus name.
21. My head From now on, life shall be easy for you, in the name of Jesus.
22. By the blood of Jesus Christ, I rise above all limitations in life and shine, in the name of Jesus.
23. Lord Jesus, show up in my affairs today in the name of Jesus.
24. I cancel every evil dreams, visions, prophesy and prayers against my life and family in the name of Jesus.
25. Talk to God about your heart desires and your situation.
26. Thank God for answered prayers.

Apostle A.O. Solomon

Confession:

"But I will deliver thee in that day, saith the Lord: and I shall not be given into the hand of the men of whom I am afraid. For God will surely deliver me, and I shall not fall by the sword, but my life shall be for a prey unto me: because I put my trust in God, says the Lord"
Jeremiah 39:17–18.

"God shall deliver me in six troubles: yea, in the seven there shall no evil touch me" Job 5:19.

Wisdom for Today:

Has anyone ever made fun of you, said bad things about or to you, or hurt you because you did the right thing or because you are a Christian? Chances are if that hasn't happened to you yet, it will someday. Those of us who love Jesus and try to do the right thing make others uncomfortable. Deep down, they realize that something is not quite right in their lives ... something is missing. As a result, they often try to make themselves look and feel better by trying to make us look and feel badly. This is what Jesus was talking about when he said this: "Blessed are you when people insult you, persecute you and falsely say all kinds of evil against you because of me. Rejoice and be glad, because great is your reward in heaven, for in the same way they persecuted the prophets who were before you" (Matthew 5:11–12, NIV). That is just one of Jesus wonderful promises for us. Even while others might treat us very badly here and now because we love Jesus, we can still do what we know is right, because we know that God will reward us later. Just as that popular phrase goes, "No pain, no gain," we can remember that whenever we endure hard times for Jesus sake, we really are being blessed with a great reward in heaven.

Read the Bible Today: Acts 7

Prayer Points:

1. I thank God for today.
2. Almighty God send your fire of deliverance into the foundation of my life, in the name of Jesus.
3. I lay hold on the divine sword of fire and cut off every power holding me in bondage, in the name of Jesus.
4. I command every internal bondage in my life to be broken by the blood of Jesus.

5. I am made in the image of Jehovah God, I am curiously made, I am fearfully and wonderfully made, I am the crown of God's creation, I am created a dominion child of God, and I am an express image of Elohim, his workmanship in Christ Jesus for good works.

6. I release myself from parental and family bondage, in the name of Jesus.

7. Almighty God of great deliverance, deliver me from every conscious and unconscious bondage, in the name of Jesus.

8. I break every covenant with bondage, in the name of Jesus.

9. Any material that has to do with bondage that is buried for my sake, be exhumed, be roasted, and relinquish your power, in the name of Jesus.

10. I walk out of bondage into God's perfect deliverance, in the name of Jesus.

11. Almighty God deliver me from any form of bondage, in the name of Jesus.

12. Almighty God by your power, separate me from every evil attachment, in the name of Jesus.

13. I command deliverance upon every department of my life, in the name of Jesus.

14. I break every curse of bondage issued against my life, in the name of Jesus.

15. I declare that no power shall be able to put my life in bondage, in the name of Jesus.

16. I live upon Mount Zion; therefore I am delivered, in the name of Jesus.

17. I shall not end my life in shame, in the name of Jesus.

18. I shall not weep over what has been giving me joy, in the name of Jesus.

19. I shall not wear rags; I shall not wear the garment of shame, in the name of Jesus.

20. I shall not turn to a beggar, in the name of Jesus.

21. Almighty God baptize me with your divine favor, in the name of Jesus.

22. By the blood of Jesus, I rise above every limitation in life and shine, in Jesus name.

23. Almighty God add your salt to every area of my life, in the name of Jesus.

24. I cancel every evil dreams, visions, prophesy and prayers against my life and family in the name of Jesus.

25. Talk to God about your heart desires and your situation.

26. Thank God for answered prayers.

Confession:

Christ has redeemed me from the curse of the law. I am free from the power of the evil ones. My freedom is guaranteed in Jesus. I am covered by his precious blood.

Wisdom for Today:

Most of the demands of scriptures cannot be seen as rational, but inside those seemingly irrational demands lies the power of God that delivers and decorates destinies. Those instructions might appear foolish to you, but the "foolishness" of God holds more wisdom than any thoughts we may have. "The foolishness of God is wiser than men; and the weakness of God is stronger than men" 1 Corinthians 1:25.

Read the Bible Today: Isaiah 1 and Genesis 26

Prayer Points:

1. I thank God for today.
2. Let every internal and external warfare in my life and family; be ended in peace, in the name of Jesus.
3. I command the weapons of my enemies to turn against them, in the name of Jesus.
4. Every satanic warfare arranged against me in the heavenly places and on earth, be dismantled by thunder, in the name of Jesus.
5. I command the weapons of war that my enemies depend on to disappoint them, in the name of Jesus.
6. Almighty God prove yourself as a man of war over my enemies, in the name of Jesus.
7. I declare in the name of Jesus that no weapon fashioned against me shall succeed in the name of Jesus.
8. I remove any protection that hovers over the enemy who is going to war against me, and I expose him to danger of death, in the name of Jesus.
9. Every power constantly challenging me to battle, thereby forcing me to live my life in a warzone, receive double destruction by fire, in the name of Jesus.
10. Any power that wants to replace my peace with war, die suddenly, in the name of Jesus.

11. I release discord into the camp of the enemies as they plan war against me, and I command them to fight themselves to death, in the name of Jesus.
12. Almighty God fight my battles for me, in the name of Jesus.
13. I go with the Lord Jesus into every battle of my life, and I come out victorious, in the name of Jesus.
14. It is well with my spirit, soul, and body, in Jesus name.
15. By the blood of Jesus Christ, I rise above every limitation in life, in the name of Jesus.
16. Lord Jesus, show up in my case today, in the name of Jesus.
17. Lord Jesus, stand in the gap for me today, in the name of Jesus.
18. I refuse to carry any evil into the New Year, in the name of Jesus.
19. Almighty God let my life attract your favor, in the name of Jesus.
20. I cancel every evil dreams, visions, prophesy and prayers against my life and family in the name of Jesus.
21. Talk to God about your heart desires and your situation.
22. Thank God for answered prayers.

Confession:

"Bless the Lord, O my soul, and forget not all his benefit: who forgiveth all mine iniquities: who healeth all my diseases. Who redeemeth my life from destruction; who crowneth me with loving kindness and tender mercies" Psalms 103:2–4.

"And the Lord will take away from me all sickness, and will put none of the evil diseases of Egypt which I know, upon me; but will lay them upon all them that hate me" Deuteronomy 7:15.

Wisdom for Today:

Thanksgiving is not only for good times alone. Even when things are not going the way you want them to go, you must still I give thanks to God! The Bible says: "In everything give thanks; for this is the will of God in Christ Jesus concerning you" 1 Thessalonians 5:18. This means we must give thanks for everything—not only a few things, but everything! Even in the face of adversity and opposition, you must give God thanks!

Read the Bible Today: Exodus 14 and 15

Prayer Points:

1. I thank God for today.
2. Every seed of sickness growing in the foundation of my life die by fire, in the name of Jesus.
3. I detach myself from every inherited sickness, in the name of Jesus.
4. Almighty God you are a great physician, heal me with your healing balm, in the name of Jesus.
5. Almighty God you are the great healer let your healing power flow through my body, in the name of Jesus.
6. I command every terminal and seasonal illness to get out of my life with all their roots, in the name of Jesus.
7. Every evil dream against my destiny, surrender your power and die, in the name of Jesus.
8. No sickness shall come near my dwelling place, in the name of Jesus.
9. I shake sickness and infirmity out of my body; I declare that I am strong, in the name of Jesus.

10. I claim divine health upon my life, in the name of Jesus.
11. Every evil challenge against my destiny be disgraced, in the name of Jesus.
12. I shall not answer the call of evil spirits, in the name of Jesus.
13. Declare Jesus Christ is Lord.
14. Holy Spirit; my comforter rule over my spirit, soul, and body in the name of Jesus.
15. I lose the blessing of God upon my life in the name of Jesus.
16. I reject every evil in this day in the name of Jesus.
17. Let the ordinances of the heaven bless and favor me today in the name of Jesus.
18. Let my destiny receive the assuring rest of heaven in the name of Jesus.
19. Blood of Jesus Christ renew my life completely in the name of Jesus.
20. Every evil counsel and satanic advice against my life; be terminated in the name of Jesus.
21. Almighty God; have mercy upon me and make me a corner stone in the name of Jesus.
22. Almighty God; give me rest from fear, sorrow, trouble, and hard labor in the name of Jesus.
23. I cancel every evil dreams, visions, prophesy and prayers against my life and family in the name of Jesus.
24. Talk to God about your heart desires and your situation.
25. Thank God for answered prayers.

Confession:

"I shall be like a tree planted by the rivers of water, that bringeth forth his fruits in his season; my leaf also shall not wither; and what-soever I doeth shall prosper" Psalms 1:3, .

"The Lord is the portion of mine inheritance and of my cup: God maintains my lot. The lines are fallen unto me in pleasant places; yea, I have a goodly heritage" Psalms 16:5–6.

"The young lion do lack, and suffer hunger: but I that seek the Lord shall not lack any good thing" Psalms 34:10.

"Thou shall increase my greatness, and comfort me on every side. Psalms 71:21

For the Lord is a sun and shield: the Lord will give grace and glory: no good thing will he withhold from me, in Jesus name" Psalms 84:11.

Wisdom for Today:

Christ is the answer to sadness and discouragement. This is a world of thwarted hopes, broken dreams, and frustrated desires. Optimism and cheerfulness are products of knowing Christ. If the heart has been attuned to God through faith in Christ, then its overflow will be joyous optimism and good cheer. You will never be free from discouragement and despondency until you have been tuned to God. Christ is the wellspring of happiness. He is the fountainhead of joy. Here is the secret of the joy of the Christians.

Read the Bible Today: Matthew 26 and Psalm 16

Prayer Points:

1. I thank God for allowing me to see the last day of the year.
2. I sing praises unto the Most High God.
3. You, the spirit of poverty assigned against my life, I cut off your head, in the name of Jesus.
4. I render powerless every spirit of fruitless effort and profitless handwork working against my life, in the name of Jesus.
5. I destroy by the blood of Jesus every power that binds me to poverty, failure, and disappointment, in the name of Jesus.

6. I refuse to wear the garment of poverty, lack, and debt, in the name of Jesus.

7. I refuse to follow the poverty pattern of my ancestors, in the name of Jesus.

8. Every power attacking my source of income be destroyed beyond remedy, in the name of Jesus.

9. Let all those who do not want to see me prosper bow to me by fire, in Jesus name.

10. You, spirit of poverty, failure, and backwardness, I am not your candidate; therefore, release your hold upon my life, in the name of Jesus.

11. I repossess my destiny, benefits, and potentials that have been stolen by anybody dead or alive, in the name of Jesus.

12. Almighty God soak me in your favor and in success and breakthrough, in the name of Jesus.

13. Almighty God rend the heavens for my sake and pour your unlimited blessings upon me, in the name of Jesus.

14. From the east, west, north and south, I keep all my possessions safe, in the name of Jesus.

15. I receive expected and unexpected financial breakthroughs today, in the name of Jesus.

16. Almighty God of heaven and earth, make haste to connect me with my divine helpers, in the name of Jesus.

17. I command the sun, moon, and stars to favor me, in the name of Jesus.

18. I rebuke every force directed against my prosperity: come out of my life, in the name of Jesus.

19. I command the ground, water, and heavens to release my blessings, by fire and by force, in the name of Jesus.

20. I command the milk and honey of my life to turn to poison in the mouth of any evil person who tries to suck them, in the name of Jesus.

21. Almighty God give me the power to prosper in all my endeavors, in the name of Jesus.

22. I rise above every limitation in life, in the name of Jesus.

23. The New Year shall bring all-round comfort for me and my family and in the name of Jesus.

24. Failure shall not be my portion in the New Year in Jesus name.

25. Sorrow, sighing, and weeping shall not be my portion in the New Year, in the name of Jesus.

26. Accident, tragedy, and death shall not be my portion in the New Year, in Jesus name.
27. This year ahead of me shall be my year of supernatural harvest, in the name of Jesus.
28. This year ahead of me shall be my year of incomparable honor and favor, in the name of Jesus.
29. This year ahead of me shall be my year of open heavens, open doors, and financial breakthroughs, in the name of Jesus.
30. From now on, life shall be easy for me, in the name of Jesus.
31. I cancel every evil dreams, visions, prophesy and prayers against my life and family in the name of Jesus.
32. Talk to God about your heart desires and your situation.
33. Thank God for answered prayers.

ABOUT THE AUTHOR

Born and raised in Nigeria, Apostle Solomon Abiodun Odejayi grew up in a Muslim home, and later gave his life to Jesus Christ. Ever since he became a Christian, his life has been filled with great blessings and wonders. He is the president and senior pastor of The Shadow of the Almighty Ministries. He also runs the church's Prayer Line, which reaches out to over 7,000 people every day. He is happily married and blessed with children. He has been in the ministry for seventeen years as a deliverance minister, a prophet, a motivator, and a sound teacher of the word of God. He is also the author of other books: *Captured by the Night*, *Defeating Marital Problems*, and *Destroying the Pregnancy (Desire) of the Enemy*.

It's time to *take over* the days of your life by the power of prayer, positive confessions, and wisdom. Jesus Christ is Lord!

CPSIA information can be obtained at www.ICGtesting.com
Printed in the USA
LVOW121100200112

264710LV00003B/7/P